Post-Horror

Art, Genre, and Cultural Elevation

David Church

Edinburgh University Press is one of the leading university presses in the UK. We publish academic books and journals in our selected subject areas across the humanities and social sciences, combining cutting-edge scholarship with high editorial and production values to produce academic works of lasting importance. For more information visit our website: edinburghuniversitypress.com

© David Church, 2021, 2022

Edinburgh University Press Ltd
The Tun – Holyrood Road
12(2f) Jackson's Entry
Edinburgh EH8 8PJ

First published in hardback by Edinburgh University Press 2021

Typeset in 11/13 Monotype Ehrhardt by
IDSUK (DataConnection) Ltd

A CIP record for this book is available from the British Library

ISBN 978 1 4744 7588 4 (hardback)
ISBN 978 1 4744 7589 1 (paperback)
ISBN 978 1 4744 7590 7 (webready PDF)
ISBN 978 1 4744 7591 4 (epub)

The right of David Church to be identified as the author of this work has been asserted in accordance with the Copyright, Designs and Patents Act 1988, and the Copyright and Related Rights Regulations 2003 (SI No. 2498).

Post-Horror

Contents

Figures vi
Acknowledgments viii

1. Apprehension Engines: Defining a New Wave of
   Art-Horror Cinema   1
2. "Slow," "Smart," "Indie," "Prestige," "Elevated":
   Discursive Struggle for Cultural Distinction   27
3. Grief, Mourning, and the Horrors of Familial Inheritance   68
4. Horror by Gaslight: Epistemic Violence and
   Ambivalent Belonging   102
5. Beautiful, Horrible Desolation: Landscape in
   Post-Horror Cinema   142
6. Queer Ethics and the Urban Ruin-Porn Landscape:
   The Horrors of Monogamy in *It Follows*   181
7. Existential Dread and the Trouble with Transcendence   213

Selected Bibliography 245
Index 260

Illustrations

Figures

1.1	Mark Korven and Tony Duggan-Smith's "Apprehension Engine"	2
3.1	Amelia moves far away from Samuel in *The Babadook*	77
3.2	Mother and twins in the high-modernist interiors of *Goodnight Mommy*	82
3.3	Ellen offers her breast to Charlie in one of Annie's miniatures in *Hereditary*	88
4.1	Dani smiles as she watches Christian burn in the final shot of *Midsommar*	114
4.2	The village women mirror Dani's anguish back to her in *Midsommar*	117
4.3	Chris drops into the cosmic void of the Sunken Place in *Get Out*	126
4.4	Chris remains in the Sunken Place in *Get Out*'s pessimistic alternate ending	131
5.1	The hare as pagan fertility symbol in *The Witch*	152
5.2	Black Phillip rams William into the woodpile in *The Witch*	153
5.3	Albrun drowns baby Martha in the bog in *Hagazussa: A Heathen's Curse*	159
5.4	Albrun spontaneously bursts into flames in *Hagazussa: A Heathen's Curse*	160
5.5	Howard peers up into the lantern room in *The Lighthouse*	172
5.6	Howard meets his Promethean fate in *The Lighthouse*	174
6.1	Hugh/Jeff explains the curse to wheelchair-bound Jay in *It Follows*	185
6.2	The "happy" monogamous couple as image of ruination in *It Follows*	195
6.3	The monster appears in *It Follows* in the form of a nude woman	205

7.1 Sophia asks her Holy Guardian Angel for the power to forgive in *A Dark Song* — 216
7.2 Mother Nature stumbles through the warzone of her former house in *mother!* — 220
7.3 The Ghost stands in an industrial building site in *A Ghost Story* — 232

Table

1.1 Provisional corpus of post-horror cinema — 14

Acknowledgments

First of all, my deep thanks to Gillian Leslie, Richard Strachan, Fiona Conn, and Peter Williams and the other good folks at Edinburgh University Press for working with me on a second book with them. It is always so wonderful to work with such a friendly, responsive, and professional publishing team. Thanks to the readers of the proposal for their kind feedback as well.

Steffen Hantke assembled a workshop at the 2018 Southwest Popular/American Culture Association Conference that provided a valuable outlet for some of my early ideas about the overall post-horror corpus. Several early readers provided wonderfully productive feedback on chapters in progress, including Eddie Falvey, Joe Hickinbottom, and Jonathan Wroot, who also invited me to contribute an earlier version of Chapter 1 to their edited collection *New Blood*; Jennifer Maher on Chapter 3; Raymond Rea, Glyn Davis, and anonymous *Cinema Journal* reviewers on Chapter 6; and Paul Donnelly on Chapter 7. A variety of other folks provided useful conversation or research recommendations along the way, including Paul Donnelly, Karen Renner, Rebecca Gordon, Diana Coleman, Joan Hawkins, Ryan Powell, Mark Hain, Stephanie Graves, and David Gray. Aisha Shelton braved several of these movies with me in the theater, which was certainly admirable.

Earlier parts of this book were written across teaching gigs at Minnesota State University – Moorhead and Northern Arizona University. As a contingent faculty member, I'm so appreciative of my colleagues at each of these schools for their friendship and support, fixed-term contracts be damned. For my comrades in NAU's Department of Comparative Cultural Studies, we'll always have the Gnostic Mass.

Most recently, Brenda Weber and Stephanie Sanders brought me in on a Postdoctoral Fellowship in the Department of Gender Studies at Indiana University, providing the luxury of additional time to complete the research and writing of this book, for which I'm very grateful.

Thanks to Mark Korven and Tony Duggan-Smith for photos of the "Apprehension Engine," and to Conor Dennison for digging out archived sketches and sharing his memories of the production design on *A Dark Song*.

ACKNOWLEDGMENTS

This book was written during a tumultuous period, including sudden uprootings from family and friends in the service of cross-country moves, the daily psychological toll of the US political scene, and the outbreak of a global pandemic. Although some of these shifts seemed strangely appropriate (such as writing about Chapter 5's "cabin fever" films during the COVID-19 lockdown), others are indicative of the ever-growing precarity both within and beyond academia. In that regard, Erika Vause's *McSweeney's Internet Tendency* piece "Critically Acclaimed Horror Film of the 2010s or Your Ph.D. Program?" (see Selected Bibliography) has proven a recurring source of pleasure, since so many of its trenchantly humorous observations apply as well to life on the non-tenure track. If this book's overall tone contains a soupçon of cynicism and despair, then there you are. Hugs to Stephanie and my family for their constant love from afar.

Portions of Chapters 1 and 2 were first published as "Apprehension Engines: The New Independent 'Prestige Horror,'" in *New Blood: Critical Approaches to Contemporary Horror*, eds Eddie Falvey, Joe Hickinbottom, and Jonathan Wroot (Cardiff: University of Wales Press, 2020), pp. 15–33. My thanks to University of Wales Press for their generous permission to reprint this material herein.

An earlier version of Chapter 6 was first published as the article "Queer Ethics, Urban Spaces, and the Horrors of Monogamy in *It Follows*," in *Cinema Journal*, 57, no. 3, pp. 3–28. Copyright © 2018 by the University of Texas Press. All rights reserved.

CHAPTER 1

Apprehension Engines: Defining a New Wave of Art-Horror Cinema

Unearthly drones, metallic whines, and ominous clanks emanate from a contraption consisting of several wooden boxes with a guitar-like neck, onto which are affixed magnets, metal wires and coils, and a hurdy-gurdy crank. "The Apprehension Engine" is the nickname for this unique musical instrument, commissioned by Mark Korven, composer of *The Witch* (2015), and designed/built by guitar maker Tony Duggan-Smith (Figure 1.1). As its name suggests, the foreboding ambience created by this device instills a deep sense of anxiety and dread in the listener, even as these eldritch sounds cannot be easily associated with conventional musical instruments or arrangements. That is, the machine's tones are all the more unsettling because their source seems more obscure, less readily pinned down via common referents in the listener's mind. Inspired by his score for *The Witch*, Korven commissioned this experimental instrument to lend his film scores a more original sound than the overused digital samples previously at his disposal.[1] And, after the machine itself came to wider attention via social media, Duggan-Smith began taking orders from other filmmakers and media producers for small runs of the instrument, each one selling for a cool $10,000.[2]

Both the ethos and the effects of this device provide a useful way to approach an emerging cycle of independently produced (and potentially profitable) horror films that merge art-cinema style with decentered genre tropes, privileging lingering dread and visual restraint over audiovisual shocks and monstrous disgust. As "apprehension engines" in their own right, these films represent "a new-wave horror that diverges from the assembly line and strays from overpitched archetypes,"[3] sharing with Korven and Duggan-Smith's instrument a sense of handmade artistry, low-budget ingenuity, and striking originality – all in the service of producing affective tones that unsettle both viewers and the genre itself. Often heralded for possessing an aesthetically "higher" tone than the average multiplex horror movie, these films have received disproportionate critical acclaim for catering to more rarefied tastes, even as viewers with more

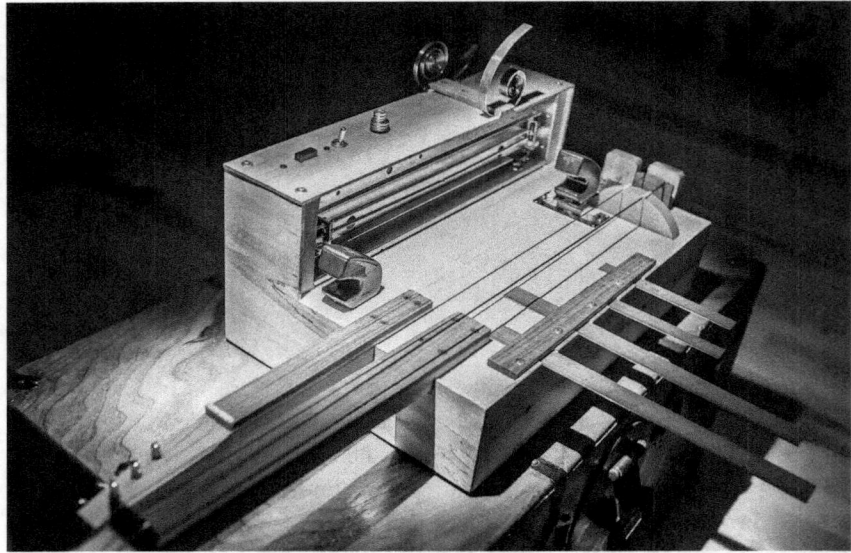

Figure 1.1 Film composer Mark Korven's "Apprehension Engine" instrument, designed and built by Tony Duggan-Smith. Photo by Kai Korven; courtesy of Mark Korven.

populist tastes have proved ambivalent or even hostile toward the films' aesthetic strategies, and dedicated horror fans have decried the critical conversation emerging around these works.

Variously dubbed "slow horror," "smart horror," "indie horror," "prestige horror," and "elevated horror," films such as *It Follows* (2014), *The Witch*, *It Comes at Night* (2017), and *Hereditary* (2018) all emerged from the crucible of major film festivals like Sundance and Toronto with significant critical buzz for supposedly transcending the horror genre's oft-presumed lowbrow status, and succeeded in crossing over to multiplexes. Meanwhile, arthouse releases like *Under the Skin* (2013) and *The Babadook* (2014) found a larger second audience on streaming video services around the same time that films like *I Am the Pretty Thing That Lives in the House* (2016) premiered on Netflix and studio-backed releases like *Get Out* (2017) and *A Quiet Place* (2018) earned critical acclaim for their intelligent takes on the genre. Collectively, these films represent one of the horror genre's most important trends since the turn of the twenty-first century, as a major site of both artistic innovation and cultural distinction. As just one example of how traditional gatekeepers of cultural taste have embraced these films, three-quarters of the entries on a recent *New York Times* list of the best

"21st Century Horror" films belong to the emerging corpus of films that, for the sake of expedience, I will refer to across this book as *post-horror*.[4]

Coined in July 2017 by *Guardian* columnist Steve Rose,[5] the term "post-horror" is one of many flawed attempts to name a corpus of recent films whose core stylistic tendencies were developed during the 1950s to 1970s "golden age" of modernist art cinema, but whose generic overlaps with horror cinema also open onto a wider range of precursors and contemporary intertexts. Because I will address the shortcomings in each of these critical labels in Chapter 2, my tentative use of *post-horror* should be taken with a large grain of salt, as less a wholesale endorsement of the term itself than as a convenient shorthand for the corpus of films concurrently labeled "smart horror," "elevated horror," and so on. (Although this book focuses primarily on Anglo-American understandings of these films, the label "elevated horror" continues to be more prevalent in the United States, while "post-horror" has become more common in British critical contexts.) In my opinion, "elevated" is a more accurate descriptor for the *aesthetic strategies* used in these films, but, as we will see, it comes freighted with elitist biases against the horror genre itself. Meanwhile, "post-horror" is also problematic, since it could erroneously imply that these are not "actual" horror films – yet its very vagueness as a term also makes it more reclaimable, for my purposes, as a ready-made placeholder label for the many tropes, themes, affects, and political concerns that together constitute the corpus.

In this opening chapter, I will argue that form and style are far more functional elements uniting these films as a shared corpus than the morass of critical labels more promiscuously applied to horror films that may or may not evince the distinctly austere aesthetic seen at the heart of the corpus. Some film critics have posited post-horror as a "new genre" or "new subgenre" – but it is far more accurately described as an aesthetically linked *cycle* within the longer and broader tradition of art-horror cinema, as longtime genre fans are more likely to point out (and as I will explain in these first two chapters). My goal for this first chapter is thus twofold: first, by enumerating some of the most common formal traits in films that critics have nominated as part of this emergent cycle, we will arrive at a provisional corpus of post-horror films; and second, we will see how such stylistic traits can generate forms of affect that may appeal very differently to different tastes. This chapter will thereby lay the groundwork for Chapter 2's more expansive reception study of how differences in aesthetic tastes – and the commingling of such divergent opinions as the lines between traditional film criticism and genre fandom have increasingly blurred – have generated voluminous discourse about post-horror's cultural value vis-à-vis its perceived closeness to, or distance from, the larger genre.

Other than pornography, horror is perhaps the most divisive of all popular genres: it garners tremendous devotion from fans who consider it their favorite type of film, while other folks avoid the genre altogether if they can at all help it. Between these two poles, however, we can posit a broad continuum, ranging from *horror-friendly* viewers on one side to *horror-skeptic* viewers on the other; the former are more likely to consider themselves fans and frequent consumers of the genre, while the latter are less frequent genre consumers but may still make exceptions for what they see as qualitatively superior texts. Canonization, for example, is a process that adheres less in choosing sets of texts than aggregating sets of valuations that associate some texts (and, by extension, the readers best suited to "properly" understand them) as more "literate" than others – hence the ability for a handful of high-minded horror texts to be canonized by horror-skeptic viewers.[6] For the purposes of this study, I will use the terms horror-friendly and horror-skeptic to describe tastes inclined toward or away from the genre, in addition to three related (albeit inevitably porous) categories of viewers/discourse who can be roughly situated along that continuum.

First, there are *professional film critics*, whose livelihood as arbiters of cultural taste depends on making aesthetic judgments and viewing recommendations for the perceived benefit of a wide readership. Although their overall numbers declined during print media's painful transition into the digital era (including the corresponding rise of freelance and unpaid critics writing in nontraditional venues), I am primarily referring to full-time film critics whose job as cultural gatekeepers has traditionally required a significant amount of cultural capital (that is, higher education in aesthetic appreciation, accumulated knowledge about culturally/historically valued texts, and so on) as justification for the value of their opinions.[7] Working for a widely read publication means that their opinions often circulate more broadly and create more discursive impact – thereby actualizing their cultural capital – in more substantial ways than highly educated writers (such as scholars) with more limited platforms at their disposal.[8] However, it is also important to note that Anglo-American film criticism has longstanding biases against the horror genre – so, even though it would be an overgeneralization to say that all film critics share a distaste for horror, it is still reasonable to position the broad category of professional film critics along the horror-skeptic axis.

Along the horror-friendly axis resides the second category of viewers/discourse discussed in these opening chapters: *genre fans*, or highly devoted aficionados whose long-term investment in a particular filmic genre typically involves acquiring a broad and deep knowledge of texts from different historical periods, national contexts, and industrial sectors. While it is possible for devoted horror fans to move into the dwindling ranks of professional film critics (and professional academics), it is far more likely for fans to circulate discourse in genre-specific venues, such as horror-related websites and magazines, where their subcultural capital (that is, an intra-subcultural sense of coolness that includes accrued knowledge, experience, and prestige) will be recognized by fellow fans.[9] Although a very small handful of writers may be able to eke out a living writing about the horror genre, genre fan discourse is typically circulated in either unpaid venues, such as blog and discussion-board postings, and/or in a freelance capacity. Without the expectation of reaching a more general readership or earning a regular paycheck from such efforts, genre fans often have more freedom – but may also be under more competitive pressure – to engage in discourse relevant to the cultivation of subcultural tastes in texts that are not widely recognized by larger society as "legitimate" or "respectable" objects. Many genre fans, however, still possess some degree of cultural capital, including an above-average amount of formal education and/or the cultivation of high-cultural tastes and reading strategies (their tastes not merely being limited to a culturally "low" genre).

Hence, both professional film critics and genre fans may know how to appreciate the "difficult" formal and stylistic qualities of art-horror films that alienate viewers with less cultural capital. Yet, when fans' high-cultural tastes and practices are nested within niche appreciation of a genre too often considered beneath "serious" aesthetic contemplation, we might use the conjunction "*(sub)cultural capital*" to connote the provisional status of cultural capitals that are not yet seen as fully "legitimate" because originally honed within the realm of subcultural tastes. Academics who are writing as an outgrowth of their genre fandom exemplify a particularly high mixture of both cultural and subcultural capital, so their voices best fall under this category as well – not least because their writing typically reaches a coterie of fellow scholar-fans.[10] Nevertheless, genre fans (both academic and non-academic) may attempt to enter the cultural conversation about post-horror, directly responding to the perceived limitations of broader film-critical discourse about such films, via online venues with a wider readership than fellow fans. As addressed in Chapter 2, this vying for expertise is partly driven by film criticism's increased reliance on freelance writers who may have dubious amounts of genre knowledge, or may be rushing their opinions into circulation for the sake of profitable clicks in the social-media era.

By contrast, the third category of viewers/discourse consists of what I am calling, for better or worse, *populist viewers* – or the wider and more mainstream range of horror-friendly viewers who may watch and enjoy horror films in a more "casual" way than the genre fan's acquisition of subcultural capital through broader and deeper knowledge of the genre's historical, cultural, and stylistic diversity.[11] Although they may consider themselves horror fans, their relative shortage of subcultural capital is more akin to the "fair-weather fans" of a sports team during a highly publicized season, or music fans whose tastes are primarily shaped by pop-radio programming. Due to this shortage of subcultural capital, they are less likely to engage with horror-specific websites or contribute to the same discursive nodes frequented by devoted genre fans, instead sharing their opinions via more generalist movie websites (such as the Internet Movie Database (IMDb) and Rotten Tomatoes) and major social-media platforms. These viewers are more likely to view and enjoy horror films that adhere closer to mainstream conventions as regards both filmic style and generic content – especially (but not exclusively) those produced by the major Hollywood studios, since those texts receive the largest market visibility. Their sharing of opinions about post-horror films on generalist websites is also populist in the sense of trying to warn other prospective viewers against seeing such films, in order to avoid similar feelings of disappointment or frustration. This criticism is sometimes framed as a reaction against the buzz that professional film reviewers and genre fans have helped generate around such texts, or may be rooted in reactions against the exhibition of arthouse-style films in multiplexes (a predominantly populist exhibition site) under misleadingly generic marketing. In this regard, my use of the admittedly charged term "populist" should connote an *aesthetic* conservatism on the part of both texts and audiences, a conventionalism in style and taste rooted in attempted appeals to a very wide viewership.

"Populist" should not be taken as synonymous with "popular," however, since the post-horror films *Get Out* and *A Quiet Place* ranked among the top twenty box-office hits of their respective years, whereas not all horror films that adhere to industry-standard norms for film form/style or generic treatment of their subject matter necessarily become major hits when released to multiplexes.[12] Nor should it be presumed that more populist horror films – for instance, the massively profitable *It* (2017/2019) and *Halloween* (2018), whose generically conventional style complements their well-known source material – are devoid of artistic, cultural, or intellectual value. Indeed, the huge body of scholarship on genre cinema has aptly demonstrated that even mainstream genre films that gain broad audiences can still speak to cultural anxieties in surprisingly fascinating ways. As we will see in Chapter 2, genre fans make precisely this claim as a means of trying to level the cultural distinctions that professional film critics often draw between post-horror and more populist horror movies. Yet, even if many horror fans may criticize this high-minded stratification of the genre, I would point out that populist audiences uphold such distinctions as well, when lacking the "double access" to appreciation of both "high" and "low" culture that fans' higher degree of (sub)cultural capital can grant.[13] If genre fans primarily have *discursive* qualms about the critical conversation around contemporary horror cinema, many populist viewers still have *textual* qualms about films that seem not to deliver the genre's conventionally expected pleasures, for reasons that this chapter will address and the next chapter will elaborate.

Post-Horror as Minimalist Art-Horror

Horror cinema has long been a popular but critically denigrated genre, capable of reaching sizable audiences but often derided for its corporeal appeals, fantastical conceits, and thematic focus on evil, monstrosity, and death. Accordingly, it is a critical commonplace for horror-skeptic film reviewers without deeper appreciation for the genre to celebrate texts that privilege haunting atmospheres and indirect chills over shocking spectacles and visceral disgust. As such, the monster conjured in the high-minded viewer's imagination has often held critical precedence over blatant images of the abject, with "psychological horror" seen as a more refined and restrained aesthetic that is more at home in the art house than the grind house.[14]

At root here are taste valuations diverging around different generic strategies for producing *affect*, or sensations which precede cognitive organization into emotions attached to particular objects or figures. Theorizations of affect tend to offer slippery definitions of the term (often by attempting to distinguish it from more common terms like emotion, feeling, mood, and so on), in part due to this sensed quality's evasion from being easily put into words.[15] Whereas *emotions*, for example, are commonly recognizable varieties of feelings that we might associate with a specific person or action, *affect* registers as a more generalized, ineffable block of sensation, such as free-floating anxieties without an apparent cause or solution. Across this book, I am far less interested in meticulously deploying affect theory (or even adhering to a specific definition of the term itself) than in exploring how the aesthetic form and narrative strategies of post-horror films produce various affects that have been subject to critical nomination (and contestation) as a supposedly "new" trend in the horror genre. Rather, my methodological approach here unites formal analysis with reception studies and cultural studies, in order to tease out how and why this corpus of recent films has emerged as one of the genre's most prominently discussed developments since approximately 2014.

As a starting point, I must clarify that my description of post-horror films as a cycle within a longer tradition of *art-horror* reflects its status as a noticeable spike in (at least) Anglo-American film markets, driven by several trailblazing hits – including *It Follows* and *The Witch* – which proved the crossover potential of films that might have otherwise remained within the realm of limited arthouse distribution that two other early examples, *The Babadook* and *Goodnight Mommy* (2014), called home.[16] That is, critical acclaim and box-office grosses after 2014 meant that more of these films were visibly circulating, creating the impression of a surge above baseline production levels for art-horror films in the marketplace.

For my purposes, the compound noun "art-horror" is far less an evaluative modification of the genre label than a much more literal means of evoking the combination of *art cinema* as a formally distinctive mode of film practice and the *horror genre* as an established set of storytelling conventions, iconography, and themes.[17] In other words, I am not using the term to effectively say "These films are 'art,' unlike most horror movies" (as the epithet "elevated horror" implies), but rather to directly allude to the stylistic methods used by these filmmakers in approaching the genre. David Bordwell influentially outlines art cinema as less a genre in its own right than a *mode* of filmmaking inspired by modernist art, and internationally popularized during the 1950s–70s with the spread of independently owned arthouse theaters. More formally challenging than classical Hollywood cinema (a far more populist filmmaking mode), modernist art films frequently include drifting, circular, and open-ended narratives; ambiguous and psychologically complex characters; and various forms of spatial and temporal manipulation (including deliberate continuity violations, durational realism, and so on).[18]

Importantly, viewing art cinema through the more nebulous classification of a "mode" allows us to see how its common formal traits can serve as a sort of conceptual umbrella beneath which many existing genres can also function. That is, virtually any popular film genre (such as gangster, science fiction, suspense, comedy, war, and so on) can be approached via art cinema's formal strategies – and horror films have proven a staple source of subject matter in this regard. Indeed, the long tradition of art-horror includes such diverse films as *The Cabinet of Dr. Caligari* (1920), *Vampyr* (1932), *Ugetsu* (1953), *Night Tide* (1961), *Repulsion* (1965), *Hour of the Wolf* (1968), *Don't Look Now* (1973), *The Tenant* (1976), *Eraserhead* (1977), *Possession* (1981), *Funny Games* (1997), *Trouble Every Day* (2001), *Pan's Labyrinth* (2006), *Antichrist* (2009), *A Girl Walks Home Alone at Night* (2014), and countless others.

In her ground-breaking book *Cutting Edge: Art-Horror and the Horrific Avant-Garde*, Joan Hawkins argues that, despite the cultural stratification of tastes that privilege higher cognition (such as vision and intellect) over lower bodily sensations, art films trade in many of the same capacities to shock, disgust, and offend as horror films – albeit framed for supposedly different, "higher" purposes (for instance, symbolism over literalism). For Hawkins, then, art-horror films represent a key site for levelling the taste hierarchies between so-called "high" and "low" culture. Most of Hawkins's examples explore how modernist art and avant-garde cinema (such as *Un Chien Andalou* (1928), *Eyes without a Face* (1959), *A Clockwork Orange* (1971), *The Act of Seeing with One's Own Eyes* (1972), *Salò, or the 120 Days of Sodom* (1975)) and "trashy" exploitation cinema similarly trade in both taboo spectacle (including gore and explicit sex) and Brechtian distanciation strategies – creating a dialectic of "high is low" and "low is high," wherein visceral affect is the uniting factor between films from seemingly opposed taste strata. As Hawkins shows, most critics have read such shock effects as signifiers of authorial intent and symbolic resonance when occurring in art and avant-garde films, but more likely dismiss them as literal-minded prurience and inadvertently sloppy filmmaking when present in genre and exploitation cinema.[19] Nevertheless, Matt Hills argues that Hawkins's own attempt to level these taste strata does not wholly deconstruct taste hierarchies so much as maintain art cinema's existing cultural repute as a tool for culturally salvaging exploitation films: "the lines of cultural demarcation around film as art are stretched as avant-garde legitimacy is discursively borrowed" when the umbrella of avant-gardism is extended to analyze seemingly "low" texts.[20]

Although Hills's criticism is more fittingly targeted at Jeffrey Sconce's concept of "paracinema" (the practice of ironically reading unintentionally "bad" exploitation movies as inadvertent avant-garde masterpieces),[21] the idea that modernist art cinema has retained its cultural repute as a qualitative yardstick among professional film critics is important for understanding how post-horror films fit into the larger realm of art cinema. Post-horror films exhibit many of the art-cinema traits noted by Bordwell, but without so many of the genre's critically countervailing traits like graphic violence/gore, unrealistic monsters, and so on. Even if some post-horror films contain gory or abject imagery consonant with Hawkins's argument (see the graphic decapitations in Ari Aster's films),

I argue that they more often share similarities with varieties of art cinema marked by visual restraint and stylistic minimalism; in other words, they tend to work in a rather different affective register than Hawkins's predominant emphasis on art-horror films which foreground shock and disgust.

Post-horror films, for instance, have fewer formal affinities with the so-called "new extremism"[22] (such as the films of Catherine Breillat, Gaspar Noé, Lars von Trier, Sion Sono), which controversially infused a new level of explicit sex and violence into international art cinema during the post-9/11 period, than affinities with one of that period's critical darlings: "slow cinema" (see Chapter 2). Hence the fact that not all art-horror films produced during the post-2014 period were critically lumped in with post-horror, since some diverged too far from post-horror's more specific subset of aesthetic strategies. Hawkins notes how any art-horror film's "affective properties tend to be divorced from its 'artistic' and 'poetic' ones, so that it's difficult to find a critical language that allows us to speak about the film as a whole."[23] Consequently, even when post-horror films bear more subtle and subdued qualities of art cinema than shock value, horror-skeptic critics still tend to compartmentalize and downplay such traits by using qualifiers like "elevated" in order to preserve the hierarchies that keep the horror genre near the bottom of the ladder of cultural taste. Hence, professional film critics less often valorize post-horror films according to what they *are* (part of the larger history of art-horror cinema) than what they are *not* (the mainstream horror film as "bad object"), much to the chagrin of genre fans who assert horror's longer history of artworthiness. Rather than being distinguished from other varieties of concurrently circulating art-horror films, then, post-horror is typically posited as highbrow counterprogramming to the supposedly trite and clichéd Hollywood horror film.

Whereas these films earned very strong reviews from most film critics on the basis of distinctions from more conventional Hollywood fare, review-aggregator websites with broad user bases (such as IMDb and Rotten Tomatoes), along with opening-night audience polling services like CinemaScore, demonstrate far less acclaim from more general viewers. *It Comes at Night* (2017) and *Hereditary* respectively earned "D" and "D+" CinemaScore grades, for example, despite earning critical plaudits; similar splits emerged on Rotten Tomatoes between high "Tomatometer" scores (compiled from professional film critics) relative to very low user-generated "Audience Scores." According to high-minded reviewers, these are "no jump-scare, teen-bait multiplex horror movie[s]," but instead "make . . . the viewer work for gratification"[24] and "cherish . . . the intelligence of [their] audience."[25]

Meanwhile, populist viewers regularly criticize the films' slow pacing, ambiguous endings, and lack of conventional monsters/thrills, deeming the films to be boring, confusing, not scary, and utterly unsatisfying; indeed, the vast majority of negative criticism from general audiences hinges precisely on the art-cinema traits that these films display. Misleadingly genre-centric trailers have been suggested as one reason for this disappointment: "One hallmark of the new wave of prestige horror is that the movies are often nothing like the trailers. [. . .] Cutting together duplicitous trailers to bait a broader audience into seeing these very good movies seems like the best of a lot of bad options."[26]

Even among the minority of professional critics with negative reviews of these films, the same traits that they might praise in an international art film – stylistic self-consciousness, mood over narrative, cryptic character motivations, depressive affect – are here deemed faults by virtue of their presence in a feature-length horror film. Hence, *The Witch* is a "witches' brew of half-formed subplots, under-baked themes, a grating score, and unlikable characters"[27] that "needs to be less proud of itself and yeah, it needs to be scarier."[28] And "[t]hose expecting a horror movie that's filled with a *lot* of those gross and scary moments will likely be disappointed" by *It Comes at Night*, "while those who might appreciate the film's less horrific storytelling will probably be scared away by the marketing. One thing's for sure: no one who sees this is going to come out of it thinking it was any kind of fun; it's one of the bleakest movies to be released this year."[29] In short, for nonplussed viewers, both casual and professional, these films may be stylish, moody, and technically accomplished – but they are not conventionally "fun," their affective tone may feel more oppressive or alienating than sensational, and their narratives may read as "yet another would-be art piece that mistakes ambiguity for complexity."[30]

In my estimation, post-horror's difference from more conventional horror films is primarily one of *tone*. As Douglas Pye argues, a film's tone resides in how a film's dramatic content is stylistically conveyed via the construction of an overall mood that shapes our affective horizon as viewers. Tone can register through a film's apparent generic or formal/stylistic distance from established norms – and is especially apparent when alternative uses of film form unsettle our conventional ways of approaching genre conventions.[31] Stylistically, post-horror films evince minimalism over maximalism, largely eschewing jump scares, frenetic editing, and energetic and/or handheld cinematography in favor of cold and distanced shot framing, longer-than-average shot durations, slow camera movements, and stately narrative pacing. In *It Follows*, for instance, David Robert Mitchell uses slow 360-degree pans, static long shots, and slow zooms that allow the viewer to share the protagonist's paranoid searching of her visual field for a perpetually approaching monster that can take anyone's form (see Chapter 6), while *The Witch* presents interiors as chiaroscuro tableaux and exteriors as distanced vistas where even a waving tree branch conjures supernatural fears among its family of early American colonists (see Chapter 5).

This tendency toward a "vulnerable stillness" increases the viewer's dread that something might occur at any moment, affectively stretching out the film as a felt temporal experience.[32] Confirming Hawkins's argument, critics often highlight the "poetic" and "dreamlike" qualities of post-horror films, while typically downplaying the more visceral moments. For instance, *I Am the Pretty Thing* is described as "a tone poem," "almost pornographic in its portent, every second of it seductive and ripe with tension, promising money shots that never come."[33] Critics also observe that these films avoid "the annoying modern tendency towards wobblicam and over-editing"[34] and "don't fit neatly into the 'rising action, jump scare, rinse, repeat' model" of mainstream Hollywood horror.[35] Whereas jump scares' sudden audiovisual shocks (as produced through quick cuts, loud aural stingers, and startling intrusions hidden by frame edges) cause visceral bodily reactions that precede and short-circuit higher forms of cognition, post-horror's distanced visual style generally eschews such "cheap" and "dumb" thrills in favor of slow-building tension and sources of fear emerging from small details in the *mise-en-scène* (such as glimpsed hints of a monster). With the de-emphasis on jump scares, there may also be more investment in developing psychologically complex protagonists; as Cary Fukunaga remarked, for example, about his abrupt departure from writing and directing the remake of *It*, "In the first movie, what I was trying to do was an elevated horror film with actual characters. [The studio] didn't want any characters. They wanted archetypes and scares."[36]

Although post-horror films can be said to occupy established horror subgenres in their underlying subject matter (ghostly hauntings in *The Babadook* and *I Am the Pretty Thing*; supernatural curses in *It Follows*; post-apocalyptic survivalism in *It Comes at Night*; demonic possession in *Hereditary*), familiar genre tropes become decentered via art cinema's formal expressiveness and narrative ambiguity, making space for characters and viewers alike to soak in contemplative or emotionally fraught moods, not be shuffled along to the next abrupt scare. In these films, for instance, the appearance of the monster itself is frequently downplayed or presented only indirectly – whether turned into an invisible or abstract force (*It Follows*, *It Comes at Night*), or presented as a potential figment of a character's overwrought imagination (*The Witch*, *I Am the Pretty Thing*) or mental illness (*The Babadook*, *Hereditary*). Even when the monster does appear, it often takes a recognizably human form, not that of a grotesquely inhuman creature. *A Ghost Story* (2017) takes this decentering of the conventional monster to an extreme, presenting its titular ghost as an actor under a white sheet with black eyeholes – thus replacing the horror genre's fear-inducing ghosts with a more comic image that marks the film's closer generic resemblance to an existential drama.

Indeed, one of the major characteristics of post-horror films is a thematic exploration of what Silvan Tomkins terms "negative affects"[37] (including grief, sadness, shame, anger), with fear serving as an affective platform for shifting to affects that might be more closely associated with the themes in "serious" arthouse dramas. *I Am the Pretty Thing* and *A Ghost Story*, for instance, use the figure of the ghost for poetically meditating on mortality, memory, and time (Chapter 7), while other films have more worldly concerns. *Hereditary*, *The Babadook*, and many other post-horror texts operate, in addition to horror films, as family dramas about grief, mourning, and monstrous reproduction (Chapter 3). In a more sociopolitical context, *Get Out* explores the hypocrisies of white liberalism as a racially charged iteration of the epistemic violence in "gaslighting" (Chapter 4), while *The Witch* uses its teenage protagonist's budding sexuality and growing defiance of her family patriarch as an exploration of puritanical paranoia about unruly female bodies (Chapter 5), as though contextualizing the historical roots of the sexual shame and control depicted in *It Follows* (Chapter 6). Of course, this is not to say that more mainstream horror films have not used similar themes in less "rarified" forms, but rather that post-horror films tend to ascribe more narrative weight to such concerns – and, more importantly, the films' stylistic minimalism distinctly enhances such themes' cumulative negative affect. To put it another way, the underlying themes in many post-horror films are not necessarily new to the genre – which may account for why so many of them, by offering recognizable generic hooks, found crossover distribution to multiplexes, in spite of their arthouse stylization. Rather, the key distinction resides in *how* these films' relatively minimalistic form activates themes and anxieties that have long existed within the genre.

Although the preceding paragraphs constitute more of a précis for the chapters to come, we can begin to sketch the contours of the post-horror corpus via three main criteria: (1) which films that critics have labeled as such; (2) which films share the aforementioned formal/stylistic characteristics; and (3) whether these texts substantially engage with themes generating negative affects. In Table 1.1, I have subdivided the post-horror corpus into those films which best represent the above criteria (the "primary" or "core" texts), and

Table 1.1 Provisional corpus of post-horror cinema

Primary/core texts	Secondary/peripheral texts
Under the Skin (Jonathan Glazer, 2013)	*Let the Right One In* (Tomas Alfredson, 2008)
It Follows (David Robert Mitchell, 2014)	*House of the Devil* (Ti West, 2009)
The Witch (Robert Eggers, 2015)	*Absentia* (Mike Flanagan, 2011)
The Blackcoat's Daughter (Oz Perkins, 2015)	*The Innkeepers* (Ti West, 2011)
The Invitation (Karyn Kusama, 2015)	*Berberian Sound Studio* (Peter Strickland, 2012)
A Dark Song (Liam Gavin, 2016)	*Only Lovers Left Alive* (Jim Jarmusch, 2013)
The Eyes of My Mother (Nicholas Pesce, 2016)	*Enemy* (Denis Villeneuve, 2013)
I Am the Pretty Thing That Lives in the House (Oz Perkins, 2016)	*The Babadook* (Jennifer Kent, 2014)
A Ghost Story (David Lowery, 2017)	*Goodnight Mommy* (Veronika Franz and Severin Fiala, 2014)
It Comes at Night (Trey Edward Shults, 2017)	*Evolution* (Lucile Hadžihalilović, 2015)
Get Out (Jordan Peele, 2017)	*Don't Breathe* (Fede Álvarez, 2016)
Hagazussa: A Heathen's Curse (Lukas Feigelfeld, 2017)	*Personal Shopper* (Olivier Assayas, 2016)
Hereditary (Ari Aster, 2018)	*Under the Shadow* (Babak Anvari, 2016)
Midsommar (Ari Aster, 2019)	*The Untamed* (Amat Escalante, 2016)
The Lighthouse (Robert Eggers, 2019)	*Raw* (Julia Ducournau, 2016)
The Lodge (Veronika Franz and Severin Fiala, 2019)	*The Neon Demon* (Nicolas Winding Refn, 2016)
Relic (Natalie Erika James, 2020)	*mother!* (Darren Aronofsky, 2017)
She Dies Tomorrow (Amy Seimetz, 2020)	*The Killing of a Sacred Deer* (Yorgos Lanthimos, 2017)
	A Quiet Place (John Krasinski, 2018)
	Suspiria (Luca Guadagnino, 2018)
	Us (Jordan Peele, 2019)
	Swallow (Carlo Mirabella-Davis, 2019)
	Gretel & Hansel (Oz Perkins, 2020)
	Amulet (Romola Garai, 2020)

those films which display only some of the aesthetic qualities or which critics have less frequently associated with the trend (the "secondary" or "peripheral" texts). This subdivision is intended to help indicate how not all films critically ascribed to "post-horror" status share all of the aforementioned stylistic traits, nor are those traits wholly new or exclusive to only the films clustered beneath that banner. In this regard, I have attempted to strike a balance between my own subjective reading of each film's formal/affective qualities and a more objective survey of which films have been critically nominated as post-horror.

The films most often identified as post-horror's core examples (such as *It Follows*, *The Witch*, and *Hereditary*) bear a distinctly slow, austere, and minimalist style for most of their duration, for instance – but I have also included less overtly restrained films like *The Invitation* (2015) and *Get Out* on the primary list due to both their ubiquity in critical discourse about post-horror and their thematic similarities to core post-horror texts. Films on the secondary list, by contrast, may initially share the claustrophobic ambience and shortage of jump scares associated with the primary texts, but eventually devote extended narrative duration to faster, action-oriented pacing (as in *Don't Breathe* (2016) and *mother!* (2017)) or uncharacteristically violent scenes (as in *Goodnight Mommy* and *Suspiria* (2018)). Likewise, critics frequently described *A Quiet Place* as "elevated horror" due to its clever narrative conceit (the characters must remain silent to avoid attracting monsters that hunt by sound), but I have relegated it to the secondary list because its overall form adheres so closely to classical Hollywood style and narration (as compared to, say, the art-film ambiguities of the similarly post-apocalyptic *It Comes at Night*).[38] Moreover, some of the secondary films – such as *The Neon Demon* (2016) and *Personal Shopper* (2016) – may appear too peripheral to the horror genre itself for some viewers to readily associate them with post-horror. Despite the table's rather schematic look, then, these subdivisions should be seen as potentially fluid, and readers are welcome to add or subtract entries on either provisional list, depending on whether one privileges (1) critical nomination; (2) formal/stylistic minimalism; or (3) thematic/affective resonance.

Narrative vs. Affect

Thus far, I have argued that post-horror is a variant of art-horror distinguished from its generic kin via a minimalist aesthetic that functionally enhances the affective impact of a set of recurring themes. Although I will elaborate in subsequent chapters on these themes and how post-horror's formal style informs their narrative meaning, a few additional words about the relationship between narrative, genre, and the generation of affect are important for understanding how these films operate as "apprehension engines" – and thereby why they have engendered such a gaping evaluative divide between, on one side, horror-skeptic film critics and horror-friendly genre fans and, on the other side, more casual and populist horror viewers. After all, it is one thing to analyze texts for their thematic content as an interpretive through-line connecting multiple films, but another to consider how affect may, in fact, be better generated by films whose narratives are more impressionistic than explicitly discerned.

Rather than the monster serving as the horror genre's conventional locus for generating emotions of fear and disgust (as Noël Carroll has argued),[39] many of these films veer closer to Tzvetan Todorov's concept of "the fantastic," as narratives rooted in hesitation over whether apparently supernatural occurrences can be explained away as mere "uncanny" events with rational elucidation or whether something truly "marvelous" is afoot.[40] As noted earlier, in classic art-cinema style, these films predominantly filter their diegetic visions through the vagaries of characters' distressed psychological states, often refusing to confirm or deny the truth of their seemingly supernatural happenings. Hence, if these films evoke a deep sense of unease, it is partly because they often retain one foot in the realm of real-world plausibility.

The Witch, for example, leaves ambiguity about whether a witch has actually beset a colonial family, whether the various travails of frontier life (child disappearances, crop and livestock failures, and so on) are mere projections of puritanical fears about Satan's invisible assaults, or even whether blame can be attributed to a hallucinogenic rot on the family's corn. This mix of epistemic registers is further suggested by the film's titular subtitle "A New England Folktale" (cuing us to expect a more mythical narrative), whereas a closing onscreen card informs us that this "folktale" was also inspired by "written accounts of historical witchcraft, including journals, diaries, and court records. Much of the dialogue comes directly from these period sources." As Aviva Briefel argues, the film's revival of a historically accurate past thus conflicts with its potential to be read as a historical counter-narrative confirming the "actual" existence of Puritan-era witchcraft.[41] In this sense, *The Witch*'s historical verisimilitude blends supernatural ambiguity with the "documentary realism" that David Bordwell associates with some examples of art cinema,[42] with the film's portrayed events occupying an epistemic shadow not unlike the so-called "spectral evidence" presented against suspected witches during colonial-era trials.

Matt Hills argues that horror cinema may be organized less around the object-directed emotions that Carroll privileges, but instead "immerse its audiences in an 'anticipatory' mood or ambience that endures across the text" – an overwhelming affect of "objectless anxiety" that may especially linger beyond the text when a film ends without a clear narrative resolution.[43] For Hills, horror should be defined more as an "event-based" than "entity-based" aesthetic experience, with narrative circumstances and the details of *mise-en-scène* and cinematography being capable of generating horror even in films like *The Haunting* (1963) and *The Blair Witch Project* (1999) where a monster is implied but never explicitly manifest.[44] In other words, because affect precedes emotion, creating diffuse sensations that may not be easily ascribed to particular characters (whether humans or monsters), the horror genre's affective impact cannot be simply reduced to abject imagery of the monster and its effects. This idea certainly fits post-horror's lessened focus on the terror-inducing monster as a clearly defined narrative locus, and its alternate focus on generating ambient states of dreadful unease.

Hence, in a film like *It Comes at Night*, there is no "it" revealed over the course of the film (a recurring complaint among populist viewers), beyond the literal nightmares among a family of plague survivors fighting off potential interlopers and an invisible disease (see Chapter 5), while *The Neon Demon* contains no "demon" beyond the insatiable consumers of youthful beauty in Los Angeles's cut-throat fashion world. In its story of a high-minded British sound designer (Toby Jones) slowly losing his mind while working on a 1970s Italian *giallo* film, *Berberian Sound Studio* (2012) even goes so far as to conceal any horrific sights whatsoever from the film's own viewers; apart from a brief glimpse of the film-within-the-film's opening title sequence, we only ever see (and feel) Gilderoy's reaction shots to the violent footage as he creates morbid Foley effects for the gory scenes that are merely described to us. Compared to the rather straightforward narrative conceit of *A Quiet Place*, then, *Berberian Sound Studio* presents a far more *formally* self-conscious play upon how sound is typically used in the horror genre. Because post-horror thus prioritizes affect over monstrous entities, it is perhaps little surprise that these texts seem more difficult for film critics to label in a satisfactory way, unlike so many entity-based subgeneric labels (such as "slasher," "zombie," and so on).

As Robert Spadoni argues, atmosphere in horror cinema is often considered secondary and subservient to narrative concerns, but affective moods like dread prove that atmosphere is functionally inseparable from narrative – operating less as accompaniment than *culmination* of certain scenes. Thus atmosphere "may have as special a relationship to the *absence* of narrative as it does to narrative."[45] He further suggests that atmosphere and narrative exist in tension with each other, with one side filling in where the other is used more sparsely.[46] In this regard, then, the relative paucity of classical Hollywood narrative structure in post-horror films allows their thick affective ambience to take precedence during the viewing experience. Also of note here are their ambient scores and claustrophobic sound design, from Rich Vreeland's eerie retro-synth vibes in *It Follows* to Mark Korven's quasi-medieval noisescapes for *The Witch*. If orchestral scores traditionally cater to object/character-based emotions, then these more affectively immersive, dread-inducing uses of music underscore the films' function as "apprehension engines" that seldom deliver the same narrative beats as populist horror films.

Much as horror films may shift from narrative to atmosphere, it is precisely this ability for horror to shift fluidly from objectless affect to object-directed emotion (and vice versa) that, I argue, allows the genre's traditional emotion (fear) to be shifted toward other negative affects in post-horror films.[47] As noted earlier, these films do not regularly deliver the steady string of jump scares that typically relieve tension, instead allowing dread to stretch across and beyond the loose progression of narrative events. Hence, even if eschewing many of the genre's most familiar means of sensationally addressing the viewer, "formal or thematic 'sophistication' seems to authorize sensation" (that is, affect) in a different mode by instead "incorporat[ing] sensation into their [arthouse] style."[48] When viscerally shocking moments do occasionally occur in post-horror films, they are more likely used to signal major traumatic events, and therefore used to greater thematic effect than as disposably "cheap" scares. In *Hereditary*, for instance, Charlie's (Milly Shapiro) sudden decapitation comes as a major shock to viewers (see Chapter 3) – but those who saw the film in theaters will likely recall audience members who emulated Charlie's dental clicks during other parts of the film, effectively trying to relieve the near-constant tension that the film refuses to temper with jump scares or comic relief.

Here, then, we also have a tension between the "quiet-attentive" mode of pleasurably concentrated viewership that Julian Hanich associates with the collective theatrical experience of slow art cinema and the "expressive-diverted" mode in which film viewers' responses become a partial focus of co-present viewers' attention.[49] The latter mode is conventionally expected of the horror genre (especially in the populist forms typically found at multiplexes), whereas the former mode can be more apt for consuming post-horror texts. As Hanich notes, dread-inducing scenes seem to stretch out time by delaying narrative momentum, but even though horror films typically use such scenes to pleasurably build up tension before a scare, such scenes can instead run the risk of generating boredom and feeling unfinished when conventionally expected scares do not come.[50] Adam Charles Hart, for example, argues that jump scares have become such a defining characteristic of the twenty-first-century horror experience that the overall genre functions as a system for prioritizing bodily responses above narrative absorption. Yet, when this "sensational address" is far less overt, when the viewer's body is not directly implicated in completing a given scene's intended effect, then a horror film may not offer the "affirming experience" that the film is being made for the viewer's entertainment.[51] Rather than being encouraged to play a game with the filmmaker over when and how the expected scares will arrive, post-horror films sometimes seem indifferent to audience response, willing to risk alienating viewers in the service of a "higher" artistic vision. As we will see in the next chapter, this stylistic flouting of generic convention vis-à-vis dread helps explain the sharp divide between populist viewers who accuse post-horror films of being "boring" and high-minded film critics who celebrate such "slowness" as their own show of elitist tastes.[52]

Unlike the jump scares that have abruptly punctuated the final frames of many Hollywood horror films since *Carrie* (1976), post-horror films more likely extend their sense of fantastic hesitation and ambient affect by way of art cinema's open endings (especially an abrupt cut-to-black), as an extension of narrative ambiguity – instead of delivering one last scare before the lights come up and thus teasing the monster's survival for a potential sequel. *The Witch*, for example, ends with its protagonist, her family's sole survivor, joining a coven of witches in the woods and levitating into the trees – but whether this is all a fantasy sequence borne of desperation or an actual event is left unclear. Likewise, the seemingly "happy" formation of the heterosexual couple at the end of *It Follows* is undercut by their ignorance that they are still quite possibly being followed by that film's titular entity, as seen in the distant background (see Figure 6.2). More often than not, such ambiguously open endings extend the post-horror film's affective power across and beyond the narrative events, leaving viewers in a more pensive position than the average horror film. Rather than a mere question of misleading marketing, then, occupying a stylistic position closer to "difficult" art cinema than populist genre cinema means that post-horror films offer audiences beyond the art house an expanded view of what the horror film can feel like, but at the cost of potentially alienating many horror-friendly viewers with less (sub)cultural capital.

The Chapters to Come

The remaining chapters in this book discuss other important aspects of the post-horror phenomenon, moving outward from the formal/aesthetic and affective traits sketched here, through the mesh of critical debates that encircle the corpus's boundaries, and into recurring threads in the thematic and social meanings engendered by such a diverse group of texts. Each chapter addresses films from both the primary and secondary lists presented in Table 1.1, in order to indicate the places where these lists aesthetically or thematically overlap. Much as the body of films in Table 1.1 should be seen as an open and fluidly shifting category, this book does not pretend to offer an exhaustive overview of all post-horror films – not least because the post-horror cycle is still in progress at the time of this writing – but also because these complex interminglings of art cinema and horror cinema readily lend themselves to many methods of scholarly analysis. Indeed, several of these films (including *The Witch*, *The Babadook*, *It Follows*, and *Get Out*) have already inspired separate academic volumes and plentiful articles of their own – with surely more to come – while multiple films that I had originally planned to analyze herein fell by the wayside as the project evolved. My own modest goal for *Post-Horror* is to provide a useful entry point into this corpus by reading across a variety of the cycle's major texts in order to account for genre history, critical/popular reception, sociocultural implications, and artistic style. Since this book is primarily a work of film criticism, I also invite readers to follow along with the mini-analyses in the following chapters, by watching the films with me and developing their own conclusions.

Building atop this chapter's focus on art-horror, Chapter 2 examines the successive critical attempts to name this emergent cycle of films as something other than the literal conjunction of art cinema and horror, including modifiers like "slow," "smart," "indie," "prestige," "elevated," and finally "post." As I will argue, the shortcomings in each of these naming attempts were driven as much by critics' difficulties to put the films' affective impact into words as by the increased speed and fragmentation of film-critical discourse during the social-media era. The immediate flak that these terms earned from genre-literate fans reflects online film criticism's collapsing of longstanding cultural lines between professional film critics as (horror-skeptic) cultural gatekeepers and genre fans as (horror-friendly) organic intellectuals, with each broad category of viewers actualizing a different degree of either (legitimate) cultural capital or (less recognized) subcultural capital. Nevertheless, by looking at the individual meanings of these critical labels, we can trace an intersecting series of historical lineages that have led into the stylistic and discursive construction of the post-horror corpus.

Chapter 3 begins to unpack some of the recurring narrative tropes in these films by exploring how familial traumas – particularly the narrativized process of mourning a lost family member – form one of the most prominent ways that post-horror encroaches on the generic territory of serious arthouse dramas. In making such a comparison, however, I am not trying to make the case, as some horror-skeptic viewers have done, that these films are "actually" something (anything!) other than "horror" movies; rather, I am interested in how these films expose fault lines between genres and modes that are too frequently considered separate categories. With the affective shape of grief at their disposal, many of these films (*Goodnight Mommy*, *The Babadook*, *Hereditary*) depict mothers and their offspring as made monstrous by their emotional response to the haunting loss of immediate family members. Moreover, drawing on Richard Armstrong's generic conception of the "mourning film," this chapter argues that themes of generationally inherited dysfunction serve as a larger metaphor for post-horror's own relationship to both the horror genre and art cinema.

Shifting the focus from familial to romantic relationships, and from the personal to the political, Chapter 4 posits that "gaslighting" serves as a common theme in post-horror films where emotional abuse cannot be immediately ascribed to intergenerational family dynamics. Whereas the couple is presented as part of an endangered out-group in both *The Invitation* and *Midsommar* (2019), the racialized possession of black bodies in *Get Out* demonstrates how gaslighting within romantic bonds can function as a form of epistemic violence that reinforces larger social inequalities beyond sexism. The affective discomfort created by films about the horrors of gaslighting is further heightened by post-horror's tendency toward epistemic hesitation, encouraging viewers to reflect on their own positionality as viewers who may or may not know more than the deceived protagonists.

Chapter 5 looks at how post-horror films use their physical settings to differently generate affect, with particular emphasis on rural areas and wilderness as spaces whose sparseness and depopulation operates in conjunction with the films' own stylistic minimalism. To call these films "spaced out" describes not only their literal locations, but also the films' generic distance from the larger horror genre and the contemplative mood that each one encourages. Witchcraft-themed films like *The Witch*, *Hagazussa: A Heathen's Curse* (2017), and *Gretel & Hansel* (2020) use wilderness settings to evoke woman's place in relation to fertile landscapes, while post-apocalyptic survival films like *It Comes at Night* and *A Quiet Place* use the countryside to invoke a paranoid "bunker mentality" against perceived or actual threats to the existing family. Meanwhile, seaside-set films like *The Lighthouse* (2019) allow us to explore post-horror's larger relationship to inhospitable realms of non-human nature as well.

Unlike the previous chapter's discussion of wild natural spaces, Chapter 6 offers an extended case study of one of the earliest and most important post-horror films, *It Follows*, whose overall aesthetic is rooted in its specifically urban, postindustrial setting. Through its ironic critique of monogamy as a monstrous force, I argue that the film advances, by way of negative example, a queer ethics of open, responsible sexuality – albeit an ethics constrained by the film's setting in a neoliberal Detroit increasingly stripped of public services. By examining the film's ambivalent nostalgia for both a generic and an urban past, this chapter argues that *It Follows*'s queer aesthetic achieves its affective tenor through imaging Detroit's decrepit (sub)urban spaces as haunted by polyvalent sexualities and socioeconomic inequalities.

Finally, Chapter 7 answers the prior reframing of sexuality as a horror of the body by examining the other side of a classic philosophical dualism: horrors of the soul. Although hardly unique to post-horror films, one of the cycle's contributions to the genre is refiguring the ghost from a vengeful, fear-inducing trope into a much more existential figure, as in *A Ghost Story* and *I Am the Pretty Thing That Lives in the House*. Meanwhile, *A Dark Song* (2016) echoes *A Ghost Story*'s concern with individual grief's relationship to cosmic realms of (non)existence, much as *mother!* and *I Am the Pretty Thing* ask whether artistic creation itself can play any role in personal or spiritual redemption. In closing the book, these stories about attempts to gain some sort of transcendence thus serve as a way of imagining post-horror's own mixed success at (for better or worse) transcending the genre itself.

Notes

1. Indie Film Maker, "Horror Musical Instrument – The Apprehension Engine," YouTube, September 30, 2016, <https://www.youtube.com/watch?v=lzk-l8Gm0MY>; Great Big Story, "Sounds of the Nightmare Machine," YouTube, June 20, 2017 <https://www.youtube.com/watch?v=1lTYPvArbGo>.
2. The Apprehension Engine, accessed June 27, 2019 <http://apprehensionengine.com/PreOrder/>.
3. Laura Birnbaum, "*The Blackcoat's Daughter*: The Film You Aren't Ready to See (But Should)," *Film Inquiry*, July 1, 2016 <https://www.filminquiry.com/blackcoats-daughter-2015-review/>.

4. Watching Staff, "21st Century Horror," *New York Times*, accessed June 24, 2019 <https://www.nytimes.com/watching/lists/best-horror-movies-21st-century>.
5. Steve Rose, "How Post-Horror Movies are Taking Over Cinema," *The Guardian*, July 6, 2017 <https://www.theguardian.com/film/2017/jul/06/post-horror-films-scary-movies-ghost-story-it-comes-at-night>.
6. See Sheila J. Nayar, "Epistemic Capital: The Etiology of an 'Elitist' Film Canon's Aesthetic Criteria," *Post Script*, 29, no. 1 (2009), pp. 27–44.
7. Pierre Bourdieu, *Distinction: A Social Critique of the Judgment of Taste*, trans. Richard Nice (Cambridge, MA: Harvard University Press, 1984), pp. 16, 27.
8. On the distinction between potential and actual subcultural capital, see Matt Hills, "Attending Horror Film Festivals and Conventions: Liveness, Subcultural Capital, and 'Flesh-and-Blood Genre Communities,'" in *Horror Zone: The Cultural Experience of Contemporary Horror Cinema*, ed. Ian Conrich (New York: I. B. Tauris, 2010), pp. 92–3.
9. Sarah Thornton, *Club Cultures: Music, Media, and Subcultural Capital* (Middletown, CT: Wesleyan University Press, 1996), pp. 11–12.
10. Jostein Gripsrud, "'High Culture' Revisited," *Cultural Studies*, 3, no. 2 (1989), pp. 196–8.
11. There are plenty of populist viewers at the horror-skeptic end of the continuum as well, but because they lack the horror-skeptic film critic's professional obligation to occasionally watch horror films, horror-skeptic populist viewers are more likely to altogether avoid viewing or sharing opinions about (post-)horror films. Therefore they will be generally left unaddressed in this book.
12. Nevertheless, these two films do veer considerably closer to the dominant Hollywood style than most post-horror films (see Chapters 4 and 5), and had the support of major Hollywood studios as distributors. Both films also feature established actors, and directors who were widely known from previous television careers as comic actors. These factors all helped contribute to their box-office success, relative to post-horror films with more modest origins and more pronounced art-cinema inspiration.
13. Gripsrud, "'High Culture' Revisited," 199. This double access surely animates my own taste-based biases toward the films under consideration in this book, even as my larger academic career has also focused on revaluing culturally "low" texts, such as exploitation and adult films, on their own terms.
14. Among others, see Gregory A. Waller, "Made-for-Television Horror Films," in *American Horrors: Essays on the Modern American Horror Film*, ed. Gregory A. Waller (Urbana, IL: University of Illinois Press, 1987), p. 148; Mark Jancovich, "Genre and the Audience: Genre Classifications and Cultural Distinctions in the Mediation of *The Silence of the Lambs*," in *Horror: The Film Reader*, ed. Mark Jancovich (London: Routledge, 2002), pp. 151–61; Joan Hawkins, *Cutting Edge: Art-Horror and the Horrific Avant-Garde* (Minneapolis, MN: University of Minnesota Press, 2000), ch. 3; Kate Egan, *Trash or Treasure? Censorship and the Changing Meanings of the Video Nasties* (Manchester: Manchester University

Press, 2007), ch. 1; Daniel Martin, "Japan's *Blair Witch*: Restraint, Maturity, and Generic Canons in the British Critical Reception of *Ring*," *Cinema Journal*, 48, no. 3 (2009), pp. 35–51; I. Q. Hunter, *British Trash Cinema* (London: British Film Institute, 2013).
15. For example, Brian Massumi, *Parables for the Virtual: Movement, Affect, Sensation* (Durham, NC: Duke University Press, 2002), ch. 1; Teresa Brennan, *The Transmission of Affect* (Ithaca, NY: Cornell University Press, 2004), ch. 1; Eric Shouse, "Feeling, Emotion, Affect," *M/C Journal*, 8, no. 6 (2005) <http://journal.media-culture.org.au/0512/03-shouse.php>; Gregory J. Seigworth and Melissa Gregg, "An Inventory of Shimmers," in *The Affect Theory Reader*, eds Gregory J. Seigworth and Melissa Gregg (Durham, NC: Duke University Press, 2010), pp. 1–25; Sara Ahmed, *The Cultural Politics of Emotion*, 2nd edn (Edinburgh: Edinburgh University Press, 2014), pp. 204–18.
16. On this model of film-cycle development, see Richard Nowell, *Blood Money: A History of the First Teen Slasher Film Cycle* (London: Continuum, 2011), pp. 42–7.
17. This literal conjunction of the art-cinema mode and the horror genre should not be confused with Noël Carroll's cognitivist use of the term "art-horror" to broadly describe emotional responses to horrific works of art (as opposed to real-world horrors) – not least because Carroll's entity-based approach to the horror genre does not usefully explain post-horror, as I elaborate below. See Carroll, *The Philosophy of Horror, or Paradoxes of the Heart* (New York: Routledge, 1990), pp. 27–42.
18. David Bordwell, "The Art Cinema as a Mode of Film Practice," in *Critical Visions in Film Theory: Classic and Contemporary Readings*, eds Timothy Corrigan, Patricia White, and Meta Mazaj (Boston: Bedford/St. Martin's, 2011), pp. 560–4.
19. Hawkins, *Cutting Edge*, 4–8, 21–8.
20. Matt Hills, "Para-Paracinema: The *Friday the 13th* Film Series as Other to Trash and Legitimate Film Cultures," in *Sleaze Artists: Cinema at the Margins of Taste, Style, and Politics*, ed. Jeffrey Sconce (Durham, NC: Duke University Press, 2007), pp. 221–2 (quoted at p. 222).
21. Ibid., pp. 220–1; Jeffrey Sconce, "'Trashing' the Academy: Taste, Excess, and an Emerging Politics of Cinematic Style," *Screen*, 36, no. 4 (1995), pp. 371–93.
22. See James Quandt, "Flesh and Blood: Sex and Violence in Recent French Cinema," *Artforum*, 42, no. 6 (2004), pp. 126–32; Joan Hawkins, "Culture Wars: Some New Trends in Art Horror," *Jump Cut*, no. 51 (2009) <https://www.ejumpcut.org/archive/jc51.2009/artHorror/>; Tanya Horek and Tina Kendall (eds), *The New Extremism in Cinema: From France to Europe* (Edinburgh: Edinburgh University Press, 2011); Mattias Frey, *Extreme Cinema: The Transgressive Rhetoric of Today's Art Film Culture* (New Brunswick, NJ: Rutgers University Press, 2016), ch. 2; Aaron Michael Kerner and Jonathan L. Knapp, *Extreme Cinema: Affective Strategies in Transnational Media* (Edinburgh: Edinburgh University Press, 2017), ch. 1.

23. Hawkins, *Cutting Edge*, 66.
24. Chris Alexander, "TIFF 2016 Review: *I Am the Pretty Thing That Lives in the House*," *ComingSoon.net*, September 12, 2016 <http://www.comingsoon.net/horror/reviews/766113-tiff-2016-review-i-am-the-pretty-thing-that-lives-in-the-house>.
25. Kiernan McLoone, "*It Comes at Night* and the Power of the Unseen Horror," *Cultured Vultures*, July 12, 2017 <https://culturedvultures.com/it-comes-at-night-horror/>.
26. Jordan Crucchiola, "Why Do Prestige-Horror Trailers Keep Lying to Us?" *Vulture*, June 13, 2017 <http://www.vulture.com/2017/06/it-comes-at-night-why-are-horror-trailers-lying-to-us.html>.
27. Ethan Sacks, "'The Witch' Casts a Spell on Critics Even Though It's Not Very Good," *New York Daily News*, February 17, 2016 <http://www.nydailynews.com/entertainment/movies/witch-casts-spell-critics-not-good-article-1.2529738>.
28. Will Leitch, "*The Witch*: Suffer the Little Children," *New Republic*, February 19, 2016 <https://newrepublic.com/article/130182/witch-suffer-little-children>.
29. Rain Jokinen, "Bleak 'It Comes at Night' is a Thoroughly Unpleasant Experience," *SFist*, June 9, 2017 <http://sfist.com/2017/06/09/bleak_it_comes_at_night_a_thoroughl.php> (original emphasis).
30. Richard Lawson, "*It Comes at Night* is a Pretty But Pointless Downer," *Vanity Fair*, June 6, 2017 <http://www.vanityfair.com/hollywood/2017/06/it-comes-at-night-review>.
31. Douglas Pye, "Movies and Tone," in *Close-Up 02*, eds John Gibbs and Douglas Pye (London: Wallflower Press, 2007), pp. 7, 21, 23, 28, 76.
32. Julian Hanich, *Cinematic Emotion in Horror Films and Thrillers: The Aesthetic Paradox of Pleasurable Fear* (New York: Routledge, 2010), pp. 179–80, 187.
33. Alexander, "TIFF 2016 Review."
34. Anne Billson, "Cheap Thrills: The Frightful Rise of Low-Budget Horror," *The Telegraph*, May 6, 2015 <http://www.telegraph.co.uk/film/it-follows/rise-of-low-budget-horror-movies-babadook/>.
35. Crucchiola, "Why Do Prestige-Horror."
36. Quoted in Ramin Setoodeh, "Cary Fukunaga Offers New Details on Why 'It' Remake Fell Apart," *Variety*, September 2, 2015 <https://variety.com/2015/film/news/cary-fukunaga-it-exit-1201584416/>.
37. Silvan S. Tomkins, *Affect, Imagery, Consciousness: The Complete Edition* (New York: Springer, 2008), vols II–III.
38. The quick, direct-to-streaming release of imitators like Netflix's *Bird Box* (2018) and *The Silence* (2019), both of which similarly use sensory-deprivation themes within post-apocalyptic milieus, also suggests how *A Quiet Place*'s success can be attributed to a gimmick that proved easily adaptable to conventional Hollywood filmmaking practices and audience expectations.
39. Carroll, *The Philosophy of Horror*, 28–30.

40. Tzvetan Todorov, *The Fantastic: A Structural Approach to a Literary Genre*, trans. Richard Howard (Ithaca, NY: Cornell University Press, 1975), ch. 2.
41. Aviva Briefel, "Devil in the Details: The Uncanny History of *The Witch* (2015)," *Film & History: An Interdisciplinary Journal*, 49, no. 1 (2019), p. 6.
42. Bordwell, "The Art Cinema," 562.
43. Matt Hills, *The Pleasures of Horror* (London: Continuum, 2005), pp. 25–7 (quoted at pp. 25, 27).
44. Matt Hills, "An Event-Based Definition of Art-Horror," in *Dark Thoughts: Philosophic Reflections on Cinematic Horror*, eds Steven Jay Schneider and Daniel Shaw (Lanham, MD: Scarecrow Press, 2003), pp. 142–4, 148–50.
45. Robert Spadoni, "Carl Dreyer's Corpse: Horror Film Atmosphere and Narrative," in *A Companion to the Horror Film*, ed. Harry M. Benshoff (Malden, MA: Wiley Blackwell, 2014), pp. 157–9, 165 (quoted at p. 165), original emphasis.
46. Robert Spadoni, "Horror Film Atmosphere as Anti-Narrative (and Vice Versa)," in *Merchants of Menace: The Business of Horror Cinema*, ed. Richard Nowell (New York: Bloomsbury Academic, 2014), pp. 109–12.
47. Hills, *The Pleasures of Horror*, 28.
48. Adam Charles Hart, *Monstrous Forms: Moving Image Horror Across Media* (New York: Oxford University Press, 2020), p. 83.
49. Julian Hanich, *The Audience Effect: On the Collective Cinema Experience* (Edinburgh: Edinburgh University Press, 2018), pp. 95, 112.
50. Hanich, *Cinematic Emotion*, 169, 187, 192.
51. Hart, *Monstrous Forms*, 28, 34, 41, 51, 68, 80 (quoted at p. 51).
52. See, for example, the discussion of *Midsommar* (2019) in Charles Bramesco, "Extended Scares: In Defense of the Two-Hour-Plus Horror Movie," *The Guardian*, July 1, 2019, <https://www.theguardian.com/film/2019/jul/01/midsommar-ari-aster-horror-movie-extended>.

CHAPTER 2

"Slow," "Smart," "Indie," "Prestige," "Elevated": Discursive Struggle for Cultural Distinction

Elevated horror is like an artisanal cheeseburger. Make the goddamn cheeseburger. If it's delicious, nobody will care what adjective you put in front of it.

– Matt Zoller Seitz[1]

It would not be a stretch to say that the loudest critical conversation about the horror genre during the first decade of the twenty-first century concerned the post-9/11 rise of so-called "torture porn" films (such as *Saw* (2004) and *Hostel* (2005)) and their graphic depictions of extreme violence. More specifically, these films were so controversial because they proved to be popular films at the American multiplex at a flashpoint in the "War on Terror," when cynically capitalizing on torture was also occurring on a national-political level.[2] When we jump forward to the second decade of the new millennium, however, the state of horror cinema seems to have changed quite substantially. As noted in the previous chapter, post-horror films are increasingly finding a home in multiplexes, more likely offering de-sensationalized takes on genre conventions, and privileging visual restraint over exaggerated displays of spectacularly opened bodies. Accordingly, the critical conversation has also moved on, with horror-skeptic film critics and horror-friendly genre fans debating to what extent these films fit into larger generic traditions, and how these films might violate the narrower sets of generic expectations that high-minded critics and populist viewers project onto the genre. In other words, if torture-porn films amped up the genre's visceral attention to abjection, post-horror films answer this excess by moving in a very different stylistic direction, albeit one that can still generate its own strong affects and receptional divisiveness when viewed by wider audiences.

In the previous chapter, I argued that "art-horror" is a more literal way to describe a *stylistic* core for post-horror cinema, rather than being used as an evaluative epithet. In this chapter, however, I will trace the shifting critical reception around these films by way of the adjectival modifiers variously applied to the corpus, including "indie," "smart," "prestige," "elevated," and finally "post." Although subject to contestation, it is important to examine the critical labels that are used to demarcate this emerging wave of art-horror films as somehow different from the presumed generic norm. As I will argue, the succession of different terms used to name the cycle is not merely a question of taste, but also a product of film critics grappling with the affective qualities of these films – trying and repeatedly failing to find a name sufficient for circumscribing the affects produced by art cinema's formal structures. Rather than merely rejecting these labels (as genre-literate fans have so often done), then, this chapter examines each one as a productive site for revealing different layers of the post-horror corpus and its influences.

These various descriptors commingled and overlapped with each other as they appeared during 2014–17, but we can still trace a rough trajectory for their prevalence within critical discourse. Among the earliest terms were "slow horror," which then ceded the discursive stage to "smart horror," "indie horror," and "prestige horror," and finally settled into "elevated horror" and "post-horror" as the most-used critical shorthand to date. Looking at each descriptor is useful for telling us something about what film critics saw in these films and how genre fans responded to these qualifiers in sometimes hostile ways.

More crucially, though, each of these sets of terms offers clues for contextualizing post-horror's historical and stylistic precursors, and understanding how their affective qualities produced the critical difficulty in landing on a satisfactory label. Despite the commonality of fan-cultural discourse accusing horror-skeptic film critics of snobbery for developing such labels, genre fans are also implicitly responding to a broader "crisis of expertise" in film criticism, wherein freelance or unpaid articles increasingly vie for online readers' clicks and retweets but are not necessarily written by authors with high amounts of either cultural or subcultural capital. As Mattias Frey observes, "from the very first film critics, including the early trade press through the postwar leading organs of film criticism, the worry over a loss of status, as well as the 'dumbing down' of film criticism, has continually reappeared in remarkably consistent language."[3] The transition from print to digital media has reactivated these longstanding critical anxieties – but rather than a wholesale "dumbing down" of film criticism, horror-friendly fans' own critical interventions attempt to reconcile post-horror's debated status as *both* art and genre. Yet, even as genre fans have knowledgably criticized high-minded critical labels – framing their correctives as a "democratizing" attack upon the perceived elitism of professional film critics with more cultural than subcultural capital – fans frequently neglect how their own high degree of (sub)cultural capital distances themselves from post-horror's rejection by more populist viewers.

"Slow Horror" and "Quiet Horror"

Among the first critical epithets in circulation was "slow horror," often used in reference to the independently produced films of Ti West, including *House of the Devil* (2009) and *The Innkeepers* (2011). These films predated those most often associated with post-horror, but nevertheless foreshadow the leisurely paced narratives, atmospheric restraint, and eschewal of graphic violence and jump scares that would become associated with the emerging cycle. Frequent comparisons between West's work and John Carpenter's films (especially *Halloween* (1978), retrospectively praised for its gore-free restraint compared to the slasher films it birthed) formed another common motif that carried forward into critical praise for post-horror films like *It Follows* (2014).[4] As Glyn Davis observes, West openly acknowledges his inspiration from the slower pacing of 1980s horror films, while his circle of creative collaborators also includes many of the micro-budget independent filmmakers associated with the slowly paced and stylistically minimalist "mumblecore" movement (which has itself frequently incorporated horror film tropes).[5] Meanwhile, a *National Public Radio* profile of West describes *The Innkeepers* as "a kind of horror movie you don't have to be a horror fan to enjoy," citing *Rosemary's Baby* (1968) and *The Shining* (1980) as other examples – and thus looks ahead to critical efforts to distance post-horror films from the genre's common associations with exploitative filmmaking and correspondingly unsophisticated tastes.[6] As we will see below and in the coming chapters, a handful of such prominent art-horror films – especially *Rosemary's Baby* and *The Shining* – have become recurring influences upon the post-horror corpus.

According to his producer Larry Fessenden, West's slowed-down approach to building tension within horror films involves not only a turn toward past films, but also resonates with "slow food," "slow scholarship," and other movements framed as reactions against the increasing speed of twenty-first-century life.[7] In this regard, the label "slow horror" can additionally be seen as an outgrowth of the critically derived category "slow cinema" that became widely discussed in cinephile circles by 2010.[8] In his influential position article, Matthew Flanagan argues that slow cinema comprises a variety of international art films which actively resist the "intensified continuity" of post-1990s Hollywood cinema's increasingly quick and chaotic editing and camera movements that bombard the viewer with audiovisual information (a supposed symptom of intensified corporate capitalism). For Flanagan, slow cinema is aesthetically distinguished by "(often extremely) long takes, decentered and understated modes of storytelling, and a pronounced emphasis on quietude and the everyday," collectively reducing "the familiar hegemony of drama, consequence, and psychological motivation" to a phenomenologically realistic experience of time and action that can border on boredom.[9]

Although horror cinema is not often associated with slow cinema (particularly due to the former's generic use of suspense, terror, and visceral affect), Flanagan's caveat that describing a film as "slow" is a "wholly relative" distinction might invite us to consider the comparative slowness of post-horror films like *I Am the Pretty Thing That Lives in the House* (2016) and *A Ghost Story* (2017) in relation to the rest of the genre – even if most post-horror works may not be as stylistically sparse as a Béla Tarr or Pedro Costa film. For instance, Ira Jaffe's mention of "a slow, perhaps mythical past" that "sidestep[s] the frenzy of modernity"[10] is reminiscent of *The Witch*'s (2015) seventeenth-century settler-colonial setting; while Flanagan's brief discussion of slow cinema as a "cinema of walking," featuring drawn-out scenes of isolated characters walking toward an unreachable horizon, might remind us of how *It Follows* inverts these *temps morts* to generate claustrophobic dread via a lone character walking slowly toward the protagonist/camera.[11]

Moreover, the reduction of jump scares and other "cheap" shock effects in post-horror cinema suggests slow cinema's turn away from an accelerationist assault on the viewer's senses. While far from exhaustive, the list of "High Jump Scare Movies" on the website Where's the Jump? is dominated by horror films made since 2003, and suggests a sharp upward trend in such scare tactics since 2009 – the same period when "slow horror" emerged as a critical term to mark this aesthetic-cum-affective distinction.[12] For example, Joshua Wise's *Slow Horror* blog offers short reviews of "pieces of slow moving horror media that don't try to scare us with chainsaws, gouting fountains of blood, or hoards [sic] of the undead," featuring many post-horror films alongside notable precursors like *Rosemary's Baby* and *The Shining*, while the *New York Times*'s list of "Slow and Creepy Horror" films *only* includes post-horror films, with the lone exception of *The Birds* (1963).[13] As a review of one such film, *The Blackcoat's Daughter* (2015), observes, "To call the story a slow burn would be a mischaracterization of the word *slow*. It's more like a meditation or a waking nightmare, the kind you're not actually sure is a dream at all until it's over and you're safe again."[14]

Not only are there examples of slow cinema that already contain elements from horror cinema – such as the purportedly haunted theater in Tsai

Ming-liang's *Goodbye, Dragon Inn* (2003), or the ghosts and forest demons in Apichatpong Weerasethakul's *Uncle Boonmee Who Can Recall His Past Lives* (2010). Davis argues that Ti West's films might also help us expand the slow-cinema canon to include films from culturally "lower" genres not often consonant with slow cinema's predominant associations with serious dramas about precarious labor and existential ennui.[15] In his July 2017 *Guardian* article coining the term "post-horror," Steve Rose also cites *Goodbye, Dragon Inn* and Weerasethakul's work (whose "entire career is basically post-horror") as more akin to the existential treatment of ghosts and hauntings being "Westernized" in *A Ghost Story* (also see Chapter 7).[16] Meanwhile, scholars have discussed several other films already associated with the slow-cinema movement as being horror films (and vice versa), including Todd Haynes's *Safe* (1995) and Gus van Sant's *Elephant* (2003).[17]

Much as Joan Hawkins does with art-horror, we might see this expansion of the slow-cinema canon as a rhetorical gesture for complicating slow cinema's frequent associations with cinephile elitism (including the underlying contradiction that so many slow films celebrated by first-world film critics evince a visual aesthetic that the films' frequently dispossessed, working-class characters would themselves likely reject in favor of more populist entertainments). This "opening up" of slow cinema via horror is especially apt since post-horror films have far more crossover potential beyond the arthouse/festival circuit, including to multiplexes and major streaming services like Netflix, than most slow films. (*I Am the Pretty Thing That Lives in the House*, for example, is an especially apt title for a film distributed as a Netflix exclusive.) After all, the critical debates about slow cinema may have been initially framed around aesthetics, but "were centered largely on matters of taste" in the end – much as early descriptors like "slow horror" soon gave way to more taste-based epithets like "prestige" and "elevated."[18] Nevertheless, I would maintain that even if post-horror films are less often confined to the festival circuit, the critical vs. popular divide in their overall reception suggests how a slow aesthetic might exacerbate the negative affects and dark themes that more conventional horror films cloak beneath the aegis of entertainment value:

> [S]low movies are hard to take not simply because they portray feelings contrary to optimism. Rather, they also inhibit the expression of such feelings, just as they restrict motion, action, dialogue, and glitter. Slow movies thus bring to the fore cheerless aspects of existence that are likely to worsen if ignored, but drape them in stillness, blankness, emptiness, and silence.[19]

The epithet "slow horror" shares additional similarities with "quiet horror" – a label borrowed from the world of horror fiction (such as the work of Charles L. Grant, who coined the term) – which Joan Hawkins associates with a post-9/11 resurgence of the Gothic tradition in horror cinema.[20] Although her use of "new Gothic" encapsulates a broader corpus of films (*Crimson Peak* (2015) and *A Cure for Wellness* (2016), for instance) than merely post-horror or independently produced productions, she locates a strong area of overlap between low-budget, direct-to-video (DTV) horror (including the early films of Ti West and Mike Flanagan) and a Gothic turn toward stories about uncanny, ghostly returns instead of torture-porn violence. For Hawkins, these films became a fully-fledged production trend by 2013, marked by soft-focus cinematography, "a heightened emphasis on sound perspective," "compelling but unreliable" POV shots, and epistemic hesitation over whether "the monster merely exists outside the protagonist's mind."[21] Even as I would note that post-horror films often evince greater visual depth of field to emphasize spatial longueur, the primary characteristic of so-called "slow horror" films, as the label implies, is the sense of quietude that overlaps with the aforementioned slow aesthetic that Davis and Hawkins both see in West's films. One of Hawkins's case studies, Mike Flanagan's *Absentia* (2011), is relatively talky and contains plenty of handheld cinematography, but its story of a legally deceased husband returning to his estranged wife, after having vanished years earlier in an underground tunnel controlled by spider-like monsters, prioritizes realistic familial tensions and a slowly unfolding narrative that downplays easy scares in favor of long scenes of family members mourning unexplained losses.

The periodization of "quiet horror" as a post-9/11 reaction to torture porn concurs with James Kendrick's comparison of the American horror genre to a pendulum swinging periodically between spiritual/supernatural and materialist/graphic tropes, with the post-*Scream* (1996) "neo-slasher" cycle followed by an early 2000s trend toward paranormal films (such as *The Sixth Sense* (1999) and *The Others* (2001)), that eventually yielded to the mid-2000s torture-porn cycle.[22] Yet, torture porn's divisively violent and nihilistic tone ultimately proved less popular (and thus less profitable) with general audiences than supernatural horror films whose visual restraint was more broadly palatable.[23] The vogue for East Asian horror films and their remakes in the Anglo-American market during this same transitional period is also notable, since Daniel Martin explains how *Ringu*'s (1998) British reception privileged its supernatural themes and lessened emphasis on gore as markers of its sophistication and good taste, much as Hawkins claims these films as a major influence on the post-2013 rise of "new Gothic"/"quiet horror" films.[24] Indeed, I would argue that Kiyoshi Kurosawa's *Pulse* (2001), one of the slower and more contemplative films from the Japanese horror boom, could just as easily be considered one of the first post-horror films in how it moves beyond the "J-horror" cycle's typical focus on technological fears in favor of constructing a depopulated world of melancholic loss and existential ennui not unlike a large-scale version of the world in *Absentia*.

Following Kendrick and Hawkins, we can likewise see a swing back toward supernatural topics in the post-torture-porn popularity of haunted-house films like *Insidious* (2011), *Sinister* (2012), *The Conjuring* (2013), *Oculus* (2013), and *Crimson Peak*. For my purposes, it is useful to see many post-horror films as an outgrowth of this supernatural revival, even as post-horror's austere style differentiates them from the more clichéd aspects of such supernatural horror films. Flanagan's *Oculus*, for example, serves as a sort of missing link between his earlier "quiet horror" film *Absentia* and his later, high-profile works, including the Netflix series *The Haunting of Hill House* (2018) and the far more conventional *Shining* sequel, *Doctor Sleep* (2019). It is notable that films like *Insidious* and *The Conjuring* initially received very positive reviews as gore-free throwbacks to old-fashioned haunted-house scares – including plaudits for former *Saw* director James Wan finally "making good" on his torture-porn roots with these two high-profile films – in a manner confirming the old pattern that horror films with higher budgets and less graphic violence tend to earn stronger critical acclaim.[25] Yet, the fact that the overuse of jump scares quickly became a target for criticism of these supernatural films suggests how even more reputable productions like *The Conjuring* can be negatively affected by subsequent imitators, and hence how fragile the horror genre's reputability ever truly is. To wit, *The Telegraph*'s Anne Billson suggests that

> [r]ecent high-profile horror films such as *Annabelle* [2014], *Jessabelle* [2014] and *The Woman in Black 2: Angel of Death* [2014] founder on sloppy storytelling and an over-reliance on hoary old methods of making us jump, but are still a welcome sign of the decline of noughties torture-porn, an unremittingly grim ordeal not only for the unfortunate characters, but for audiences as well.[26]

What we have in post-horror films, then, are a number of stylistic traits and genre conventions that might resonate in differing proportions with either arthouse denizens or multiplex audiences – but finding huge overlaps in cultural taste between those demographics has not always proven easy. Had these films not followed a festival-to-multiplex trajectory driven by positive critical word-of-mouth, gradually earning a platformed release onto screens beyond either the arthouse circuit or the DTV market, then they would have likely remained niche-interest texts primarily seen by devoted genre fans, and their apparent difference from Hollywood's more populist horror films would not have registered so noticeably. Even as terms like "slow horror" and "quiet horror" both evoke something of post-horror's style and affect, they ultimately proved insufficient for signaling these films' difference to prospective viewers – hence the move toward critical labels that more explicitly invoke reified tastes and higher levels of cultural capital, such as "smart" and "prestige."

As much as these films can be seen as counterprogramming to several different types of "excess" (explicit gore and jump scares, respectively) within the horror genre during the post-9/11 period, I would argue that their coalescence into a perceivable trend after 2013 cannot be wholly reduced to market trends or sociohistorical factors. Rather, the speed and fragmentation of film-critical discourse in the social-media era bears much responsibility for the cycle's debatability (as was also true of "slow cinema"). With the economics of film criticism now largely driven by web traffic, for instance, festival coverage increasingly leans into hyperbole for the sake of clicks (for example, *The A.V. Club*'s early hype about *Hereditary* (2018) as "pure emotional terrorism").[27] Whereas David Edelstein's coinage of "torture porn" in a January 2006 *New York* article very quickly gained widespread currency,[28] demonstrating a single film critic's ability to influence the conversation about genre through a simple act of naming, the following decade saw an explosion of social media and (micro)blogging platforms, proliferating far more voices than the small coterie of professional film critics who once served as cultural gatekeepers. Genre fans, for instance, can now use online platforms (subculturally dedicated or otherwise) to quickly rip apart the flaws in critical attempts to name post-horror cinema, as if trying to prevent such a reductive label as "torture porn" from taking root again.[29] Therefore, despite the hostility that genre fans frequently level at professional film critics from major newspapers and magazines (such as *The Guardian*'s coiner of "post-horror," Steve Rose), the debate around post-horror is actually a symptom of traditional gatekeepers' loosened grip on film-critical discourse as journalism's economic model shifts, begetting a plethora of freelance and unpaid content producers who may be more horror-friendly than salaried film critics, but who may or may not possess the genre fan's deeper pool of film-historical knowledge.

Mattias Frey points out that professional film critics' recommendations "only ha[ve] an effect on certain type[s] of productions ('legitimate' genres such as art-house) or certain types of readers/viewers (those who seek to refine a discriminating sensibility for art)."[30] Hence, it makes sense that critics might attempt to reassert their eroding cultural authority via the naming of "arthouse"-type films within a genre whose most popular texts are nevertheless deemed "critic-proof." Of course, movie-going during the 1950s–70s golden age of modernist art cinema inspired immediate discussion about the films' textual ambiguities and cultural value – but these debates casually unfolded in person in theater lobbies, coffee shops, and college dorms. Other than salaried film critics working against a publication deadline, those ideas and opinions were not immediately shared with the greater public as social-media "hot takes" and half-thought "think-pieces," whereas one can now seek or share online opinions about post-horror's formal and thematic ambiguities as soon as possible. Because social-media usage in first-world countries has become de rigueur in the second decade of the twenty-first century, the critical attention devoted to debating post-horror's texts and paratexts (including its various labels) has been largely fueled by the drive for social capital (for example, more social-media followers) in the so-called "attention economy" – thus rendering post-horror's cultural prominence an ironic byproduct of the very accelerationism that the films themselves stylistically oppose.

By the 2010s, not only have professional critics felt their authority threatened by online film criticism's invasion by freelancers and amateurs, but genre fans also fear a qualitative decline in film-critical discourse at a time when so many artistically significant horror films are gaining broad exposure – with the important difference that fans' frequently well-informed opinions have seldom been valued as authoritative to begin with. As genre fan Andrew Carroll aptly explains:

> I'm writing this before some hard[-]done[-]by writer at *Buzzfeed* or *GQ* or *VICE* publishes an article entitled "Horror Only Meant Something After 2000." Do I blame them? Partly[,] but the blame mostly falls on Google and Facebook for devouring the digital ad market and leaving hate clicks as one of the few ways for online media to survive. That's the real horror.[31]

This quote suggests that, with the shift from print to digital film criticism and the corresponding focus on number of clicks over quality of content, unsalaried writers with less historical and generic knowledge are cluttering the cultural conversation about horror – thus putting increased pressure on genre fans to flex their subcultural capital in broader online venues beyond those targeted primarily to fellow fans. However, genre fans' use of these same types of digital platforms – blogs, social media, freelance-driven websites – to offer intelligent rebuttals belies the common argument that the erosion of print media has necessarily "dumbed down" the overall state of film criticism. Rather, the inclusion of more voices within the sphere of digital film criticism includes both the "hard-done-by writer" gigging for a few extra bucks and the highly knowledgeable horror fan defending the genre from oversimplification by professional critics and uninformed bloggers alike.

"Smart Horror"

The pressure to quickly say something smart for the sake of accruing social capital has therefore encouraged the multiple (unsuccessful) attempts to find a sufficiently fitting name for the post-horror cycle, including the very name "smart horror."[32] Many of post-horror's stylistic choices recall the American "smart films" described by Jeffrey Sconce as an "indie" aesthetic developed in the late 1990s that favors "long-shots, static composition, and sparse editing" to suggest a hip, ironic distance from white, middle-class conformity and the "horrors of life under advanced capitalism."[33] Although filmmakers like Todd Solondz, Wes Anderson, Paul Thomas Anderson, and Alexander Payne most commonly used this style to produce a quirky or darkly comedic tone, Todd Haynes's deadly serious *Safe* (which, again, has also been deemed a "slow film") perhaps comes closest to evoking post-horror's nebulously defined (and possibly imagined) threats, the overwhelming sense of dread, and narrative ambiguity.

Filmed in a coldly detached style, *Safe*'s protagonist, upper-class 1980s housewife Carol White (Julianne Moore), increasingly develops a mysterious environmental illness (likened to AIDS), which her fellow sufferers compare to a "monster" that suddenly attacks when one is exposed to invisible toxins. Carol leaves her vaguely supportive husband (Xander Berkeley) to become an in-patient at a cult-like recovery center, but she keeps physically deteriorating even after she removes herself from modern industrial society, and the film ends with a long, frontally centered take of Carol repeating "I love you" to herself in the mirror. With its gaslighting themes (many people dismiss Carol's illness as simply in her head), its oppressive atmosphere of unseen menace, and its abrupt, ambiguously open ending, *Safe* offers the best link between 2010s post-horror films and the deeply ironic 1990s sensibility that Sconce describes as having been (temporarily) shaken by sociopolitical rhetoric about the "end of irony" during the same post-9/11 period that Hawkins associates with the uncanny returns of the "new Gothic."[34] J. A. Bridges also cites Paul Thomas Anderson's *There Will Be Blood* (2007) as a stylistic precursor to the almost post-apocalyptic starkness found in some post-horror films, displaying a more "mature" visual aesthetic than Anderson's earlier "smart films" like *Magnolia* (1999) and *Punch-Drunk Love* (2002).[35]

Indeed, with its focus on Gothicized environments of male labor, Robert Eggers's *The Lighthouse* (2019) is perhaps the best point of comparison here (see Chapter 5).

Although mostly comedic, smart films also tend to evince what Sconce calls "a sense of *dampened affect*" whose opposition to the intensified "dumbness" of mainstream Hollywood movies flatters the "smart" viewer's aesthetic discernment.[36] It is little surprise, then, that 2010s post-horror films emerged from a similar indie milieu with the sobriquet "smart horror," albeit with affect less "dampened" than diffused throughout (and beyond) the text. As Julian Hanich notes, films built around dread are often seen as culturally "higher" works, since dread's "extended, anticipatory character and its gradual coming-into-being grant the viewer a certain freedom to act, while the in-your-faceness of horror and shock is bound to an aesthetics of overwhelming."[37] Hence, like 1990s-era smart films, post-horror's visual style and slow pace may suggest a cold and ironic distance from conventional horror tropes themselves, as though their filmmakers are visually signaling the space they wish to occupy between the (post)modernist art film and the more populist horror film. Stephanie Graves further observes that epithets like "smart" create "a false, binary divide between these films and those that must, then, be 'dumb' – the very kind of high/low art that films designated as 'smart' routinely problematize."[38]

Although age-based "generations" as demographic categories are notoriously debatable, it is notable that so many post-horror filmmakers belong to the younger, "Millennial" generation (born 1981–2000) instead of the "Generation X" filmmakers (born 1965–80) behind 1990s smart films, suggesting a sort of generational inheritance evinced as less of an ironic than a "post-ironic" tone. Whereas Gen-X hipsters used irony as a subcultural gesture to demonstrate their knowing superiority to mainstream consumer culture and culturally hegemonic lifeways, the concept of *post-irony* has been described as a post-9/11 re-embrace of so-called "New Sincerity" in response to irony's wider mainstreaming as a default mode for understanding the world. Post-irony is less a wholesale rejection of irony than a sensibility that takes an ironic worldview as a given, but attempts to also look beyond irony with a side-eyed reappraisal of more earnest and serious ways of experiencing life.[39] The relationship between irony and "post-irony" is therefore much like the relationship between horror and "post-horror," with horror's well-established generic tropes and themes taken as read, but stylistically revamped in such a way as to prioritize (negative) affect differently. In other words, "post-horror" operates similarly to aesthetic labels like "postmodern" or "post-punk," in that it should not signify a definitive break from what came before, but rather a stylistic approach that attempts to both contain and move beyond the ethos of whichever existing term "post" modifies.

Using Raymond Williams's terms, I would therefore maintain that the overall "structure of feeling" encouraged by post-horror's formal minimalism is more post-ironic than ironic. If the ironic sensibility behind smart films represented "affective elements of consciousness" that were emergent during the mid-1990s but have since become dominant, then post-irony bespeaks "characteristic elements of impulse, restraint, and tone" that emerged with the more recent generational shift from Gen-X to Millennials.[40] Here, for example, we might contrast the eternally "cool," hipster vampires living in (and feeding off) postindustrial Motown in Jim Jarmusch's *Only Lovers Left Alive* (2013) as genre tropes being "smartly" revisioned through Jarmusch's ironic Gen-X sensibility, whereas the protagonists of *In Follows*, part of a younger generation facing more economic precarity, earnestly drift through Detroit's dying suburbs in search of sexual trust (see Chapter 6).

The horror genre's proximity to humor is notable here, since the expectation of familiar generic pleasures is precisely why post-horror films have proven so divisive in flouting convention. It is important to note that most post-horror films are not "smart" in the self-parodic winking sense of humorously oversaturated closeness to genre conventions flaunted in meta-horror films like *Wes Craven's New Nightmare* (1994), *Scream* (1996), *Tucker and Dale vs. Evil* (2010), *The Cabin in the Woods* (2012), or *The Final Girls* (2015). Whereas meta-horror films use heavily allusive intertextuality to "smartly" and comedically play with the genre's more tired conventions, presuming a viewer's sense of ironic superiority over generic clichés, post-horror films often seem less blatantly indebted to popular horror cinema for direct inspiration – hence the fact that they are often described as looking and feeling more like character-driven dramas. Post-horror films taken on their own terms are typically framed as no laughing matter, by way of their chilly decentering of all-too-familiar genre tropes and their verging on other genres where sincere explorations of life beyond irony might flourish. To put it another way, if the postmillennial mainstreaming of irony sees the whole world in quotation marks by default, then post-horror's own tendency to register the genre as "horror" has less to do with wallowing in genre clichés to the point of (self-)parody, but rather distancing the viewer from horror conventions by way of intersections with more "respectable" genres that are not necessarily associated with a humorously fun time.

Even in Jordan Peele's *Get Out* (2017), a film that does use black humor to great effect, its critical nomination as a "smart" horror film came less from playing with longtime conventions (though it does that as well) than from using the horror genre as a timely platform to "smartly" intervene in American racial-equality debates during the Black Lives Matter movement. Although *Get Out*'s explicit relevance to its sociopolitical moment marks its difference from the less urgent themes in many other post-horror films, the fact that *Get Out* was viewed as a post-horror film while Peele's follow-up *Us* (2019) was, as I elaborate below, more often considered "just" a horror movie – despite both films incorporating a mixture of humor and social commentary – tells us something about the different tone struck by each film. In particular, I will argue in Chapter 4 that gaslighting themes – central to *Get Out*'s sociopolitical commentary – engender negative affects that are more easily perpetuated through *uncomfortable* laughter (rather than ironically superior laughter) at the epistemic incongruities sensed by our protagonist(s), while the negative affects generated by other varieties of post-horror are far less conducive to humor at all.

"Indie Horror" and "Prestige Horror"

In critical discussions of post-horror, the modifier "smart" is very often used in conjunction with the additional qualifier "indie" – although sometimes the latter term alone suffices to distinguish post-horror from its more "mainstream" brethren.[41] This critical marker of cultural elevation is unsurprising, given the lower-budget, quasi-generic status of "indie" as a buzzword "whose meanings – alternative, hip, edgy, uncompromising – far exceed the literal designation of media products that are made independently of major firms."[42] Claire Perkins observes that the milieu that fostered the smart-film cycle – largely developed from the 1990s rise of film festivals like Sundance and distributors like Miramax – has been in decline since 1999, due to media conglomeration that saw major studios taking up indie films as a potentially profitable niche market.[43] Yet, if the term "indie" was subsequently adopted by the short-lived "Indiewood" specialty divisions developed within the major studios in the early 2000s, post-horror films have emerged at a moment when the majors have again retracted from inroads into the independent film market.[44]

Jamie Sexton argues that the idea of "indie-horror" frequently serves as a conceptual Other to American independent cinema, since the various qualities attributed to indie cinema (including authorial originality, formal innovation and self-consciousness, inclusion of marginalized characters/voices, and so on) are not often attributed to horror, particularly given the genre's common association with well-trodden generic conventions, commercial motivations, and lower bodily appeals. Indeed, apart from character-centered dramas, horror films constitute perhaps the most prolific genre within the annual output of American independent filmmakers – but only certain types of films are discursively positioned as "indie," regardless of whether truly produced independently from the major studios.[45] For instance, genre-centric producer-distributors like Lionsgate and Blumhouse have been responsible for leveraging independently produced horror films into mainstream distribution deals, thereby helping shape several of the largest horror trends during the first decade of the twenty-first century (such as the torture-porn and found-footage cycles). And yet, due to their commercially accessible styles, these companies' films are seldom labeled "indie" in the same way that label has been applied to many post-horror films. (Given its distribution deal via Universal Pictures, it is perhaps no coincidence that Blumhouse's productions *Get Out* and *A Quiet Place* (2018) hew closer to Hollywood's industry-standard style than most other post-horror films.)

Post-horror films, for example, have seemingly transcended their generic roots by evincing a less populist style at the blurred borderline of art-cinema form and indie distribution practices. As noted in the previous chapter, this new wave of art-horror resembles an emergent trend because multiple films have followed the same trajectory from festival to multiplex since 2014, as also exemplified by the newness of their young directors. Although some of these films also played at Fantastic Fest, Fantasia Film Festival, and other genre film festivals populated by independent horror films, the fact that many of them broke out at prominent non-genre-specific festivals is noteworthy. Even as some of the major film festivals have sidebars dedicated to cultish genre films (for example, Toronto's "Midnight Madness" series), many post-horror films screened in regular competition – a testament to their inability to be qualitatively segregated based on genre alone. Former Midnight Madness programmer Colin Geddes, however, deems this part of a longer pattern of cultural gatekeepers periodically flirting with the horror genre as a redeemable object.[46] David Andrews also notes how "promoters of genre-branded art movies . . . often stress the art-cinema affiliations of their movies when speaking within art-cinema contexts, as if art cinema were a place of refuge from genre affiliations and their low status – even if those low affiliations can, in other more commercial contexts, help their films circulate."[47]

Major-studio acquisitions of completed, independently produced films have become less common over the 2010s, but the brick-and-mortar exhibition industry has still taken chances on films with more promotable genre elements than the typical indie drama. A 2017 American Film Market report heralds "clear-concept horror films" as the prime category of low-budget films best able to break out into mainstream success.[48] But while post-horror films are "far more likely to blur the line between scary movie and bleak drama" than their trailers and posters may suggest,[49] they often have enough of a recognizable generic hook to be seen as possessing more crossover potential than the average arthouse offering. This becomes especially clear in cases where filmmakers did have an earlier dramatic film under their belts before achieving wider renown with post-horror – such as David Robert Mitchell's *The Myth of the American Sleepover* (2010), David Lowery's *Ain't Them Bodies Saints* (2013), and Trey Edward Shults's *Krisha* (2015) – with such previous films often evincing similarities in theme and tone to their post-horror films that achieved broader circulation.

Hence, many of these films earned distribution deals for limited and expanded release into major theater chains – especially via distributors with more cultural capital than Lionsgate or Blumhouse – such as indie distributor A24 (founded in 2012), which gained significant repute as the producer-distributor of the Best Picture Oscar winner, *Moonlight* (2016).[50] A24 would also release *The Witch*, *The Blackcoat's Daughter*, *It Comes at Night* (2017), *A Ghost Story*, *The Killing of a Sacred Deer* (2017), *Hereditary*, *In Fabric* (2018), *Midsommar* (2019), and *The Lighthouse* – thus making it as close to a devoted home for post-horror as Blumhouse has been for paranormal-themed films, despite recurring criticism of A24's "rather recognizable habit ... of somewhat misrepresenting movies with an idiosyncratic '*art house*' bent in their marketing."[51] *The Witch*'s director Robert Eggers notes, however, that A24's marketing strategies can also offer interesting opportunities for filmmakers: "This may sound crass, but it's like ... how can I write something that's withholding, but still offers enough interesting imagery that you can put in a trailer?"[52]

In 2016, *The Witch* was the seventh-highest grossing horror film of the year at the US box office, earning over $25 million, well above more established properties like *Blair Witch* (2016).[53] Hence such independently produced, low-budget films clearly demonstrated their earning potential, especially given their outsized budget-to-return ratios, by contending alongside major-studio productions. Industry watchers have compared this crossover potential to independent horror productions from the New Hollywood era, such as *Night of the Living Dead* (1968) and *The Texas Chain Saw Massacre* (1974), arguing that well-made, low-budget films that engage with serious themes periodically arise in reaction to studio-produced horror films ostensibly made for a "quick buck"[54] – although this comparison neglects how such earlier independent productions made their outsized grosses over many years of theatrical reissues in the drive-in and midnight movie markets, rather than the quick path from major film festivals to mainstream multiplexes trod by many post-horror films.

Much as Joan Hawkins observes that horror-skeptic critics tend to separate "high" from "low" culture in their evaluations of art-horror, Sexton argues that critical engagement with indie-horror tends to separate auteurism from genre, with each angle respectively mapping onto the high/low divide.[55] Indeed, in Douglas Pye's theorization of cinematic tone, he notes how tone is often conveyed through the author's implied attitude toward their subject matter and toward the reader, which can encourage "smart" viewers to reflect on the figure of the auteur.[56] However, many post-horror directors were previously unknown quantities – even as promotional materials might position them as major new talents, such as singling out Eggers's meticulous seventeenth-century verisimilitude in *The Witch*.[57] Without an already established auteur at the helm, even audiences attuned to auteurism typically had a less specific frame of reference for what to expect from these films, meta-textually extending the films' own mysterious sense of fantastic hesitation. Viewers with more cultural capital, for example, might see the A24 logo at the start of a trailer and have some expectation of an art-horror viewing experience, but more populist viewers might not pick up on such branding cues. Hence the art/auteur vs. horror/genre divide is most strongly reflected in the disjunction between the high praise from viewers with higher amounts of cultural capital (including film critics and genre fans) and the disappointment expressed by more populist viewers as these films crossed over to multiplexes with genre expectations as the main point of reference. After all, much as Sconce's smart films can still offer strongly affective viewing experiences, in spite of their distanced takes on genres like comedy and melodrama, post-horror also operates in a way that divides audiences into "those who 'get it' and those who don't."[58]

Yet, even though the horror genre's cultural disrepute helped set a low aesthetic bar for post-horror filmmakers to vault above, Sexton observes that "art films which incorporate horror may be viewed as dealing too seriously with material that does not warrant such an approach, whereas horror films which take an overly 'arty' approach may be seen as pretentious."[59] As such, viewers with high amounts of cultural capital might not unanimously praise a post-horror film's ambiguities as properly "earned." Appreciative reviews of *The Blackcoat's Daughter*, for instance, privileged the affective qualities of its "suffocating mood" and use of "stillness, quiet, and isolation – the elements that . . . feel like lying alone and awake in a dark house, letting your mind play tricks on you."[60] But other critics described it as "built around elliptical vagaries," unable "to channel the story through emotion, spreading itself thin across themes of alienation, mourning, and fears of abandonment."[61] Dismissing it as "pseudo-intellectual horror," another critic complains that "setting a bunch of people loose on the screen and telling them to mope until something supernatural emerges, then calling it a tone poem about loss, is no way to keep an audience entertained."[62]

Given this critical fallback position on trying to reconcile art with entertainment value, it remains important to remember that there is an existing lineage of "prestige" horror films produced and released by major Hollywood studios, usually with the imprimatur of an established auteur or major star, high production values, or widely known source material. Indeed, some of the most canonical horror films – including *Frankenstein* (1931), *Dracula* (1931), *Cat People* (1942), *The Spiral Staircase* (1946), *Psycho* (1960), *The Innocents* (1961), *The Haunting* (1963), *Rosemary's Baby*, *The Exorcist* (1973), *Don't Look Now* (1973), *The Shining*, *The Silence of the Lambs* (1990), *Bram Stoker's Dracula* (1992), and *The Sixth Sense* – emerged from such industrial and publicity strategies, with their "prestige-ness" generally constructed against the monolithic image of a young, male, uncouth horror viewership. *Dracula* and *The Spiral Staircase*, for example, were celebrated as more attuned to the pleasures of female viewers, with women more often expressing tastes for "Gothic, suggestive, and atmospheric modes" of horror cinema.[63] Meanwhile, *Cat People* and *The Haunting* were heralded for their visual restraint in keeping monsters off-screen altogether.[64] In many cases, professional film critics claimed these films to be more oriented toward "adult" viewers than the genre's dominant reputation as juvenilia, especially in cases of literary adaptations or participation by above-the-line personnel who might "elevate" such an otherwise lowly genre.[65] This is not to say, of course, that prestige horror films are bereft of shock value or have enjoyed unanimously positive critical reception – take Michael Powell's career implosion for directing *Peeping Tom* (1960), for instance, or the various complaints about sexual perversity in *Psycho* or sacrilegious imagery in *The Exorcist* – but that the aforementioned qualities of prestige-ness have frequently served as mitigating factors against negative criticism.

Given these generic predecessors in cultural reclamation, it is little surprise that post-horror films have also earned the sobriquet "prestige horror," especially from horror-skeptic reviewers.[66] Indeed, even if they do not (yet) have the auteur status associated with many directors of earlier prestige-horror films, it is quite common for post-horror directors to cite the influence of the aforementioned films (and a variety of art films) in interviews and other promotional paratexts. Meanwhile, as noted earlier, horror-skeptic film critics frequently mention films like *Rosemary's Baby* and *The Shining* as precursors to post-horror's slow pace, claustrophobic moods, and narrative lacunae.[67] Likewise, critics often remark upon the fact that Oz Perkins, writer-director of *The Blackcoat's Daughter* and *I Am the Pretty Thing*, is the son of *Psycho* star Anthony Perkins, in a more literal claim of artistic/generic lineage (see Chapter 7).[68]

Many of horror's earlier "prestige" films were promoted as singular, high-profile events, often appearing years apart from each other, and capable of appealing to broad – or at least middlebrow – tastes. Whether seen as transcending generic mediocrity or marketed as new entries to the generic canon, film critics less often posited these movies as somehow elevated "beyond" the genre than still situated at its core. By contrast, post-horror more closely resembles a trend because so many of these films have appeared across a tighter cluster of years, while also bearing greater stylistic affinities with modernist art films than with major-studio productions – thus bespeaking the corpus's less populist register. After all, most earlier prestige-horror films predominantly obey classical Hollywood narrative conventions (with a few notable exceptions such as *The Shining*'s slow, coldly distant aesthetic and ambiguously time-bending epilogue), not the potentially confounding qualities of modernist art cinema that are more frequently seen in post-horror texts.

Designating post-horror films as "prestige" therefore differs from that label's earlier application to middlebrow horror films aimed at a broad-based movie-going public. By primarily hailing viewers who are presumed to have more sophisticated aesthetic tastes than the mainstream audience, this newer application of "prestige" leaves the value of legitimate cultural capital unchallenged, even as horror-skeptic critics may be tenuously associating that value with a few seemingly exceptional texts from an otherwise lowly genre.[69] Nevertheless, as Laura Mee notes, "It would be disingenuous to suggest that more viewers were attracted to *Hereditary*'s 'elevated' horror than its promise to be the 'scariest movie in years,' just as it is dismissive to champion *The Shining* for transcending a disreputable genre."[70]

"Elevated Horror" and "Post-Horror"

Meanwhile, horror-friendly fans astutely observe that "[b]y calling something 'prestige horror' or 'smart horror,' we [fans] are inadvertently (or maybe intentionally, for some) putting down other equally valid movies in the genre – and subsequently the fans who like them."[71] As this quote suggests, horror-skeptic and horror-friendly viewers often concur about post-horror's aesthetic value – but the latter contingent are more likely to see these films as evidence of the genre's collective value, not as texts divisively positioned above it. These efforts to intercede between the horror-skepticism of post-horror's critically coined qualifiers and the genre's predominant association with unsophisticated audiences finally brings us to the crux of the controversy – a controversy that has been driven by not only populist viewers' alienation from post-horror's core style, but also longtime horror fans' own insecurities as viewers rich with *subcultural* capital earned around a disreputable genre with low *cultural* capital.

Nowhere has the fan-cultural backlash against post-horror's critical labels – and the implied or actual snobbery of such distinctions – been stronger than in debates about the term "elevated horror." As with "prestige," this modifier suggests a raising of horror up to a certain degree of respectability, but I would stress that horror's "elevation" also implies raising the genre to a level where it might mix with genres already associated with "higher" aesthetic strata, such as character-based dramas. Horror fans are apt to observe that "elevated" is a qualification not similarly expected or applied to other genres, regardless of whether other genres contain more than their fair share of either populist or poor-quality texts.[72] Genre fan Michael Brown, for example, proposes that "[r]ather than claiming that horror is having a 'prestige' drama moment, maybe we should say that drama is once again having a horror moment."[73]

By contrast, horror-skeptic film critics who profess a general dislike of the genre defend these modifiers as useful in denoting qualitatively exceptional texts of the sort that Mark Jancovich has called horror movies for "people who don't like horror."[74] Whereas many horror fans suggest that "elevated" and "post" demean the genre as a whole by implicitly upholding its presumed lack of cultural capital – which fans' own deep knowledge of the genre's historical and artistic diversity would challenge – it is unsurprising that professional critics are more sympathetic to such labels. After all, their (economic) *raison d'être* primarily resides in making evaluative judgments of *individual* texts – although, by potentially coining and circulating new genre labels for emerging trends, critics might enhance their overall social and cultural capital as well. (Of course, not all professional film critics agreed with this need for such labels, as Matt Zoller Seitz's epigraph opening this chapter indicates.) Indeed, Shellie McMurdo argues that qualifiers like "elevated" or "post" serve to "distance the 'serious' critic from the historically distasteful, and possibly deviant, position of horror fan, in their key suggestion that if a non-horror fan enjoys a horror film, then that film cannot possibly belong to the horror genre, which is [seen as] a 'bad' genre."[75]

Rather than using such qualifiers, some horror-skeptic film critics instead profess a sort of "genre agnosticism" by downplaying their use of the generic label "horror" altogether – though this rhetorical gesture usually requires more explanation on a critic's part. In Richard Brody's glowing *New Yorker* review of *Us* (2019), for instance, he says the film is "[s]tructured like a home-invasion drama," but ultimately "is a horror film – though saying so is like offering a reminder that *The Godfather* [1972] is a gangster film or that *2001: A Space Odyssey* [1968] is science fiction. Genre is irrelevant to the merits of a film, whether its conventions are followed or defied."[76] Although it is more common for horror-skeptic critics to place a discursive asterisk beside the word "horror," critics might also use other genre labels altogether. Shane Danielsen's review of *Hereditary*, for example, describes the film as "actually a psychological drama of surprising acuity" – shortly after admitting "I'm not a big fan of horror movies – in part because they're usually not ambiguous *enough*, but mostly because they achieve their effects too cheaply" via jump scares and so on.[77] The horror genre is thus positioned here as a rhetorical straw person, rejectable because it has been grossly oversimplified and reduced to only its "undesirable" or "unsophisticated" traits. In a twist on this dissembling gesture, negative criticism of the deeply populist horror film *It: Chapter Two* (2019) stresses its reliance on "blockbuster CGI window dressing and faux-jump scares," resulting in "a bad horror movie, but it works rather well as a *comedy* – or rather, a comic *drama* about adults trying to come to terms with their lingering childhood traumas."[78]

With post-horror films, "drama" and "thriller" are the most common alternate genre labels used by critics – but there is a longer tradition at play here. Jancovich notes how establishment film critics referred to *The Silence of the Lambs* as a "suspense drama," a "thriller," or by any number of "ambivalent adjectives" in order to avoid the lowbrow connotations of "horror" – especially due to the film's "prestige" components, such as a major director (Jonathan Demme) and stars (Jodie Foster, Anthony Hopkins), and its subsequent sweep of the year's top Academy Awards.[79] Similar critical dissembling occurred when *Get Out* was nominated for four Academy Awards in 2018, including Best Picture, Best Director, Best Actor, and Best Original Screenplay – a tremendous degree of critical and industry acclaim for a horror film, not seen since *Lambs* – though some critics' avoidance of the term "horror" was driven by Jordan Peele's own description of *Get Out* as a "social thriller."[80]

In this respect, horror-skeptic film critics have gained leverage in their discursive struggles to avoid the term "horror" due to the marked amount of dissembling by post-horror filmmakers themselves. Oz Perkins notes, for example:

I find myself much more turned on by mood and color and shadow and being observational [. . .] But I think I couch these movies enough in [genre] – "oh, it's a demonic possession movie," "oh, it's a ghost story" – so you can kind of feel the edges, and then be inside that with the character, and feel the human experience within that framework.[81]

Similarly, Jennifer Kent says, "I didn't think about genre when I made" *The Babadook*. "And I certainly didn't think of it as a horror film."[82] This assertion of "genre agnosticism" is shared by *It Comes at Night*'s Trey Edward Shults, who claims, "I didn't set out to make a horror movie per se . . . I just set out to make something personal and that's what it turned into. I put a lot of my fears into it, and if fear equates with horror then, yeah, it's horror."[83] Perhaps most notorious, though, were Peele's self-applied "social thriller" tag and Ari Aster's deliberate avoidance of describing the very horrific *Hereditary* as a horror film: "The people that were on the crew, or even the people that I was pitching the film to, I would describe it as a family tragedy that curdles into a nightmare."[84]

Much like horror-skeptic critics' avoidance of "horror," these moves to distance one's work from the genre's air of cultural disrepute are not unique to the 2010s post-horror cycle; rather, we can also see precedents among the makers of earlier "prestige" horror films. For example, Michael Powell asserted that *Peeping Tom* is "not a horror film" but rather "a film of compassion, of observation and of memory," while William Friedkin recalls that "I thought it [*The Exorcist*] was a film about the mystery of faith . . . but I didn't set out to make a horror film."[85] Perhaps most notably, when William Castle produced *Rosemary's Baby* for Columbia Pictures, he carefully avoided tainting the film with his existing reputation as the impresario behind gimmicky, kid-friendly horror movies like *The Tingler* (1959) and *Homicidal* (1961), minimizing his name in publicity materials and instead playing up the film's middlebrow source material (Ira Levin's novel), its acclaimed art-cinema auteur (Roman Polanski), and its rising star (Mia Farrow). As Kevin Heffernan argues, these combined efforts helped establish *Rosemary's Baby* as one of the first "adult" horror movies, distancing the film from horror's generic associations with juvenilia; with its similar emphasis on parents struggling with demonic children, *The Exorcist* would repeat this strategy five years later, becoming one of the first blockbusters of the 1970s.[86]

Small wonder, then, that Jason Zinoman alternately labels post-horror films as "grown-up horror" films, which, through their thematic focus on parental crises and overwhelming grief, "are more likely to try to make adults tremble than children giggle."[87] When post-horror filmmakers make dissembling remarks about their work as something other than straightforward "horror," then, they may be trying to avoid being pigeonholed as "simply" horror filmmakers from an early career stage, or may be making bids for greater amounts of legitimate cultural capital than the horror genre is generally expected to grant, due to its lingering reputation as a genre primarily aimed at the tastes of youth and/or infantilized adults. Much as these upcoming filmmakers frequently cite *Rosemary's Baby* and other earlier examples of "prestige" horror as inspiration, the crossover success of such earlier films with middlebrow audiences may be a means for upcoming filmmakers to indicate their film's box-office potential to would-be financiers. Robert Eggers, for example, acknowledges the debate about whether *The Witch* is a "horror" film (he maintains it is), but instead describes *The Lighthouse* as a "weird tale" (in reference to the subgenre of fantastic fiction to which the story would belong during its 1890s setting).[88] He continues:

> Being a wannabe auteur and my favorite filmmakers being part of the dead canon of European, Japanese art-house masters, I want to say that I don't want to care about genre and how it's limiting and all of that stuff. [. . .] I think where genre is limiting is that in the marketplace, you have to put things in a box to create expectations to make a profit, and that's where you run into trouble. There are people who really do say, "Give me my money back because I paid to get scared and I didn't ever once throw my popcorn in the air." That's fair enough. [. . .] On the other hand, I wouldn't have the incredible opportunity to be making cinema if it wasn't for genre. Genre gave me the opportunity to get a movie fucking financed.[89]

Eggers's ambivalence in this quote encapsulates how genre may be a practical benefit to filmmakers with a personal investment in the auteur tradition, even if the longstanding assumption that auteurs somehow "transcend" the genres in which they work means that the resulting film might prove divisive to populist viewers with a narrower view of a given genre.

Professional film critics thus tend to defer to a longer tradition of "auteur-driven" horror films in attempting to contextualize post-horror's "extremely intimate, ethereal, non-conventional approach to scares" as evidence of budding auteurs instead of already established ones.[90] As Richard Brody maintains, "good filmmakers are given credit for elevating something that never should have descended in the first place. But it's the directors themselves whose elevation matters."[91] Although this rhetorical move may position the professional film critic as a knowledgeable arbiter of older traditions within which to position newer directors, it still demonstrates what Nia Edwards-Behi deems an "out-dated reliance on authorship as a mark of quality."[92] Fans may criticize this apparent inability to look beyond an established canon of horror films already considered "safe" enough to endorse – despite the fact that genre fans, and even some post-horror filmmakers, are also prone to cite many of the same precursors in their own bids to convert subcultural capital into accepted cultural capital. April Wolfe, for example, cites the many established Hollywood directors who made horror movies early in their careers, but nevertheless speculates:

> Although horror fans have little incentive to keep this genre to themselves – and will probably continue to evangelize to anyone who will listen – we fear that with its wave of popularity, horror might become too safe and averse to the experimentation that made it special, when studios left it to its own devices.[93]

Meanwhile, as much as professional film critics celebrate post-horror films for their "originality" (that is, these films are not sequels, remakes, reboots, or franchise entries seemingly made for crassly commercial reasons), the films themselves may still bear enough resemblance to financially proven genre tropes – at least for marketing purposes – to be seen as less risky for investors at both the production and distribution levels.

Genre fans are therefore more likely to challenge the alleged ahistoricism of qualifiers like "elevated" and "post" by pointing to a historically wider range of films that have engaged with not just similar genre tropes, but also – and more importantly – similar types of repressed cultural anxieties (including familial traumas, gender/race/class inequalities, and so on) at a deeper thematic level. In addition to listing past examples of horror's intersection with art cinema, then, the genre's defenders assert that horror has *always* been a genre of ideas, especially "transgressive" or "subversive" ideas that have allegedly contributed to the genre's denigration by exposing too much of what bubbles to the surface from the cultural unconscious.[94] As one self-professed fan says, "The term 'elevated horror' is pure snobbery. [. . .] The truth, *as any sincere horror fan knows*, is that horror is as important a genre as any other. There have been artistically ambitious horror films since the beginning of cinema, and through every decade."[95] Whereas horror-skeptic film critics like Steve Rose suggest that, "[m]ore than any other genre, horror movies are governed by rules and codes,"[96] fans offer the corrective that "[h]orror is quick to adapt and change more so than any other genre" as society itself changes. "Horror has always had layers to it, even the cheap gore movies of the '60s and '70s."[97] Put another way, horror-skeptic critics are more likely to see auteurs working in the older arthouse and prestige traditions as exceptions to the presumed rule of horror's disposability, while horror-friendly fans more often cite a wider range of films in positing horror's cultural value as a more sociological phenomenon than a strictly aesthetic one.

As Matt Hills observes, it is common for horror fans to justify their love for a devalued genre by privileging connoisseurship – whether framed through genre history, formal traits, cultural-symptomatic readings, expanded notions of authorship, and so on – and hence their ability *not* to be as easily scared as non-fans and more "casual" or "naive" viewers supposedly are. This often means privileging certain horror films for their capacity to inspire affects beyond simply fear, particularly when those other affects allow fans to uphold horror as more of a "mind genre" than a "body genre."[98] It is not difficult to see how post-horror films, with their minimalist tone and their uses of narrative ambiguity over the mechanics of delivering jump scares, would seem ready-made for this fan-cultural rhetoric – especially for fans who wish to mark themselves off as possessing more "refined" tastes than populist viewers for whom horror cinema should foremost equal "scary."

But even as fandom privileges breadth of subcultural knowledge over professional film criticism's underlying purpose of evaluating the merits of individual films, this does not preclude horror fans with high amounts of genre literacy from ranking post-horror texts among the year's best horror films on genre-specific websites and social media. On Reddit's "Horror" board, for instance, *It Follows*, *The Witch*, and *Hereditary* topped the fan rankings of top films for 2015, 2016, and 2018 (respectively), with other post-horror movies placing highly alongside subculturally respected crowd-pleasers like *It: Chapter One* (2017) and *Halloween* (2018).[99] If anything, genre fans with high amounts of (sub)cultural capital may be best equipped to balance the respective merits of both populist and art-horror films on these year-end lists, due to their recognition of how past horror films, including ones that pursued very different aesthetic strategies, now commingle within the genre-historical canon.

Again, the social-media era's commingling of film-critical voices (professional, freelance, or otherwise) with very different levels of expertise specific to the horror genre – plus the increased speed of film-critical discourse (including breathless coverage of opening-weekend box-office buzz) in pursuit of click-based ad revenue – too often leads to what genre fans consider insufficiently historicized claims about post-horror's overall newness or novelty.[100] In their own intelligently developed counter-discourse, genre fans instead observe that 2010s post-horror does not necessarily equate to the "golden age of horror"[101] proclaimed by horror-skeptic critics, since qualifiers like "elevated" and "post" may drop off as vestigial once more historical distance from their moment of coinage has accrued, and once a select few post-horror films move to the center of the generic canon. After all, the horror canon does not simply include art-horror and prestige entries, but rather a wide range of films that span the gamut from populist to popular to texts once (and sometimes still) seen as downright disreputable (such as *The Last House on the Left* (1972), *The Texas Chain Saw Massacre*, *Cannibal Holocaust* (1980), *Hostel*, and many more). As genre fan Jacob Knight says, "[I]t's not going to be audiences, critics, or even filmmakers who end up defining what these movies are called ten, fifteen, or even fifty years in the future, but the pictures themselves."[102] Q. V. Hough concurs: "Twenty years from now, cinephiles will probably laugh at all the tidy film categorizations, like 'elevated horror,' from social media's early years."[103]

As previously noted, both horror-skeptic film critics and horror-friendly genre fans tend to concur about the *aesthetic* value of post-horror films, but their differing levels of (sub)cultural capital animate a discursive struggle over whether or not the horror genre needs "saving" in the first place. Possessing more subcultural capital than horror-skeptic film critics may allow fans to offer correctives to critics' ahistorical and reductive claims about the genre, but because critics who would otherwise sneer at taking horror films seriously are willing to admit a relatively small number of art-horror texts into the realm of "high culture," fans who position themselves as speaking on behalf of the overall genre's complexity may still feel marginalized in this conversation. This is because subcultural capital is more difficult to convert into recognizably "legitimate" cultural capital when accrued around media genres that are already considered culturally disreputable. Consequently, fans' assertions that horror has always been an artistically valid and sociologically important genre are a "democratizing" gesture that allows fans to (at least partially) imagine themselves more aligned with populist viewers than elitist guardians of cultural taste. Jostein Gripsrud explains: "Denunciation of high culture, often accompanied by populist attacks on 'elitism' . . . may have the dubious function of presenting the writer or speaker in question as no-different-from-the-rest, as some sort of ordinary and authentic [horror]-watcher in general."[104] That is, genre fans may rhetorically situate themselves as cultural intermediaries speaking on behalf of a mainstream horror viewership, but this is ultimately less a defense of what Pierre Bourdieu calls the "barbarous" tastes of the "common people" (such as privileging content over form, entertainment over contemplation, and so on) than a self-defense of fans' underrecognized sophistication in the face of lingering stereotypes about the overall horror audience as immature, sensation-seeking heathens.[105]

Gripsrud points out that (bourgeois) viewers with above-average amounts of cultural capital typically consume both "high" culture (classical music, contemporary art, and so on) and "lower" (or at least more broadly popular) forms of film and television, while "the majority of film and television audiences will never go to the opera; or visit places like museums of contemporary art, certain theatres," and other rarified venues. The former group's "double access" to different cultural-taste strata is thus a form of social privilege that is partly reflected – and yet disavowed – in the rhetorical stance of culturally educated viewers who imagine themselves interceding between highbrow elites and common media viewers.[106] In other words, horror fans with high enough (sub)cultural capital to seriously appreciate both arthouse and grindhouse product may posit professional film critics as the "enemy" in this debate over what to call post-horror films, but these fans nevertheless overlook the extent to which their correctives are elitist gestures in their own right.

After all, because they are far more likely to concur with horror-skeptic critics' high opinions of individual post-horror texts than the low CinemaScore and Rotten Tomatoes "Audience Score" ratings generated by populist viewers, genre fans' defenses of the overall horror genre (coming from both outside and inside the academy) have far less to say about post-horror's frequent rejection by wide swaths of the mainstream audience – other than fleeting acknowledgments en route to privileging genre fans as the true arbiters of horror's cultural value. When Jane Hu, for instance, speculates that "the low CinemaScore ratings of 'elevated horror' might be right in maintaining loyalty to horror's independent roots,"[107] she dubiously attributes high levels of subcultural capital (historical knowledge about "horror's independent roots") to the same populist viewership whose generalized dislike of art-cinema style actually fuels such disproportionately low scores in the first place. Furthermore, Nia Edwards-Behi admits, "Now, I have no doubt that there are *some people* who like their horror to look, sound, and feel a certain way, but for the most part *fans* of horror are fans of it precisely because of how broad and all-encompassing it can be."[108] Minus the gesture toward revaluing the genre as a whole, this all sounds quite similar to horror-skeptic critics who "argue that you [detractors] need to reconsider your expectations for 'horror,' but I can understand if the mainstream movie-goer would take the upcoming *Annabelle: Creation* [2017] over a more contemplative film."[109]

Gripsrud's mention of different consumption venues is notable here, since post-horror's exhibition in multiplexes instead of merely the arthouse/festival circuit means that "difficult" films formally akin to art cinema actually are reaching populist audiences who might not otherwise visit high-cultural venues. But these films' presence in multiplexes frequently leaves populist viewers feeling tricked into having seen something far less satisfying than what was marketed or what they expected to find playing on the same screens as the latest Disney/ Marvel movies. Genre fans' acknowledgment of populist resistance to post-horror texts therefore resembles an ambivalent shrug: "To me, when work is polarizing, when audiences are divided – some hateful and upset, others inspired and enlightened – the filmmakers are onto something."[110] The dominant counter-discourse thus finds horror aficionados asserting their own (sub)cultural connoisseurship by criticizing the cherry-picking practices of "pretentious" film critics for whom post-horror's art-cinema form makes specific texts "safe" for celebration – even as fans' advocacy on behalf of the broader genre does not adequately account for post-horror's rejection by the populist viewers in whose name they implicitly speak.

The Defense of Disreputability

Nevertheless, an important subcurrent of counter-discourse exists among fans who specifically frame the horror genre's value not despite, but precisely because, of its cultural reputation as a "low" and/or populist form. For instance, Dan Berlinka says:

> Horror fans are like music fans who complain that their favorite indie band isn't popular, but then get upset when it is. We like the slightly forbidden nature of horror. We like the fact that it's often crude and exploitative and appeals to our worst instincts. And, at heart, that's why we get so touchy about "elevated horror." We don't want our horror to be elevated.[111]

Likewise, Jason Zinoman expresses "a concern that many fans, including myself, have about the growing respectability of the genre," inaugurated by post-horror's critical acclaim. "Has horror lost some of its disreputable pleasures, not to mention its single-minded determination to terrify?"[112] Although these fans share the stance that horror does not need qualitative modifiers like "elevated" and "post," the doubt they cast on post-horror's critical embrace is rooted less in advocating for the overall genre as always-already worthy of cultural esteem than a nagging feeling that cultural esteem is an undesirable goal in itself: "[H]orror *should* be disreputable; the great horror classics, from *Night of the Living Dead* to *Texas Chainsaw Massacre* to the original *Suspiria* [1977], all were."[113]

Post-horror's outsized critical acclaim has therefore led to a backlash from some fans who claim that these films are "overrated" or stray too far from an imagined generic core (sometimes dubbed "straight-up" horror) associated with scariness, monsters, gore, entertainment value, and other traits that post-horror texts may seem to eschew. In some respects, this stance aligns them more closely with populist viewers' reaction to post-horror texts, but its refusal of critical reclamation is also a "reverse-elitist" reassertion of subcultural capital – hence Berlinka's analogy of an "indie" band that becomes too popular. Rather than a conflict framed between fans and critics, this is primarily a strategy of intra-subcultural distinction over the desirability of horror's inclusion vs. exclusion from broader cultural acceptance. That is, the horror fans discussed in the previous section celebrate post-horror texts, but resent how the critical praise lavished on these select films does not so much universalize the genre's overall cultural standing as preserve the genre's status as a "bad object" allegedly transcended by a prestigious few texts.

Whereas genre fans who celebrate post-horror (despite their quibbles over the use of such labels) ultimately align themselves with horror-skeptic film critics' tastes toward the "higher" end of the cultural spectrum, other genre fans more clearly embrace the horror genre's predominant association with "barbarous" tastes by arguing that "there is a sense of fun missing in some of the tasteful scary movies."[114] This smaller contingent of horror fans espouses their preference for generically "purer" texts with more minoritizing potential to *épater la bourgeoisie* – but it is important to note that horror's "disreputable" pleasures are not necessarily synonymous with its most popular or populist texts. (Recall how supernatural horror films, such as the *Conjuring* franchise, have gained broader box-office success than the far more "crude and exploitative" torture-porn cycle that preceded them.) Rather, for some fans, a large part of horror's subcultural appeal may reside in graphic gore and abject or "extreme" imagery – content that, while on the opposite end of the cultural-taste spectrum from post-horror, might also seem poorly suited to middle-of-the-road multiplex tastes, and instead find their "correct" audience in an alternative venue (for instance, the DTV market).

Both fan-cultural stances, however, privilege one end of the spectrum over the other by seeking some degree of distance from the nebulously defined "middle" range – which might vary, according to each viewer, from negligible populist texts to middlebrow texts aspiring too hard for prestige – and its perceived shortage of subcultural capital. Though hardly unique to horror fandom, this disdain for the cultural middle is evinced by accusations that "elevated" and "post" also function as trendy marketing labels; such complaints implicitly acknowledge post-horror's potential for box-office success beyond the arthouse/festival circuit, while also trying to distance the films from populism's taint of capitalist commodification and "easy" consumption.[115]

Even as post-horror auteur Robert Eggers confirms that "elevated" might be a useful term for independent filmmakers to use in pitching aesthetically "difficult" projects to potential financiers, a too broad application of "elevated" might backfire when appended to more populist texts. When the directors of *Pet Sematary* (2019), for example, described it as "elevated horror" during pre-release interviews, even horror fans with high expectations for the film complained that the qualifier likely "stem[med] from the fact that they tackle some pretty heavy thematic material" – even if it was deemed an unnecessary appellation, since "[m]ost horror films deal with death and trauma in some way or other."[116] Yet, when film critics and genre fans alike panned the resulting picture as a "woefully, sometimes irritatingly average" horror movie, the mismatch between the filmmakers' self-applied label and post-horror's stylistic core became all too apparent. Horror fan Jason Bailey argues that, despite having a "high-caliber cast" and themes about "familial grief and parental responsibility" similar to *Hereditary*, "if anything should get to just be regular ol' horror, it's a film adaptation of an '80s Stephen King book. [. . .] [Y]ou don't get to throw in a bunch of cheap jump scares and other pat devices, and then insist that you're above the genre fray."[117] Similar issues affected *The Shining* sequel *Doctor Sleep*, which makes deliberate homages to scenes from the original film, but whose significant departures from the stylistic minimalism and narrative ambiguity of Kubrick's film inadvertently highlight the original film's far greater influence on the post-horror corpus than on populist King adaptations like *It*.[118] This failure of "elevated" to adhere to an all too conventional Hollywood horror film with a populist aesthetic thus proves that post-horror cannot be simply defined by its "heavy" or "serious" themes, but *must* evince the tonal and formal influence of art cinema. Moreover, these comments suggest that some genre material deserves to be given the "regular ol' horror" treatment, not be filtered through art cinema's aesthetic register – implying that films aiming for a mainstream audience should simply embrace the term "horror" without qualification.

Released two weeks after *Pet Sematary*, Jordan Peele's *Us* presents another interesting example of this fan-cultural pushback against a potential mismatch between text and generic label. Peele acknowledged his earlier, much disparaged labeling of *Get Out* as a "social thriller" by declaring on Twitter, several days before *Us*'s release, that "*Us* is a horror movie."[119] Although genre fans generally acclaimed the film, *Get Out*'s critical nomination as "elevated horror" continued to cast a long shadow over Peele's follow-up film. "[M]ost critics within the genre community agree that it's good," says Robert Skvarla's review for *Diabolique Magazine*. "The bad news: so do most mainstream critics. The problem here isn't that *Us* doesn't deserve praise outside genre circles. [. . .] But the nature of the praise the film is receiving is precisely the problem." For Skvarla, "*Us* is a horror film through-and-through," and does not "transcend" its genre (here he cites Richard Brody's aforementioned dissembling over its generic status) so much as wholly embodies it.[120] Likewise, K. Austin Collins argues that *Us* "is much more loaded with straightforward scares than *Get Out* was. It is much bloodier" and "also, to my mind, funnier . . . But there's little doubt that this is unabashedly a horror movie, no matter how eager it is to pivot and sway between multiple subgenres, from funhouse horror to home-invasion thriller to slasher, sci-fi, and horror comedy." Collins situates the film's admixture of subgeneric conventions squarely inside the horror genre, but he also argues that the film doesn't work as well as *Get Out* because Peele allegedly internalized high critical expectations to the point of cramming too many ideas into a more conventionally generic package:

> [I]f we don't accept that *Us* is plain, simple, corny, "don't overthink it" horror – if we insist on making it elevated, or treating it like a film that surpasses its generic roots . . . it simply doesn't work. [. . .] It isn't that horror films cannot have ideas without sacrificing their legitimacy as horror. It's that *Us* feels too eager to prove, on *Get Out*'s coattails, that horror can have ideas to begin with – a concept that doesn't really need proving.[121]

This quote implicitly suggests that film critics and more erudite genre fans are to blame for encouraging Peele's (arguably) less successful attempt to "elevate" a story that, in contrast to *Get Out*'s more focused concept and execution, "trades elegance for abundance" and cannot seem to settle for being "just" a horror movie.[122] Whereas *Pet Sematary*'s filmmakers explicitly adopted the "elevated" label but glaringly failed to pair it with the expected art-cinema aesthetic, Peele's deliberate avoidance of such qualifiers for *Us* paradoxically haunted the reception of a film with social commentary galore but a less contemplative aesthetic than its predecessor.

What these two examples suggest, then, is that the presence or absence of generic qualifiers like "elevated" and "post" ultimately matters less than a filmmaker's tonal treatment of their subject matter. Contra Edwards-Behi, I would argue that, despite their shortcomings, authorship-based approaches to post-horror remain an important means of understanding how a filmmaker's specific formal/stylistic choices filter horror's generic tropes and themes through the art-cinema mode, giving them a different affective resonance than if presented via a more classical, populist mode of filmmaking. Genre fans may hem and haw about how horror-skeptic critics' taste-based blinders obscure horror's longer history as a genre containing artistically and sociologically sophisticated texts, not just movies appealing to the lowest common denominator. Yet, if they have accrued high levels of subcultural capital, fans' own blinders obscure the extent to which populist viewers have rejected so many post-horror films on the basis of these texts' rarified and minimalist aesthetic that fails to deliver enough sense of fun. Even trade publications like *The Hollywood Reporter* began speculating in early 2019 that, with "auteur craftsmanship and prestige horror" garnering so much attention, "it's becoming increasingly necessary to come back up for air and explore the horror that exists on the surface," especially via "a possible return to form for serialized horror franchises of the popcorn entertainment variety" – regardless of the fact that populist horror films had not declined in overall number or box-office success upon post-horror's dive "deeper into contemporary examinations of fears concerning race, culture, parenthood, and sexuality."[123]

In conclusion, film critics, genre fans, and a broader swath of mainstream viewers all remain haunted by horror's predominant reputation as a populist genre – albeit for different reasons. Post-horror's divisive reception ultimately demonstrates that art-horror's disrepute may have less to do with horror's visceral appeals to the body, as Joan Hawkins argues, than its expected appeals to entertainment value.[124] Following Jamie Sexton, if viewers with high degrees of cultural or subcultural capital are far more likely to engage with one side of the art/genre binary when encountering culturally "lower" genres than higher ones, then horror's widespread cultural disrepute will likely remain upheld, rather than the binary truly collapsing. Despite some horror fans' fears that critical acceptance or mainstream box-office success will somehow spoil the genre's disreputable appeal, other fans observe that the genre has always fostered critical and popular exceptions to the divisive cultural status that has long made it an object of subcultural dedication. The fact that generic appeals can allow post-horror films to find larger audiences beyond the arthouse/festival circuit does show how aesthetically different uses of the genre can still achieve some (limited) mainstream visibility. As Robert Eggers optimistically notes, "As the audience grows wider, people who wouldn't necessarily be a part of . . . the A24 core art-house audience might be exposed to this stuff – and they might find that it's more accessible than some people thought."[125] Whether mainstream audiences with populist tastes will adjust their generic expectations by gradually accepting post-horror's arthouse stylization is still an open question – but it also remains to be seen whether horror's most dedicated fans would genuinely accept this potential dismantling of subculturally constitutive taste hierarchies between "high art" and "low genre."

Notes

1. Matt Zoller Seitz, Twitter post, March 24, 2019, 9:13 p.m., <https://twitter.com/mattzollerseitz/status/1110032050126503936>.
2. Aaron Michael Kerner, *Torture Porn in the Wake of 9/11: Horror, Exploitation, and the Cinema of Sensation* (New Brunswick, NJ: Rutgers University Press, 2015), ch. 1.
3. Mattias Frey, "The New Democracy? Rotten Tomatoes, Metacritic, Twitter, and IMDb," in *Film Criticism in the Digital Age*, eds Mattias Frey and Cecilia Sayad (New Brunswick, NJ: Rutgers University Press, 2015), p. 83. Also see Mattias Frey, *The Permanent Crisis of Film Criticism: The Anxiety of Authority* (Amsterdam: Amsterdam University Press, 2014).
4. For example, Michael Nordine, "'It Follows' is the Best Horror Film in Years," *VICE*, March 4, 2015 <https://www.vice.com/en_us/article/5gk77n/it-follows-is-the-new-horror-movie-about-a-sexually-transmitted-monster-456>; and Alessio Marinacci, "*Halloween/It Follows* (atmosphere)," YouTube, February 12, 2017 <https://youtu.be/-KOXw8YDKDE>.
5. Glyn Davis, "The Speed of the VCR: Ti West's Slow Horror," *Screen*, 59, no. 1 (2018), pp. 54–5. Also see Amy Nicholson, "Mumblegore: Meet the Smart Young Misfits Who Are Revolutionizing Indie Horror Movies," *LA Weekly*, October 28, 2013 <https://www.laweekly.com/how-mumblegores-smart-young-misfits-are-revolutionizing-indie-horror-films/>.
6. Neda Ulaby, "Director Ti West Talks Slow Horror, 'The Innkeepers,'" *National Public Radio*, February 4, 2012 <https://www.npr.org/2012/02/04/146343636/director-ti-west-talks-slow-horror-the-innkeepers>.
7. Ibid.
8. Tiago de Luca and Nuno Barradas Jorge, "Introduction: From Slow Cinema to Slow Cinemas," in *Slow Cinema*, eds Tiago de Luca and Nuno Barradas Jorge (Edinburgh: Edinburgh University Press, 2016), p. 2.
9. Matthew Flanagan, "Towards an Aesthetics of Slow in Contemporary Cinema," *16:9*, 6, no. 29 (2008) <http://www.16-9.dk/2008-11/side11_inenglish.htm>. On intensified continuity, see David Bordwell, "Intensified Continuity: Visual Style in Contemporary American Film," *Film Quarterly*, 55, no. 3 (2002), pp. 16–28.
10. Ira Jaffe, *Slow Movies: Countering the Cinema of Action* (London: Wallflower Press, 2014), p. 6.
11. Flanagan, "Towards an Aesthetic of Slow."
12. "High Jump Scare Movies," Where's the Jump?, accessed July 16, 2017 <https://wheresthejump.com/high-jump-scare-movies/>.
13. Joshua Wise, "What Is Slow Horror?" *Slow Horror* (blog), accessed June 26, 2019 <https://www.slowhorror.com/single-post/2017/08/10/What-is-Slow-Horror>; The Watching Staff, "Slow and Creepy Horror," *New York Times*, accessed June 27, 2019 <https://www.nytimes.com/watching/lists/horror-movies-slow>.

14. Jordan Crucchiola, "Let's Talk about the Ending of *The Blackcoat's Daughter*," *Vulture*, March 31, 2017 <http://www.vulture.com/2017/03/blackcoats-daughter-ending.html> original emphasis.
15. Davis, "The Speed of the VCR," 42, 49. On the role of ghosts in these two canonical examples of slow cinema, also see Nicholas de Villiers, "Leaving the Cinema: Metacinematic Cruising in Tsai Ming-liang's *Goodbye, Dragon Inn*," *Jump Cut*, no. 50 (2008), <https://www.ejumpcut.org/archive/jc50.2008/DragonInn/>; and Mitsuyo Wada-Marciano, "Showing the Unknowable: *Uncle Boonmee Who Can Recall His Past Lives*," in *Cinematic Ghosts: Haunting and Spectrality from Silent Cinema to the Digital Era*, ed. Murray Leeder (New York: Bloomsbury Academic, 2015), pp. 271–89.
16. Steve Rose, "How Post-Horror Movies are Taking Over Cinema," *The Guardian*, July 6, 2017 <https://www.theguardian.com/film/2017/jul/06/post-horror-films-scary-movies-ghost-story-it-comes-at-night>.
17. See Jaffe, *Slow Movies*, 45–59, 102–8; Jennifer A. Rich, "Shock Corridors: The New Rhetoric of Horror in Gus Van Sant's *Elephant*," *Journal of Popular Culture*, 45, no. 6 (2012), pp. 1310–29; Pamela Craig and Martin Fradley, "Teenage Traumata: Youth, Affective Politics, and the Contemporary American Horror Film," in *American Horror Film: The Genre at the Turn of the Millennium*, ed. Steffen Hantke (Jackson, MS: University Press of Mississippi, 2010), pp. 77–8, 94; Laura Christian, "Of Housewives and Saints: Abjection, Transgression, and Impossible Mourning in *Poison* and *Safe*," *Camera Obscura*, 19, no. 3 (2004), pp. 93–123.
18. Davis, "The Speed of the VCR," 44.
19. Jaffe, *Slow Movies*, 9.
20. A. C. Wise, "Quiet Horror," *A.C. Wise* (blog), July 30, 2016, <http://www.acwise.net/?p=2217>.
21. Joan Hawkins, "'It Fixates': Indie Quiets and the New Gothics," *Palgrave Communications*, 3:17088 (2017): doi: 10.1057/palcomms.2017.88 (pp. 2–6).
22. James Kendrick, "A Return to the Graveyard: Notes on the Spiritual Horror Film," *American Horror Film*, 142–4, 155–6.
23. Blair Davis and Kial Natale, "'The Pound of Flesh Which I Demand': American Horror Cinema, Gore, and the Box Office, 1998–2007," in *American Horror Film*, 46–9.
24. Daniel Martin, "Japan's *Blair Witch*: Restraint, Maturity, and Generic Canons in the British Critical Reception of *Ring*," *Cinema Journal*, 48, no. 3 (2009), p. 43–9; Hawkins, "'It Fixates,'" 3.
25. For example, Justin Chang, "Film Review: 'The Conjuring,'" *Variety*, June 22, 2013 <https://variety.com/2013/film/markets-festivals/film-review-the-conjuring-1200500864/>; Sheri Linden, "*The Conjuring*: LAFF Review," *Hollywood Reporter*, June 22, 2013 <https://www.hollywoodreporter.com/review/conjuring-laff-review-573656>.
26. Anne Billson, "Cheap Thrills: The Frightful Rise of Low-Budget Horror," *The Telegraph*, May 6, 2015 <http://www.telegraph.co.uk/film/it-follows/rise-of-low-budget-horror-movies-babadook/>.

27. A. A. Dowd, "*Hereditary* is the Most Traumatically Terrifying Horror Movie in Ages," *A.V. Club*, January 23, 2018 <https://www.avclub.com/hereditary-is-the-most-traumatically-terrifying-horror-1822352430>.
28. David Edelstein, "Now Playing at Your Local Multiplex: Torture Porn," *New York*, January 26, 2006 <http://nymag.com/movies/features/15622/>.
29. Compare, for example, the titles of Adam Lowenstein, "Spectacle Horror and *Hostel*: Why 'Torture Porn' Does Not Exist," *Critical Quarterly*, 53, no. 1 (2011), pp. 42–60; and Jacob Knight, "There's No Such Thing as an 'Elevated Horror Movie' (And Yes, 'Hereditary' is a Horror Movie)," *SlashFilm*, June 8, 2018 <https://www.slashfilm.com/elevated-horror/>.
30. Mattias Frey, "Introduction: Critical Questions," in *Film Criticism in the Digital Age*, 5. Also see Wesley Shrum, "Critics and Publics: Cultural Mediation in Highbrow and Popular Performing Arts," *American Journal of Sociology*, 97, no. 2 (1991), p. 369.
31. Andrew Carroll, "Horror Means Horror: The Fallacy of 'Elevated Horror,'" *Headstuff*, March 28, 2019 <https://www.headstuff.org/entertainment/film/elevated-horror-get-out-us/>.
32. For example, Wendy Ide, "The Rise of Smart Indie Horror Films," *The Times*, February 27, 2015 <https://www.thetimes.co.uk/article/the-rise-of-smart-indie-horror-films-ps7mbrs28qd>; Frankie Taggart, "The Rise of Smart, Low-Budget Horror," *AFP*, August 20, 2016 <https://www.afp.com/en/news/206/rise-smart-low-budget-horror>; Graeme Virtue, "Why Smart Horror is Putting the Fear into Sequel-Addicted Hollywood," *The Guardian*, April 12, 2018 <https://www.theguardian.com/film/2018/apr/12/horror-quiet-place-get-out-hollywood>.
33. Jeffrey Sconce, "Irony, Nihilism, and the New American 'Smart' Film," *Screen*, 43, no. 4 (2002), pp. 358–60, 364, 368 (quotes at pp. 359, 368).
34. Ibid., pp. 353–8.
35. J. A. Bridges, "Post-Horror Kinships: From *Goodnight Mommy* to *Get Out*," *Bright Lights Film Journal*, December 20, 2018 <https://brightlightsfilm.com/post-horror-kinships-from-goodnight-mommy-to-get-out/>.
36. Sconce, "Irony," pp. 358–9 (quoted at p. 359, original emphasis).
37. Julian Hanich, *Cinematic Emotion in Horror Films and Thrillers: The Aesthetic Paradox of Pleasurable Fear* (New York: Routledge, 2010), p. 193.
38. Stephanie A. Graves, "Jordan Peele's *Get Out* (2017) – Smart Horror," in *Horror: A Companion*, ed. Simon Bacon (Oxford: Peter Lang, 2019), p. 132.
39. Among others, see Zoe Williams, "The Final Irony," *The Guardian*, June 27, 2003 <https://www.theguardian.com/theguardian/2003/jun/28/weekend7.weekend2>; Steven Shaviro, "Prophecies of the Present," *Socialism and Democracy*, 20, no. 3 (2006), pp. 5–24; Christy Wampole, "How to Live Without Irony," *New York Times*, November 17, 2012 <https://opinionator.blogs.nytimes.com/2012/11/17/how-to-live-without-irony/>; Jonathan D. Fitzgerald, "Sincerity, Not Irony, is Our Age's Ethos," *The Atlantic*, November 20, 2012 <https://www.theatlantic.

com/entertainment/archive/2012/11/sincerity-not-irony-is-our-ages-ethos/265466/>; Lee Konstantinou, *Cool Characters: Irony and American Fiction* (Cambridge, MA: Harvard University Press, 2016). On the New Sincerity, also see Jim Collins, *Architectures of Excess: Cultural Life in the Information Age* (New York: Routledge, 1995), ch. 3.

40. Raymond Williams, *Marxism and Literature* (New York: Oxford University Press, 1977), p. 132.
41. For example, Eric Kohn, "Is 'It Follows' Paving the Way to a New Era for Indie Genre Films?" *IndieWire*, May 1, 2015 <https://www.indiewire.com/2015/05/is-it-follows-paving-the-way-to-a-new-era-for-indie-genre-films-62470/>; Brandon T. Gass, "Indie Horror: The Rise of a Meta-Genre," *The Artifice*, November 24, 2015 <https://the-artifice.com/indie-horror-recent-rise-of-a-meta-genre/>; Frederick Bleichert, "What's Next for the Indie Horror Movie Wave," *VICE*, June 9, 2017 <https://www.vice.com/en_us/article/kzq7kz/heres-what-to-watch-next-if-youre-riding-the-prestige-horror-wave>.
42. Michael Z. Newman, "Indie Culture: In Pursuit of the Authentic Autonomous Alternative," *Cinema Journal*, 48, no. 3 (2009), p. 16.
43. Claire Perkins, *American Smart Cinema* (Edinburgh: Edinburgh University Press, 2012), pp. 1–2.
44. On these shifts, see Yannis Tzioumakis, "'Independent,' 'Indie,' and 'Indiewood': Towards a Periodization of Contemporary (Post-1980) American Independent Cinema," in *American Independent Cinema: Indie, Indiewood, and Beyond*, eds Geoff King, Claire Molloy, and Yannis Tzioumakis (London: Routledge, 2013), pp. 28–40.
45. Jamie Sexton, "US 'Indie-Horror': Critical Reception, Genre Construction, and Suspect Hybridity," *Cinema Journal*, 51, no. 2 (2012), pp. 69–71, 81–3.
46. Blichert, "What's Next."
47. David Andrews, *Theorizing Art Cinemas: Foreign, Cult, Avant-Garde, and Beyond* (Austin, TX: University of Texas Press, 2013), p. 27.
48. Stephen Follows and Bruce Nash, "UPDATE: What Types of Low Budget Films Break Out?" *American Film Market*, accessed June 28, 2019 <https://americanfilmmarket.com/update-types-low-budget-films-break-out/>.
49. Jason Zinoman, "Home Is Where the Horror Is," *New York Times*, June 7, 2018, <https://www.nytimes.com/2018/06/07/movies/hereditary-horror-movies.html>.
50. Zach Baron, "How A24 is Disrupting Hollywood," *GQ*, May 9, 2017 <http://www.gq.com/story/a24-studio-oral-history>.
51. Knight, "There's No Such Thing" (original emphasis).
52. Quoted in David Ehrlich, "How Ari Aster, Robert Eggers, and Jordan Peele are Using Horror Movies to Fix Hollywood," *IndieWire*, November 6, 2019 <https://www.indiewire.com/2019/11/oscar-worthy-horror-movies-midsommar-lighthouse-us-1202187720/>.

53. Figures taken from The Numbers, "Box Office Performance for Horror Movies in 2015" <http://www.the-numbers.com/market/2015/genre/Horror> and "Box Office Performance for Horror Movies in 2016" <http://www.the-numbers.com/market/2016/genre/Horror)>; both accessed July 12, 2017.
54. Tyler Aquilina, "Why Horror is Having Its Moment," *Hollywood Reporter*, August 28, 2018 <https://www.hollywoodreporter.com/heat-vision/suspiria-why-horror-is-thriving-once-more-1137706>.
55. Sexton, "US 'Indie-Horror,'" 75.
56. Douglas Pye, "Movies and Tone," in *Close-Up 02*, eds John Gibbs and Douglas Pye (London: Wallflower Press, 2007), pp. 14–15.
57. For example, Lauren Duca, "How Robert Eggers Wove the Nightmares of *The Witch* Out of Historical Documents," *Vulture*, February 18, 2016 <https://www.vulture.com/2016/02/how-robert-eggers-researched-the-witch.html>.
58. Perkins, *American Smart Cinema*, 12.
59. Sexton, "US 'Indie-Horror,'" 85.
60. A. A. Dowd, "*The Blackcoat's Daughter* Finally Rises from Release-Date Purgatory to Give Everyone the Creeps," *A. V. Club*, March 30, 2017 <http://www.avclub.com/review/blackcoats-daughter-rises-release-date-purgatory-g-252881>.
61. Justine Smith, "*The Blackcoat's Daughter*," *RogerEbert.com*, March 29, 2017 <http://www.rogerebert.com/reviews/the-blackcoats-daughter-2017>.
62. Jordan Hoffman, "*February* Review – Pseudo-Intellectual Horror of the Dullest Kind," *The Guardian*, September 14, 2015 <https://www.theguardian.com/film/2015/sep/14/february-film-review-kiernan-shipka-osgood-perkins-horror>.
63. See Rhona J. Berenstein, *Attack of the Leading Ladies: Gender, Sexuality, and Spectatorship in Classic Horror Cinema* (New York: Columbia University Press, 1996), ch. 3; Tim Snelson, "'From Grade B Thrillers to Deluxe Chillers': Prestige Horror, Female Audiences, and Allegories of Spectatorship in *The Spiral Staircase* (1946)," *New Review of Film and Television Studies*, 7, no. 2 (2009), pp. 173–88; Brigid Cherry, "Gothics and Grand Guignols: Violence and the Gendered Aesthetics of Cinematic Horror," *Participations: Journal of Audience and Reception Studies*, 5, no. 1 (2008), <http://www.participations.org/Volume%205/Issue%201%20-%20special/5_01_cherry.htm> (quoted); Alison Peirce, "The Feminine Appeal of British Horror Cinema," *New Review of Film and Television Studies*, 13, no. 4 (2015), pp. 385–402.
64. See Mark Jancovich, "Relocating Lewton: Cultural Distinctions, Critical Reception, and the Val Lewton Horror Films," *Journal of Film and Video*, 64, no. 3 (2012), pp. 21–37; Mark Jancovich, "'Antique Chiller': Quality, Pretention, and History in the Critical Reception of *The Innocents* and *The Haunting*," in *Cinematic Ghosts*, 115–28; Mark Jancovich, "Beyond Hammer: The First Run Market and the Prestige Horror Film in the Early 1960s," *Palgrave Communications*, 3:17028 (2017): doi: 10.1057/palcomms.2017.28.

65. See Kyle Edwards, "'House of Horrors': Corporate Strategy at Universal Pictures in the 1930s," in *Merchants of Menace: The Business of Horror Cinema*, ed. Richard Nowell (New York: Bloomsbury Academic, 2014), pp. 13–30; Kevin Heffernan, *Ghouls, Gimmicks, and Gold: Horror Films and the American Movie Business, 1953–1968* (Durham, NC: Duke University Press, 2004), ch. 8; Stacy Abbott, "High Concept Thrills and Chills: The Horror Blockbuster," in *Horror Zone: The Cultural Experience of Contemporary Horror Cinema*, ed. Ian Conrich (London: I. B. Tauris, 2010), pp. 29–34.
66. For example, Ira Madison III, "The Prestige Horror Revival," *MTV.com*, April 26, 2017 <http://www.mtv.com/news/3006220/the-prestige-horror-revival/>; Jacob Trussell, "Prestige Horror Has Arrived," *Film School Rejects*, June 30, 2018 <https://filmschoolrejects.com/prestige-horror-movies/>; Harry Pages, "Hollywood's Frightening Future: Prestige Horror Films," *Film Daily*, July 2, 2019 <https://filmdaily.co/obsessions/hollywood-prestige-horror-films/>.
67. For example, Rose, "How Post-Horror Movies are Taking Over Cinema"; Ulaby, "Director Ti West Talks Slow Horror."
68. For example, Matt Hagerholm, "A Movie Can Be a Poem: Oz Perkins on 'The Blackcoat's Daughter,'" *RogerEbert.com*, March 20, 2017 <https://www.rogerebert.com/interviews/a-movie-can-be-a-poem-oz-perkins-on-the-blackcoats-daughter>.
69. Jane Hu, "Can Horror Movies Be Prestigious?" *The Ringer*, June 15, 2018, <https://www.theringer.com/movies/2018/6/15/17467020/hereditary-elevated-horror-get-out-a-quiet-place-the-witch>.
70. Laura Mee, "*The Shining* and the Spectre of 'Elevated Horror,'" *In Media Res*, March 8, 2019 <http://mediacommons.org/imr/content/shining-and-spectre-elevated-horror>.
71. Jess Hicks, "Everybody Be Cool: How to Rise Above Genre-Fan Backlash," *Blumhouse.com*, July 5, 2017, <http://www.blumhouse.com/2017/07/05/everybody-be-cool-how-to-rise-above-genre-fan-backlash/>.
72. For example, see Adam Epstein, "'Hereditary' is Not 'Elevated Horror.' It's Just a Good Horror Movie," *Quartzy*, June 11, 2018 <https://qz.com/quartzy/1302187/hereditary-is-not-elevated-horror-its-just-a-good-horror-movie/; Aaron Neuwirth and Anne McCarthy, quoted in David Ehrlich, "The Evils of 'Elevated Horror': *IndieWire* Critics Survey," *IndieWire*, March 25, 2019 <https://www.indiewire.com/2019/03/elevated-horror-movies-us-1202053471/>.
73. Michael Brown, "The Problem with 'Post-Horror,'" *Overland*, May 15, 2019 <https://overland.org.au/2019/05/the-problem-with-post-horror/>.
74. Mark Jancovich, "'A Real Shocker': Authenticity, Genre, and the Struggle for Distinction," *Continuum: Journal of Media and Cultural Studies*, 14, no. 1 (2000), p. 31. For examples of this critical defense of "elevated," see Monique Jones, Joanna Langfield, and Don Shanahan, quoted in Ehrlich, "The Evils of 'Elevated Horror.'"

75. Shellie McMurdo, "The Problem with Post-Horror," *In Media Res*, March 4, 2019 <http://mediacommons.org/imr/content/problem-post-horror>.
76. Richard Brody, "Review: Jordan Peele's 'Us' is a Colossal Cinematic Achievement," *New Yorker*, March 23, 2019 <https://www.newyorker.com/culture/the-front-row/review-jordan-peeles-us-is-a-colossal-cinematic-achievement>.
77. Shane Danielsen, "The Elevated Horror of Ari Aster's 'Hereditary,'" *The Monthly*, June 2018, https://www.themonthly.com.au/issue/2018/june/1527775200/shane-danielsen/elevated-horror-ari-aster-s-hereditary#mtr> (original emphasis).
78. Alex McLevy, "*It Chapter Two* Is a Bad Horror Movie, But It's a Pretty Decent Comedy," *A. V. Club*, September 9, 2019 <https://film.avclub.com/it-chapter-two-is-a-bad-horror-movie-but-it-s-a-pretty-1837937721> (emphasis mine).
79. Mark Jancovich, "Genre and the Audience: Genre Classifications and Cultural Distinctions in the Mediation of *The Silence of the Lambs*," in *Horror: The Film Reader*, ed. Mark Jancovich (London: Routledge, 2002), pp. 156–9 (quote at p. 156).
80. Quoted in Michael Phillips, "Jordan Peele's 'Social Thriller' Launches a Directorial Career," *Chicago Tribune*, February 24, 2017 <https://www.chicagotribune.com/entertainment/movies/ct-jordan-peele-get-out-interview-20170224-column.html>.
81. Quoted in Katie Rife, "Horror is a Trojan Horse for *The Blackcoat's Daughter* Director Oz Perkins," *A. V. Club*, March 30, 2017, <http://www.avclub.com/article/horror-trojan-horse-blackcoats-daughter-director-o-252538>.
82. Quoted in Michael O'Sullivan, "'Babadook' Director Jennifer Kent Talks About Women Making Horror Movies," *Washington Post*, December 12, 2014, <https://www.washingtonpost.com/lifestyle/style/babadook-director-jennifer-kent-talks-about-women-making-horror-movies/2014/12/12/11dba89a-8082-11e4-9f38-95a187e4c1f7_story.html?noredirect=on>.
83. Quoted in Rose, "How Post-Horror Movies are Taking Over Cinema."
84. Quoted in Britt Hayes, "'Hereditary' Director Ari Aster on Why He Avoided Calling His Terrifying Debut a 'Horror Film,'" *Screen Crush*, June 7, 2018 <https://screencrush.com/ari-aster-interview-hereditary/>.
85. Powell, quoted in Carol J. Clover, *Men, Women, and Chainsaws: Gender in the Modern Horror Film* (Princeton, NJ: Princeton University Press, 1992), p. 169; Friedkin, quoted in Ryan Parker, "'The Exorcist' Director William Friedkin: 'I Didn't Set Out to Make a Horror Film,'" *Hollywood Reporter*, October 28, 2015 <https://www.hollywoodreporter.com/news/exorcist-director-william-friedkin-i-835016>.
86. Heffernan, *Ghouls, Gimmicks*, ch. 8. Castle did, however, reserve a brief but blatant cameo for himself in *Rosemary's Baby* as a quick nod to his public persona.
87. Zinoman, "Home Is Where the Horror Is."

88. Nancy Tartagloione, "*The Lighthouse*'s Robert Eggers, Willem Dafoe, & Robert Pattinson on 'Something More Dreadful Than Horror' – Cannes Studio," *Deadline*, May 19, 2019 <https://deadline.com/2019/05/the-lighthouse-robert-pattinson-willem-dafoe-robert-eggers-cannes-video-1202618609/>.
89. Quoted in Zach Sharf, "Robert Eggers Rejects 'Elevated Horror,' But Embraces the Freedom of 'Genre Films,'" *IndieWire*, September 3, 2019 <https://www.indiewire.com/2019/09/robert-eggers-lighthouse-elevated-horror-1202170649/>.
90. For example, Aquilina, "Why Horror Is Having Its Moment"; Dom Nero, "Hallowed Grounds: Auteur-Driven Horror Films Have Always Led the Genre," *Esquire*, October 3, 2018 <https://www.esquire.com/entertainment/movies/a23494447/auteur-driven-horror-movies/>.
91. Richard Brody, quoted in Ehrlich, "The Evils of 'Elevated Horror.'"
92. Nia Edwards-Behi, "A Response to Post-Horror," *Wales Arts Review*, July 9, 2017 <https://www.walesartsreview.org/cinema-a-response-to-post-horror/>.
93. April Wolfe, "With 'A Quiet Place' and 'Get Out,' Horror Is Having a Mainstream Moment. Will That Alienate Fans?" *Washington Post*, April 13, 2018 <https://www.washingtonpost.com/entertainment/with-a-quiet-place-and-get-out-horror-is-having-a-mainstream-moment-will-that-alienate-fans/2018/04/13/99bbcbb0-3db1-11e8-974f-aacd97698cef_story.html>.
94. Among others, see Edwards-Behi, "A Response to Post-Horror"; Knight, "There's No Such Thing"; Hu, "Can Horror Movies Be Prestigious?"; Carroll, "Horror Means Horror"; Brown, "The Problem with 'Post-Horror'"; K. Austin Collins, "Jordan Peele's *Us* Is Just a Horror Movie, and That's a Good Thing," *Vanity Fair*, March 22, 2019 <https://www.vanityfair.com/hollywood/2019/03/jordan-peeles-us-dont-overthink-it>; Robert Skvarla, "Among Us: On Jordan Peele and Elevated Horror," *Diabolique Magazine*, March 27, 2019 <https://diaboliquemagazine.com/among-us-on-jordan-peele-and-elevated-horror/>. On horror as a sociocultural "return of the repressed," also see Robin Wood, *Hollywood from Vietnam to Reagan . . . and Beyond* (New York: Columbia University Press, 2003).
95. Mike McGranaghan, quoted in Ehrlich, "The Evils of 'Elevated Horror'" (emphasis mine).
96. Rose, "How Post-Horror Movies are Taking Over Cinema."
97. Carroll, "Horror Means Horror."
98. Matt Hills, *The Pleasures of Horror* (London: Continuum, 2005), pp. 74–6, 82 (quoted at p. 82).
99. See "Dreadit's Top 20 Films of 2015" <https://www.reddit.com/r/horror/wiki/bestof2015>; "Dreadit's Top 20 Films of 2016" <https://www.reddit.com/r/horror/comments/5re1dl/dreadits_top_films_of_2016/>; "Dreadit's Top 25 of 2018" <https://www.reddit.com/r/horror/comments/ab792o/rhorrors_top_25_films_of_2018/>; all accessed June 25, 2019.

100. See Chuck Tryon, *Reinventing Cinema: Movies in the Age of Convergence* (New Brunswick, NJ: Rutgers University Press, 2009), pp. 128–30, 135–6.
101. Kevin Maher, "*Midsommar* Review – All Hail the New Golden Age of Horror," *The Times*, July 4, 2019 <https://www.thetimes.co.uk/article/midsommar-review-all-hail-the-new-golden-era-of-horror-3bfq3btr9>.
102. Knight, "There's No Such Thing."
103. Q. V. Hough, quoted in Ehrlich, "The Evils of 'Elevated Horror.'"
104. Jostein Gripsrud, "'High Culture' Revisited," *Cultural Studies*, 3, no. 2 (1989), p. 198.
105. Pierre Bourdieu, *Distinction: A Social Critique of the Judgment of Taste*, trans. Richard Nice (Cambridge, MA: Harvard University Press, 1984), pp. 30–1.
106. Gripsrud, "'High Culture' Revisited," 198–9.
107. Hu, "Can Horror Movies Be Prestigious?"
108. Edwards-Behi, "A Response to Post-Horror" (emphasis mine).
109. Kiernan McLoone, "*It Comes at Night* and the Power of the Unseen Horror," *Cultured Vultures*, July 12, 2017, <https://culturedvultures.com/it-comes-at-night-horror/>.
110. Richard Thomas, "The H Word: How *The Witch* and *Get Out* Helped Usher in the New Wave of Elevated Horror," *Nightmare Magazine*, February 2019 <http://www.nightmare-magazine.com/nonfiction/the-h-word-how-the-witch-and-get-out-helped-usher-in-the-new-wave-of-elevated-horror/>.
111. Quoted in Nicholas Barber, "Is Horror the Most Disrespected Genre?" *BBC*, June 14, 2018 <http://www.bbc.com/culture/story/20180614-is-horror-the-most-disrespected-genre>.
112. Zinoman, "Home Is Where the Horror Is."
113. Jason Bailey, "'Pet Sematary' and the Sticky Wicket of 'Elevated Horror,'" *Flavorwire*, April 4, 2019 <https://www.flavorwire.com/616170/pet-sematary-and-the-sticky-wicket-of-elevated-horror> (original emphasis).
114. Zinoman, "Home Is Where the Horror Is."
115. For example, Knight, "There's No Such Thing"; Epstein, "'Hereditary' Is Not 'Elevated Horror'"; Brown, "The Problem with 'Post-Horror'"; Carl Broughton, quoted in Ehrlich, "The Evils of 'Elevated Horror.'"
116. Kate Gardner, "Please, Stop Calling Your Scary Movies 'Elevated Horror,'" *The Mary Sue*, March 18, 2019 <https://www.themarysue.com/stop-calling-scary-movies-elevated-horror/>.
117. Bailey, "'Pet Sematary' and the Sticky Wicket of 'Elevated Horror.'"
118. Unsurprisingly, most of *The Shining*'s stylistic qualities that later influenced the post-horror cycle are the very qualities that King harshly criticized about Kubrick's adaptation.
119. Jordan Peele, Twitter post, March 17, 2019, 11:57 a.m., <https://twitter.com/JordanPeele/status/1107355349177257984>.
120. Skvarla, "Among Us."
121. Collins, "Jordan Peele's *Us* Is Just a Horror Movie."
122. Ibid.

123. Richard Newby, "How 'Final Destination' Reboot Can Fill a Horror Void," *Hollywood Reporter*, January 14, 2019 <https://www.hollywoodreporter.com/heat-vision/how-final-destination-reboot-can-bring-dumb-fun-back-movies-1175855>.
124. Joan Hawkins, *Cutting Edge: Art-Horror and the Horrific Avant-Garde* (Minneapolis, MN: University of Minnesota Press, 2000), ch. 1.
125. Quoted in Ehrlich, "How Ari Aster."

CHAPTER 3

Grief, Mourning, and the Horrors of Familial Inheritance

During the first two chapters of this study, I explored the "anxiety of influence" with which filmmakers, critics, and audiences must, in their own way, grapple with post-horror's uneasy relationship to precursors drawn from multiple genres and modes. Yet, because genres are systems of quasi-familial relationships between texts, these uncanny resemblances might disturb and disappoint viewers expecting more straightforward thrills than extended meditations on "the ominous danger of overwhelming grief." "A character coping with the death of a loved one is the new car of teenagers heading to a cabin in the woods," remarks *New York Times* critic Jason Zinoman, observing that post-horror's reliance on grief is now an almost rote narrative setup.[1] J. A. Bridges likewise notes how many post-horror films feature a tragic death during the first act in order to establish the emotional depth of middle-class family dramas, before the haunting quality of such traumas introduces more supernatural circumstances in later narrative acts. Such originating traumas may also account for why many post-horror films feature a major character who seems trapped in an emotional limbo that they are unable to get beyond.[2]

Indeed, nearly all of the films listed as primary/core post-horror texts (see Table 1.1) prominently feature the loss of at least one immediate family member, and many of the secondary texts do as well. In some of these films (such as *The Babadook* (2014), *Goodnight Mommy* (2014), and *The Eyes of My Mother* (2016)), the suddenness of the initial loss registers as a trauma, while in others (such as *Hagazussa: A Heathen's Curse* (2017) and *Hereditary* (2018)), a later traumatic event reactivates the grief lingering from a prior, more gradual loss of a family member. As early as Freud's seminal 1917 essay "Mourning and Melancholia," *grief* has named an emotion that can open onto other affects in potentially messy ways, while *mourning* names a process of overcoming loss (via the ego's gradual withdrawal from its prior cathexis with the lost object) that can lend itself to narrative. Eugenie Brinkema explains that grief is typically expected to remain an interior emotional state, while mourning corresponds to the external work, such as social and family rituals, that (ideally) traces one's progress back toward a healthy psychological state.[3]

Depictions of grief and mourning are not, however, sufficient to mark off post-horror from more populist fare, since there is no shortage of less "rarified" horror films that feature bereaved characters, including *The Tomb of Ligeia* (1964), *Deathdream* (1974), *The Changeling* (1980), *Friday the 13th* (1980), *Pet Sematary* (1989), and many more. Tony Williams argues that the family has long served as a major locus for the modern horror genre because the nuclear family breeds paranoia about external threats to its coherence, while also serving as the site of psychosexual development (including all of that process's potentially horrific detours into neuroses).[4] Likewise, Vivian Sobchack posits that horror films since *Rosemary's Baby* (1968) have thematically shifted from monstrous children (a symptom of the 1960s "generation gap") toward monstrous parents (à la *The Shining* (1980)) – these two oft-cited precursors to post-horror films representing modern horror's affinity with the family melodrama's anxieties over threats to the continuance of the familial line.[5] Meanwhile, the recurring trope of the lost child gains its cultural power because childlessness seems an affront to the dominant ideology of "reproductive futurism" (that is, personal/social reproduction, as embodied in the symbol of the Child), as a threatened terminus of the family line.[6]

Richard Armstrong's concept of the "mourning film" as a distinct genre marked by many of the formal structures of modernist art cinema (with strong inspiration from both horror and melodrama) offers a rich starting point for explaining how post-horror often makes mourning a central theme and grief a dominant affect – much to the displeasure of viewers expecting horror films about familial loss to translate into a "fun" experience. Indeed, Armstrong describes mourning films as a "post-genre," as their extended focus on the "post-life" moment "drags down" classical narrative momentum in favor of externally visualizing states of psychological interiority – which adds an additional gloss to the "postness" of post-horror.[7] Yet, whereas Armstrong privileges the widow as the mourning film's primary (female) protagonist,[8] I find it notable that post-horror's primary texts are twice as likely to foreground the mourning of a *parent* or *child* as a spouse or sibling, thus suggesting a thematic preoccupation with linear generational inheritance.

In this chapter, I will explain how the mourning film's combination of modernist formal practices and horror genre influence provides a useful means of approaching how post-horror films create unpleasant viewing affects by formally evoking anxieties about sudden breaks and reappearances in the chain of generational inheritance – familial and generic alike. As Lucy Fischer argues, the very concept of "genre" has more often been gendered as masculine, via common associations with scientific classification systems, yet the word's etymological connections to the word "gender" actually share the more feminine connotation of endless generative potential.[9] Hence, much as *Hereditary* focuses on the horror of traits atavistically passed along to successive generations, thinking of the horror genre as a maternal entity giving birth to progeny that bear uncertain resemblances to earlier generations allows us to further explain post-horror's divisive reception as indicative of these films' seemingly dysfunctional place within their own generic family.

In other words, if we consider that post-horror films already have a fraught relationship with their cinematic forebearers as the seemingly unlikely offspring of both art and horror cinema, then that same dynamic is also reflected in the potentially monstrous relationships between mothers and children in so many of these texts. Instead of representing a direct familial line of genetic/generic continuity, the post-horror cycle's development may be better described as a genealogy constituted by unpredictable breaks and deviations from generic/familial tradition – as previously suggested by the web of influences that inform the various generic descriptors discussed in Chapter 2.[10]

Although other post-horror films involving grief and mothers will be taken up later in this book, this chapter begins with a brief overview of how modernist aesthetic devices have been used to figure tropes of trauma and mourning. Deploying close readings of family dynamics in three key films, I will argue that different formal approaches to trauma narratives – particularly the presence or absence of narrative closure that depicts successfully completed mourning – allow the audience to differently *feel* the breaks in generic/familial tradition that have proven so divisive among different audience segments. That is, the further that post-horror films deploy art-cinema devices to break from the generic templates popularized by more conventionally Hollywood-style horror films, the more affectively powerful their narratives about traumatic disruptions to the familial line can be felt.

For my case studies, I start with several of the earliest entries retrospectively identified as part of the post-horror corpus: Jennifer Kent's *The Babadook* and Veronika Franz and Severin Fiala's *Goodnight Mommy*. Both released in 2014, a year before *It Follows* (2014) and *The Witch* (2015) demonstrated the emerging cycle's crossover potential, these films both played on the arthouse circuit in the United States (not least because each film was an international import, from Australia and Austria, respectively). Whereas *The Babadook* presents a more conventional depiction of trauma from its opening scene, followed by a reassuringly successful completion of the mourning process, *Goodnight Mommy* uses unreliable narration to conceal the trauma's source until late in the film's duration, thereby allowing other traumatic events to transpire as its characters fail to "properly" grieve.

Arriving shortly before critics claimed post-horror to be a newly blossoming branch of the genre's proverbial family tree, these particular progeny of art and horror cinema still remain haunted by then-recent trends in Hollywood cinema. Because, for instance, *The Babadook*'s trauma narrative adheres more closely in style and narrative form to the classical tradition, these traits make it more of an outlier to the post-horror corpus than most of the other films discussed in this book. By contrast, *Goodnight Mommy*'s more ambiguous narrative and nihilistic ending allows it to feel like a defamiliarizing break from the norm. Nevertheless, they each look ahead to the stylistic austerity and dark familial themes that coalesce in the later core examples.[11]

Hence the chapter concludes with a close reading of one of "the most archetypal"[12] post-horror films, *Hereditary*, which quickly jumped from a high-profile Sundance premiere to a wide multiplex release by A24 in 2018, thereby following a more representative distribution trajectory once post-horror had already become an established market trend. Because it more solidly evinces post-horror's stylistic and thematic core, I argue that *Hereditary*'s unrelentingly grim depiction of its eponymous themes thus represents the film's own relationship to its cross-generic progenitors at a time when post-horror had coalesced into a much-debated mutation of art and horror cinema.

The Shape of Grief

According to Richard Armstrong, cinema's status as an image-based medium makes it more adept than literature for depicting grief, since grief (and especially the traumatic loss of a loved one) already operates more strongly in the realm of affect than words. Much as death as a metaphysical transition/state cannot be cinematically represented with any degree of surety, the survivor's grief often evades linguistic representation. Cinematic spectatorship and grief share the state of being powerfully affected by spectral images of who/what is no longer there, with the cinematic image's status as ontologically present and absent at once (that is, the photographic frame is already vanished from our vision by the time our brain can cognitively process it) echoing the experience of the bereaved person trying to make sense of absence.[13] As Eugenie

Brinkema argues, however, grief also poses formal problems for cinema, since it involves looking for a now-absent thing from which light can no longer be indexically reflected into the camera lens – hence the fact that conventional strategies for figuring grief will paradoxically reinscribe the dead person's absence as presence by depicting them as ghosts, by framing the loss as a gaping hole in the *mise-en-scène* of everyday life (shots of empty chairs), or via visual doublings (shots of the mourner looking in mirrors).[14]

For Armstrong, mainstream genre films typically depict death as either a sensationalized event whose emotional consequences are seldom dwelt upon (as is true in many examples of the horror genre), or as a melodramatic event that can be reassuringly overcome to achieve a sense of classical narrative closure that corresponds with the successfully completed mourning process.[15] It is less common for films to focus on grief in itself, since grief's negative affect is certainly not "fun" to wallow in, evincing "the brute facticity of the impression something foul has made on celluloid" (especially if one is expecting an entertaining viewing experience).[16] In this regard, modernist art cinema (such as *Hiroshima Mon Amour* (1959), *Cries and Whispers* (1972), and others) provides a more instructive model for the "post-generic" qualities of mourning films: from their alienated and passive protagonists wandering through the modern, secular world; to their quiet and contemplative moods, evoking the slow process of working through grief; to narrative ellipses and blurred epistemic lines between memory/fantasy and reality; to formal devices (including freeze frames, slow motion, and long-shot durations) that can read as stylistic excess.[17] Brinkema also stresses how (selectively) darkened imagery suggests grief's emotional darkening of the survivor's world – which would seem especially amenable to the low-key lighting used in most horror films.[18]

As Armstrong continues, the mourning film's focus on hauntings, visionary imagery, *memento mori*, and the susceptibility of women (and children) to supernatural influence demonstrates these texts' deep indebtedness to the horror genre, especially the Gothic tradition of films already more often considered "prestige" or "art-horror" films (as discussed in the previous chapter). He specifically cites *Rebecca* (1940), *The Spiral Staircase* (1946), *The Innocents* (1961), *Carnival of Souls* (1962), and *The Haunting* (1963) as examples of Gothic horror films that are thematically invested in mourning characters, especially women whose grief manifests as fear and apprehension over what will happen next – thus also aligning these texts with the so-called "woman's film."[19]

Largely associated with 1930s–1950s melodramas featuring the domestic travails of female protagonists, the "woman's film" typically focuses on themes of maternal self-sacrifice, spousal paranoia, medicalization, and romantic dysfunction. According to Mary Ann Doane, these films are defined more by their emphasis on female subjectivity and their address to a female viewership than by generic consistency; the melodramatic "weepie" may be emblematic of the form, but the woman's film "is frequently combined with other genres – the film noir and the gothic or horror film."[20] For example, *Rebecca*, *Gaslight* (1944), *The Spiral Staircase*, *Dragonwyck* (1946), and *Caught* (1949) all exemplify the Gothic melodrama as woman's film. Mark Jancovich observes, however, that many of these films were explicitly understood as part of the larger horror genre at the time of their release, not as a separate category of "Gothic" films.[21] Sarah Arnold, too, describes how the self-sacrificing "Good Mother" of the melodramatic woman's film and the overbearing "Bad Mother" of the maternal horror film represent flip sides of the same generic coin, connected by Gothic tropes that figure a domestic relationship of longing between maternal figure and child.[22] David Greven likewise argues that the woman's film effectively "went underground" by the early 1960s, its maternal themes resurfacing in the mother/child conflicts undergirding much of modern horror cinema. In Hitchcock's work, for example, apparent hauntings by a deceased female ancestor/predecessor thematically link *Rebecca* to *Vertigo* (1958) to *Psycho* (1960), and thence to the latter's many generic progeny.[23] Armstrong summarizes the mourning film's generic links between horror and melodrama as follows:

> Preoccupied with scenarios of loss and sacrifice, animated by themes of masochism, the lachrymal gesture, chance, coincidence, and the uncanny, the horror film and the woman's picture together bequeath particular sentiments and attitudes to the mourning film as surely as both genres reproduced such traditional notions of the "feminine" as passivity, emotionalism, and intuition.[24]

Perhaps Armstrong's most notable example for the purposes of this chapter is Nicolas Roeg's *Don't Look Now* (1973), which not only unites Gothic horror themes with the formal traits of modernist art cinema, but also prominently features parents mourning a recently drowned daughter (as opposed to the mourning spouses in many of Armstrong's other case studies). Because John (Donald Sutherland) realizes too late that he experiences premonitions (including both his daughter's and his own demise), he wanders through Venice's labyrinthine streets, trying to find a red-coated figure resembling his daughter. Yet, in the film's final scene, this figure is revealed to be an elderly dwarf woman who stabs John to death. In light of its shocking twist ending, the film's use of symbolic motifs (often visualized via graphic matches and red objects) and proleptic editing suggest the blurring of temporalities that viewers may have previously suspected to be John's grief-induced delusions about his lost daughter. Using fragmented editing and recurring colors enhances the viewer's sense that, despite trying to change future events, John's death is already predestined – thus creating what Tarja Laine calls a "hopeless hope" that affectively threads between John and the viewer.[25]

Appearing at a moment when Gothic horror in British cinema was largely confined to the schlocky excesses of late-period Hammer films, *Don't Look Now*'s thematic focus on "continuities between the solidity of earthly spaces and the ideal spaces of a transcendent perfection" echoes its own hauntingly tenuous position between the European arthouse drama and the horror genre.[26] Yet *Don't Look Now* also differs from many mourning films in its predominant focus on the grieving *father*, whereas the maternal melodrama's "scenarios of separation, of separation and return, or of threatened separation – dramas which play out all the permutations of the mother/child relation" – more accurately describe the fraught relationship between mothers and children in numerous post-horror films.[27]

Many of the same formal traits that Armstrong and Brinkema associate with grief-laden films also resonate with critical theorists' privileging of modernist formal techniques as the most "appropriate" way to depict the fragmentary memories and hallucinations left in the wake of a major trauma.[28] These claims that fragmentary and elliptical narratives marked by absence, indirection, and repetition best convey trauma's "affect aesthetic" follow from Cathy Caruth's theorization of trauma as a catastrophic event whose powerful suddenness and magnitude bypass ordinary cognition and mnemonic inscription, becoming rendered as an unspeakable gap in one's memory. For Caruth, trauma's impact resides less in the event itself than in the event's inability to be properly processed; the catastrophe always threatens to be re-enacted in the form of recurring flashbacks, nightmares, hallucinations, and other breaks from everyday consciousness.[29]

Indeed, cinema's visual grammar provided much of the vocabulary (such as flashbacks, screen memories, and so on) for Freud and other early elucidators of psychic trauma, while art cinema's formal innovations would later prove especially amenable to depicting trauma's distortions of memory/reality. *Don't Look Now*'s disorienting use of graphic matches and intrusive images – though eventually revealed to be flash-forwards instead of flashbacks – are a case in point. Roger Luckhurst, for example, argues that *Hiroshima Mon Amour* effectively "invented the traumatic flashback" in 1959, years before intrusive flashbacks were added to the *Diagnostic and Statistical Manual*'s (*DSM*) definition of trauma in reference to Vietnam veterans' post-traumatic stress disorder (PTSD).

Moreover, the flashback was already imbued with Freudian implications in German Expressionist films like *The Cabinet of Dr. Caligari* (1920), influencing the 1940s woman's film and Gothic horror films indebted to the Expressionist tradition. For Luckhurst, then, developments in cinematic style do not merely mimic, but actually precede and help inform, common psychiatric understandings of trauma.[30]

Although undoubtedly influential in the critical humanities, Caruth's theory has since been critiqued as an overly narrow definition of trauma. Clinical literature, for example, shows that dissociative amnesia and belated recall are actually quite rare in trauma survivors; if elements of a traumatic event are not clearly recalled after the fact, it may be less because trauma is a special occurrence than because memory ordinarily fails to register all events fully or accurately to begin with.[31] Moreover, Caruth has been accused of misreading Freud, for whom the traumatic event is not re-experienced as a literal replay of the past so much as repressed into the unconscious and subsequently filtered through fantasies and memories, such that "a memory becomes traumatic when it becomes associated, later, with inadmissible meanings, wishes, [and] fantasies."[32]

Furthermore, Susannah Radstone notes that, rather than figuring it as an extraordinary event originating wholly outside the self, refocusing attention on trauma as a product of the unconscious mind allows us to better account for sources of "darkness" within oneself,[33] much as E. Ann Kaplan and Ban Wang argue that depicting trauma as somehow beyond the scope of aesthetic representation "may push trauma into the mystified circle of the occult."[34] As the rest of this chapter will explore, some post-horror films (such as *The Babadook*) adhere more closely to a Caruthian vision of trauma, while other films (such as *Hereditary*) figure grief and mourning as less the product of sudden losses re-experienced than as slowly building fantasies "which might include an identification with the aggressor."[35]

Following Freud's focus on shell-shocked war veterans and train accident survivors, Caruth also emphasizes the sudden and catastrophic event as a "punctual" trauma that violently intrudes upon one's everyday experience and hence manifests as PTSD symptoms. By contrast, Laura S. Brown describes "insidious trauma" as caused not by "an event that is outside the range of human experience" (as the *DSM* defines "trauma") than as caused by the structural violence and micro-aggressions experienced within the daily experience of women, people of color, people with disabilities, and queer and gender-nonconforming folks.[36] Melodrama's exposure of domestic female suffering, however, marks a familiar generic home for depicting such insidious traumas. Post-horror's frequent thematic focus on mother/child grief, influenced by the maternal melodrama, thus complicates the horror genre's common association as a "masculine" genre, bringing together differently gendered connotations of trauma's horrific effects as manifested within the space of the (film-generic) home.

The Babadook: Trauma Revealed

Largely set within enclosed domestic spaces and (indirectly) focused on the loss of a family member in a car accident, both *The Babadook* and *Goodnight Mommy* use the grieving mother and the misbehaving child to explore different reactions to trauma and different means of narrativizing its effects. Both films are also variants of the "maternal Gothic" tradition inaugurated by *Rosemary's Baby* (1968), in which "the mother often becomes an unwilling puppet" to a child from which she feels alienated – and she frequently becomes figured as somehow monstrous in the process.[37] In both films, the home is rendered an "unhomely" (*unheimlich*) place by the experience of grief, and a young boy accuses his mother of no longer seeming to be herself. Yet, it is ultimately disavowal or repression of the originating trauma that renders the main character monstrous in both films.

On a pragmatic level, the family themes and fraught domestic spheres found in so many post-horror films are partly due to these films' budgetary scale as independent productions featuring small casts, a limited number of settings, and so on. On the other hand, while the home figures as a space under threat from within or without in many horror films, grief has the capacity to make mourners no longer feel at home in such spaces as they "struggle to reconcile fragile interiority with an uncomprehending or indifferent world, one from which the character is psychologically and physically isolated."[38] Such uncanny spaces blur the boundaries between inside and outside, comfort and threat, creating "a third space where new dwelling places emerge from the uncertainty of the present"[39] – a description that also evokes post-horror's liminal position between the art film and the horror genre.

Both films depict the Caruthian trauma symptom of dissociation, but while *Goodnight Mommy* conceals and displaces the trauma's origin through unreliable narration, *The Babadook*'s opening scene reveals the inciting trauma through another classic symptom: the recurring flashback/nightmare. The film opens with Amelia (Essie Davis), filmed in medium close-up, dreaming about the car accident that killed her husband Oskar (Ben Winspear) while she was being driven to the hospital to give birth to their son Samuel (Noah Wiseman), seven years earlier. This sequence's status as a nightmare is revealed as we see Amelia float back down onto her bed as Samuel calls her awake; suffering from recurring

GRIEF, MOURNING, AND FAMILIAL INHERITANCE

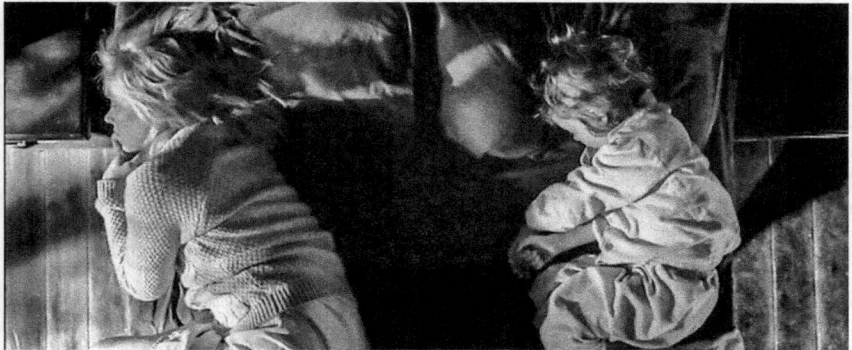

Figure 3.1 Struggling to sleep, Amelia moves as far away as possible from Samuel, suggesting her maternal ambivalence in *The Babadook*. (Source: DVD.)

nightmares himself, Samuel climbs into bed next to her, and she promptly slides to the far side of the bed to distance herself from him, just before a cut to the title card (Figure 3.1). By appearing just before the written name of the film's eponymous monster, this sequence also functions as a sort of thesis statement for *The Babadook* as whole: the recurring nightmares and insomnia propagated by Amelia's emotional resentment toward her son – whom she implicitly blames for her husband's death – lead to the monster's emergence as a threat to the surviving family members.

After the mysterious pop-up book *Mister Babadook* (about a top-hatted monster with blade-like fingers) appears in her son's room, Samuel's nightmares (and consequently his mother's insomnia) increase. Meanwhile, Amelia appears unable to balance her life as a single mother working as a caretaker at a retirement home (suggesting her capacity for supporting dependent people at the other end of the life cycle) and "the gendering of emotional labor" that she is expected to maintain.[40] When school authorities chastise Amelia for allowing Samuel to bring home-made weapons to class, for example, she becomes defensive, asserting that her son merely needs some emotional empathy. However, this reaction seems an act of projection on her part, since Amelia herself refuses to talk about Samuel's father, becomes embarrassed when he openly mentions his father's death to strangers, does not celebrate Samuel's birthday on the anniversary of the car crash, and generally refuses to complete the grieving process. She is the one who shuts out the catastrophic loss, while her son is far more willing to do the difficult work of mourning. Unlike the various tropes of the evil child used in so many horror films, Samuel acts out because of a desperate desire for his mother's attention and emotional support, not because something monstrous is being channeled through him.[41] These issues become more acute once she takes Samuel out of school and stops going to work, further isolating them from potentially supportive family and friends.

Although Amelia eventually destroys the book, it keeps reappearing with more threatening messages about the specter's incursion into their home. As the mother of a young boy with behavioral problems, long-suffering Amelia at first seems far more oppressed, but she eventually becomes the most monstrous character as her resentment toward him turns increasingly violent. She imagines a roach-filled, yonic slit in the wall behind her refrigerator (an allusion to *Repulsion* (1965)), which vanishes upon later inspection. Likewise, she slips into a series of nightmares while watching late-night television, in which she alternately sees the Babadook appear in Georges Méliès films, looks over to see Samuel's throat slit, and then sees herself in the window of a building in a news report about a mother who has stabbed her seven-year-old child to death. In another dream, the Babadook appears to Amelia in the basement in the form of her dead husband, asking her to give him Samuel as an offering. Now possessed by this embodiment of trauma, she tells Samuel that she wishes he had died instead of Oskar, attempts to strangle her son to death, and vomits black bile on the basement floor. Eventually, Samuel will use the same weapons on her that he made to defend against his imagined bedtime monsters.

In Amelia's case, her increased delusions of the Babadook and other seemingly supernatural manifestations – suggesting that her son's paranoia about domestic monsters has somehow infected her as well – imply her gradual mental breakdown from insomnia and other PTSD effects. Rather than the conscious process of mourning, Amelia's psychological state is closer to Freud's conception of melancholia, in which the survivor unconsciously refuses to withdraw her ego from the lost loved one – her sense of self-regard henceforth becoming impoverished through delusions of moral inferiority, deflections of responsibility for the death, and symptoms including "sleeplessness and refusal to take nourishment." While mourning may involve neurotic fantasies of having been somehow to blame for the death, melancholia generates a more ambivalent range of emotions (including mixtures of love and hate) directed elsewhere.[42]

Much as *Rosemary's Baby* has "all the earmarks of the Gothic mode (the naïve young heroine, her opaque husband, the awesome mansion, the supernatural events)" that initially seem to be psychological symptoms of parturition,[43] *The Babadook* depicts the home as a claustrophobically enclosed, Gothic space haunted by frustration and grief (see the obvious Freudian metaphor of the monster dwelling in the basement, where Oskar's boxed-up belongings are stored).[44] Although Michael Reiff argues that the film's visual grammar posits the Babadook as simply an imagined externalization of psychic trauma, especially since our sightings of the monster are almost entirely focalized through Amelia's eyes,[45] other scholars have noted that the book's supernatural reappearance, its newly created pages (presaging her murder of the family dog and attempted murder of Samuel), and the *Exorcist*-style (1973) imagery in the film's final act all seem to confirm the presence of the supernatural.[46] Yet, if films like *The Exorcist* or, better yet, *The Shining* (in which a physically isolated parent becomes murderous towards his child) figure supernatural possession as an external force invading the family from without, *The Babadook* depicts this possession as the internal force of unresolved grief.[47]

Like the story of maternal ambivalence in *Rosemary's Baby*, which ends with Rosemary (Mia Farrow) acquiescing to raise the surrogate demon child that she has begotten via marital rape, Amelia (whose wan appearance also resembles Rosemary) finally decides to do what is best for Samuel. Turning against her murderous temptations amid a climactic confrontation with the Babadook, during which Oskar's traumatic death is replayed, she suddenly snaps from melancholia into proper mourning. Now processing the loss of her husband by seeing Samuel as a symbol of survival instead of death, she refuses to give the monster any more power over her. But, during the film's happy epilogue (their relationships mended, Amelia finally talks openly about Oskar's death and Samuel gets to celebrate his birthday before returning to school), the Babadook remains chained in the shadows of the basement, where Amelia keeps it alive on a modest diet of worms. Although ending on a less bittersweet note than Polanski's film (Rosemary still gets to mother her child, even if it is the Antichrist!), *The Babadook* at least tempers its Hollywood-style narrative closure with the suggestion that Amelia may have overcome her trauma but will never be able to completely stop nursing the pain of Oskar's loss.

Compared to the modernist-inspired mourning films discussed by Richard Armstrong, *The Babadook* hews far closer to the tropes that Eugenie Brinkema associates with classical Hollywood depictions of grief as an "overcoming" narrative – especially its far more reassuring narrative closure compared to *Goodnight Mommy*'s hauntingly bleak denouement.[48] Fran Pheasant-Kelly also observes that Amelia's trauma is formally conveyed through "instances of fast motion and slow motion editing, and amplified non-simultaneous and asynchronous sound associated with" Amelia – all conventional cinematic tropes for depicting PTSD symptoms.[49] Moreover, unlike the relatively slow and cold visual aesthetic used in *Goodnight Mommy*, *The Babadook*'s energetic editing, inclusion of jump scares, and prioritization of dialogue over silence more closely resembles Hollywood's post-torture porn turn toward paranormal horror movies like *Insidious* (2010), *Sinister* (2012), and *Mama* (2013) – all of which "present eerie child figures that seem to be evil and possessed, before proceeding to deconstruct this trope, presenting visions of uncanny childhood which subvert the evil/innocence dichotomy that underpinned seminal possessed child films" like *The Exorcist*.[50]

Because *The Babadook* thereby "expresses clear and conscious links to popular Hollywood horror films of the past decade," these similarities are "perhaps part of the reason why critics and audiences overseas [outside Australia] so readily engaged with the film."[51] Due to its conventional visual grammar and comforting sense of narrative closure – with grief overcome and a healthy mother/child relationship restored – *The Babadook* feels like a very "Hollywood" film in many respects, despite its exclusive play on the arthouse circuit. This generic familiarity may have also encouraged the Babadook's ironic, paratextual appropriation as a "gay icon" (in my opinion, a queer reading that, compared to several films discussed in Chapters 5 and 6, *The Babadook* does not compellingly support on a textual level), as spread through online memes after the film moved onto Netflix and other streaming services.[52]

Yet, where *The Babadook* differs from more populist horror films – in which parents almost consistently act as benevolent protectors of their children – is the more disturbing theme of maternal indifference, whose discomforting affect for much of the film may outweigh the narrative's relatively happy ending. As Shelley Buerger argues, it is all too common for the horror genre to depict the "monstrous-feminine" figure as a mother overly attached to her children (for example, *Psycho*, *Alien* (1979), *The Brood* (1979), *Mama*) or as a woman threatening to control and destroy the male characters. Amelia's alienation from motherhood and her emotional indifference to Samuel is, however, not only a more novel way of marking her monstrosity, but can also be especially troubling for viewers wanting to sympathetically respond to Samuel's unanswered cries into the emotional void once his mother (or rather her unprocessed grief) becomes the true antagonist.[53] Comparing Amelia to the mother grieving for the horrific actions of her mass-shooter son in *We Need to Talk About Kevin* (2011), Paula Quigley notes that Amelia finally overcomes her maternal ambivalence by, at the film's end, mothering both the child and the monster. Via "generic assimilation . . . the victimized protagonist of the Female Gothic (whose male child assumes the role of persecutor hitherto occupied by her husband) transforms into the horror mother in both her 'Good' and 'Bad' modes, and finally reconciles with those aspects of herself that are more typically concealed and/or reviled in mainstream cinema."[54]

Although both *Goodnight Mommy* and *The Babadook* were critically acclaimed for infusing the horror genre with similar themes about grief and a mother altered by her response to a devastating loss, Australian critics tried to distinguish *The Babadook* from the generic label "horror" by contrasting it with a culturally "lower," Australian-made horror film then occupying domestic theaters, *Wolf Creek 2* (2014). As Jessica Balanzategui observes, *Wolf Creek 2*'s torture-porn aesthetic and status as a commercially motivated sequel both seemed too closely aligned with the Hollywood horror ethos for critical appreciation, not despite but precisely because of its greater box-office success than *The Babadook* (which was released in only a handful of Australian art houses).[55] Balanzategui continues by explaining how Australian horror's critical reception tends to ascribe films into either the highbrow "Australian Gothic" tradition (considered to successfully "transcend" the horror genre by localizing the European Gothic tradition into rural Australian landscapes) or the lowbrow "Ozploitation" tradition (considered as crassly commercial films wallowing in exploitative genre conventions, and at least partly intended for the international market) – despite the same film (*Wake in Fright* (1971) or *Wolf Creek* (2005), for instance) potentially being slottable into either taste-laden camp, depending on the critic doing the naming. *The Babadook*, for instance, displays clear influence from the Gothic tradition, but is not specifically tied to exploring the Australian national psyche via rural settings – hence its ability to more closely resemble the American paranormal horror film.[56]

As noted in the previous chapter, critics attempting to distinguish one film as more "artworthy" than another frequently use rhetorical caveats to label post-horror as "psychological drama" or some less debased genre. Nevertheless, I would maintain that, even as its maternal indifference themes likely generate more negative affect than Hollywood cinema's fervent child protectionism, *The Babadook*'s closer adherence to the overall style of Hollywood paranormal films primarily differentiates it from many of the core post-horror texts that followed. Much like the emotional closeness restored between mother and child at its conclusion, *The Babadook*'s stylistic proximity to mainstream Hollywood horror represents less of a disturbing break in the generic line than another bud easily fostered on the family tree.

Goodnight Mommy: Trauma Concealed

Unlike the Gothicized suburban home in *The Babadook*, *Goodnight Mommy*'s largely daylit setting in a high-modernist house (its angular, minimalist design consisting of elegant glass panes, metal fixtures, and bare stonework) suggests the film's own position between the trappings of high art and the territory of genre. Isolated amid the summery Austrian countryside, its architectural sterility is only rarely violated by the abject imagery of the escaped cockroaches kept as pets by its protagonists: identical-twin brothers Lukas and Elias (Lukas and Elias Schwarz). Indeed, Lies Lanckman argues that "the film seems aware of the contradiction between its setting and the viewer's expectations of a horror film, and often plays with these expectations by visiting and then rejecting particular spaces more typical to its genre." Lukas and Elias make very brief incursions to crypts, cellars, churches, and other typically Gothic locations, only to return to the wide-windowed modernist house where their mysterious Mother (Susanne Wuest), her face bandaged into an uncannily strange visage after recent cosmetic surgery, holds court (Figure 3.2).[57]

The film opens, however, with a pre-credit clip from the conclusion of *The Trapp Family* (1956) as Maria (Ruth Leuwerik) sings Brahms's "Lullaby" to the children (and the viewer); presented without context, the archival clip's film stock is badly worn, this physical degradation ironically undercutting the song's syrupy tone (as well as Maria von Trapp's fame as an idealized maternal figure) by rendering it one of ominous foreboding. Only in the film's final stretch do we learn that this lullaby was Lukas's favorite song, and that Lukas – recently killed in a car accident – has been either a ghost or a projection of his brother's imagination for the whole film. Aside from his Mother, no other family members or friends are present to dissuade Elias from his delusion (and upon escaping to seek help from a priest, he is promptly driven home to her).

Figure 3.2 Mother plays a guessing game with Elias (and Lukas) amidst the cold, high-modernist interiors in *Goodnight Mommy*. (Source: Blu-ray.)

Much as *The Babadook* presents us with many scenes of a young boy left without parental supervision because his mother has emotionally withdrawn from him, Mother in *Goodnight Mommy* shuts herself away during the day and tells Elias to stay quiet while she recuperates. In the film's opening scenes, we see both brothers playing in the countryside – with Lukas always seeming to slip away from Elias unnoticed (such as vanishing beneath the surface of a nearby lake or a darkened underpass), which foreshadows how Elias has refused to process his brother's death. We also see the twins jumping on waterlogged soil, the ground undulating beneath their feet, as they first walk toward the house – visually suggesting the unstable epistemic ground upon which the narrative is positioned. Indeed, unlike many post-horror films, *Goodnight Mommy* operates less through Todorovian fantastic hesitation about whether supernatural events are actually happening, and more through what Matt Hills terms the "ontological shock" of a major narrative twist.[58] Much as the grieving parents in *Don't Look Now* "fail to read and anticipate danger in time," the film's twist conveys traumatic affect to the viewer via "the horror of" both the character's and audience's "failure to read the experience or the narrative correctly."[59]

Much like *The Cabinet of Dr. Caligari*, *Don't Look Now*, *The Sixth Sense* (1999), or *The Others* (2001), *Goodnight Mommy* is premised on a reality-shifting revelation that has been previously concealed from the viewer by strategies of unreliable narration first developed in the art-cinema tradition. Focalized through Elias's perspective, not only does he believe that his twin brother is still alive, but he becomes increasingly convinced that their Mother has been replaced by an imposter (possibly an unnamed woman spotted beside her in a scrapbook photo). When disturbing things happen – such as Elias finding the corpse of a sick cat he had brought home from a nearby crypt – he attributes them to his Mother's subtly changed demeanor. After all, traumatized characters may be (or at least seem) unreliable, but this unreliability is likely a defense against their own fears of further loss; moreover, these characters may be difficult to sympathize with, because they manifest aberrant behavior stemming from feelings of shame or helplessness.[60]

First shown shutting the house's blinds as she locks herself away to convalesce from the surgery, Mother's strange and emotionally cold behavior is fundamentally based in Elias's misrecognition of how grief has altered her psyche. (As a professional television host, the cosmetic surgery is presumably intended to correct a facial injury sustained during the car accident, but it can also be read as a part of her mourning process: an attempt to rejuvenate her physical appearance as a symbolic "restart" for her life.)

She refuses to make meals for Lukas, set aside clothes for him, or acknowledge him in conversation; further, she says she will not play along with her son's games. At first, the viewer is led to believe that she is passive-aggressively ignoring Lukas in response to some past tomfoolery or her own trauma, but she only explains the truth about the accident after Elias takes her hostage and tortures the supposed "imposter" into explaining what she did with his true Mother.

Importantly, rather than being told from the mother's perspective (as in *The Babadook*), *Goodnight Mommy* is focalized through the child's perspective, albeit with their relationship to the traumatic event reversed: here, Mother is far more able to properly grieve than her son. Yet, if this focalization through Elias's eyes has made Mother seem uncanny to him, the revelation that he is actually the one unable to properly grieve for his lost brother creates a marked shift in the viewer's sympathies. Richard Armstrong notes that the mourning woman may herself come to seem "supernatural" because, in her grief, she is not mentally inhabiting the same plane as everyone else, instead living a parallel life with the dead loved one who haunts her.[61] In *Goodnight Mommy*, however, the "haunted one" is actually the surviving son, effectively ventriloquizing his deceased twin as a product of either paranormal happenings or mental illness. (Unsurprisingly, children are also common characters in mourning films because, as in so many horror films, they are far more prone to magical thinking than adults.)[62]

For Freud, the uncanny is not only associated with "homely" people and places that become rendered strange, but also with doubled characters (doppelgängers), especially when those uncomfortably similar characters seem telepathically linked. Such fantasies about doubling originate early in life and attempt to shore up the ego by warding off fears of death – which is also why doubles and mirror imagery become common tropes in mourning films.[63] As Nicholas Royle notes, the uncanny "has to do with a sense of ourselves as double, split, at odds with ourselves," hence its affective prevalence in films about hauntings and grief alike.[64]

Although the viewer has previously come to fear Mother, she eventually becomes a far less uncanny figure than the doubled child. Once she unbandages her face halfway through the film's duration, for example, Elias and "Lukas" decide to begin dressing identically in order to confuse her about which twin is which; likewise, Elias is never referred to by name until the film's final act, when Mother attempts talk her way out of bondage, whereas Lukas is named from the opening scene. If one discounts a potentially supernatural explanation, the film's implication is that the surviving twin's identity has been so bound to his now-deceased brother that he has undergone a severe form of psychic splitting in order to repress the traumatic separation. Delusions are not uncommon in mourning films, since the dead loved one often appears to the mourner in a recognizably everyday form – but hallucinations of the dead are typically presented as momentary aberrations in consciousness, not as severe and persistent breaks in one's identity.[65] However, despite the extreme rarity of dissociative identity disorder (DID), psychiatric diagnoses of DID began becoming attributed to childhood trauma after the film *Sybil* (1976) popularized the dubious links between them.[66]

During the film's final third, Mother is tied to her bed and tortured by Elias with a magnifying glass (he burns a black spot onto her cheek akin to the birthmark removed during her surgery – one of the reasons for his lingering suspicion of an imposter), in addition to sawing her gums with dental floss and gluing her lips shut before later cutting them apart. Recalling how Amelia gradually emerges as the most monstrous character in *The Babadook*, a similar shift in sympathies occurs in *Goodnight Mommy*, but from the opposite direction: the film finally shifts its focalization to the tortured woman's perspective (shots from her point of view first appear here) and Elias emerges as the truly monstrous character, his childish refusal to properly mourn blinding him to the new trauma that he now instigates. Despite his Mother's offer to play along with the illusion in exchange for her freedom, Elias (imagining himself as Lukas) sets fire to the curtains, stating that their real mother would be able to see what "Lukas" was doing. If *The Babadook* primarily presents the violence of mother upon child, then *Goodnight Mommy* ultimately presents the threat of the child's violence toward his mother.

On one hand, *Goodnight Mommy*'s minimalist aesthetic complements the architectural form of the modernist house at its center, maintaining a generic tone more akin to Michael Haneke than Eli Roth for the first two-thirds of its duration (Haneke's *Funny Games* (1997) was a recurring point of comparison among critics, not least as another Austrian film). On the other hand, the extended scenes of bondage and torture in this final act also betray *Goodnight Mommy*'s closer generic relationship to "torture porn" than most of the post-horror films that followed, indicating its status as a transitional text between the post-9/11 decade's major generic trend and post-horror's 2010s coalescence into a trend of its own. These (not-unfounded) critical comparisons to torture porn were generally received from *Goodnight Mommy*'s detractors as a means of (again) using that post-9/11 trend as a scapegoat for the horror genre's worst impulses.

The film ends with the house going up in flames, and Elias coming together with his brother and mother in the nearby cornfield – their hauntingly idyllic pose, looking directly into the camera, not only recalling the film's opening *Trapp Family* clip, but also suggesting that they have all died and been reunited in the afterlife. J. A. Bridges notes that many post-horror films feature such circular or cyclical narratives, since so many of these films figure the reverberations of traumatic loss as roadblocks to emotional progress.[67] Unlike *The Babadook*'s repression of its titular monster into the basement, purging the once-Gothicized house of grief's threatening effects, *Goodnight Mommy* destroys the modernist house at its center and no one escapes alive. Although overwhelming death can serve as a type of narrative closure in its own right, it is not difficult to imagine (populist) viewers coming away from *Goodnight Mommy*'s nihilistic conclusion feeling far less satisfied, especially given the unreliability of its preceding narration.

Much like Armstrong describes *Don't Look Now* as a mourning film liminally positioned between formal strategies and generic strata with different taste connotations, these two early examples of the post-horror cycle seem "elevated" above the horror genre's less reputable connotations by virtue of their serious and, at times, distinctly discomforting depictions of grief's psychological effects, as conveyed through techniques inherited from dramas about trauma and mourning. For different reasons, however, both *The Babadook* and *Goodnight Mommy* differ from the sustained minimalism and visual restraint associated with the core post-horror texts (such as *It Follows* and *The Witch*) that followed them into the (mainstream) marketplace as heralds of the emergent cycle – especially since each arthouse film bears an uncanny familial resemblance to a Hollywood-based genre trend (whether paranormal films or torture porn, respectively).

Hereditary: "Mother, Can't You See I'm Burning?"

Perhaps the best example of post-horror cinema about mourning, trauma, and maternal influence is Ari Aster's aptly named *Hereditary*, which roots its story of demonic possession in a mother's fears about inheriting and passing along mental illness to her children. Marking its status as a film centrally about grief, the film opens with a title card reproducing the obituary notice (one of the public signifiers of the modern mourning process) for Ellen Leigh, the mother of our protagonist, Annie Graham (Toni Collette). Annie is an artist who works in miniature tableaux reconstructed from her own life, as we see from the film's first shot: a view of her pre-teen daughter Charlie's (Milly Shapiro) treehouse framed through Annie's workshop window, with the camera slowly pulling back, panning across the workshop, and tracking into a scale model of the Graham house itself. After the camera finally settles on her teenage son Peter's (Alex Wolff) room, the miniature seems to come to life via a seamless transition into an identical shot of his father Steve (Gabriel Byrne) entering to wake Peter for his grandmother's strangely well-attended memorial service.[68]

This deeply uncanny moment, featuring an inanimate doppelgänger of the home itself becoming animate, recalls Freud's discussion of the word *Heimlich* as meaning "belonging to the house" or "the members of the household," even as it can also imply concealment and secrecy (for example, magic as "the *Heimlich* art") – thus potentially shading into the epistemic hesitation characteristic of the *Unheimlich* as an affect generated by literary fictions that blur the lines between natural and supernatural occurrences.[69] Indeed, as the film continues and we increasingly see evidence of ritual magic instead of mental illness, we also see distant exterior shots of the Graham house, rendered via selective focus to resemble one of Annie's miniatures. Much as symptoms of mental illness can seem to render a person's behavior uncanny (especially when evil intent is superstitiously ascribed to such symptoms) and the "daemonic character" of repetition-compulsion can produce uncanny sensations in people reminded of a traumatic loss,[70] the haunting visions experienced by Annie and her children prove to be no mere symptoms of grief, but rather clues to a diabolical conspiracy against her family.

Attending a grief-recovery group after her mother's burial, Annie delivers a long, expositional monologue about the history of mental illness in her family. The camera slowly tracks in from an extreme long shot to a medium shot and then back out again as she explains how her psychotically depressed father had died from self-starvation when she was still a baby; how her schizophrenic teenage brother committed suicide in their mother's room; and how Annie herself had been estranged from her mother (a sufferer of DID and dementia) until close to Ellen's death. We also learn that Ellen had lived in a spare bedroom in the Graham home (where a magic triangle remains etched in the floor) shortly before her death, and that Annie feels guilty for having allowed her mentally ill mother to be part of Charlie's life: "I realize that I am to blame. Or not that I'm *to* blame, but . . . I am *blamed*."[71] While unable to articulate exactly what she feels blamed for, her grammatical shift toward a free-floating culpability for some unknown misdeed is not only consistent with grief symptoms, but also makes more sense when, late in the film, she learns the true cause of her family's disposition toward mental illness: Ellen was the "queen" of a group of demon worshippers, and had long been invoking Paimon, one of the sub-Luciferian kings of Hell, to possess one of her male family members.

Figure 3.3 Grandmother Ellen offers her breast to nourish infant Charlie in one of Annie's miniatures, evoking art as a means of mourning and *Hereditary*'s own atavistic influences from an earlier cinematic generation. (Source: Blu-ray.)

Because Steve, in his capacity as a psychiatrist, had enforced a no-contact rule between Ellen and Annie up until Annie's pregnancy with Charlie, Charlie is far more affected by her grandmother's death than either Steve or Peter. One of the first miniatures shown in Annie's workshop is a scene of the grandmother offering her own breast to nurse infant Charlie in place of Annie – an offering of nourishment that, in most modern Western cultures, breaks an unspoken taboo about the cross-generational limits of childrearing (Figure 3.3). Only later in the film do we realize that Charlie, who mentions that her grandmother had wanted her to be a boy, was used as a temporary host for Paimon – but, because Paimon prefers a male host body, the demon must later be transferred into Peter's body to successfully complete his corporeal invocation. The fact that neither of the actors portraying Charlie or Peter bear a close physical resemblance to Toni Collette or Gabriel Byrne merely enhances the discomforting sense that repressed traits are resurfacing within the Graham family after atavistically skipping a generation, much like *Hereditary*'s own relationship to its textual predecessors in both art and horror cinema. In a July 2019 episode of *The A24 Podcast*, for example, Ari Aster and Robert Eggers spend as much time discussing Ingmar Bergman and Andrei Tarkovsky as their own post-horror films, with Aster citing *Carrie* (1976) and *Autumn Sonata* (1978) as direct influences on *Hereditary*.[72]

Ellen continues to haunt the Graham family, in part because Annie and especially Annie's children have unknowingly become carriers of Ellen's dark secret; with Ellen's own husband and son having already died in failed attempts to conjure Paimon, the next generation of the family line has become new potential hosts. When Annie eulogizes her mother at the film's opening, she begins: "My mother was a very secretive and private woman. She had private rituals, private friends, private anxieties. It honestly feels like a betrayal just to be standing here talking about her." Yet, her apparent inability or refusal to mourn her mother also foreshadows what will soon be Annie's inadequate attempt to properly mourn her own daughter through her artwork.

In their revision of Freud's foundational theories on mourning and melancholia, Nicolas Abraham and Maria Torok describe the psychic "crypt" created in the survivor's mind when a lost loved one has carried a shameful or unspeakable secret to the grave; this is especially common when a child unconsciously inherits his or her deceased parent's secrets. When the survivor has some degree of vicarious identification with the secret-keeper (such as Annie's identification with Ellen in their shared role as mothers) but does not properly mourn them, she seals off the lost person as if still existing somewhere within her mind. Yet, this psychic gap left by a parent's unresolved secrets allows the dead person to haunt her child, as if a phantom that "give[s] [her] strange and incomprehensible signals, making [her] perform bizarre acts, or subjecting [her] to unexpected sensations." The surviving family member unconsciously grappling with the deceased person's unresolved secrets may thus seem manipulated by this psychic phantom until the secret comes to light and the dead can be properly mourned.[73] If we consider *Hereditary* to be as much a horror film as a portrait of how grief affects different family members, then the tropes of haunting-cum-possession that emerge over its duration speak to how Ellen's phantom presence has passed down the family line. For Abraham and Torok, the phantom's influence can also gradually fade as the original secret becomes entirely forgotten across successive generations – but the members of Ellen's coven, periodically appearing to cast influence on the Graham children from afar (much like the neighborly Satanists in *Rosemary's Baby*), will not allow that to happen.[74]

Although occult knowledge has historically been passed down via a master/apprentice system, as if from parent to (symbolic or actual) child, Ellen's demonic penetration of multiple generations of family members recalls the insidious trauma of incest (also see Chapter 5) – a theme that Ari Aster had previously explored in his short horror film *The Strange Thing About the Johnsons* (2011), whose story of a son's longtime sexual abuse of his own father prefigures Ellen's unexpected abuse of her grandchildren. The Paimon sigil first glimpsed on Ellen's necklace during her open-casket service, for instance, reappears on the telephone pole where Charlie is "accidentally" decapitated as Peter speeds home from a party after Charlie has suffered a severe food allergy. Echoing an earlier scene where a bird strikes

Charlie's classroom window, after which Charlie beheads the bird with a pair of scissors, there are early intimations that Charlie's tragic death has been predestined all along, much as Peter's high-school class discusses how *Women of Trachis* is made all the more tragic because predestination means that Sophocles' characters are "pawns in this horrible, hopeless machine."[75]

Throughout the film, Aster affectively conveys the "mechanical" feeling of inevitably unfolding events via his predominant use of slow camera movements, as if largely indifferent to the raw human emotions on display, and a soundtrack composed of woodwinds and electronic drones, punctuated by uncomfortably long moments of silence – plus an almost subliminal, low-frequency throbbing during many scenes of emotional tension. The film's very rare use of jump scares largely comes from the sound design, specifically when Annie and Peter keep hearing Charlie's dental clicks at varying volumes after her death.

Emma Wilson describes how "the grief of mourning parents is popularly reckoned an ultimate horror," a trauma so intense that it seems to exceed the limits of cinematic representation – hence the trope of the "missing child" in films like *Don't Look Now* and many others.[76] Aster visually tarries on the immediate aftermath of Charlie's death, from a lingering close-up of Peter in the stopped car after realizing what has happened; to a shot of him lying in bed staring at the camera as he waits and listens for his mother to discover Charlie's body in the car the next morning; to a long shot of Annie wailing abjectly in her bedroom as Steve attempts to comfort her, the camera slowly tracking out the door and into the hallway where Peter stands listening to her pain. Although Aster punctures the seemingly unrepresentable trauma of child death with a gratuitous shock cut to a close-up of Charlie's ant-covered head resting at the side of the road, much of the film's remaining duration focuses on how Annie and Peter differently mourn Charlie's death, with mother and son passive-aggressively playing their resentments off each other.

Emotions boil over during a tense family dinner at which Peter seeks a cathartic confrontation that will release him from the burden of guilt for causing the "accident" that killed his sister. After Peter suggests that Charlie would still be alive if Annie had not made him take his sister to the party, Annie refuses to forgive Peter or allow the event to bond them all together in grief; not only does Peter refuse to accept responsibility for Charlie's death, but Annie also associates his very existence with her mother's lingering influence over the family. As we soon learn, Annie only carried Peter to term because Ellen pressured her to do so – even though Annie's prevention of Ellen from emotionally connecting with her firstborn child is what eventually necessitated Charlie's sacrifice. Like Freud's melancholiac, whose ambivalent feelings engender "self-reproaches to the effect the mourner [her]self is to blame for the loss of the loved object, i.e. that [s]he has killed it," Annie refuses to give up her lost daughter because doing so feels like having indirectly played some part in killing her.[77] Meanwhile, Peter's post-traumatic symptoms include haunting visions of Charlie in his bedroom; an intrusive flashback of the car's rear-view mirror (with Charlie's headless body in the back seat) dangling above him as he sits at his school desk; and his throat becoming mysteriously constricted – all of which are actually signs of his increasing fall under Paimon's influence.

Much as its predestination themes recall *Don't Look Now* (another acknowledged influence on *Hereditary*), the young daughter's death serves as the primary source of grief in this film as well – and the second-act turning point toward more supernatural plot elements as Annie returns to the grief-recovery group.[78] There Annie meets Joan (Ann Dowd), unbeknownst to her a member of Ellen's coven who, under the guise of reconnecting Annie with her daughter's spirit, tricks Annie into opening the conduit through which Paimon enters first her and then Peter.

Peter himself comes to embody what psychoanalytic theory terms "replacement children" – a common response to the traumatic loss of a child, wherein parents idealize the dead child whose loss they do not properly mourn because the surviving sibling comes to stand in for the previous child's existence. Much like Elias in *Goodnight Mommy*, the replacement child involuntarily inherits their parents' trauma by being denied a stable identity of their own, and may feel dislocated in time and space, or confused about their identity, when seemingly haunted by a phantom sibling with whom they must tacitly compete. As Gabriele Schwab describes, this phenomenon recalls Abraham and Torok's theory of the phantom from the crypt, since it is often associated with a sibling whom the replacement child did not personally know or may not have been aware existed.[79] Although Peter played a more active (if ultimately predestined) role in Charlie's death than the cases of children's deaths in war or genocide that Schwab analyzes, Charlie's eerie and mysterious nature as the previous host for Paimon – and having herself been the replacement child for Annie's dead brother – shows how the unnatural (or, here, supernatural) expectations placed on the replacement child can evoke deeper anxieties about familial reproduction.

In her own fantasy of replacing Charlie, Annie begins sneaking out of bed to sleep in Charlie's treehouse as a displaced act of childhood regression, and she also reverts to her former habit of sleepwalking.[80] In one of the film's most disturbing scenes, she dreams of walking into Peter's bedroom to find his head covered with ants. She then "wakes" from that nightmare to find herself standing at the foot of his bed, where she confesses that she "never wanted to be [his] mother" and had repeatedly attempted to miscarry. Much like Amelia's resentment of her son in *The Babadook*, this maternal ambivalence turns potentially murderous when Aster's use of shot/reverse-shot editing suddenly reveals both Peter and Annie dripping with paint thinner and going up in flames as Annie strikes a match. At this point, Annie wakes to realize that this was also part of a nightmare – but one that has re-enacted a prior sleepwalking event during which she had indeed awoken at the moment of striking a match, just before igniting Peter with flammable chemicals.

This waking from a nightmare into another fright recalls the famous dream of the burning child, discussed in Freud's *The Interpretation of Dreams* as a father's nightmare that his recently deceased child appears at his bedside, tugging at his arm and remarking "Father, can't you see I'm burning?" The father wakes from the nightmare to discover that a candle has fallen over and burnt the arm of the child's corpse, which is lying in repose in the adjacent room. Cathy Caruth argues that this dream commingles the father's wish to sleep (and therefore escape the reality of his child's death) with the fantasy of the child's return to life – and yet, when the post-traumatic nightmare wakes the dreamer with the imperative to remember the reality of the loss, the trauma's affective force recurs upon awakening to find that he is again too late to save his child (in this case, from the burning candle).[81]

In *Hereditary*, then, Annie's awakening from one nightmare into another one – in which she incinerates Peter and herself – bespeaks how her repressed resentment toward Peter has monstrously returned in the wake of Charlie's death. When, just before she strikes the match in the dream, Peter cries out "You tried to kill me!" in response to her confession of the miscarriage attempts, it is as if he says "Mother, can't you see I'm burning?" in order to wake Annie to the supernatural threat that she also proves too late to prevent. (We might see the fatal conflagration that ends *Goodnight Mommy* as another example of a mother responding too late to prevent a traumatic loss, much as John in *Don't Look Now* is not so much attempting to forget or repress the original trauma as anxiously dreading its future recurrence.[82])

Nevertheless, Richard Armstrong notes that grieving women in mourning films often "attempt to express [their] experience in art or another exacting endeavor," meta-textually reflecting on such films' own spectatorial potential as "vehicles for the mourning process."[83] Eugenie Brinkema's description of tableaux as a privileged form for cinematically depicting grief's heaviness is especially apt here, since the stillness of forms like Annie's miniatures reduces living things to their status as mere objects.[84] Although it disgusts her husband as an unseemly means of mourning Charlie's death, Annie's creation of a miniature depicting (in her words) "a neutral view of the accident" can be read as an attempt to use artistic creation as a "transformational object . . . to carry the task of mourning and integration beyond replacement and substitution."[85]

Because Annie reproduces in her miniatures even the subtle demonic invocations that her mother Ellen had scrawled on the walls of the Graham house, the fact that the film is bookended by shots of Annie's miniatures suggests that, on some level, Annie herself is the creator of this "family tragedy that curdles into a nightmare" (to use Aster's description of the film), as if confirming Annie's fears about being (indirectly) responsible for generating such horrors.[86] Yet, much of this blame seems to fall on her in particularly gendered ways. Hence, Katherine Fusco sees the film as demonizing creative mothers like Annie, who seems to focus more on her art than on supporting her family – unlike, say, the "nurturing domestic angel" of *A Quiet Place* (2018), who is also mourning a lost child but pours her energies into improving the male-led homestead (see Chapter 5). Ellen's posthumous note left for Annie to find ("Our sacrifice will pale next to the rewards") also suggests a longer legacy of sacrificing family to one's (witch)craft, with Annie's uncanny miniatures as "the art of someone drawn to detail and who wants things arranged just so." Fusco argues that when women pursue such artistic activities, it is considered aberrant (see the paint thinner from Annie's workshop as a potential murder-suicide method), whereas such craftsmanship is both expected and celebrated when it comes from burgeoning male auteurs like Ari Aster.[87]

In addition, *Hereditary* seems more apt to blame Annie and other maternal figures for unleashing horror upon the family due to their participation in spiritualism – a mourning practice historically tied to women's presence in seances, either as mediums or as expressors of public grief. Much as Freud associated the uncanny with the then-popular practice of spiritualism, Richard Armstrong notes how cinema and spiritualism arose in tandem as means of conjuring spectral presences, with women's lachrymal responses to such events as a trope inherited by the maternal melodramas of the 1940s and beyond. Akin to scenes of looking through a deceased person's belongings, seances become a common setting in mourning films, with other characters' skepticism about contact with the dead serving as a means of strengthening the viewer's empathy with grieving female protagonists.[88] In the context of a horror film, though, the seance scenes in *Hereditary* also serve as a narrative turn toward the full emergence of demonic possession during the film's final act.

Having demonstrated to Annie how she uses a small chalkboard to spiritually contact her dead grandson, Joan provides Annie with instructions on how to seemingly make contact with Charlie through an object owned by the dead person and a spoken invocation requiring the co-presence of the other Graham family members. Unbeknownst to Annie, this act binds the Grahams to Paimon via Charlie's sketchpad, which begins to manifest uncanny images of Peter with his eyes crossed out – another instance of monstrous art. Shortly after finding her disinterred mother's corpse lying headless in their attic, Annie tries to burn the sketchpad and Steve goes up in flames instead. Steve is, then, the "offering" that, according to Goetic grimoires, must be made to Paimon when the demon is summoned alone.[89] Now possessed by Paimon herself, Annie chases Peter into the attic, where she levitates and saws her own head off (one of the few viscerally gory scenes in the post-horror corpus) as the members of Ellen's coven converge on the house.

Even in these most straightforwardly horrific scenes, Aster uses very few jump scares, instead relying on long and wide shots to reveal particularly haunting details – such as Annie levitating, out of focus but still visible in the shadows, in the corners of the house as she stalks Peter, or the nude coven members standing motionless in and around the home. After Annie's self-beheading, Paimon finally passes into Peter's body, and he follows his mother's corpse as it silently floats up into Charlie's treehouse, where the coven has posed Ellen and Annie's headless bodies genuflecting toward a statue of Paimon. Although these ritual beheadings have no correspondence in the Goetic literature, the soundtrack in this final scene prominently features the cymbals and trumpets associated with Paimon's arrival.[90] With the Graham family destroyed and evil utterly triumphant, the film's final image before abruptly cutting to black is the treehouse scene rendered as yet another miniature tableau.

In this film about monstrous inheritances, then, art itself is foregrounded as a possible vehicle for mourning, as well as for considering *Hereditary*'s own admixture of influences from different generations of art and genre cinema, including atavistic inheritances from maternal melodramas and arthouse classics. It is notable that Annie repeatedly uses "going to a movie" as her alibi for secretly visiting the grief-recovery group, suggesting the role that post-horror films like *Hereditary* might themselves play as artistic sites for exploring grief (unlike Annie's sculptural work that, through its association with feminine labor, apparently fails to serve as an adequate tool for mourning). Although E. Ann Kaplan cautions that viewing cinematic representations of trauma can only ever provide mild experiences of "vicarious trauma" (as opposed to the intensity of real traumatic experiences) by encouraging viewers to empathize with a character's pain, post-horror's refusal to provide the conventionally entertaining genre experiences expected of simply "going to a movie" points toward how these films might operate more akin to art cinema's mourning dramas.[91]

Indeed, trauma victims – whether sadistically blamed or masochistically identified with – can become objects of voyeuristic fascination if the sources of their trauma seem so far removed from the viewer's everyday experience as to be reassuringly consumed, which would seem a potential pitfall for any genre rooted in the fantastic.[92] When trauma becomes treated as just another part of the horror genre's repertoire of recreational effects, it thus threatens to become "dispensable and always subjected to an economy of accelerated obsolescence," much like the replacement child as a figure of inherited trauma represents wider cultural anxieties about humans being reduced to objects of capitalistic exchange.[93] Small wonder, then, that (as noted in the previous chapter) a planned reboot of *Final Destination* (2000) – a film series that treats traumatic catastrophes as just another funhouse ride – has been proposed as a populist return to "popcorn horror" after post-horror's grim portrayals of loss and grief.[94]

By depicting trauma and loss through aesthetic and narratological choices that affectively disturb, rather than mollifying the experience of grief, post-horror films like *Hereditary* emerge as all the more monstrous embodiments of art and horror cinema's unexpectedly prolific progeny. Nevertheless, much as Peter seeks the cathartic release that his mother ultimately denies him, some viewers argue that these films can feel oppressively heavy and even cruel to both characters and viewers alike, working against the purgation of grief that the genre's expected pleasures might instead provide. In a mournful think-piece, for example, Scout Tafoya reflects on watching Aster's *Midsommar* (2019) shortly after several friends' deaths, and finding it far too claustrophobic compared to the crowd-pleasing catharsis and closure provided by the alligator-horror movie *Crawl* (2019) concurrently in theaters. Tafoya remarks that, while watching *Midsommar*, "I remember Toni Collette cutting her head off fifteen minutes before the end of *Hereditary*. 'What was the point of watching her try and deal with her issues if you were just going to kill her?' I all but scream at the screen."[95] As we will see in the next chapter, when post-horror films stretch their protagonists' traumas across a narrative that denies them (and us) a classically satisfying resolution, the films' creators may themselves seem uncomfortably complicit with characters who consistently undercut the protagonists' emotional selfhood, enhancing the sense of psychological violence committed against those already suffering from grief.

Notes

1. Jason Zinoman, "Home Is Where the Horror Is," *New York Times*, June 7, 2018 <https://www.nytimes.com/2018/06/07/movies/hereditary-horror-movies.html>.
2. J. A. Bridges, "Post-Horror Kinships: From *Goodnight Mommy* to *Get Out*," *Bright Lights Film Journal*, December 20, 2018 <https://brightlightsfilm.com/post-horror-kinships-from-goodnight-mommy-to-get-out/>.
3. Eugenie Brinkema, *The Forms of the Affects* (Durham, NC: Duke University Press, 2014), pp. 57–8, 72, 74, 94–5. Also see Sigmund Freud, "Mourning and Melancholia," in *The Standard Edition of the Complete Psychological Works of Sigmund Freud*, Vol. XIV, ed. James Strachey (London: Hogarth Press, 1964), pp. 243–58.
4. Tony Williams, *Hearths of Darkness: The Family in the American Horror Film* (Jackson, MS: University Press of Mississippi, 2014), pp. 13, 16.
5. Vivian Sobchack, "Bringing It All Back Home: Family Economy and Generic Exchange," in *The Dread of Difference: Gender and the Horror Film*, ed. Barry Keith Grant (Austin, TX: University of Texas Press, 1996), pp. 147, 149–50, 152, 156, 159.
6. Lisa Downing, "On the Fantasy of Childlessness as Death in Psychoanalysis and in Roeg's *Don't Look Now* and Von Trier's *Antichrist*," *Lambda Nordica*, 16, no. 2/3 (2011), p. 48. Also see Chapters 6 and 7 for more on reproductive futurism.
7. Richard Armstrong, *Mourning Films: A Critical Study of Loss and Grieving in Cinema* (Jefferson, NC: McFarland, 2012), p. 98.
8. Ibid., p. 23.
9. Lucy Fischer, *Cinematernity: Film, Motherhood, Genre* (Princeton, NJ: Princeton University Press, 1996), pp. 6–8.
10. See Michel Foucault, "Nietzsche, Genealogy, History," in *The Foucault Reader*, ed. Paul Rabinow (New York: Pantheon Books, 1984), p. 81.
11. *The Blackcoat's Daughter* (2015), for example, also uses unreliable narration – albeit focalized more through the perpetrator of trauma than the victims – to conceal the ambiguities of the potentially supernatural killings at its center, while *Hagazussa*'s already mourning mother follows through on the child murder that *The Babadook* only threatens (see Chapter 5).
12. Bridges, "Post-Horror Kinships."
13. Armstrong, *Mourning Films*, 11–12, 15, 41, 151.
14. Brinkema, *The Forms of the Affects*, 55, 95–6.
15. Armstrong, *Mourning Films*, 129, 168.
16. Ibid., p. 12.
17. Ibid., pp. 39, 70, 74, 122, 172, 183, 185.

18. Brinkema, *The Forms of the Affects*, 54–5, 109.
19. Armstrong, *Mourning Films*, 12, 14, 23, 53–7, 60–6, 148, 179.
20. Mary Ann Doane, *The Desire to Desire: The Woman's Film of the 1940s* (Bloomington, IN: Indiana University Press, 1987), pp. 2–4, 34, 36, 73 (quoted at p. 4).
21. Mark Jancovich, "Bluebeard's Wives: Horror, Quality, and the Gothic (or Paranoid) Woman's Film in the 1940s," *Irish Journal of Gothic and Horror Studies*, no. 12 (2013), pp. 25–6, 43. Also see Guy Barefoot, *Gaslight Melodrama: From Victorian London to 1940s Hollywood* (London: Continuum, 2001), p. 71; and Tim Snelson, *Phantom Ladies: Hollywood Horror and the Home Front* (New Brunswick, NJ: Rutgers University Press, 2015).
22. Sarah Arnold, *Maternal Horror Film: Melodrama and Motherhood* (New York: Palgrave Macmillan, 2013).
23. David Greven, *Representations of Femininity in American Genre Cinema: The Woman's Film, Film Noir, and Modern Horror* (New York: Palgrave Macmillan, 2011).
24. Armstrong, *Mourning Films*, 23.
25. Tarja Laine, *Feeling Cinema: Emotional Dynamics in Film Studies* (New York: Continuum, 2011), p. 42.
26. Armstrong, *Mourning Films*, 88–96 (quoted at p. 91).
27. Doane, *The Desire to Desire*, 73.
28. Among others, see Joshua Hirsch, *Afterimage: Film, Trauma, and the Holocaust* (Philadelphia, PA: Temple University Press, 2004), p. 3; Adam Lowenstein, *Shocking Representation: Historical Trauma, National Cinema, and the Modern Horror Film* (New York: Columbia University Press, 2005), p. 4; Linnie Blake, *The Wounds of Nations: Horror Cinema, Historical Trauma, and National Identity* (Manchester: Manchester University Press, 2008), p. 3; Alan Gibbs, *Contemporary American Trauma Narratives* (Edinburgh: Edinburgh University Press, 2014), pp. 17, 25–6, 32; Joshua Pederson, "Trauma and Narrative," in *Trauma and Literature*, ed. J. Roger Kurtz (Cambridge: Cambridge University Press, 2018), pp. 98, 100–1, 106.
29. Cathy Caruth, *Unclaimed Experience: Trauma, Narrative, and History* (Baltimore, MD: Johns Hopkins University Press, 1996), pp. 4, 6, 11, 17–18, 91. The phrase "affect aesthetic" derives from E. Ann Kaplan, *Trauma Culture: The Politics of Terror and Loss in Media and Literature* (New Brunswick, NJ: Rutgers University Press, 2005), p. 76.
30. Roger Luckhurst, *The Trauma Question* (New York: Routledge, 2008), pp. 178, 180–3, 185, 205, 208 (quoted at p. 185); Gibbs, *Contemporary American Trauma Narratives*, 4; Marie Kruger, "Trauma and the Visual Arts," in *Trauma and Literature*, 258.
31. Kaplan, *Trauma Culture*, 34; Gibbs, *Contemporary American Trauma Narratives*, 11–13.
32. Ruth Leys, *Trauma: A Genealogy* (Chicago: University of Chicago Press, 2000), pp. 270–2; Kaplan, *Trauma Culture*, 32, 35–8; Gibbs, *Contemporary American*

Trauma Narratives, 10; Susannah Radstone, "Trauma Theory: Contexts, Politics, Ethics," *Paragraph*, 30, no. 1 (2007), pp. 15–18 (quoted at p. 17).
33. Radstone, "Trauma Theory," 19.
34. E. Ann Kaplan and Ban Wang, "Introduction: From Traumatic Paralysis to the Force Field of Modernity," in *Trauma and Cinema: Cross-Cultural Explorations*, eds E. Ann Kaplan and Ban Wang (Hong Kong: Hong Kong University Press, 2004), p. 8.
35. Radstone, "Trauma Theory," 17.
36. Laura S. Brown, "Not Outside the Range: One Feminist Perspective on Psychic Trauma," *American Imago*, 48, no. 1 (1991), pp. 120–2, 128 (quoted at pp. 120 and 122).
37. Andrew Scahill, *The Revolting Child in Horror Cinema: Youth Rebellion and Queer Spectatorship* (New York: Palgrave Macmillan, 2015), pp. 91–4 (quoted at p. 94).
38. Armstrong, *Mourning Films*, 176–8 (quoted at p. 176).
39. Dwayne Avery, *Unhomely Cinema: Home and Place in Global Cinema* (London: Anthem Press, 2014), p. 17.
40. Bridges, "Post-Horror Kinships."
41. See Karen J. Renner, *Evil Children in the Popular Imagination* (New York: Palgrave Macmillan, 2016).
42. Freud, "Mourning and Melancholia," 244–6, 251 (quoted at p. 246).
43. Fischer, *Cinematernity*, 77–89 (quoted at p. 78).
44. Jessica Balanzategui, "*The Babadook* and the Haunted Space Between High and Low Genres in the Australian Horror Tradition," *Studies in Australasian Studies*, 11, no. 1 (2017), pp. 27–8. For a more culturally specific example of post-horror's linkage between Gothic setting and motherhood, see Babak Anvari's film *Under the Shadow* (2016). Set during the Iran–Iraq War, a young Iranian woman is trapped at home with her daughter as supernatural events begin transpiring within their Tehran apartment block. She initially suspects that her daughter's contact with a djinn is a manifestation of post-traumatic grief over the father's disappearance during his military service. Meanwhile, she has been blacklisted from resuming medical school due to her pre-Revolution political activities, and is forbidden by sharia law from leaving home without a male companion. The film's specific historical-cultural setting offers a more politicized take on many of the more secular issues around motherhood in *The Babadook*.
45. Michael C. Reiff, "Mediating Trauma in Jennifer Kent's *The Babadook*," in *Terrifying Texts: Essays on Books of Good and Evil in Horror Cinema*, eds Cynthia J. Miller and A. Bowdoin Van Riper (Jefferson, NC: McFarland, 2018), p. 128.
46. Balanzategui, "*The Babadook* and the Haunted Space," 28; Aviva Briefel, "Parenting Through Horror: Reassurance in Jennifer Kent's *The Babadook*," *Camera Obscura*, 32, no. 2 (2017), pp. 13–14; Fran Pheasant-Kelly, "Trauma, Repression, and *The Babadook*: Sexual Identity in the Trump Era," in *Make*

America Hate Again: Trump-Era Horror and the Politics of Fear, ed. Victoria McCollum (London: Routledge, 2019), p. 88.
47. Williams, *Hearths of Darkness*, 98; Laura Mee, *The Shining* (Leighton Buzzard: Auteur, 2017), p. 94; Shelley Buerger, "The Beak That Grips: Maternal Indifference, Ambivalence, and the Abject in *The Babadook*," *Studies in Australasian Cinema*, 11, no. 1 (2017), p. 42.
48. Brinkema, *The Forms of the Affects*, 95–6.
49. Pheasant-Kelly, "Trauma, Repression, and *The Babadook*," 81.
50. Balanzategui, "*The Babadook* and the Haunted Space," 29.
51. Ibid., p. 28.
52. See Renee Middlemost, "Babashook: *The Babadook*, Gay Iconography, and Internet Cultures," *Australasian Journal of Popular Culture*, 8, no. 1 (2019), pp. 7–26.
53. Buerger, "The Beak That Grips," 34, 38–40. On versions of this monstrous-feminine trope, also see Barbara Creed, *The Monstrous-Feminine: Film, Feminism, Psychoanalysis* (London: Routledge, 1993).
54. Paula Quigley, "*The Babadook* (2014), Maternal Gothic, and the 'Woman's Horror Film,'" in *Gothic Heroines on Screen: Representation, Interpretation, and Feminist Enquiry*, eds Tamar Jeffers McDonald and Frances A. Kamm (New York: Routledge, 2019), p. 196.
55. Balanzategui, "*The Babadook* and the Haunted Space," 20–2.
56. Ibid., pp. 22–9.
57. Lies Lanckman, "'I See, I See . . .': *Goodnight Mommy* (2014) as Austrian Gothic," in *Gothic Heroines on Screen*, 178.
58. Matt Hills, *The Pleasures of Horror* (London: Continuum, 2005), p. 44.
59. Jessica Gildersleeve, *Don't Look Now* (Leighton Buzzard: Auteur, 2017), pp. 55, 75.
60. Laurie Vickroy, *Reading Trauma Narratives: The Contemporary Novel and the Psychology of Oppression* (Charlottesville, VA: University of Virginia Press, 2015), pp. 47, 183.
61. Armstrong, *Mourning Films*, 31–2, 39.
62. Ibid., p. 148.
63. Sigmund Freud, "The Uncanny," in *The Standard Edition of the Complete Psychological Works of Sigmund Freud*, Vol. XVII), ed. James Strachey (London: Hogarth Press, 1955), pp. 234–6, 249. Also see Brinkema, *The Forms of the Affects*, 95–6.
64. Nicholas Royle, *The Uncanny* (Manchester: Manchester University Press, 2003), p. 6. Although more often deemed a "thriller" than a horror film (albeit its ending clearly relies on horror), Denis Villeneuve's *Enemy* (2013) can be effectively read as another post-horror film capitalizing on such doppelgänger themes.
65. Armstrong, *Mourning Films*, 152.
66. Richard J. McNally, *Remembering Trauma* (Cambridge, MA: Harvard University Press, 2003), pp. 11–13; Luckhurst, *The Trauma Question*, 181–2.

67. Bridges, "Post-Horror Kinships."
68. *The Lodge* (2019) opens in a similar manner, as the camera roves inside what is revealed to be a dollhouse model of the titular location, while also providing clues to another extraordinarily grim narrative outcome, courtesy of *Goodnight Mommy* co-directors Veronika Franz and Severin Fiala.
69. Freud, "The Uncanny," pp. 222–4, 230, 244, 249 (quotes at pp. 222, 224).
70. Ibid., pp. 238, 243.
71. With *Get Out* (2017) having shown the prior year that post-horror films could earn Academy Award nods, many film critics deemed Toni Collette's portrayal of Annie as worthy of a Best Actress nomination. Despite winning multiple awards from film critics' associations, however, she was not nominated for *Hereditary* – though she had previously earned a Best Supporting Actress nomination for playing another mourning character in *The Sixth Sense*.
72. "Deep Cuts with Ari Aster & Robert Eggers," *A24.com*, July 17, 2019 <https://a24films.com/notes/2019/07/deep-cuts-with-robert-eggers-and-ari-aster>.
73. Nicolas Abraham and Maria Torok, *The Shell and the Kernel: Renewals of Psychoanalysis, Vol. 1*, ed. Nicholas T. Rand (Chicago: University of Chicago Press, 1994), pp. 130–1, 141–2, 171–3, 181 (quoted at p. 130). Also see Armstrong, *Mourning Films*, 89, 142; Gabriele Schwab, *Haunting Legacies: Violent Histories and Transgenerational Trauma* (New York: Columbia University Press, 2010), pp. 126, 143, 145.
74. Abraham and Torok, *The Shell and the Kernel*, 176.
75. In Sophocles' play, Heracles is prophesied to be killed by someone who is already dead. After his wife Deianeira accidentally poisons Heracles with what she thinks is a love spell, she kills herself; he begs to be burned alive upon realizing that the prophesy has been fulfilled, since the "love spell" had been supplied to Deianeira by a romantic rival whom Heracles had slain years earlier.
76. Emma Wilson, *Cinema's Missing Children* (London: Wallflower Press, 2003), pp. 2–4, 9–11, 157 (quoted at p. 157).
77. Freud, "Mourning and Melancholia," 251, 257 (quoted at p. 251).
78. Dom Nero, "Nicolas Roeg's *Don't Look Now* is a Masterwork of Psychological Horror," *Esquire*, November 26, 2018 <https://www.esquire.com/entertainment/movies/a25309246/dont-look-now-nicolas-roeg/>.
79. Schwab, *Haunting Legacies*, 121, 123–6, 143–5.
80. In Aster's darkly comic short film *C'est La Vie* (2016), a homeless man explicitly references Freud's *Unheimlich* to describe America – just after he mentions how, as a child, his parents died in a fire, but he survived because he was sleeping outside in a treehouse, at just the right height to hear their screams.
81. Caruth, *Unclaimed Experience*, 92–100. Also see Sigmund Freud, *The Interpretation of Dreams*, 3rd edn (New York: Macmillan, 1913), pp. 403–4, 422–3, 435; Wilson, *Cinema's Missing Children*, 4–9; Armstrong, *Mourning Films*, 11–12.

82. Gildersleeve, *Don't Look Now*, 32, 74–5.
83. Armstrong, *Mourning Films*, 175–6.
84. Brinkema, *The Forms of the Affects*, 56, 109.
85. Schwab, *Haunting Legacies*, 145.
86. Quoted in Britt Hayes, "'Hereditary' Director Ari Aster on Why He Avoided Calling His Terrifying Debut a 'Horror Film,'" *Screen Crush*, June 7, 2018 <https://screencrush.com/ari-aster-interview-hereditary/>.
87. Katherine Fusco, "*Hereditary* and the Monstrousness of Creative Moms," *The Atlantic*, July 11, 2018 <https://www.theatlantic.com/entertainment/archive/2018/07/hereditary-and-the-monstrousness-of-creative-moms/564815/>.
88. Armstrong, *Mourning Films*, 15, 21, 44–5, 51, 53, 176, 181–2. Also see Freud, "The Uncanny," 242; and Jeffrey Sconce, *Haunted Media: Electronic Presence from Telegraphy to Television* (Durham, NC: Duke University Press, 2000), pp. 26–7, 44–56.
89. For example, Aleister Crowley, *The Book of the Goetia of Solomon the King* (Leeds: Celephaïs Press, 2003 [1904]), p. 15.
90. Ibid. Unlike *Hereditary*, *A Dark Song* (2016) depicts a magical operation as a mother's redemptive process for mourning a lost child, as one of the few successful turns toward spirituality or mysticism in post-horror cinema (see Chapter 7).
91. Kaplan, *Trauma Culture*, 90.
92. Brown, "Not Outside the Range," 129; Radstone, "Trauma Theory," 23.
93. Schwab, *Haunting Legacies*, 142.
94. Richard Newby, "How 'Final Destination' Reboot Can Fill a Horror Void," *The Hollywood Reporter*, January 14, 2019 <https://www.hollywoodreporter.com/heat-vision/how-final-destination-reboot-can-bring-dumb-fun-back-movies-1175855>.
95. Scout Tafoya, "The Pain Needs to Mean Something: On Horror and Grief," *RogerEbert.com*, August 26, 2019 <https://www.rogerebert.com/balder-and-dash/the-pain-needs-to-mean-something-on-horror-and-grief>.

CHAPTER 4

Horror by Gaslight: Epistemic Violence and Ambivalent Belonging

"Gaslighting" is a concept that first gained prevalence in 1940s America, but was revived as a pop-psychology term during the period of post-horror's 2010s emergence. Broadly speaking, it describes a destructive pattern of emotional manipulation achieved by consistently undercutting a person's psychological selfhood to the point of affecting their sense of reality, especially through accusations of being "mistaken," "paranoid," or "crazy." Whereas grieving an immediate family member (especially a lost parent or child) provides one of the major dramatic engines for post-horror films, as we saw in the previous chapter, films with gaslighting as a central dramatic focus tend to be structured around romantic or intimate-partner relationships. When we consider that post-horror cinema's minimalist tone prioritizes feelings of apprehension and dread over shock and disgust, this dynamic can help us account for post-horror films in which grief may be dramatically present, but does not necessarily occupy the dominant affective register. As this chapter will explain, gaslighting is another recurring thread in the post-horror corpus for evoking discomfort in viewers for whom these films may feel less like entertaining diversions than painfully recognizable emotional scenarios.

Yet, much like the films analyzed in Chapter 3, many post-horror films about gaslighting still open with a grieving protagonist, encouraging the audience to sympathize with a character already in an emotionally vulnerable state. Lacking family members to turn toward as an emotional support network when strange events begin to transpire merely encourages these characters to side with a gaslighting partner, more out of romantic affection than long-established trust. Eventually, the gaslighted protagonist comes to grieve not only a lost family member, but also their temporarily lost sense of self. As Kate Abramson observes, the gaslightee "griev[es] the loss of her independent perspective, her ability to form and maintain her own reactions and perceptions, the loss of the friendships that became or turned out to be mere gaslighting relations, and her own largely blameless complicity in all of this."[1] The state of mourning, then, can potentially make a person more susceptible to gaslighting, while severe cases of gaslighting effectively rebound into forms of grief in their own right.

While Chapter 3 traced a genealogical thread of maternal anxieties from 1940s woman's films through art-horror precedents like *Rosemary's Baby* (1968) and down to post-horror films, we should consider how *Rosemary's Baby* provides a similar link in its powerful depiction of Rosemary's continual gaslighting by her husband (John Cassavetes) and the kindly cabal of Satanists next door. Assured that she is merely suffering from prepartum "nerves" and driving herself toward a psychiatric breakdown, Rosemary's pregnancy is repeatedly described as anything *but* supernatural, despite her (ultimately correct) suspicions to the contrary. Even when mourning her supposedly stillborn baby, others blame these epistemic doubts on her grief – before she hears the baby crying next door and discovers the ghastly truth.

Nevertheless, whereas the post-horror films qua mourning films discussed in the previous chapter tend to use post-traumatic distortions of reality as a means of generating epistemic hesitation about whether something truly supernatural is happening, post-horror films about gaslighting most often fall more clearly on the side of the Todorovian "uncanny" by revealing all-too-human sources of horror – such as characters who exploit knowledge of the protagonist's past trauma in order to gaslight them. In many respects, the result is the same – the protagonist increasingly doubts their sense of sanity as horrific events unfold – but the underlying source of such self-doubt originates less within the survivor's own grief than the machinations of their romantic partner. For example, Ari Aster's *Midsommar* (2019) effectively begins where *Hereditary* (2018) leaves off: at the moment of the nuclear family's destruction, save a sole survivor. Even as the grieving American protagonist, Dani (Florence Pugh), soon finds herself a fish out of water amid the pagan rituals of an isolated Swedish midsummer festival, the locals ultimately prove less of a direct threat to her than the emotionally abusive boyfriend, Christian (Jack Reynor), who grudgingly invited her along. If post-horror films create discomfort in viewers via our emotional connections to well-developed protagonists, then such films about gaslighting may be especially uncomfortable viewing for those who recognize elements of this common phenomenon from their own lives.

Throughout the films discussed in this chapter, a deceptively welcoming in-group preys upon the insecurities of a visiting outsider whose ambivalent sense of belonging is exacerbated less by grief itself than by gaslighting from their romantic partner. Unlike the family trauma films discussed in the previous chapter, these films often isolate the protagonist in an unfamiliar place outside their own home, albeit still remaining faced with upholding social graces as guests; as one of *Get Out*'s (2017) taglines states, "Just because you're invited, doesn't mean you're welcome." Indeed, in all three films, a lack of cellular phone reception prevents those within an increasingly horrific situation from seeking external perspectives for psychological support, leaving them struggling to escape their emotional and physical confinement – a dynamic inherited from the namesake film *Gaslight* (1944).

This chapter will begin by locating the conceptual roots of gaslighting in the same strand of 1940s paranoid Gothic woman's films that (as discussed in Chapter 3) influenced mourning films, before then exploring how the concept has been taken up and expanded in recent years. I will then turn toward *Midsommar* as a post-horror film that represents gaslighting in one of its most classical forms: the heterosexual male's psychological abuse of his female partner. However, because gaslighting is not exclusively experienced by women, *The Invitation* (2015) puts its traditionally gendered dynamics into relief by depicting a male protagonist as a gaslightee who struggles to maintain the bourgeois social graces of being a good party guest after suspecting that his wealthy hosts are members of a suicide cult. Like all of the films discussed in this chapter, *The Invitation* demonstrates how gaslighting relies, in part, on both physically and emotionally isolating the victim to better prey upon their vulnerabilities, despite the gaslighter(s) often seeming outwardly sympathetic and hospitable toward the person whom they are subtly undercutting. Finally, these tensions come to the fore in perhaps the most overtly political film of the post-horror cycle, *Get Out*, which shows how gaslighting can be fueled by structural inequalities beyond its common association with gender. Each of these three case studies thus progressively expands outward from the romantic dyad toward exploring gaslighting's larger implications as a form of epistemic violence.

From *Gaslight* to "Gaslighting"

Although multiple psychologists have latterly claimed to have coined the term "gaslighting," always in reference to the film *Gaslight*, it had already passed into popular slang as early as the 1940s, due to that film's tremendous critical and popular success, and thence into psychoanalytic literature.[2] Patrick Hamilton's 1938 play *Gas Light: A Victorian Thriller* (staged in the US under the title *Angel Street*) had been adapted for the screen several times before the 1944 version earned even bigger box-office receipts and nominations for the year's top Academy Awards. As in *Rebecca* (1940), the "Bluebeard" folktale as Gothic narrative device informs *Gaslight*'s focus on a husband as a potentially violent threat toward a younger and less worldly wife, generating suspense through the extent to which the character and viewer alike do not truly understand the ominous events afoot. This use of epistemic hesitation therefore allows *Gaslight* and other paranoid Gothic woman's films to also verge on the narrative and affective territory typically occupied by the horror film.[3]

Directed by George Cukor, the 1944 version of *Gaslight* depicts the aftermath of naive young Paula Alquist's (Ingrid Bergman) rushed marriage to older sophisticate Gregory Anton (Charles Boyer). Gregory immediately moves them into Paula's childhood house on London's Thornton Square, which Paula has inherited from her aunt Alice who had been strangled in the house ten years earlier. Still traumatized from the childhood memory of having discovered her aunt's corpse, Paula hopes her recurring nightmares about the house will cease with Gregory there as emotional support. Yet, he soon begins going out at night on vague errands, leaving Paula secluded at home with a resentful maid. During Gregory's nocturnal jaunts, the gas lights seemingly dim on their own and Paula hears noises coming from the locked attic, which she imagines to be her aunt's ghost. Unbeknownst to Paula, though, Gregory was her aunt's murderer, and has deliberately acquired both Paula and the Alquist house so that he can surreptitiously enter the attic through an adjacent home, in search of the aunt's unrecovered jewels. Only when a handsome detective (Joseph Cotten) realizes that something fishy is happening at the site of the unsolved murder does he help Paula turn the tables and capture the criminal, reassuring her that there was "nothing real from the beginning." Yet, whereas Cukor's film adaptation attributes Gregory's evil to his search for the lost jewels, Hamilton's original play hints at more ambiguous motives, implying that Gregory is a "criminal maniac" closer to the serial killers of the horror genre.[4]

The heroic detective may spell out the pattern of psychological manipulation in which Paula has been slowly and deliberately driven out of her mind, but *Gaslight*'s viewer has already witnessed how Gregory has consistently challenged her sense of reality. Among other strategies, he has secretly hidden valuables and then "found" them in Paula's possession, claiming that she suffers from kleptomania; as further justification, he lies that Paula's mother had been committed to an asylum, instilling the fear that she has inherited a mental illness. Because Paula was effectively orphaned from a young age and is now sequestered within the house, she lacks other family members or friends as a support network for reaffirming her perception of events. Much as *Rebecca* initially hints that the second Mrs de Winter (Joan Fontaine) is being haunted by her titular predecessor and threatened by her overly controlling husband Maxim (Laurence Olivier), *Gaslight* also hints at the supernatural, only to later disprove those explanations. *Rebecca* ultimately reveals that the housekeeper, Mrs Danvers (Judith Anderson), has been trying to drive the new Mrs de Winter to suicide, whereas *Gaslight* depicts Gregory angling for Paula's involuntary psychiatric commitment in order to gain full possession of the house and jewels. In both films, though, the isolated Gothic heroine suffers until an empathetic (male) outside party corroborates her experience.[5]

Guy Barefoot notes that *Gaslight* was "not seen as anything more than entertainment" during its initial reception, even if its title soon leant its name to a form of emotional abuse primarily suffered by women driven to paranoia over their husbands' true intentions.[6] Early in the film, Paula shares a train car with a matronly older woman also her way to Thornton Street; not realizing that she is talking to the younger Alquist, the older woman describes the Bluebeard-type novel she is reading, ghoulishly telling Paula how she "enjoys a good murder" and wishes that she had lived on Thornton Street back at the time of the unsolved homicide. Horror fiction is thus positioned within the film itself as little more than titillating entertainment consumed by readers with few ethical qualms – but this reflexive moment of aesthetic self-deprecation would be complicated by "*Gaslight*'s" subsequent appropriation as a term for a serious and endemic issue. In classical Hollywood style, the film may end happily with Paula saved via the intervention of a morally upstanding man (and potential romantic suitor), but Diane Waldman notes that the film at least affirms the woman's suspicions that something very wrong has indeed been going on, contrary to her malevolent husband's attempts at psychological manipulation.[7]

As Diane Shoos argues, *Gaslight* was ahead of its time for not only depicting a variety of different forms of gaslighting, dating from the beginning of Paula and Gregory's relationship, but also by depicting domestic violence as psychological at a time when it was commonly understood as physical.[8] Andrea Walsh further suggests that *Gaslight*, among other examples of the paranoid Gothic woman's film, proved resonant by tapping into women's anger, suspicion, and distrust toward men at a moment when the post-World War II "cult of domesticity" was displacing women from their temporarily assumed role in the national workforce – and not least because the female protagonists of these films often fight back against their (male) psychological oppressors.[9] Small wonder, then, that Adrienne Rich wrote in an influential 1975 essay, "Women have been driven mad, 'gaslighted,' for centuries by the refutation of our experience and our instincts in a culture which validates only male experience. The truth of our bodies and our minds has been mystified to us."[10]

Later writers who have taken up and developed gaslighting as a concept generally concur that, unlike its namesake film, gaslighting may not be done consciously. Still, even if intentional, gaslighting is rarely done with a specific end goal (such as driving someone insane). Psychoanalysts Victor Calef and Edward M. Weinshel, for example, describe it as an unconscious process wherein the gaslighter "dumps" their own anxieties (feelings of greed, guilt, or shame) onto the gaslightee as a form of projective identification, exteriorizing those inner emotional conflicts in order to wrest control over them in another person.[11] Likewise, in her book *The Gaslight Effect*, Robin Stern argues that the gaslighter has a flawed sense of self, disavowing or repressing their insecurities in order to shore up their fragile feelings of power. Because the gaslightee already seeks the gaslighter's approval or affection, the gaslightee's existing anxieties or self-doubts can be passive-aggressively exploited and exacerbated to the gaslighter's advantage.[12] Furthermore, Kate Abramson clarifies how by refusing or thwarting genuinely empathetic communication, gaslighters thus go beyond simply accusing a person of being wrong or mistaken; rather, they destructively induce such profound self-doubt that the gaslightee questions their own rationality and loses the epistemic standing on which to protest such abusive treatment in the first place.[13]

Although Stern notes that male/female romantic pairings are where the gaslighter/gaslightee dyad most often occurs in actual practice,[14] other works of pop psychology claim that men and women are equally prone to being gaslighters, with men less likely to report being the victim in an emotionally abusive relationship.[15] Given their respective genres, self-help books about gaslighting are more likely to stress the gaslightee's need to take personal responsibility by withdrawing their empathy for the gaslighter and becoming willing to end the relationship altogether – even as this advice implicitly blames the victim for having chosen and stuck with the "wrong person" for too long.[16]

By contrast, feminist scholars more often stress the structural inequalities that make women, people of color, and queer or gender non-conforming people more vulnerable to gaslighting. For instance, Abramson argues that gaslighters can leverage "appeals to ungrounded authority" rooted in hierarchies of social power – such as the sexist stereotype of women as more prone to emotionality (accusations of "hysteria," for example).[17] Rachel McKinnon similarly discusses the resulting "epistemic injustice circle (of hell)" as a self-fulfilling feedback loop in which "an identity prejudice based on emotion is treated as a reason to discount a speaker's testimony, whereby a normal response to this testimonial injustice is to become *more* emotional (e.g., angry, frustrated, etc.). But this subsequent emotionality is treated as a *further* reason to discount the speaker's testimony."[18] As we will see during the rest of this chapter, structural inequalities color the unethical dynamics of gaslighting that are depicted in post-horror films and, I would argue, discomfortingly sensed by their viewers.

Midsommar: Gaslighting's "Most Unholy Affekts"

Midsommar opens with several long, placid shots of snowy landscapes at night, soundtracked by a female soloist singing a gentle Swedish folksong – but this deceptively peaceful tone is interrupted by a loud, unanswered phone ringing as the camera cuts in toward the Ardor residence with each ring. Dani is calling her parents to check in about a cryptic social-media message left by her sister. Her boyfriend Christian seems unconcerned about "the sister situation," more interested in hanging out with his graduate-school friends, and blames Dani for letting her sister drive her "straight to crisis mode . . . every other day" as an "obvious ploy for attention." She responds, "You're right. I just needed to be reminded – thank you." But despite this instance of how anxious gaslightees "align themselves with a partner . . . giving up their own perception as quickly as they can in order to win the other person's approval and thereby prove to themselves that they're good, capable, lovable people,"[19] Dani is ultimately proven correct.

Shortly before receiving the call informing her that her sister has, in fact, killed both herself and their parents with carbon monoxide poisoning, Dani calls a female friend and tearfully confides that she fears her need for emotional support is driving Christian away. Sure enough, we cut to Christian contemplating how to break up with Dani, goaded on by his friends Josh (William Jackson Harper) and Mark (Will Poulter). Josh asks whether "a masochistic part" of Christian is keeping him unconsciously tied to Dani to avoid writing his Ph.D. prospectus, while Mark encourages Christian to find a partner who "actually likes sex" and does not "literally [*sic*] abuse" him with panicked phone calls.

Upon receiving Dani's call about the multiple suicide, Christian goes to her apartment to console her. Inside, the wide shot very slowly tracks in and indifferently passes out through the window as she wails abjectly, soundtracked by the rise of discordant strings and tribal drumbeats. During this lengthy pre-credit sequence, Ari Aster thus foreshadows several important threads that run throughout the film: Dani's correct intuition about impending danger, which Christian continually discounts through gaslighting; the camera's willingness to uncomfortably linger on Dani in moments of emotional torment; and the anxieties induced through modern technologies like cellular phones and social media, both of which will be conspicuously absent – thus further cutting off Dani from outside emotional support – once the story shifts to a remote area of central Sweden.

The following summer, Josh casually remarks to Dani that he and his friends are about to leave for several weeks in Hälsingland, Sweden, having been invited by their fellow anthropology student Pelle (Vilhelm Blomgren) to visit his home village during his community's traditional midsummer festival. Later at her apartment, Dani calls it "really weird" that Christian has already agreed to go without consulting with her, for which he insincerely apologizes. When Dani says, "You didn't apologize – you said 'Sorry,' which sounds more like 'Too bad,'" he passive-aggressively threatens to go home, to avoid the discussion:

> DANI: I'm not trying to attack you.
> CHRISTIAN: It really feels like you are.
> DANI: Well, then, *I'm* sorry. I just got confused.

Dani also attempts to justify Christian's decision to herself by remarking that the trip could inspire his yet-to-be-determined thesis. (In the director's cut, the scene continues with Dani tearfully apologizing again, attributing her paranoia to her recent family tragedy; when Christian guiltily invites her along on the trip, she second-guesses his motives as false sympathy, and he lies that the invitation was meant to be a romantic surprise.) Christian thus fits the mold of what Robin Stern calls the "Good-Guy Gaslighter," a partner who seems to be good and to act reasonably, but who does not really compromise when he seems to do so.[20] Stephanie Sarkis also describes gaslighters as masters of the "conditional apology" (a non-apology intended to deflect criticism), using superficial displays of empathy while avoiding responsibility for their own actions. Moreover, they may triangulate their communication through third parties, enlisting others to unknowingly assist in the gaslighting process – as we see when Christian tells his friends to play along with Dani's ad hoc invitation to Sweden, erroneously presuming that she will back out at the last minute.[21]

However, even after Pelle leads Dani, Christian, and his friends to the isolated Hårga village, the gaslighting continues – whether in minor forms (such as Christian lying about having forgotten Dani's birthday) or the major betrayal that occurs when Christian deflowers Maja (Isabelle Grill), one of the village maidens, during the film's final act. In a scene only in the director's cut, Dani even confronts Christian with her awareness that their relationship has been in a "devaluation phase" for a long time, which he rejects as "textbook psychology keywords." Sarcastically remarking that "it looks like you've got this all figured out," Christian then accuses her of being conniving by giving him little gifts like flowers to make him feel indebted to her. This scene suggests how Dani is not naive about his treatment of her, even as he doubles-down on his manipulative reversals.

Yet, unlike in *Gaslight* and *Rebecca* (or, for that matter, *The Invitation* and *Get Out*), *Midsommar*'s audience is not initially confused or misled about the gaslighter's motives: we already know from the pre-credit sequence that a pattern of gaslighting is present, so our discomfort lies less in sharing Dani's epistemic hesitation over Christian's true motives than our being privy to more narrative information than she is. As Julian Hanich observes, horror films produce dread by oscillating between not only our heightened empathy (feeling with) for all-too-realistic protagonists like Dani, but also our sympathy (feeling for) when we care enough about a character to fear and pity the misfortune that we know is coming.[22]

By contrast, the Hårgas' true motives are more shrouded in mystery early in the film – but simply knowing that this is a horror film should cue the first-time viewer to expect the worst from the conspicuously welcoming villagers. Aster's use of an overhead tracking shot that slowly and vertiginously turns upside-down, rendering an inverted image of the highway as the group's car first drives into Hälsingland, suggests how their world will soon be turned topsy-turvy. The gaslighting relationship at the film's emotional core is thus complemented by *Midsommar*'s roots in the folk-horror subgenre, which features slow and ritualistic forms of death in adherence to the arcane, pre-modern beliefs of an insular community whose isolated, agrarian landscape needs to be "occultivated" with bloodshed. As Adam Scovell notes, these communities' folkloric beliefs may include supernatural components, but their violent actions are ultimately the product of local theologies. As in *The Wicker Man* (1973), a chain of narrative events inevitably leads toward peak violence by the film's end, with outside representatives of modernity drawn inexorably toward a macabre fate.[23]

Indeed, the very first image in *Midsommar* is a painted Hårga tableau (inspired by actual painted farmhouses in Hälsingland) depicting the coming narrative in miniature; much like *Hereditary*'s classroom discussion about cruel predestination, Aster seeds plenty of early hints about the slow inevitability of the coming deaths (including images of bears and flower crowns) and how Dani's post-traumatic grief has (over)sensitized her to impending threats. Despite her reluctance, for example, Christian (and Mark) pressure Dani into ingesting psilocybin mushrooms after Pelle dubs it a traditional Hårga way to connect with nature before the festivities begin – and Dani soon has a bad trip, seeing visions of her dead sister.

This is the first of several instances of hallucinogenic flora's use in drugging the Americans – and an indication that it is not just Dani who is being gaslighted in the context of the ensuing festival. As eventually becomes clear, Pelle and his brother Ingemar (Hampus Hallberg) have deliberately invited guests because the close-knit Hårga community needs fresh blood from outside, both by breeding with and ritually sacrificing foreigners. As in torture-porn films like *Hostel* (2005) or *Turistas* (2006), locals first invite the visitors with open arms – responding to Christian's query if anyone can participate in the ceremonies, Pelle replies, "You're an American; jam yourself in there" – and then the locals consistently discount the waylaid travelers' growing concerns as mere cultural misunderstandings. Yet, *Midsommar*'s post-horror tone also modulates the generic results by focusing more on the emotional stakes for Dani and Christian's relationship than the threats to Americans traveling abroad.

If *Midsommar* sounds like a mix of *The Wicker Man* and *Hostel*, that was how Aster was first pitched the premise by the Swedish producers who approached him to write and direct the script after having read *Hereditary*'s script. While initially hesitant, Aster was then in the aftermath of a breakup, and accepted the project-for-hire in order to "smuggle a breakup movie" into "a throwaway folk-horror movie" wherein the typical generic appeal for audiences is speculating how the characters will inevitably be sacrificed in grotesque ways. Although Aster describes Dani as his onscreen surrogate, achieving "a wish-fulfillment fantasy" of retribution against a former partner, he also admits to having been on both sides of the central couple's emotionally mismatched relationship.[24] Much as he described *Hereditary* as "a family tragedy that curdles into a nightmare," he calls *Midsommar* "more of a fairy tale than a horror film,"[25] while also noting its indebtedness to melodrama's tradition of "having the movie be as big as the feelings that the characters are feeling." The opening family tragedy was intended to be

> bad enough, traumatic enough, to hang over the whole film. And that was necessary because I wanted to make this big operatic breakup movie where the breakup itself is not that special. He's not the worst guy in the world. And she's very needy. But she's needy because she's navigating this unfathomable situation.[26]

When releasing the director's cut to digital services, A24 even offered viewers the chance to win three months of couples therapy, implying (with tongue firmly in cheek) that the film's depictions of gaslighting, infidelity, and retribution might strike too close to home for some couples.[27] YouTube comments also suggest how strongly many women relate the Dani/Christian scenes to their own past relationships, often describing these scenes as textbook examples of gaslighting.

Following Aster's "fairy-tale" comparison – and with rare exceptions like *The Witch* (2015, discussed in Chapter 5) – most folk-horror films, including *Midsommar*, do not depict a culturally accurate folkloric tradition, more often inventing their own.[28] Even if set in the real province of Hälsingland and featuring pagan-derived elements of European midsummer festivals (such as maypoles), Aster and his Swedish collaborators Martin Karlqvist and Patrik Andersson mixed further influences from Scandinavian mythology, including Elder *Futhark* runic magic, the *Hårgalåten* dance (based on a legend about the Devil dancing the Hårga people to death), and the *Ättestupan* senicide ritual. Although historians have discounted the purported existence of pre-modern suicide cliffs, this latter ceremony marks *Midsommar*'s first significant engagement with folk horror, depicting two village elders casting themselves to their deaths upon reaching the end of the Hårgas' seventy-two-year lifecycle.[29] The scene unfolds with a slow track along the villagers' upturned faces as they duly wait, while Pelle and Ingemar's American and British guests stand nearby, unaware of what is to come. (As if a sly wink to the audience, a young villager standing at a distance from the ceremony conspicuously turns to stare directly into the camera before the first jump.) Consistent with post-horror's minimalist tone, the slow, almost silent build-up to violent death – particularly during the second jump – induces a strong sense of dread, even as Aster's quick juxtaposition between extreme long shots and gory close-ups of the aftermath enhances the scene's visceral power. Given her recent tragedy, Dani is deeply disturbed by the ritual, but the distraught British guests Simon (Archie Madekwe) and Connie (Ellora Torchia) are far more vocal about how "fucked" they find the senicide. Village matriarch Siv (Gunnel Fred) counters that it is a joyful, long-honored ceremony, more humane than merely hiding away their elders to deteriorate in old age.

If, true to pagan beliefs, the *Ättestupan* ritual is meant to be as much about rebirth as death, it certainly plants a thesis-shaped seed in Christian's mind. Although Josh (the only member of the party who previously knew what an *Ättestupan* was) accuses Christian of lazily appropriating his thesis topic on European midsummer festivals, Christian offers to either collaborate or simply work separately. Gaslighters like Christian may attempt to take credit for others' work but, ironically, Josh is the one killed for sneaking into the temple to photograph the *Rubi Radr*, or the Hårga holy books, after being previously forbidden.[30] (Whether he would have stooped to this unethical data collection unless in sudden competition with Christian is unclear.) Unlike the reprehensible travelers in *Hostel*, though, *Midsommar* features only one blatantly "ugly American" character, Mark, who occasionally provides comic relief – until he learns too late the true objective of the Hårga game "Skin the Fool," after the faux pas of urinating on a sacred tree containing the Hårga elders' ashes.

Moreover, the overwhelming whiteness of the Hårga community, even down to their attire, complicates the threat from ethnic or cultural Others often found in torture-porn films (save their ruralness, which provides one area of generic overlap between torture-porn and folk-horror films).[31] Indeed, their ominously cheerful whiteness implicitly hides an underlying commitment to white supremacy (a dynamic that becomes explicit in *Get Out*); Christian and Dani, for example, are ultimately invited to contribute their genetic material to the community, while the non-white visitors (Josh, Simon, and Connie) are all dispatched as mere flesh to be burnt asunder. As Adam Scovell notes, films of the post-millennial folk-horror revival, such as *The Witch* and *Midsommar*, often reveal and villainize the historical roots of contemporary far-right political attitudes.[32] Sure enough, Sophie Lewis observes that, en route to the village, *Midsommar*'s characters drive beneath a xenophobic banner that translates as "Stop Mass Immigration to Hälsingland," an allusion to the 2010s rise of the *Sverigedemokraterna* (Swedish Democrats), which began as a fascist and white-nationalist party.[33]

Whereas torture-porn films encourage (American) viewers to sadomasochistically savor the violence done to their closest onscreen counterparts, Dani remains our emotional lodestone here. Especially as the other outsiders eventually become sacrificed, due to their inability to properly recognize the Hårgas's true designs, we never lose sight of the gendered epistemic violence in Dani's relationship with Christian. Despite his name, Christian repeatedly (and insincerely) jumps to a cultural-relativist defense of the Hårga ceremonies ("Yeah, that was really, really *shocking* ... I'm trying to keep an open mind, though") whenever Dani expresses her desire to go home – thus giving him a further excuse to neglect her as he conducts his research, and foreshadowing his later acceptance of Siv's invitation to mate with Maja.[34]

After both surviving Americans are drugged with another hallucinogenic tea, Dani wins the *Hårgalåten* contest and is crowned May Queen. While she is taken away to bless the year's crops, Christian performs some fertilization of his own during the sex ritual with Maja, surrounded by much older, nude village women. Dani discovers his infidelity upon returning to the village, and Christian is subsequently paralyzed with another drug in advance of the festival's culminating ceremony, in which the May Queen must select the final human sacrifice: either one of the remaining outsiders (Christian) or a randomly selected villager. Christian's infidelity, then, cements the film's focus on the effects of gaslighting, and also seals his doom.

Much like the reversal at the end of *Gaslight*, in which Paula torments the tied-up Gregory by momentarily pretending to have actually been driven insane, Dani reverses the "Emotional Apocalypse" (an ended relationship) that gaslighters hold over their targets' heads when challenged too much.[35] Sewn into a freshly slaughtered bear carcass and joined with the other human sacrifices to be collectively immolated in a wooden pyramid, Christian's retributive death follows both the folk-horror tradition of *The Wicker Man* (a "Christian" outsider lured in to be sacrificed by the pagan revelers) and, filtered through that generic context, self-help books' advice that gaslightees cannot fully take back their power until willing to terminate their abusive relationships. The Hårga frame the bear-man's sacrifice as purging their community's "most unholy affekts" [*sic*], an allusion to the system of sixteen "affekts" comprising the runic language of the *Rubi Radr*. It is no coincidence that the sign for "grief" is the only one specifically pointed out when the *Rubi Radr* is explained, foreshadowing how Dani will seemingly purge her own grief through the final sacrifice that bonds her to the Hårga.[36] First shown wailing and retching as she stumbles beneath the weight of a mountainous, flower-laden dress, *Midsommar*'s final shot is a close-up of Dani's face slowly breaking into a wide smile as she continues to watch the pyramid burn, while liltingly happy strings rise on the score before a cut-to-black (Figure 4.1).

Figure 4.1 Perhaps driven mad, Dani smiles as she watches Christian burn inside the pyramid, in the final shot of *Midsommar*. (Source: Blu-ray.)

Earlier in the film, Pelle had made subtle romantic advances toward Dani, asking whether Christian "feel[s] like home" to her, and framing his interest as empathy over having also lost his parents as a child (quite possibly during an earlier midsummer ritual), with the rest of his village having become his surrogate family. This is where Dani now finds herself at the film's end, destroying her last link to life back home in order to gain a new family in the Hårga.[37] As Pelle explained earlier, the Hårga life cycle is separated into four "seasons": spring (age 0–18, or childhood), summer (age 18–36, or pilgrimage age), fall (age 36–54, or working age), and winter (age 54–72, or mentorship age). The film's title is telling because, per this periodization, twenty-something Dani has found herself navigating the "midsummer" of her own life (she repeatedly remarks on her upcoming birthday) without the traditional support network of a family and reliable partner, whose shed blood has now occasioned her "rebirth" as a member of the Hårga.

Yet, however much Christian's death may serve as a revenge fantasy for viewers who have also experienced gaslighting relationships, this fantasy is complicated by the distinct possibility that, unlike how *Gaslight*'s Paula briefly "exorcize[s] her madness as a return to sender," Dani may have indeed gone mad. Hence, it is unclear whether the viewer's own negative affects are "purged" in this potentially cathartic ending, or discomfortingly extended via ambiguity about her underlying mental state.[38] Cultural relativism notwithstanding, the Hårgas's belief system has already been called into question by the film itself – whether because they use inbred offspring with severe intellectual disabilities as their "oracles" for producing the *Rubi Radr*; or when several self-sacrificing Hårga scream in agony while being burnt alive in the final conflagration, after having just been told that taking yew poison will help them "feel no pain." By aligning herself with the film's most blatantly monstrous characters, Dani's questionable choice to join the Hårga thus undercuts our *own* epistemic ground by potentially demonizing our primary locus of identification. (Here, we might also recall how *Hereditary* implicitly blames Annie for setting in motion her family's destruction, while simultaneously eroding our previous empathy with her grief as she becomes a monstrous threat to them in the end.) In other words, despite the fact that *Midsommar*'s gaslighting narrative has encouraged us to sympathetically uphold Dani's threatened perception of events in the face of Christian's constant gaslighting, the film itself ends on a note that questions if and when Dani actually *has* lost the epistemic ground from which to make such dire choices.[39]

In one sense, then, Dani's decision to sacrifice Christian suggests personal victory over her main gaslighting relationship, yet she also surrenders her emotions to the collective social body that has been gradually drugging and coercing her into joining them. As Kate Abramson argues, part of gaslighting's epistemic violence derives from its victims' loss of the independent standing from which to speak as a full member of the moral community.[40] Writ large, this dynamic can be seen in the Hårgas' mimesis of their fellow villagers during emotionally distressing rituals – as first seen when the male elder crushes his leg during his *Ättestupan* jump and the Hårga mimic his anguish; when the older village women mimic Maja's moans of pain and pleasure during her ritual deflowering; and when the entire community begins screaming and rending their garments during the fiery, final sacrifice.

Much as Maja previously cast a love spell on Christian by leaving a rune beneath his bed and baking her pubic hair into his pie, the Hårgas' emotional mimesis is a form of what James George Frazer, in his classic study *The Golden Bough* (also one of Aster's cited inspirations), termed "sympathetic magic," or magical beliefs based in ideas of imitation and contagion. Although such forms of mimesis are typically discounted as primitive superstition, Michael Taussig argues that sympathetic magic – including its revival via mimetic technologies like cinema – offers a means of reconsidering the "silly if not desperate place between the real and the really made-up [that is, the socially constructed] . . . where most of us spend most of our time as epistemically correct . . . beings."[41] When Dani, for instance, returns from performing the May Queen blessing and spies on the sex ritual, she breaks down in anguished cries that the young Hårga women uncannily mirror back to her (another indication of Dani's growing acceptance into the community). Sandra Huber optimistically claims that the women imitating Dani's cries are "not there merely to listen to or comfort her, but to mirror her rage, to conjure it up and throw it out into exteriority, to awaken and vanquish it."[42] Yet, I would argue that *Midsommar* consistently depicts the Hårgas's "bodily copying of the other," in which "one tries out the very shape of a perception in one's own body," as a source of (folk-)horror, as is first established during the *Ättestupan* sequence.[43] Dani, after all, looks doubly distraught by the wailing women's refusal to let her private emotional pain remain her own (Figure 4.2).

Rather, Dani's choice to join an isolated cult commune – if it can even be said to be the fully volitional choice of an "epistemically correct" person, since the Hårga will not simply let the outsiders leave – sees her effectively replacing one gaslighting relationship with another. Dani's slow, possibly crazed smile during the controlled chaos of the final conflagration – the film's most operatically pitched moment – suggests that her initial horror at the Hårgas's emotional mimesis has been replaced by psychological submission. Whether the rest of us share her apparent joy in this substantial

Figure 4.2 The village women mirror Dani's anguish back to her as a communal form of emotional mimesis, in *Midsommar*. (Source: Blu-ray.)

loss of autonomy – as communicated via cinema's own mimetic function of encouraging us to vicariously share her fraught emotions – or whether we see it as Dani remaining trapped within the "epistemic injustice circle (of hell)" remains an open question. Although it may function as a cathartic ending for many viewers (especially women), to simply read Dani's expression as one of liberation strikes me as shortsighted in light of just what sort of new "family" she has gained. As if complicit with Dani's gaslighting, Aster's reluctance to definitively resolve the litany of emotional torment with which we have so strongly empathized and sympathized (a testament, as well, to Florence Pugh's nuanced performance) can therefore be seen as exacerbating post-horror's "most unholy affekts."

The Invitation: Cast Out of Eden

As we have seen, gaslighting can render one's own emotions usurped by others, destroying one's overall sense of psychological selfhood. *Midsommar*'s Hårga (whom Mark jokingly compares to the Branch Davidians) illustrate Stephanie Sarkis's argument that cults and other closed communities structured on extremist beliefs employ gaslighting on a wider scale to emotionally and psychologically control their members. Some symptoms of cult gaslighting, among others, include isolation from outsiders, division from family and friends, forced dependence on authority figures, and unquestioning adherence to strict rules or expectations of criminal behavior.[44]

Unlike *Midsommar*'s focus on an isolated pagan community operating well outside the norms of modern Swedish society, though, Karyn Kusama's *The Invitation* opens onto a larger vista of social inequality in contemporary Los Angeles. Depicting a dinner party thrown by members of a Heaven's Gate-inspired suicide cult, the film focuses on the gaslighting of a grieving *male* protagonist who has also been displaced from an upper-class milieu. While one guest initially quells his suspicions that their hosts are anything but a few rich "L.A. weirdos" – common enough but apparently harmless – one of the major sources of discomfort in watching the film comes from the protagonist's navigation of bourgeois social etiquette as he (and we) increasingly fear that something about the party is dangerously awry.

The film opens with Will (Logan Marshall-Green) and his girlfriend Kira (Emayatzy Corinealdi) driving to a dinner party, to be held with a group of old college friends at the posh modernist home of Will's ex-wife Eden (Tammy Blanchard) and her new husband David (Michiel Huisman). The group has not been together since a birthday party two years prior, when Will and Eden's young son Ty was accidentally killed by another child. During the intervening period, Eden attempted suicide and met David at a grief-recovery retreat in Mexico as her marriage to Will disintegrated.

Some of this exposition comes through dialogue en route to the party, while some comes through Will's flashbacks as he explores his former domain. We also learn that there was "a lot of money in Eden's family," which is why she still owns the house to which Will is now a visitor; later, when Will comments on the newly-equipped bars on the windows and David's habit of locking the doors, David replies, "I just keep the house a little differently, that's all. It's *my* house." Now effectively "cast out of Eden" when cut off from the money into which he married, Will's former house has become *Unheimlich* – as has his ex-wife's outwardly flirtatious behavior. Clearly still enamored with her, Will's prior romantic relationship leads him to seek her shared emotional recognition of his grief as the night proceeds – which Eden repeatedly rebuffs, having apparently found an emotional renewal in David that Will could not give her.

Although graciously welcomed to the party with sympathetic comments, Will immediately looks uncomfortable and is the first to notice an unexpected guest, Sadie (Lindsay Burge), an eccentric young woman introduced to the group of old friends as someone that Eden and David met in Mexico. Another strange guest, David's conspicuously older friend Pruitt (John Carrol Lynch), soon joins the proceedings as well, and the old group of friends begin to wonder why these outsiders have been invited to the intimate gathering. From these opening scenes, we repeatedly see these old college friends commiserating over the tribulations of adulthood – yet we also see Will's refusal to temporarily disengage from his grief for the sake of collective levity. Alluding to her time in Mexico, for instance, Eden tells Will and Ben (Jay Larson) that "grief, anger, [and] depression" are all "useless pain" that can be physiologically expelled from the body to regain happiness – but when Ben jokes that "shitting out the pain . . . sounds fucking crazy," she suddenly slaps him and states that nobody cares what he thinks. Ben says that Eden and David have been acting strangely all night, but that at least Will "didn't lose [his] mind." "Oh, I didn't?" Will responds, questioning his own mental state and sadly admitting that he "do[es]n't even know how to act" at the party.

On one level, like the other protagonists discussed in this chapter, we alternately empathize and sympathize with Will because grief's effects, including its distortions of reality, are rendered through tropes and stylistic conventions familiar from the mourning film – such as themes of self-delusion, the home as a now-uncanny setting, the sudden intrusion of flashbacks, the muffling or silencing of subjective sound, slow fades to/from black or white, and so on.[45] But since gender norms seldom associate cishet men with "feminine" displays of (over)emotionality – a reason, as noted earlier, why men may underreport being gaslightees – Will's dramatic position akin to that of a female gaslightee registers as particularly striking. In other words, the structural inequalities that typically premise gaslighting as especially (but not exclusively) a female experience are put into sharp relief when a male protagonist experiences similar forms of emotional manipulation, potentially heightening the viewer's discomfort.

Despondent and increasingly suspicious throughout the evening, Will's persistence in isolating himself and looking askance at seemingly normal social interactions even causes his friends to become frustrated with him, projecting their own discomfort over being unable to understand his grief. Tommy (Mike Doyle), for example, tells him: "Of course it doesn't feel safe. You're letting your mind run away with things. I love you, Will, but you've got to stop acting so fucking weird. It's freaking people out." This quick slippage from sympathy to disparagement is not so different from how David initially expresses empathy with Will's grief, but later corners Will, explaining, "You've been acting so suspicious of our hospitality that, frankly, it upsets me a little. [. . .] You seem very distant, very just *off* somehow." Rather, the difference is one of intent: Will's friends may inadvertently gaslight him by second-guessing his intuition that something malicious is unfolding behind the scenes, whereas Eden and David (and Sadie and Pruitt) do so quite intentionally. As in *Midsommar*, Will's grief already marks him out as epistemically vulnerable, and the cultists use this fact to triangulate their own aims by pitting friend against friend. Eden, for example, pulls Kira aside to ask about Will's "agitation," and confides to Kira that "he can be self-destructive" (despite Eden being the one with the prior suicide attempt); later, Sadie questions Will's relationship with Kira, remarking that Kira seems "really distant," and then suddenly offers to fuck him.

At such moments where former members of the friend in-group suddenly find themselves outsiders (and vice versa), when inklings of their hosts' strange responses to very private emotions like grief or lust shine through, then the fault lines between inadvertent and intentional gaslighting become clearer. As the guests sit chatting over pre-dinner drinks, Eden and David effusively praise the positive emotional effects of "The Invitation," the recovery group where they met in Mexico. Although Ben offhandedly refers to having heard it described as a "new EST," David calls The Invitation – a group in which every member has lost someone – more of a "science" than a "weird religious cult." (Again, the post-horror motif of grief, and especially grief turned monstrous by its inadequate discharge, is present here.) He then pulls out a laptop to show the guests what Claire (Marieh Delfino) uncomfortably anticipates is a "recruitment" video. The video depicts cult leader Dr Joseph (Toby Huss) using New Age platitudes to vaguely describe The Invitation as a "family" for overcoming trauma, before cutting to a home-video clip of a group member on her deathbed as Dr Joseph eases her toward passing. When several guests object to having just been shown an actual death video – especially at a dinner party – Pruitt, like the Hårga defending the *Ättestupan*, counters that the video is about "communion" and overcoming the fear of death. David then apologizes to his guests that it was not party material, saying he does not want them to think he is trying to force his beliefs on them. As Kate Abramson notes, though, "Any given gaslighter . . . might be able to tolerate challenges to some aspects of his views (say, literature or restaurant quality) but not others," much as they may tolerate more disagreement from some people over others, based on social standing.[46]

Nevertheless, Eden proposes a game of "I Want" (as in "I want to . . ."), during which she and Sadie kiss Ben and Gina (Michelle Krusiec), and then Pruitt explains how he went to prison for accidentally killing his wife in a drunken fight. As these erotic and violent undercurrents emerge, Claire again becomes uncomfortable and decides to leave early – but, much like Simon and Connie in *Midsommar*, leaving early is not an option. Whereas *Midsommar*'s guests to the Hårga festival try to avoid unnecessary faux pas, here it is the hosts themselves also testing the limits of decorum under the guise of generous hospitality. In other words, unlike *Martha Marcy May Marlene*'s (2011) sympathetic portrayal of a woman who has escaped a Mansonesque cult group but still struggles with its deep psychological effects on her interpersonal skills, *The Invitation*'s active cultists cloak their malicious intent in a thick veneer of bourgeois social graces. Eden and David are such magnanimous hosts that they repeatedly invite Will to rejoin the party after his escalating series of emotionally fraught disruptions.

Viewers are encouraged to share the non-cultists' discomfort over these awkward moments – but, in contrast to mourning-themed films like *Goodnight Mommy* (2014) or *The Babadook* (2014), Will's emotional isolation actually proves a boon by keeping him from being lulled into a false sense of security as the party proceeds. After all, shortly after arriving at the party, Will was teased for the "dirty dishrag look" of his long hair and unkempt beard (grown during his mourning phase), and also for not recognizing the "ridiculously expensive" vintage of the evening's wine selection. Marked off as having less economic and cultural capital than his friends, Will interrupts dinner by loudly asking "Why is everyone acting so fucking polite?" and accuses them of disavowing the evening's strangeness just because David broke out some good wine. In a sense, then, *The Invitation* depicts class status – and especially classed forms of social etiquette – as a sort of "death cult" in their own right, as another means of denying pain in search of a false sense of security and conformity.

As in *Midsommar*, the main gaslightee's intuition ultimately proves correct, when Gina drinks a lethal dose of phenobarbital (taken from a medicine bottle that Will found when snooping in Eden's bedroom) during a toast intended for the whole party. At this turning point to the film's third act, *The Invitation* shifts into more generic horror territory as the remaining guests begin violently fighting against the cultists to escape the house, physically isolated by the lack of reliable cell service. The film's overall style also shifts at this moment, with Kusama's predominant use of long, slow shots giving way to more frenetic handheld cinematography and quick editing during the ensuing fights and chases. By the film's end, all four cultists are dead, leaving only Will, Kira, and Tommy as survivors. Just before her death, Eden confesses to Will that, despite The Invitation's best efforts, she still feels the pain of her son's death.[42]

But despite this potential moment of cathartic release in shared recognition of grieving their former life together, the film's last image sees Will and Kira overlooking the Los Angeles hills as the chaotic sounds of nearby screams, police sirens, and helicopters build on the soundtrack before a cut-to-black. The red outdoor lantern that Will earlier spied David raising had been a signal to other members of The Invitation in the surrounding hills to begin a coordinated mass murder-suicide. Even as the film depicts the bourgeois elite primarily preying on their own kind (instead of upon the lower classes, as in *The Purge* franchise (2013–21), for example), the film thus ends without full narrative closure. The overall effects of The Invitation's efforts are left unclear to us, but their murder-suicide plot nevertheless represents an ultimate negation of others' epistemic-cum-ontological ground – one that Will's grief and class status have ironically sensitized him to resist.

Get Out: Gaslight to the Sunken Place

Although gaslighting will appear in several of the films discussed in later chapters, I close this chapter with perhaps the most popularly acclaimed post-horror film, *Get Out*, whose critical and commercial success derived from its political urgency amid the rising Black Lives Matter (BLM) movement, its somewhat closer stylistic adherence to classical norms than more minimalistic post-horror films, and writer-director Jordan Peele's prior renown from his comedy sketch show *Key & Peele* (2012–15). Of course, these contextual factors should not downplay the quality of the film's Oscar-winning screenplay and skilled direction by a black director deliberately making a watershed film about racial violence with a black horror audience in mind – especially at a time when horror films about the experiences of black people had largely migrated to the direct-to-video market.[48]

Nevertheless, even if more popularly accessible than slower and more austere post-horror films, *Get Out*'s nomination for "post-ness" also derives from a timeliness that seemingly elevated it above the genre's common reputation among horror-skeptic viewers as little more than populist trifles. Indeed, when developing the screenplay, Peele asked himself whether horror's cultural disrepute would complicate the film's political message: "Is it my responsibility to address this issue through entertainment, or *because it's a horror film*, will it be viewed as trivializing the very thing it's about?"[49] For the purposes of this chapter, I will focus on the gaslighting that undergirds the film's central dramatic relationship – the interracial romance between its black protagonist Chris (Daniel Kaluuya) and his white girlfriend Rose (Allison Williams) – as a means of explicating some of the film's ethical-affective stakes for viewers across racial lines, including stakes that may be complicated by the film's own status as an "elevated" text so readily celebrated by white, liberal-minded film critics.

The film opens with a young black man, Andre Hayworth (Lakeith Stanfield), walking around a predominantly white, middle-class suburb, trying to find his way out – especially once a strange car ominously pulls up beside him, its driver's face and intentions obscured. "Not today . . . not me," he whispers to himself as he backtracks in the opposite direction, but it is too late: the driver (later revealed to be Jeremy Armitage (Caleb Landry Jones)) violently abducts Andre, stuffing him into the car trunk as the opening credits roll. Reversing the horror genre's typical depiction of the white suburbs as an idyllic place disrupted by the monster's appearance (as in slasher films like *Halloween* (1978)), Peele instead depicts the suburbs as a place of confusion, fear, and potential danger for people of color (and especially black men) as outsiders to such racialized zones. Although Peele cannot recall whether this scene was written before or after the February 2012 murder of Trayvon Martin (an unarmed black teenager traversing a white neighborhood in Florida) that killing – one of the inciting events for the BLM movement – would have been an unmistakable allusion for *Get Out*'s viewers upon its early 2017 release, as well as alluding back to the longer history of racist violence in "sundown towns" across the Deep South.[50]

Ryan Poll argues that conventional horror films work for their implicitly white audience because of those viewers' privilege to "fundamentally imagine the [everyday] world without horror," to possess a cultural identity not always subject to constant surveillance or threat.[51] Here we might also recall Laura Brown's discussion of "insidious trauma" as more ambient, everyday sources of trauma additively experienced by people of color, women, and other populations who may desperately hope that "it will never happen to me."[52] The film thus opens by centering a worldview more likely shared by horror's oft-neglected black audience, even as the film's underlying critique also addresses an audience of white "allies." As Michael Jarvis summarizes:

> By representing and validating a counter-hegemonic black paranoia that in many ways transcends a strictly horror-film application, *Get Out* disrupts the dominant epistemological grounds attributed to white-centric constructions of the normative theatrical film audience. It is in this way that the race of the film's ideal viewer is less important than their access to a type of oppositional, racialized knowledge – that is, in common parlance, their "wokeness."[53]

Yet, whereas Andre is abducted by direct force, Chris will be subdued through gaslighting's more subtle strategies of coercion by white characters who perform their "wokeness" as a ruse.

We are initially introduced to Chris as a New York City-based photographer with a keen eye for capturing urban life, in an apartment scene soundtracked by the "Stay Woke" chorus of Childish Gambino's 2016 song

"Redbone."⁵⁴ Chris's nervous preparations to meet his white girlfriend's family – who, Rose assures him, are "not racist," just "lame" – during a weekend visit to their country estate, call back to the gender-based paranoia and gaslighting in Ira Levin's novels and their film adaptations. From the urban-based photographer quickly weirded out by the titular suburban automatons in *The Stepford Wives* (1975) to the deceptively friendly but ultimately evil husband and neighbors in *Rosemary's Baby*, Levin's way of "disguis[ing] the monster as something more common place, more relatable and almost comforting" was a major influence on Peele's thematic shift from gender to race in *Get Out*.⁵⁵

Moreover, the film's New England setting (albeit filmed in Alabama) defies pat associations between racism and the American South, refocusing attention on racism in the comparatively "liberal" North. According to Peele, it would be too easy to critique the hypocrisies of white liberalism by having Rose's parents express a "not in my house" attitude toward the interracial couple; rather, it would be more unnerving for Chris to be invited into their home with conspicuously open arms.⁵⁶ Even then, however, it does not take long for Rose's father Dean (Bradley Whitlock) to make things awkward, whether by showing off his collection of Balinese souvenirs ("It's such a privilege to experience someone else's culture"); noting how he would have voted for Barack Obama a third time; going out of his way to acknowledge how bad it looks that they are a white family with black servants; or referring to a deer that Rose and Chris struck during the drive out as "rats taking over the ecosystem."

As we soon learn, the mortally wounded deer reminded Chris of his mother, killed in a hit-and-run accident when he was still a child – a traumatic grief that he has not fully processed, and soon a source of susceptibility to mental control by Rose's psychotherapist mother Missy (Catherine Keener).⁵⁷ Much as these early scenes foreground Chris's subjectivity when responding to an increasing onslaught of micro-aggressions, these scenes also seem to gaslight the viewer into trusting Rose as a political ally. Rose, for example, endears herself to Chris and the audience alike when she pushes back against a white cop's suspicious demand to see Chris's identification – even as Rose's evasiveness with the cop (itself a product of white privilege) also hides her true agenda of keeping Chris's presence secreted away from the authorities. Later, after an awkward dinner with the whole Armitage clan, Rose wonders aloud to Chris whether her family is any less prejudiced than the cop was, to which he calmly replies, "I told you so." According to Peele, this scene was originally drafted with Chris vocalizing his growing unease about Rose's family, but by altering the conversation to have Rose (supposedly) expressing disbelief at the first subtle glimpses of racism that Chris knows all too well from everyday experience, the scene maintains the audience's investment in both Chris's perceptiveness and Rose's trustworthiness.[58] Yet, as Rachel McKinnon argues, gaslighting's epistemic violence can be especially painful when coming at the hands of a self-proclaimed "ally," a figure of trust who might nevertheless downplay the severity of emotional harm from structural inequalities, due to those ambient hurts not affecting that person as much.[59]

Meanwhile, the Armitages' servants Walter (Marcus Henderson) and Georgina (Betty Gabriel) recall Levin's robotic Stepford wives, for a horrific reason that only becomes clear in the film's final act: they express older white mannerisms in young black bodies because the brains of Rose's grandparents have been transplanted into them through the "Coagula procedure." Originally developed by her grandfather Roman (Richard Herd), a black person's back brain remains in place, trapping some remnant of their original identity as a "passenger" in their own body, while the majority of a white person's brain lives on in perpetuity in these host bodies; the procedure thus reinforces the racist association of blackness with the "primitive" brain and whiteness with "more evolved" cognition. Indeed, the procedure's name alludes to the alchemical maxim *solve et coagula* ("dissolve and congeal"), or the Hermetic process of reducing base materials to their "essence" in order to re-condense their transmuted and purified qualities – thus connecting eugenics to a metallurgical-cum-spiritual metaphor.

Even as Walter and Georgina behave in an uncanny way (not unlike a Frankensteinian spin on the demonic body-snatching in *Hereditary*), media-literate viewers will also note Peele's casting choices as canny allusions to other texts: whether Catherine Keener's role in *Being John Malkovich* (1999), another film about transplanted psyches trapped inside host bodies; Bradley Whitford again playing a scientist/orchestrator character, as in *The Cabin in the Woods* (2012); or Allison Williams portraying the darker side of the bourgeois-hipster white girls in HBO's *Girls* (2012–17). Unlike Rose, however, Missy's true colors are revealed during the first night, when she hypnotizes Chris against his will, exploiting traumatic memories of his mother's death in order to plant posthypnotic triggers for later inducing a state of waking paralysis. Commanded to sink into his chair, he slips into a cosmic void where he remains helplessly trapped as the world, framed as the image on a television set, slips away (Figure 4.3). For Chris, this nightmarish image derives from his shameful memories of having stayed inside watching TV for hours after his mother was struck by the car, afraid that confronting the accident scene would "make it real," and now leaving him guilt-ridden that she might have survived had he taken

Figure 4.3 Chris drops into the cosmic void of the Sunken Place, trapped by his post-traumatic memory of the television set, in *Get Out*. (Source: Blu-ray.)

action. This traumatic neglect of his mother thus triggers his descent into "a psychic space of subjugation and ontological evacuation" manifested as both "a form of individual control and the attempted obliteration of blackness itself."[60]

Indeed, Chris's surreal drop into the "Sunken Place" recalls Avery Gordon's evocative description of racism as a "sad and sunken couch that sags in just that place where an unrememberable past and an unimaginable future force us to sit day after day."[61] Peele himself cites Saidiya Hartman's work on the "afterlife of slavery," tying the Sunken Place to Afro-pessimism's recognition of how, despite the cruel optimism of "post-racial" rhetoric, contemporary black life remains structured by the legacy of chattel slavery.[62] Complementing the "post-ness" of post-horror, Kimberly Nichele Brown argues that "*post-black*" is a more appropriate counterpoint to such dubious claims about a "post-racial" present. As a useful descriptor for Peele's aesthetic, post-black instead implies "both a generational delineator" and "satirical and surrealist techniques" that, as in postcolonial fiction, create "a more effective mode [for political critique] than social realism."[63] Much like Chris's wide-eyed, weeping state of hypnotic paralysis, we soon see the real Walter and Georgina struggling to emerge from their zombified physical/psychic entrapment, the emotional strain on their faces suggesting this "suppressed trauma in symptomatic gestures that are simultaneously blocked and expressed."[64] Effectively reduced to slaves within their own bodies, they also represent Peele's post-black "repatriation" of the zombie from an Americanized horror trope back to its origins in *Vodou* beliefs in the *zombi* as a living-dead residue of Haiti's history of slavery.[65]

The following day, Chris wakes with a vague recollection of the previous night, while old family friends begin arriving at the Armitage estate for an annual party. The predominantly white guests repeatedly objectify Chris's blackness with micro-aggressive "flattery" about the supposed benefits of his racial status (athleticism, sexual virility, and so on); for example, one guest offhandedly remarks, "Fairer skin has been in favor for the past couple of hundred years, but now the pendulum has swung back. Black is in fashion." In this scene as originally filmed, Chris replies, "Sorry, but I don't know what the *fuck* you're talking about," and walks away. As Michael Jarvis notes, however, Peele wisely omitted Chris's comeback, since it would imply a sudden break in his pained restraint to be a good guest.[66] As in *The Invitation*, then, maintaining bourgeois social mores goes along with the larger dynamic of gaslighting that invalidates a marginalized person's perception of the world. Yet, unlike in *Get Out*, Will's privileged status as a white man allows him to repeatedly disrupt *The Invitation*'s party and still be re-welcomed back into the fold, whereas Chris feels the need to tread far more lightly.

The film's overall style up to this point queasily enhances the party's veneer of bourgeois restraint and decorum, effectively stranding its black protagonist within an aesthetically "higher" form not often associated with genre-centered sites of black representation. Aside from several jump scares early in the film's duration, the party scene exemplifies the slower pace (à la *Rosemary's Baby*) and distanced visual framing that continues until the film's final act. For instance, Stephanie Graves compares Peele's long shot lengths and wide, static compositions to lily-white "smart films" like *Safe* (1995), especially the Armitage house's ominously "blank" production design and Chris's frequent isolation in the center of the frame.[67]

Put another way, the film's "indictment of a white liberal self-absolution that manifests itself overtly as a form of cultural capital"[68] arguably extends into the film's overall look by rendering this horror film more amenable to viewers with more cultural capital. Small wonder, then, that the only white person with whom Chris connects at the party is the blind art dealer Jim Hudson (Stephen Root), an admirer of Chris's photography, whose high-art bona fides presumably make him less "ignorant" than the other guests, and whose literal blindness to Chris's race marks him as a potential ally. (Drawing a rough parallel between race and disability, Hudson describes his disability as the result of an unfair "genetic disease," a condition that the other party guests would not understand.) During the film's final scenes, however, Hudson will demonstrate that high-minded cultural gatekeepers – including some of the white, liberal film critics who championed *Get Out* for its "elevated" and "comedic" take on the horrors of modern black life – are not necessarily innocent of such fetishization themselves.

Chris's only major point of party disruption comes after a lone Japanese guest bluntly asks him, "Do you think being African American has more advantage or disadvantage in the modern world?" Chris defers to the only other guest of African descent at the party, "Logan King" (actually the abducted Andre Hayworth), whose older white mannerisms and submissive demeanor paint him as an Uncle Tom figure ("I find that the African American experience, for me, has been, for the most part, very good").[69] Suspicious about Logan's true identity, Chris surreptitiously snaps photos to send to his friend Rod (Lil Rel Howery), a Transportation Security Administration (TSA) officer – but the camera-phone flash triggers Logan's panicked outburst warning Chris to "Get out!" For Peele, this scene's alternation between Chris's desire to find someone else to corroborate his experience and a subsequent ratcheting up of his paranoia plays upon a "sort of gaslighting effect that's always inching you closer to the inevitable, horrific conclusion."[70] Moreover, the camera flash that allows the real Andre to momentarily shine through not only gives voice to the black viewer's potential frustration with our otherwise rational protagonist, but also hints at the use of personal cameras as a contemporary tool for capturing the forms of anti-black brutality that authority figures have too often ignored or disbelieved – a larger form of cultural gaslighting that BLM activism had raised to nationwide awareness by the time of *Get Out*'s release.[71]

Feeling increasingly alienated from the party, Chris retreats with Rose to the nearby lakeside, where he expresses discomfort with both his fetishization and the traumatic memories lingering from the previous night's hypnosis session. Much as Chris tearfully admits to her about his childhood refusal to leave the TV set to help his dying mother, he chooses to remain sitting beside the lake with her for hours as the sun sets around them, rather than following Andre's command to "get out" before it is too late. Hence, it is particularly ironic that the white party guests are busy bidding on Chris in a silent slave auction during this very scene where he acknowledges mass media's role as (in Peele's words) another "modern form of abduction," but yet again sits and delays for too long instead of decisively taking action.[72]

Only once the couple returns to the Armitage house, as the party guests leave, are Rose's true motives fully revealed: Chris finds a box of photos of her former romantic conquests, then Rose prevents his escape by refusing to turn over her car keys. Despite her initial characterization as an anti-racist ally, Chris discovers that Rose has repeatedly dated a series of black people (including Walter and Georgina) as a ploy to acquire new bodies for the Coagula procedure.[73] As Ryan Poll and Michael Jarvis both note, Chris and these other ensnared folks may have been more readily gaslighted because they imagined themselves in a "post-racial" romance like *Guess Who's Coming to Dinner?* (1967), one of the film's other major intertexts – but a horror audience likely intuits, based on generic context, that far darker intentions are at work.[74] For example, Chris originally attributed Walter and Georgina's strange behavior to potential jealousy or disapproval over his relationship with Rose – much as *Guess*'s African American maid Tillie (Isabel Sanford) resents the interracial romance at that film's center ("Civil rights is one thing, [but] this here is something else!") – while also recalling the malevolently envious housekeepers in *Rebecca* and *Gaslight*. Furthermore, several times during *Get Out*, Rose jokes about starting a new relationship with another black person (such as Rod) – thus subtly gaslighting Chris with the veiled threat of her ending the relationship. Indeed, the tense tone of the lakeside conversation, during which she guilts him for resolving to head home without her, hints that their relationship may be reaching a breaking point from which she must quickly reel him back in.[75]

As in *The Invitation*'s revelation of the cult's true intent, Rose's revelation that she will not let Chris leave is *Get Out*'s turning point into a final act marked by a far more kinetic visual style and more explicit gore, as Chris similarly fights to escape from an enclosed domestic space. Again hypnotized into waking paralysis by Missy's techniques, Chris finds himself strapped to a chair adjacent to the basement operating room where Jim Hudson, who won Chris in the silent auction, is being prepped to undergo the Coagula procedure. Hudson explains to Chris that, unlike the other party guests' explicit fetishization of black bodies, he does not care what color Chris is. Yet, this purported "cultural colorblindness" is belied by Hudson's admission that he wants Chris's literal and figurative eyes: the photographic artistry that he envies in Chris. Denials aside, Hudson ultimately seeks the same goal as the other guests – a superficial appropriation of blackness under the guise of liberal, "post-racial" inclusion – thus making Hudson and Rose not so different in their gaslighting strategies. After all, the film is not demonizing interracial couples per se (both Peele and his own parents had interracial marriages), but rather the practice of cultural (and physical) appropriation conducted solely on white people's terms.[76]

Chris eventually breaks free from his bondage, self-defensively killing most of the Armitage family in the process (including stabbing Dean with the antlers of a mounted deer head – a symbolic revenge of the trophy "buck"), as Hudson dies on the operating table and a fire spreads through the house. Chris steals Jeremy's car to speed away, but accidentally strikes Georgina in the driveway; remembering his mother's hit-and-run death, he hesitates and goes back to collect her, while Rose and Walter give chase on foot. After Chris flashes Walter with his camera phone, the real Walter emerges from the Sunken Place long enough to shoot Rose and then himself. Chris begins choking Rose to death, but is interrupted by flashing police lights. At this point, much of the audience likely presumes that police officers witnessing this apparent act of black-on-white violence will abruptly kill Chris – much like an ignorant sheriff's posse guns down Ben (Duane Jones) at the end of *Night of the Living Dead* (1968), mistaking him for a zombie – but it is actually Rod arriving in a TSA vehicle. Leaving Rose to die from her gunshot wound, much as Chris's mother had been left to die in the street, Rod jokes, "I told you not to go in that house" – and they drive off.

As with *The Babadook*'s more conventional style and largely reassuring ending, *Get Out* ends with our protagonist surviving and the monstrous threat seemingly destroyed, providing a modestly triumphant note of narrative closure. However, Peele's alternate ending (included as a DVD/Blu-ray bonus feature) was much more ambivalent in tone. In that ending, Chris succeeds in strangling Rose just as two police officers arrest him for murder. Six months later, Rod visits Chris in prison, seeking more information about the Armitage party guests. Yet, knowing that the criminal justice system is already biased against his testimony, Chris is resigned to do his time, having at least brought down the "Red Alchemist Society" and made an effort to save Georgina. This is, then, an ending where Chris nominally succeeds but still ends up trapped within the prison-industrial complex as yet another iteration of the Sunken Place, where black bodies are allowed to remain enslaved under the Thirteenth Amendment's caveat about criminal conviction (Figure 4.4).[77] According to Peele, this was intended as the film's original ending, written to be a "gut punch" to the "post-racial lie" of Barack Obama's presidency – but was later changed to the more optimistically heroic ending as a counterpoint to the racist strains of political populism fomented by Donald Trump's 2016 presidential campaign.[78] (*Get Out* was released the month after Trump's inauguration – a period in which Trump's divisive political messaging also inspired rampant comparisons to gaslighting.[79])

Figure 4.4 Chris remains trapped in a different version of the Sunken Place in *Get Out*'s non-humorous, far more pessimistic alternate ending. (Source: Blu-ray.)

Evoking longstanding debates over the political efficacy of either "aspirational" or "realistic" representation in black cinema, Peele's decision to theatrically release the film with the more heroic, comedic, and, in many respects, escapist ending has inspired considerable discussion. In my estimation, the downbeat ending featuring Chris's incarceration would have thematically bookended the film's BLM resonances by calling back to the opening scene of Andre's abduction. In either ending, Chris has made personal progress by processing through the underlying familial trauma that helped render him psychologically vulnerable – but the insidious trauma of racism, of course, remains intact. Poll concurs that the downbeat ending is ideologically consistent with the rest of the film, but also cautions that because works of Afro-pessimism can evoke similar feelings of entrapment and dehumanization as the Sunken Place itself, the glimmer of hope offered by the theatrical ending may be more welcomed by black viewers – even as it can simultaneously play into the white "liberal fantasy" of "solution and escape from slavery."[80] Put another way, unlike gaslighting's epistemic violence, Afro-pessimism corroborates the truth of one's circumstances as a black person living in the long shadow of slavery – but this recognition does not necessarily make for a crowd- (or critic-) pleasing movie, since it may feel disempoweringly oppressive.

On the one hand, the creators of post-horror films about gaslighting may seem subtly complicit with the psychological cruelty inflicted on their protagonists by denying them (and us) a classical sense of narrative closure, as seen in *Midsommar* and *The Invitation*. On the other hand, satisfyingly resolved endings run the risk of throwing a bone to the Jim Hudsons of the world – those self-congratulatory arbiters of cultural value who would prefer to live in a state that Diane Shoos calls "post-awareness." Like "post-racial" rhetoric, this form of "ideological gaslighting" allows liberal viewers to feel themselves savvy about the existence of structural inequalities – thereby absolving themselves of its perpetuation – but still fall back on outdated ideas about who is truly to blame (the proverbial "few bad apples").[81] Peele verges on doing this by implying that Roman Armitage developed the Coagula procedure as retribution for having been defeated by Jesse Owens in the 1936 Olympic qualifying rounds ("He almost got over it," Dean says). Still, to Peele's credit, he excised a subplot about the Red Alchemist Society's origins in the Knights Templars' search for immortality. In other words, Peele tiptoed close to attributing the film's sources of evil to personal vengeance or esoteric weirdness, rather than racism's endemic effects across American society.

Linda Williams argues, however, that American racial melodramas dating back to *Uncle Tom's Cabin* (1852) still share Gothic horror's condensation of moral oppositions into the characters of the good person who suffers and the evil person who creates suffering. Such narratives of spectacle and pathos may be used to generate sympathy for black people's historical plight, but:

> Though white viewers want to think that their crossracial sympathy is a reaction to a violence that is external to themselves, the inescapable logic of the dialectic of the melodrama of black and white is that violence is necessary both to keep the black man in his place *and* to generate the recognition of virtue that seeks to get him out of this place.[82]

Williams argues that melodrama is a sort of *Ur*-genre subtending many other popular film genres, including both horror and comedy, which raises the question of how *Get Out*'s use of humor functions in relation to its gaslighting themes.[83] Despite Peele's declaration of the film as a "social thriller," *Get Out* was notoriously nominated for a Golden Globe award in the category of "Best Motion Picture – Musical or Comedy." Although hardly the first time that the Hollywood Foreign Press Association has dubiously consigned a film to one of its two Best Motion Picture categories ("Horror" being so far beyond the pale as to merit categorical inclusion in its own right, of course), Peele famously tweeted in response: "'Get Out' is a documentary."[84] He continued elsewhere, "The reason for the visceral response to this movie being called a comedy is that we are still living in a time in which African American cries for justice aren't being taken seriously. It's important to acknowledge that though there are funny moments, the systemic racism that the movie is about is very real."[85]

While likely due in part to Peele's prior renown as a comedian, this generic (mis)labeling raises questions about who found what elements "funny" in the film, and what kind of laughter might have been generated. On one level, films about gaslighting are adept at creating nervous laughter at moments when the gaslightee struggles within interpersonal situations, or even light chuckles of recognition when we are privy to more information than the protagonist or detect clues about the true motives of a gaslighter.[86] More so than other types of post-horror films, then, films about gaslighting may feature a dark kind of "cringe" humor that borders on the anxious or painful. A folk-horror film like *Midsommar* lends itself to this humor because, much like Chris's status as an outsider awkwardly looking in (and being scrutinized in return by the in-group members), cross-cultural misunderstandings can breed moments when the culturally different perspectives held by a collective group undercut an isolated protagonist's existing worldview.[87]

Yet, *Get Out* differs because of its inclusion of much broader humor, as epitomized by the figure of Rod. Spatially and technologically separated from Chris for most of the film due to unreliable cell reception, Rod nevertheless puts enough of the clues together and offers a humorous running commentary on the action from afar, culminating in his "told-you-so" moment at the end. Peele has repeatedly stressed Rod's narrative function as both a source of comic relief, by offering levity at the film's darkest moments, and as an internalized stand-in for the black horror viewer. Peele, for instance, acknowledges the "true stereotype" of "black horror fans being very vocal about how dumb the [typically white] lead character is being. I think this comes from frustration of lack of representation, not just of our skin, but our sensibility."[88] The contrast between these two types of humor emerges, for example, when Rod calls Rose, hoping to record an incriminating admission of her role in the abductions – but Rose (her facial expression uncannily blank as her vocal affect changes in emotional tone) flips the conversation by accusing Rod of calling her out of sexual interest. Flustered, Rod hangs up and exclaims, "She's a fucking genius!" Of course, by this late point in the film, Rod's comically outsized reaction to his frustrated plan comes after the viewer has already recognized Rose as a skilled gaslighter; only at rare moments like this do the cringe-inducing humor created by the overwhelming whiteness of the Armitage estate and the humor of Rod's (black oppositional viewing) sensibility converge.

On the one hand, Rod serves as a concession to Peele's existing audience, who might be expecting comedic elements in his first major work after *Key & Peele*. On the other hand, Rod's comic relief also lightens the emotional discomfort that liberal-minded white viewers might experience if watching an unrelentingly grim film about racial violence in the presence of black viewers.[89] Rod's narrative presence – especially the closing comedic beat that he provides in the "liberal fantasy" of the theatrical ending – helps explain why, by making the film more accessible to a broader (white) audience, so many film critics lauded *Get Out* as a "satire on white liberal elitism." That is, providing white viewers with a "release valve" via comedy allowed them to (in Victoria Anderson's words) more easily and "unwittingly repeat the dynamics parodied in the film, invalidating the black experience and ignoring the possibility that the film might not be primarily about the experience of whiteness, nor created specifically for the edification of white audiences."[90] Not unlike Jim Hudson's unreflexive celebration and attempted appropriation of Chris's "authentic" black vision, white film critics could still defer to generic labels like "comedy" or "satire" if the higher cultural capital of adjectives like "elevated" or "post" were insufficient to raise Peele's film from (black) horror cinema's existing ghettoization. In either case, though, *Get Out*'s effusive critical acclaim could effectively gaslight the black horror audience if white critics leveraged their presumed aesthetic authority in order to undercut or diminish black viewers' experience of the film as horrifically and all too seriously true to life.

As we have seen in this chapter, post-horror films about gaslighting often depict the darker side of adhering to social mores – despite these films themselves achieving acceptance from horror-skeptic film critics for their "higher," more "respectable" approach to a largely denigrated genre. Julian Hanich describes the pleasure of collective horror viewing as rooted in sensations that both isolate oneself in one's own affective state and yet cause us to temporarily seek comfort in shared moments of dread when "we tacitly presuppose that the other viewers not only see and hear but also think and feel alike."[91] If these expected pleasures are not delivered, post-horror films may feel too boring, ambiguous, or emotionally oppressive to sit through, and they may inspire responses not unlike self-help guides' recommendations for how to escape gaslighting relationships: severing the experience by walking out. (Anecdotally, I have witnessed a number of such walkouts for many films discussed in this book – presumably from boredom or frustration, but occasionally from feelings of anger or distress, if the timing of these exits was any indication.) Hence the anxious feelings of ambivalent belonging felt by the protagonists of these films could also be implicitly felt by populist viewers who find themselves wondering, "Do I belong in the audience for this movie? What is this movie doing in the multiplex? Why did the critics/trailers make this movie out to be so scary?" and so on.

Yet, because Peele was adamant about keeping his film accessible, *Get Out*'s use of humor as a leavening agent allowed it to find a considerably larger (cross-racial) audience than post-horror films that can seem alienatingly ambiguous or even cruel to their protagonists (especially without the benefit of satisfying narrative closure). Thus viewers themselves did not necessarily "get out" of the theater, but what different viewers truly got out of the film, as regards the proportion of horror to humor, is more open to debate. Despite those shared moments of dread inspired by Peele's depiction of racial inequality as a structural influence on gaslighting, the film's critical response – as a horror text made aesthetically "safe" for high-minded white critics, but at the potential cost of downplaying its black viewers' experiences – suggests how this concession to entertainment value may also complicate how much white and non-white viewers indeed "thought and felt alike" in response to its provocations. Regarding Peele's initial reservations about potentially trivializing its deadly serious subject matter, the film's closeness to the horror genre was ultimately less of a threat to its overall political message than its closing appeals to comedy and emotional uplift.

In this sense, post-horror films about ominous shifts in epistemic ground might also reflect their own uneasy standing between genres and modes – yet, as we saw in Chapter 2, they more often do so to greater critical than widely popular success. For a film with an explicitly political message, achieving popular success – as *Get Out* certainly did – may be especially efficacious, but many other post-horror films appear more content to exist in a more aesthetically rarified, less overtly politicized realm (perhaps due, in some small part, to identity-based privileges already enjoyed by many of their creators, including whiteness or cishet maleness). In some cases, this rarified realm is also connoted by the films' desolate and depopulated settings, generating dread through feeling immersed in the natural sublime. Much as all three of the gaslighting-themed films discussed in this chapter rely on physically isolating their protagonists from potential corroborators of their experience, the next chapter examines how post-horror's frequent use of rural and especially wild landscapes heightens the emotional desolation sensed by audience members.

Notes

1. Kate Abramson, "Turning Up the Lights on Gaslighting," *Philosophical Perspectives*, 28 (2014), p. 23.
2. Andrea S. Walsh, *Women's Film and Female Experience, 1940–1950* (Westport, CT: Praeger, 1984), p. 177.

3. Diane Waldman, "'At Last I Can Tell It to Someone!': Feminine Point of View and Subjectivity in the Gothic Romance Film of the 1940s," *Cinema Journal*, 23, no. 2 (1984), pp. 31–2; Mary Ann Doane, *The Desire to Desire: The Woman's Film of the 1940s* (Bloomington, IN: Indiana University Press, 1987), pp. 123–5, 127.
4. John Fletcher, "Primal Scenes and the Female Gothic: *Rebecca* and *Gaslight*," *Screen*, 36, no. 4 (1995), p. 358.
5. Waldman, "At Last I Can Tell It to Someone!," 36.
6. Guy Barefoot, *Gaslight Melodrama: From Victorian London to 1940s Hollywood* (New York: Continuum, 2001), pp. 4–5. Quote at p. 5.
7. Waldman, "At Last I Can Tell It to Someone!," 36–8. *The Invisible Man* (2020), in which a woman's abusive husband fakes his own suicide and then attempts to drive her insane (and thereby deprive her of an inheritance) under the ghostly guise of invisibility, represents a contemporary Hollywood take on the *Gaslight* narrative. In that film, however, the sadistic husband is already wealthy and deliberately leaves his wife the inheritance with the main objective of psychologically torturing her.
8. Diane L. Shoos, *Domestic Violence in Hollywood Film: Gaslighting* (New York: Palgrave Macmillan, 2017), pp. 5, 55.
9. Walsh, *Women's Film and Female Experience*, 183, 190–1.
10. Adrienne Rich, "Women and Honor: Some Notes on Lying," in *On Secrets, Lies, and Silence: Selected Prose 1966–1978* (New York: W. W. Norton, 1979), p. 190.
11. Victor Calef and Edward M. Weinshel, "Some Clinical Consequences of Projection: Gaslighting," *Psychoanalytic Quarterly*, 50, no. 1 (1981), pp. 47, 52, 64.
12. Robin Stern, *The Gaslight Effect: How to Spot and Survive the Hidden Emotional Manipulation Others Use to Control Your Life* (New York: Harmony Books, 2018), p. 3, 5, 8–9.
13. Abramson, "Turning Up the Lights on Gaslighting," 2, 6, 8, 11–12.
14. Stern, *The Gaslight Effect*, 3.
15. Stephanie Sarkis, *Gaslighting: Recognize Manipulative and Emotionally Abusive People – and Break Free* (Boston: Da Capo, 2018), p. 27.
16. Stern, *The Gaslight Effect*, 45, 156–7. Also see Shoos, *Domestic Violence in Hollywood Film*, 5, 11–12, 57, 161.
17. Abramson, "Turning Up the Lights on Gaslighting," 3, 22.
18. Rachel McKinnon, "Allies Behaving Badly: Gaslighting as Epistemic Injustice," in *The Routledge Book of Epistemic Injustice*, eds Ian James Kidd, José Medina, and Gaile Pohlhaus, Jr (New York: Routledge, 2017), p. 191 (original emphasis).
19. Stern, *The Gaslight Effect*, 41. People with borderline personality disorder, such as Dani's sister, commonly use gaslighting to exert power (Sarkis, *Gaslighting*, 226), which suggests that Dani may already be susceptible due to past gaslighting from within her own family.

20. Stern, *The Gaslight Effect*, 20–1.
21. Sarkis, *Gaslighting*, 12–13, 19, 23.
22. Julian Hanich, *Cinematic Emotion in Horror Films and Thrillers: The Aesthetic Paradox of Pleasurable Fear* (New York: Routledge, 2010), pp. 180, 183–6.
23. Adam Scovell, *Folk Horror: Hours Dreadful and Things Strange* (Leighton Buzzard: Auteur, 2017), pp. 7, 17–18, 22, 24, 80 (quote at p. 80).
24. Emily Yoshida, "'I Really Don't Know What I've Done': Director Ari Aster Attempts to Explain How He Got from *Hereditary* to *Midsommar* in Two and a Half Years," *Vulture*, July 1, 2019 <https://www.vulture.com/2019/07/ari-aster-midsommar-interview.html>.
25. Sonia Rao, "The Horrifying 'Midsommar' is a Breakup Movie, According to Director Ari Aster," *Washington Post*, July 11, 2019 <https://www.washingtonpost.com/arts-entertainment/2019/07/11/horrifying-midsommar-is-breakup-movie-according-director-ari-aster/>. This "fairy tale" comparison did not, however, become a major means for critics to distance *Midsommar* from "horror," because the film's horrific elements remained foregrounded. By contrast, the critical success of *The Shape of Water* (2017) was due, in part, to its far closer resemblance to a fairy-tale romance than a horror film.
26. Yoshida, "I Really Don't Know What I've Done."
27. "Win Couples Therapy from *Midsommar* and Talkspace / Official Promo HD / A24," YouTube, September 25, 2019 <https://www.youtube.com/watch?v=qQ3qxTIsOhQ>.
28. Scovell, *Folk Horror*, 7, 28–9. On the film's deeper connections to folkloric and mythic traditions, also see Sandra Huber, "Blood and Tears and Potions and Flame: Excesses of Transformation in Ari Aster's *Midsommar*," *Frames Cinema Journal*, no. 16 (Winter 2019) <https://framescinemajournal.com/article/blood-and-tears-and-potions-and-flame-excesses-of-transformation-in-ari-asters-midsommar/>.
29. Birgitta Odén, "Ättestupan – Myt eller Verklighet?" *Scandia: Tidskrift för Historisk Forskning*, 62, no. 2 (1996), pp. 221–34.
30. Sarkis, *Gaslighting*, 64.
31. See Aaron Michael Kerner, *Torture Porn in the Wake of 9/11: Horror, Exploitation, and the Cinema of Sensation* (New Brunswick, NJ: Rutgers University Press, 2015), chs 5–6.
32. Scovell, *Folk Horror*, 184.
33. Sophie Lewis, "The Satanic Death-Cult is Real," *Commune*, no. 4 (Fall 2019) <https://communemag.com/the-satanic-death-cult-is-real/>.
34. An extended scene in the director's cut makes it clearer that, although Christian is initially hesitant due to Dani's presence, he is already willing to go through with the sex ritual, regardless of later being drugged by the Hårga during the process itself. Siv additionally frames it as providing "a unique glimpse into our sexual rites" for his research – though his agreement to participate indicates his unethical approach to ethnographic protocols.
35. Stern, *The Gaslight Effect*, 35.

36. In a director's cut scene, a young Hårga boy offers to drown himself in the river to appease their Goddess's hunger. Occurring on the same evening after the *Ättestupan*, Dani fears a repeat of the disturbing suicide, but several villagers call off the sacrifice, the boy having proved his bravery. Although all part of the ritual-as-performance, the boy's gesture ironically prefigures Dani's later willingness to sacrifice Christian to prove her newfound belonging to the community.
37. In the wake of the epistemic violence she has experienced as a woman, Dani's decision to join the community may also stem from its more equal standing between men and women. Earlier, Father Odd (Mats Blomgren) explains that the men's "somewhat girly" frocks are meant to evoke the "hermaphroditic" qualities of nature, and he clearly shares village seniority with Siv.
38. Fletcher, "Primal Scenes and the Female Gothic," 368.
39. However, a pre-credit close-up of Dani ingesting the commonly abused anti-anxiety drug lorazepam provides an early clue that she may already be less mentally stable (and thus her perception of events less reliable) than the viewer suspects, even before her family tragedy occurs.
40. Abramson, "Turning Up the Lights on Gaslighting," 16.
41. Michael T. Taussig, *Mimesis and Alterity: A Particular History of the Senses* (New York: Routledge, 1993), pp. xv, xvii–xix (quoted at p. xvii), 19–32, 46–7, 52–4, 58. Also see James George Frazer, *The Golden Bough: A Study in Magic and Religion*, 3rd edn (New York: Macmillan, 1913); and Mekado Murphy, "Ari Aster on the Bright and Dark Sides of 'Midsommar,'" *New York Times*, July 3, 2019 <https://www.nytimes.com/2019/07/03/movies/midsommar-ari-aster.html>.
42. Huber, "Blood and Tears and Potions and Flame."
43. Taussig, *Mimesis and Alterity*, 46.
44. Sarkis, *Gaslighting*, 116–18.
45. Richard Armstrong, *Mourning Films: A Critical Study of Loss and Grieving in Cinema* (Jefferson, NC: McFarland, 2012), pp. 169, 176–9, 183–6, 193.
46. Abramson, "Turning Up the Lights on Gaslighting," 10.
47. As if picking up where *The Invitation* leaves off, *The Lodge* (2019) imagines what might become of a sole surviving suicide-cultist who, despite seeming to have been rehabilitated, reverts to her murderously fanatical ways when isolated with her stepchildren-to-be within the eponymous mountain retreat.
48. Robin R. Means Coleman, *Horror Noire: Blacks in American Horror Films from the 1890s to Present* (New York: Routledge, 2011), pp. 205–15.
49. Jordan Peele, "Notes on the Screenplay," *Get Out: The Complete Annotated Screenplay* (Los Angeles: Inventory Press, 2019), p. 17 (emphasis mine).
50. Peele, "Annotations," *Get Out*, 168 n1–2; Ryan Poll, "Can One *Get Out*? The Aesthetics of Afro-Pessimism," *Journal of the Midwest Modern Language Association*, 51, no. 2 (2018), pp. 73–6; Elizabeth A. Patton, "*Get Out* and the Legacy of Sundown Suburbs in Post-Racial America," *New Review of Film and Television Studies*, 17, no. 3 (2019), pp. 3–4.

51. Poll, "Can One *Get Out?*," 69–70, 91 (quote at p. 69).
52. Laura S. Brown, "Not Outside the Range: One Feminist Perspective on Psychic Trauma," *American Imago*, 48, no. 1 (1991), p. 128.
53. Michael Jarvis, "Anger Translator: Jordan Peele's *Get Out*," *Science Fiction Film and Television*, 11, no. 1 (2018), p. 102.
54. The music video for Childish Gambino's "This Is America" (2018), directed by Hiro Murai, can be read as a thematic counterpart to *Get Out*, depicting sudden eruptions of violence as an everyday threat that a young black man ultimately struggles to flee.
55. Peele, "Annotations," 174 n36. Also see Jarvis, "Anger Translator," 98, 101. Character names like "Rose" and "Roman" Armitage also allude back to character names from *Rosemary's Baby*.
56. Peele, "Annotations," 170 n14.
57. Chris's sympathy for this supposed vermin resembles a very similar scene in *The Invitation* when Will and Kira (another interracial couple) hit a coyote during their drive to the dinner party. Will kills the wounded animal with a tire iron, which David endorses as "mercy" – although this ostensible expression of humanity foreshadows the cult's nefarious goal of achieving "peace through death."
58. Peele, "Annotations," 169 n13, 171 n23; Jordan Peele, director's commentary track, *Get Out*, DVD/Blu-ray (Universal City, CA: Universal Studios, 2017).
59. McKinnon, "Allies Behaving Badly," 192–3.
60. Christopher Lloyd, "'I Told You Not to Go into That House': *Get Out* and Horror's Racial Politics," in *Make America Hate Again: Trump-Era Horror and the Politics of Fear*, ed. Victoria McCollum (London: Routledge, 2019), p. 113.
61. Avery F. Gordon, *Ghostly Matters: Haunting and the Sociological Imagination* (Minneapolis, MN: University of Minnesota Press, 2008), p. 4.
62. Peele, "Notes on the Screenplay," 17; Poll, "Can One *Get Out?*," 70–1. Also see Saidiya Hartman, *Lose Your Mother: A Journey Along the Atlantic Slave Route* (New York: Farrar, Straus, and Giroux, 2008); and Lauren Berlant, *Cruel Optimism* (Durham, NC: Duke University Press, 2011).
63. Kimberly Nichele Brown, "'Stay Woke': Post-Black Filmmaking and the Afterlife of Slavery in Jordan Peele's *Get Out*," in *Slavery and the Post-Black Imagination*, eds Bertram D. Ashe and Ilka Saal (Seattle, WA: University of Washington Press, 2020), p. 107.
64. Tarja Laine, "Traumatic Horror Beyond the Edge: *It Follows* and *Get Out*," *Film-Philosophy*, 23, no. 3 (2019), p. 296.
65. Among others, see Wade Davis, *The Serpent and the Rainbow* (New York: Simon & Schuster, 1985).
66. Jarvis, "Anger Translator," 100.
67. Stephanie A. Graves, "Jordan Peele's *Get Out* (2017) – Smart Horror," in *Horror: A Companion*, ed. Simon Bacon (Oxford: Peter Lang, 2019), pp. 131–2. Also see Laine, "Traumatic Horror," 299.

68. Jarvis, "Anger Translator," 103.
69. "Logan's" response hints that the Japanese man may symbolize how Asian Americans are often upheld as a "Model Minority" that African Americans should supposedly emulate. The Japanese guest is also an allusion to the lone Japanese man among *Rosemary's Baby*'s Satanists.
70. Peele, "Annotations," 174 n39.
71. Ibid., pp. 173–4 n30, 176 n52.
72. Peele, "Notes on the Screenplay," 18.
73. The final reveal of Rose's photo with Georgina, accompanied by a loud musical sting, unfortunately casts this "shock" into a homophobic light. However, we might also read the Armitages' acceptance of Rose's apparent bisexuality as yet another nefarious example of (homonormative) liberal hypocrisy, by effectively "pinkwashing" over their white-supremacist goals.
74. Poll, "Can One *Get Out?*," 83–5; Jarvis, "Anger Translator," 99, 102.
75. In an earlier draft of this scene, Rose confesses to Chris that she suspects she is pregnant, further attempting to persuade him from leaving (Peele, "Deleted Scenes," *Get Out: The Complete Annotated Screenplay*, 200).
76. Christian's lazy appropriation of Josh's academic work in *Midsommar* is another intertextual connection here. In both films, Josh and Chris are black outsiders looking in on a deceptively welcoming white culture, unaware that their labor/bodies are about to be stolen from them under the guise of cross-cultural contact.
77. According to this 1865 amendment to the US Constitution, "Neither slavery nor involuntary servitude, *except as a punishment for crime whereof the party shall have been duly convicted*, shall exist within the United States, or any place subject to their jurisdiction" (emphasis mine).
78. Peele, "Alternate Ending" Director's Commentary, *Get Out*, DVD/Blu-ray. Also see Jarvis, "Anger Translator," 108.
79. Among others, see Amanda Carpenter, *Gaslighting America: Why We Love It When Trump Lies to Us* (New York: Broadside Books, 2018). In one of the alternate takes of Rod's ad-libbed final line, included as a DVD/Blu-ray bonus feature, he jokes that Rose was probably a Trump voter.
80. Poll, "Can One *Get Out?*," 91–3 (quote at p. 92).
81. Shoos, *Domestic Violence in Hollywood Film*, 7, 161.
82. Linda Williams, *Playing the Race Card: Melodramas of Black and White from Uncle Tom to O. J. Simpson* (Princeton, NJ: Princeton University Press, 2001), pp. 20, 44, 308 (quote at p. 308, original emphasis).
83. Ibid., p. 23.
84. Jordan Peele, Twitter post, November 15, 2017, 8:56 a.m. <https://twitter.com/jordanpeele/status/930796561302540288>.
85. Peele, quoted in Mike Fleming, "*Get Out*'s Jordan Peele Responds to Golden Globe Category," *Deadline*, November 17, 2017 <https://deadline.com/2017/11/jordan-peele-get-out-golden-globes-comedy-explanation-statement-1202211276/>.

86. On these different types of laughter, see Julian Hanich, *The Audience Effect: On the Collective Cinema Experience* (Edinburgh: Edinburgh University Press, 2018), pp. 196–7, 200–2.
87. See, for example, Marah Eakin, "Director Ari Aster and Jack Reynor Kind of See *Midsommar* as a Dark Comedy," *A. V. Club*, July 2, 2019 <https://film.avclub.com/director-ari-aster-and-jack-reynor-kind-of-see-midsomma-1836044455>; Andy Paciorek, "The Last Laugh: The Comedic Nature of Folk Horror," in *Folk Horror Revival: Field Studies*, 2nd edn, eds. Andy Paciorek, Grey Malkin, Richard Hing, and Katherine Peach (Durham, UK: Wyrd Harvest Press, 2018), pp. 536–42.
88. Peele, quoted in Tananarive Due, "*Get Out* and the Black Horror Aesthetic," in *Get Out: The Complete Annotated Screenplay*, 8. On such active resistance to being "cinematically 'gaslighted,'" also see bell hooks, "The Oppositional Gaze: Black Female Spectators," in *Black Looks: Race and Representation* (Boston: South End Press, 1992), p. 120.
89. See Hanich, *The Audience Effect*, 158–9.
90. Victoria Anderson, "*Get Out*: Why Racism Really is Terrifying," *The Independent*, March 26, 2017 <https://www.independent.co.uk/arts-entertainment/films/features/get-out-why-racism-really-is-terrifying-a7645296.html>.
91. Hanich, *Cinematic Emotion*, 247.

CHAPTER 5

Beautiful, Horrible Desolation: Landscape in Post-Horror Cinema

"What went we out into this wilderness to find?"

This rhetorical question – posed by patriarch William (Ralph Ineson) to the Puritan authorities about to banish his family into the untamed frontier beyond a New England colony's walls – is the first line of dialogue uttered in Robert Eggers's *The Witch* (2015). Among the most influential films to inaugurate the post-horror cycle, *The Witch* is also one of many post-horror films that use wild, unpopulated landscapes as an affective adjunct to their minimalist form, heightening the viewer's dreadful apprehension that larger forces will soon descend upon the temporary human inhabitants of such spaces. And, sure enough, William and his family find plenty of sources of physical and spiritual horror out in the forest, despite his prideful pledge that "We will conquer this wilderness. It will not consume us."

In Chapter 1, I suggested that post-horror films frequently use longer-than-average shot durations and distanced shot framing in order to meta-filmically connote a post-ironic distance from conventional genre tropes themselves. Yet these distanced vistas also invite the viewer to contemplate the forests, seas, and other ominously *vacant* (but not empty) spaces whose pictorial beauty complements post-horror's reputation as a "higher" aesthetic form. Karl Schoonover argues that horror film scholars rarely discuss the genre's uses of wide-open, vacant space, despite how often it helps visually to figure the protagonist/viewer's fears of the unknown or the unknowable. Darkness and claustrophobically enclosed spaces are more conventionally privileged settings, since they so strongly exploit genre-specific uses of offscreen space for generating suspense over the monster's presence.[1] Julian Hanich further explains that atmospheres of constriction and isolation heighten our feelings of dread about what might lurk around the filmic corner – but the endless spaces suggested by deep woods and vast oceans can generate similar affects by feeling constrictive and isolating in their own right, leading viewers to seek relief by imagining possible ways out.[2]

In previous chapters, we have seen how post-horror films generate dread by isolating their protagonists within Gothically enclosed interiors or at a physical distance from sympathetic allies. These examples have included several films where some of the most horrific events unfold in bright, summery daylight, from *Goodnight Mommy* (2014) to *Get Out* (2017) to *Midsommar* (2019). The latter film's setting amid the Scandinavian "midnight sun" in fact became a recurring plaudit, with critics often alluding to so-called "daylight horror" in order to claim Ari Aster's film as more sophisticated and unnerving than horror films predictably unfolding in nocturnal darkness. More to the point for this chapter, *Midsommar* depicts the land itself as less of a threat than the folk beliefs tied to its cultivation – although many of the films explored in the coming pages also figure the natural world as an inhospitable force in its own right. Whereas the previous two chapters explained the fraught interpersonal dynamics at the heart of post-horror films about trauma and gaslighting, this chapter focuses on how landscape shapes the generic spaces that their characters inhabit, in terms of both the human element and the natural world as intertwined sources of horror.

To begin, this chapter briefly notes the importance of "the sublime" as an affective mix of awe and terror when confronted with wild landscapes, plus the recurring influence of Stanley Kubrick's *The Shining* (1980) on the post-horror corpus. As I will argue, *The Witch*, *Hagazussa: A Heathen's Curse* (2017), and *Gretel & Hansel* (2020) share gendered concerns over who is seen as "legitimately" cultivating the early-modern landscape, with women laying special claim to forested areas that become wellsprings of patriarchal anxiety about "monstrous" generativity. While these witchcraft-themed films use the onset of womanhood as a purported threat from within, *It Comes at Night* (2017) and *A Quiet Place* (2018) shift survivalist themes onto external, post-apocalyptic threats along the thinly constructed line between forest and homestead. Much like the films discussed in Chapter 3, these two films use "the building and destruction of the home" to not only symbolize barriers around emotional intimacy, but also to demarcate potential threats to the (familial) future.[3] Finally, I close with a seaside film, *The Lighthouse* (2019), that depicts the ocean as a terrifying void where one's humanity can erode away like so much flotsam, especially if one retains a violently masculine bulkhead against other undercurrents. Although the narrative conflicts within these films often play out in gendered terms, neither men nor women emerge wholly triumphant over the natural world, thus suggesting the limits of the human as a source of both horror and aesthetic contemplation.

Dread and the Natural Sublime

Throughout the films addressed in this chapter, we can see post-horror's frequent use of beautiful but desolate settings as a means of evoking the sublime, in which nature's grandeur – as figured by mountains, forests, oceans, and so on – is both wondrous and terrifying in its cold indifference to the human forms which it dwarfs. Small wonder that so many early progenitors of Gothic-cum-horror fiction, such as Ann Radcliffe, relied on such landscapes as settings. Tom Cochrane argues that the sublime's inspiration of both fear and attraction can be attributed to an emotional sense of self-negation, wherein one celebrates the sublime landscape by imagining one's own smallness and softness in relation to it. In following Noël Carroll's oft-critiqued theory that horror in art must inspire both fear and disgust (the latter of which is absent in the sublime), however, Cochrane explicitly differentiates the natural sublime from the fear created by horror films, contrasting enjoyably thrill-seeking forms of fear (such as safely riding a rollercoaster) with the experience of actually being in the physical presence of vast and potentially perilous environments.[4] Film spectatorship, of course, can only provide a vicarious experience of actually being in filmed locations – but I would answer Cochrane that post-horror's aestheticized contemplation of vast and perilous landscapes still veers closer to the sublime's evocation of self-negation, or at least as close as any other film genre (for example, the *Bergfilm*) might conjure, than the rollercoaster-like thrills of more populist horror movies. Such sublime landscapes may not inspire disgust per se, but they can still heighten our affective experience of post-horror's generic elements that may mix disgust with other varieties of fear.

To wit, much as *Rosemary's Baby* (1968) was a recurring reference point for many of the films discussed in the past two chapters, *The Shining* is an important art-horror precursor for the post-horror films in this chapter. Kubrick's film memorably opens with sweeping helicopter shots of the Torrance family's car traveling toward the Overlook Hotel in the snow-capped Rockies, set to Wendy Carlos's eerily synthesized rendition of Berlioz's "Dies Irae." For both Tarja Laine and Rick Warner, these serpentine shots of the tiny car dwarfed by the sublime landscape, and seemingly followed by an unseen force, immediately conjure a sense of dread tied to the characters' physical isolation amid the craggy peaks, without yet knowing what the impending disaster will be. Even before any point of identification with the main characters, the viewer feels exposed to potentially destructive forces associated with the onscreen environment, but without any means of discharging these potentially overwhelming feelings of powerlessness.[5] Of course, *The Shining* soon presents us with ample (if semi-ambiguous) justification for this sublime dread: from Jack's (Jack Nicholson) incipient madness, partly stemming from his physical enclosure within the labyrinthine, snow-bound hotel, to the time-shifting influence of the hotel's various ghosts, culminating in the final, *mise-en-abyme* image of Jack among the Overlook's 1921 party guests.

Indeed, we can trace a line of cinematic influence from *The Shining* (and, to a lesser degree, *2001: A Space Odyssey* (1968)) through two other films that have proven influential on the post-horror corpus: *There Will Be Blood* (2007) and *Under the Skin* (2013). Warner argues that Kubrick's slow, methodical building of atmospheric dread through the use of flowing camera movements, symmetrical images, unnerving close-ups of blank-faced actors, and avant-garde music (especially Krzysztof Penderecki) influenced *There Will Be Blood*'s spare formalism, including its inhospitable natural landscapes, Jonny Greenwood's eerie score, and its depiction of a father monstrously turning upon his family.[6] For instance, when Daniel Plainview (Daniel Day-Lewis), fixed in a close-up, bursts into cruel laughter after explaining his misanthropic worldview ("I've built up my hatreds over the years, little by little. [. . .] I can't keep doing this on my own, with these . . . *people*"), it is difficult not to be reminded of Jack breaking into a mad cackle at the camera while drinking at the Overlook bar; while Plainview's bowling-pin murder of Eli Sunday (Paul Dano) at the film's conclusion echoes the darkly humorous violence of Jack's axe-wielding rampage and subsequent death in the snow.[7] Both *The Shining* and *There Will Be Blood* also feature conspicuously light music over their end credits (Ray Noble and his Orchestra's "Midnight, The Stars and You" and Brahms's "Violin Concerto in D Major," respectively), suggesting the filmmakers' coldly ironic distance from the immediately preceding horrors. Even *The Shining*'s iconic elevators full of blood (implicitly originating somewhere deep below, such as the Indigenous burial ground beneath the Overlook) finds echoes in *There Will Be Blood*'s many scenes awash with dark oil gushing up from the earth.

As Jason Sperb notes, Paul Thomas Anderson repeatedly referred to *There Will Be Blood* as a "horror film" (instead of, say, a historical drama) on the publicity circuit, even premiering it at Fantastic Fest instead of at a less genre-centric film festival.[8] Greenwood's score, directly inspired by *The Shining*'s extensive use of Penderecki, plays a major role here. George Toles explains that Greenwood's dissonant strings ominously rise upon the film's opening fade-in to a barren New Mexico desert, suggesting the landscape's own opposition to any human intruders who, like lone prospector Plainview, would be unstable enough to even be out there.[9] As noted in Chapter 1, post-horror films often use such atonal scores to heighten the viewer's objectless apprehension – hence the use of musical abstraction and non-traditional instrumentation to refocus the viewer's attention on physical environments rather than people. Saige Walton, for instance, argues that Mark Korven's dissonant score in *The Witch* creates an aerial density complementing the fog and clouds that obscure the surrounding forest, thus evoking a heavy atmosphere of dread tied to the moody landscape itself.[10]

Much like the almost wordless, 15-minute opening sequence of *There Will Be Blood*, during which we are given little more information than the foreboding landscape and Greenwood's score, Jonathan Glazer's *Under the Skin* opens with a long, largely abstract sequence depicting what appears to be the formation of a human eyeball, accompanied by Mica Levi's own Pendereckian score. For Warner, *Under the Skin* inherits *The Shining*'s use of not only avant-garde music, but also its serpentine landscape shots, tiny human figures engulfed by sublime landscapes, and tight shots of a blank-faced protagonist – plus *2001*'s shifts into more abstract, elliptical imagery when humans become possessed by extraterrestrial forces.[11] Reversing the notorious ocular destruction that opens *Un Chien Andalou* (1928), these avant-garde opening shots of a newly created eye suggest a new way of seeing the landscape when Glazer abruptly cuts to a stream raging amid snowy Scottish fields at night, an extreme long shot of a motorcycle careening along a country road in the distance, and finally a head-on close-up of the motorcyclist's helmet as he speeds along. As Ara Osterweil observes, the film's "cinematography revels in penumbral shadow, rendering geography as mysterious as ontology. Fog drapes terrain, corporeal and otherwise. Figures drown in mist; headlights sparkle and blur. Weather speaks, more frequently and comprehensibly than the film's embodied characters."[12]

Only credited as "The Bad Man" (Jeremy McWilliams), the motorcyclist is the silent handler of our extraterrestrial protagonist, the Female (Scarlett Johansson), who hunts young men for their meat. Glazer's very minimalist adaptation strips away the larger scope and more conventional characterization in Michel Faber's science-fiction novel about an underground farm of aliens harvesting human flesh to ship home as a delicacy. Instead, much of the film oscillates between urban and exurban scenes as the Female drives her unmarked white van in and around Glasgow, while the Bad Man tails her from afar to help cover up the abductions.

Most of her prey are men picked up in transit between the urban core and the exurban outskirts, whom she seductively lures into a mysterious black space located in an isolated house, where the disrobed men sink down into a liquid void until ready to be processed. (Several years later, *Get Out*'s "Sunken Place" would replicate this imagery to evoke another horrific limbo where humans are reduced to meat.) Meanwhile, many of the van scenes were filmed with hidden cameras, capturing the Female/Johansson's interactions with non-actors as she feigns being lost (but has actually found what she is looking for). Thus the film not only features a Freudian, womb-like Terrible Place where sex and death commingle, but *Under the Skin* also "renders the terrestrial landscape exquisitely alien" because "the viewer's own gaze is at least triply mediated to see the world simultaneously through alien eyes, the van's windshield, and the lens of the camera."[13]

The most notable exception to such urban-centered scenes during the first half of the film's duration comes when the Female makes a detour to a rocky ocean shoreline, just after we have seen her trap her first victim. Mostly filmed in extreme long shots, she walks along the windswept beach and meets a Czech camper (Kryštof Hádek), on vacation in Scotland because, as he tells her, "it's nowhere." When the parents of an infant child are swept away by a riptide and the camper swims out in a vain attempt to rescue them, the Female bludgeons the camper with a rock when he washes back ashore, too exhausted to move. She drags him off to her van as her newest prize, walking indifferently past the infant (as does the Bad Man when he arrives that night to break down the abductee's camp), who is left to die on its own. Set amid a beautifully desolate landscape, the extraterrestrials' blatantly inhuman treatment of the baby mirrors the cold indifference of the pounding surf that has orphaned the child only hours earlier. Even as *Under the Skin*'s largely blank-faced protagonist might hold us at an identificatory distance from either the monster or its victims, such disturbing scenes leave "spectators . . . too preoccupied with the effect that the film itself exercises upon them" as a work that threatens to affectively wash us away (unless we decide to altogether abandon the screening).[14]

It is only after the Female picks up a Deformed Man (Adam Pearson) with neurofibromatosis that she displays more empathetic traits, by not reacting to his disability with revulsion or hostility, and later allows him to escape the black void instead of processing him. The Female has apparently empathized with someone whose physical appearance makes him seem comparatively "alien" to the other men. However, the Deformed Man ultimately does not make it far: after he wanders nude across a hilly field, in an almost idyllic moment of predawn calm, the Bad Man violently intercepts him at the first line of suburban houses. It is no coincidence that the Female's meeting of the Deformed Man – and the subsequent pastoral moment marking her abandonment of professional duties – comes shortly after we see an image consisting of countless shots of Glasgow life superimposed atop each other, forming an almost psychedelic, amber-tinted mass out of which the Female's face slowly emerges. From this abstract image of extreme oversaturation by urbanity, the Female can only turn back toward a "subsumption by or alignment with or attunement to the 'natural' or non-human environment."[15] Indeed, Faber's novel makes it clear that, of all the extraterrestrials working on Earth, she alone fully appreciates the planet's natural grandeur, her growing sense of oneness with the landscape becoming the sole factor that makes her thankless job worthwhile.[16]

Immediately after the Deformed Man barely misses his safe return to human settlement, Glazer cuts to a strikingly sublime shot of harsh wind sweeping a line of fog across a lake, the fog curling against some rocks below snowy cliffs. The Female stops her van in the middle of the country road and wanders off into the fog, vanishing into a white void that contrasts with the black void she has controlled back at her home base. Having abandoned the van, we next see her framed in extreme long shot, increasingly becoming part of the landscape by traveling on foot (as opposed to the Bad Man's continued use of the motorcycle). Overall, *Under the Skin* gradually moves further away from Glasgow-heavy scenes toward more rural settings as the film proceeds – and, in doing so, the Female becomes increasingly silent as she becomes more attuned to the less populated landscapes around her.[17] After letting the Deformed Man go, for example, she ceases chatting up potential victims and even has a brief relationship with a Quiet Man (Michael Moreland) who takes her on a walk through the woods, past several people on horseback, to some nearby ruins – these archaic buildings and forms of transportation implying her continued move away from modern civilization.

Despite the film's shift toward rural areas and tiny villages, no true wilderness appears until the end, when the Female flees to a dense forest after having abandoned an attempt at sex with the Quiet Man. After passing a suspiciously friendly Logger (Dave Acton), she journeys alone into the moss-covered trees and goes to sleep in a rustic hikers' shelter. Thematically inverting the earlier image of her face emerging from teeming urbanity, now the image of her sleeping form is inset upon a distant shot of windswept trees, implying that her journey toward becoming part of the landscape is nearly complete. The Logger soon returns, attempts to rape her, and exposes part of her true alien form beneath her torn human-skin disguise. For Osterweil, the once-powerful Female tragically becomes reduced to little more than a horror movie cliché – just another woman chased through the forest by a male attacker – that is, the genre's victim instead of its seductive monster. Either way, the active female character becomes "punished" by patriarchal power for little more than being a woman on her own.[18] Returning from his truck, the Logger immolates the Female and, after an extreme long shot as her burnt form collapses in a clearing, the camera slowly tilts up to the sky, following the rising smoke as snow falls onto the lens. As Elena Gorfinkel notes, the Female's body has now effectively become inseparable from the landscape – even its weather – as the snow that slowly blots out the camera's vision bookends the film's opening shots of the newly created eyeball.[19]

Largely stripped of the novel's science-fiction trappings, *Under the Skin* more closely embodies post-horror's discomforting affect through an aesthetic that feels distinctly "spaced out" in terms of not just the cosmic, but also the slowness and distance evoked as the noise of urban space gradually gives way to wilder landscapes. Glazer's film may not seem as squarely in horror territory as *The Shining*'s grand haunted-house narrative, but its dread-inducing exploration of the limits of (human) embodiment more closely approaches the realm of body-horror than, say, *There Will Be Blood*'s more psychologized take on male greed. Distributed by A24 a year before that company's crossover success with *The Witch*, *Under the Skin* thus represents a transitional film in multiple ways, looking ahead to the contemplation of wilderness and other eerily depopulated settings in many works of the emerging cycle. Moreover, in post-horror's witchcraft-themed films, we can see *Under the Skin*'s thematic emphasis on female protagonists who threaten patriarchal order in their desire to merge with the landscape – even as the very shortage of human civilization paradoxically licenses the retributive threat of misogynistic violence toward them.

Witches of the Woods

The Witch, *Hagazussa: A Heathen's Curse*, and *Gretel & Hansel* all associate their protagonists' menarche with the journey toward witchcraft, thus linking the onset of womanhood to the female body's supposed openness to (super)natural influence. From longstanding associations between lunar cycles and the "curse" of menstruation, to fears of women's impregnation by invisible forces, the female body has long been deemed in need of patriarchal control because seen as closer to nature than culture. This patriarchal control has historically included the demonization of gynocentric occult beliefs such as some forms of paganism.[20] In this regard, all three films use the early-modern forest as a setting for the tension between (unruly) female generativity and (ordered) male cultivation of the landscape toward a yet-to-be-determined future. For Gaston Bachelard, immense depth is one of the forest's primary attributes, quickly creating the impression of not only a limitless world, but also a "before-me, before-us" temporality that human-cultivated spaces (such as fields and meadows) typically lack.[21] This anxiety about cultivation also implicitly connects these films back to Chapter 3's concerns around threats to the continuance of the family line, especially when women (such as *Hereditary*'s (2018) Ellen and Annie) become blamed for "selfishly" generating new forms that do not prioritize children's needs. Indeed, Tony Williams argues that the family horror film is indebted to an American Gothic tradition that stretches all the way back to early-colonial witch trials, when women (and some men) were persecuted for alleged ungodly endeavors secreted away in the woods outside the home.[22]

Filmed in northern Ontario, Robert Eggers's *The Witch* opens with our teenage protagonist Thomasin (Anya Taylor-Joy) praying for forgiveness for sinful thoughts amid her family's trial, during what is likely the 1630s Antinomian controversy. As Brandon Grafius explains, Antinomians like William "believed that only the individual could judge his (or her) inward beliefs," which challenged the colonial authorities' position that "only officially recognized ministers of the church could determine who was truly 'converted,' and thus who was to be treated as a full member" of the Massachusetts Bay Colony.[23] Notably, these opening scenes all occur indoors, with the first exterior shot filmed from the family's wagon, looking back at the closing gates of the colony from which they have just been banished; although initially following the wagon in a wide reverse shot, the camera stops to let the wagon recede against the distant underbrush, as if becoming swallowed up by the wilderness. After spending the night in the woods, the family arrives in a clearing where they will erect their homestead; William kisses the ground and leads his family in prayer while Pendereckian choral wails ominously rise on the score. Much like egotistical writer Jack Torrance, then, it is the patriarch's (religious) pride that drives his family into the insecurity of an untamed landscape where, as a temporal ellipsis reveals, "the land itself has rejected them, refused them even its most basic resources."[24]

Months later, the family's crops and gardens lie conspicuously fallow in wide shots of the unfinished homestead as Thomasin takes her infant brother Samuel into the yard to play peekaboo. Visually linking the family's failing crops to its endangered children, this image of failed cultivation immediately precedes Samuel's disappearance, who is silently snatched away by an unseen presence; as Thomasin panics, the camera tilts upward from the blanket where the baby sat, seeing only a branch swaying at the edge of the forest that the children are barred from entering. Adam Charles Hart observes how this scene and several others in the film use alternating edits and the violation of scenographic space to build tension similarly to a jump scare – but to somewhat opposite effect: instead of the monster's shocking emergence, the viewer is suddenly left with a devastating void.[25] Combined with the film's slow pace and contemplative attention to historical and natural detail, such moments help explain why (as noted in earlier chapters) *The Witch* disappointed some populist viewers expecting more conventional generic pleasures.

Indeed, much like the films discussed in Chapter 3, *The Witch* begins with this traumatic loss of an immediate family member, and pre-teen brother Caleb (Harvey Scrimshaw) recalls *The Babadook*'s (2014) Samuel when protesting how his mourning parents refuse to even say their lost loved one's name. However, I would argue that, due to the family's uncertain capacity to keep propagating after their banishment, *The Witch* is centrally about the threat of incest – which also thematically connects it back to the Hårgas's use of both selective inbreeding and genetic harvesting from outsiders in *Midsommar*. Thomasin's mother Katherine (Kate Dickie) observes that her daughter "hath begat the sign of her womanhood" – and, with no extrafamilial women around, Caleb has already begun sneaking glimpses of his older sister's cleavage. As Aviva Briefel notes, we see him looking down her dress and even touching her breasts while roughhousing, just after the siblings have discussed their desire for apples – thus linking his interest in Thomasin's own budding "apples" to the biblical symbol of temptation.[26] Even though Thomasin herself is blameless for her brother's repressed desires, late in the film, her mother attributes the family's slow disintegration to her teenage daughter's sexuality: "You bewitched thy brother, proud slut! [. . .] And thy father next!"

Despite Katherine having also called William's competence into question, her Puritanical worldview is more apt to ascribe blame to unruly female desires, including a conflation of incest and Satanic seduction as monstrous causes of (female) generativity associated more with the forest than the farm. Although Black Phillip, the goat host for Satan's presence on the farm, repeatedly steals the show, the recurring image of the hare – a pagan symbol of fertility later rechristened as a symbol of the Easter holiday – has received less scholarly attention. First glimpsed in the woods where William fails to shoot the animal for food, Thomasin later spies the hare in the family's barn just after having been accused of stealing her mother's heirloom silver cup

Figure 5.1 The hare, a pagan fertility symbol, bests the Puritan patriarch and hints at the threat of incest in *The Witch*. (Source: Blu-ray.)

(a metonym for Katherine's family and former home back in England), and the hare will also lead Caleb toward the witch in the woods when the family dog Fowler chases the animal.[27] Often filmed at ground level and centered in the frame, ominously staring directly at the viewer, the hare as witch's familiar arguably plays as much of a role in the film as the goat (Figure 5.1).[28]

Despite his best efforts to maintain his family's survival, the patriarch is repeatedly bested by a pagan symbol of untrammeled fertility that dwells in the forest – and, to discharge his growing frustration, William frequently turns to chopping wood. Not only is this an act of trying to process the surrounding forest into usable material, but chopping wood is also an activity associated with sublimating erotic energy into physical labor (even being prescribed by the anti-masturbation treatises of later centuries).[29] William's wood-chopping as "masturbatory" behavior thus figures as a form of misdirected masculine energy that could be better spent siring a replacement child for Samuel. Upon Caleb's death, William tries to console Thomasin by describing the wheat field and fat cow they will raise over the next growing season, but she eventually confronts her father with his failures: "You cannot bring the crops to yield! You cannot hunt! [. . .] Thou canst do nothing save cut wood!" And, shortly thereafter, Black Phillip kills William by goring and ramming him into the woodpile, the mountainous stack of logs collapsing upon him in long shot as a visual signifier of his impotent expenditure (Figure 5.2).

Figure 5.2 Black Phillip rams William into the woodpile, covering him with signifiers of his masturbatory expenditure in *The Witch*. (Source: Blu-ray.)

The Witch occupies the folk-horror tradition by not only rooting horror in and around the tiny plot of rurality surrounded by wild woods, but also by intricately depicting the folk beliefs of its Puritan protagonists – especially their paranoia about supernatural assaults resulting from any sins in either thought or deed. Recalling scenes from Benjamin Christensen's *Häxan* (1922), the first fully-formed folk-horror film,[30] Eggers's images of the witch grinding up Samuel and greasing her broomstick with the salve could, for instance, be projections of what the family members imagine has happened to their youngest member, much as the depiction of Caleb's seduction by the witch (taking the fairy-tale form of a seductive young woman bearing an apple) could well be the projection of a character whom we already know is both nutritionally and sexually starved.[31] This is especially possible since, as Hart argues, the woods as witch's domain are represented as a dreamier space, marked by more fluid camera movement and spatial disorientation compared to the static shots and drab realism of the supposed bewitchment on the farm itself.[32] In addition, Saige Walton observes how, after an early close-up of William examining the farm's moldy corn, hanging bunches of harvested corn are present in the *mise-en-scène* of many scenes of possession (such as Caleb's death) – a visual allusion to the now-discredited theory that the Salem witch panic was partly attributable to an outbreak of ergot poisoning (another example of unruly flora overwhelming the human element).[33]

As *The Witch* proceeds, the film invites us to adopt what Adam Lowenstein terms a "subtractive spectatorship," or the horror viewer's desire to subtract human characters from the landscape (through a rising body count) in order to leave the natural world undisturbed by these intruders. Notably, he associates this subtractive pleasure with a "becoming-landscape" desire to lose oneself in the depicted environment.[34] Thomasin herself, for example, only kills one character – her mother – and then only in self-defense, after which she passes out in the nearby shed and Satan finally manifests to offer his pact. In the film's closing scene, she signs the devil's book, disrobes, and walks (in extreme long shots emphasizing immersion in the forest) with Black Phillip to a witches' sabbath, where she joins them in reveling before the fire as they magically rise into the air. Having now become the film's eponymous witch, Thomasin's supernatural levitation into the ether represents a radical break from her father's Puritanical wood-chopping and cultivation of the soil, instead achieving a blasphemous unity with nature (the angles of her arms, in a Christ-like pose, match those of the upper tree limbs) as Eggers abruptly cuts to black.[35] Unlike, say, the ending of *Carrie* (1976), in which the demonized, menstruating teen with supernatural powers destroys her Puritanical mother but also herself in the process, *The Witch* seems to offer a qualified optimism about Thomasin's survival in the absence of a destructively patriarchal family unit.[36]

Yet we can complicate this common feminist reading of the film's denouement (as a liberatory instance of subverted patriarchy and reclaimed femininity) because Eggers's use of historical verisimilitude extends to affirming the Puritans' own "ontology of the witch" as "no less real or tangible than how 'a tree is a tree' or 'a rock is a rock.'"[37] For instance, Thomasin's slow transformation into a witch follows the same stages of possession described in witch-hunting guides like the influential *Malleus Malleficarum* (1486), as if confirming that her opening confession of sinful thought was indeed an opening to supernatural influence. Meanwhile, the film also "embraces Puritanism" by only depicting the fully-formed witches in the dualistic roles of either seductress or hag.[38] Laurel Zwissler compellingly argues that, although *The Witch* can be read as superficially "feminist" by illustrating women's oppression under a patriarchal ideology, the film's own historical reconstruction of the "diabolical witch" more often figures witches as sources of horror instead of empowerment. Thomasin, after all, believes herself to be "evil," and therefore has little choice but to acquiesce to the limited role left to her in the wake of her family's destruction – much as Rosemary in *Rosemary's Baby* acquiesces to her circumscribed role as the Antichrist's mother.[39] When Thomasin, for example, angrily confronts her father about his failings, shouting "You let Mother be as thy master," this accusation does not speak an unambiguously feminist ethos so much as indicate Thomasin's adherence to the same Puritanical worldview that she also chafes against.

Much as *The Babadook* and *Hereditary* implicitly blame their female protagonists' maternal ambivalence as sources of supernatural intrusion, early-modern conceptions of witchcraft saw any negative emotions in women (such as resentment or hate) as potential signs of Satan's voice speaking through them. Thus, for Zwissler, critics who project contemporary feminism's reclaimed figure of the witch-as-rebel onto non-feminist Puritans like Thomasin participate in a historical telescoping that "is on a continuum with the silence of actual victims [of witch trials], part of a broader cultural project of putting words in dead women's mouths. They may be different words than those forced on women through the historical witch trial process, but that does not make them any more authentic."[40]

Put another way, Thomasin's turn toward witchcraft (and the lack of guaranteed survival facing any witch during the colonial era) is less a wholesale act of empowerment than a deferral to Satan as an alternate, masculine-coded figure of spiritual power. Left with no other options for survival, Thomasin has little choice but to turn toward Satan, who has effectively been stalking her throughout the film; like a triumphant gaslighter, he has gradually whittled away her only other sources of support.[41] Hence the joyous look on Thomasin's face in the final shots is not unlike Dani's ambiguous smile in *Midsommar*'s final shot: loosed of her abusive interpersonal relationships in a cathartic moment of becoming "both mythical and vegetal,"[42] but also giving herself up to a new (and dubiously healthy) belief system in the process. Moreover, by second-guessing Thomasin's own epistemic ground in projecting an anachronistic feminist ethos onto her, the viewer subtly colludes with this gaslighting dynamic, attempting to "rescue" from past oppression a woman who would not recognize – and might well reject – that rhetorical move.[43]

By contrast, Lukas Feigelfeld's *Hagazussa* is somewhat less ambiguous about the fate of its titular protagonist, especially given the subtitle appended for its US release: *A Heathen's Curse*. Although its title is an Old High German word for "witch," Feigelfeld allegedly had not seen *The Witch* while working on his debut feature, set high in the Alps during the fifteenth century. As Kwasu Tembo argues, both films depict the horrors of being labeled and persecuted as a witch in an early-modern Christian society, but Feigelfeld maintained that "in the end [*Hagazussa*] is the story of a woman struggling with a mental disorder" (possibly inherited from her mother, à la *Hereditary*) that encourages her to *imagine* herself a witch. Rather than confirming the existence of the supernatural and offering tentative nods to female liberation, as *The Witch* arguably does, *Hagazussa* depicts its protagonist Albrun (Aleksandra Cwen) as ultimately destroyed by madness, social ostracism, and sexual abuse.[44] Her family line is also broken, but unlike Thomasin's self-defensive killing of her mother, Albrun's disaster comes, in part, at her own volition.

Much like *The Eyes of My Mother* (2016), another post-horror film about a daughter turned monstrous by her deceased mother's continuing influence, *Hagazussa* foregrounds its stylistic self-consciousness through four onscreen chapter headings. The first of these chapters, "Shadows," depicts how Albrun's mother Martha (Claudia Martini) died from the plague, leaving her newly adolescent daughter (Celina Peter) to grow up in the shadow of her mother's reputation as a witch. A daughter thus remains haunted by the traumatic childhood loss of her mother, isolating herself from the world to the point of insanity.[45] From the film's first image – an overhead shot looking down on Martha pulling her daughter on a sled across the snow-laden hillsides, set to a simple but ominous guitar drone by composers MMMD – the film's reliance on static shots, slow motion, and extreme-long shots of the alpine wilderness recalls Werner Herzog's early films, as well as *The Shining*'s linkage of physical isolation and incipient madness (including the potential murder of one's own child). *Hagazussa* is even more immersed in sublime landscapes than *The Witch*, and indeed the Alps were the very subject of many early theories about the natural sublime. Throughout the film, spoken dialogue is used far more sparsely than heavily atmospheric sound design that exaggerates creaking trees, blowing wind, distant voices, heavy breathing, and grotesque mouth sounds.

In the film's opening scene, Martha hurries home to her cabin to avoid the threat of local men costumed as "Ugly *Perchten*," or monstrous consorts of the Alpine witch-goddess Perchta. In this Twelfth Night tradition, men masked as monsters visit each home as revelers, ceremonially embodying the threat of evil in order to drive evil away.[46] Here, however, the Ugly *Perchten* bang on Martha's cabin door, threatening to burn down the accused witches' home. Whereas the Puritan family in *The Witch* has been banished beyond the colony for their antinomianism, Martha and Albrun are more explicitly figured as scapegoats within their own community. (This film's recurring goat imagery is no coincidence here.) When, in the next scene, Martha collapses in the snow while gathering wood, having fallen ill with the plague, the Catholic authorities consider it little more than divine punishment toward those secluded mountain dwellers who have been tempted to "touch the darkness" (as the local priest says).

Suddenly forced into becoming a caregiver to her mother, young Albrun is thrust into a maternal role at a moment that coincides with her own menarche – her ability to bear children thus overlapping with her mother's impending death. Throughout *Hagazussa*, Feigelfeld repeatedly depicts such traumatic role reversals between mothers and daughters, but he also does so by accentuating the monstrous violation of parent/child relationships. Albrun's first menses, for example, is shown when her delirious mother calls Albrun to snuggle in bed, but this momentarily tender scene turns disturbing when Martha forces her hand between Albrun's legs and begins bestially sniffing and tasting her daughter's menstrual blood. After this act of sexual violation, we next see Albrun walking across a bog in slow motion, where she finds her mother's body collapsed beside an uprooted tree, a snake crawling across the corpse's frozen face. The "Shadows" chapter ends here, contrasting the sublimely beautiful shots of Alpine landscape viewed at a distance with more horrific images of nature on a human scale.

The next chapter, "Horn," jumps ahead to Albrun as the young mother of an infant daughter (also named Martha), years later. Still living alone in the cabin, with no companionship except her small flock of goats, she remains outcast as an alleged witch. After being harassed by local boys who claim that no one wants to buy her "rotten milk" (a foreshadowing of her doomed motherhood), Albrun is summoned to the local priest, who returns her mother's painted skull from an ossuary of plague victims, as a warning against further sacrilege – yet she will enshrine this memento mori in the corner of her cabin. So desperate is Albrun for companionship that she caresses one of her goats like a lover, fondling its udders and spraying its milk across her hands like ejaculate while she masturbates herself. Filmed in slow-motion close-ups set to her heavy breathing, this eroticized scene depicts Albrun's relationship with her goats as far closer than Thomasin's relationship to Black Phillip – much as her tasting of the milk recalls her mother's tasting of Albrun's menstrual blood. For this scene to appear immediately after she has received her mother's skull suggests that Albrun's mourning for her lost mother is tied to incestuous thoughts inseparable from her prior molestation. Rather than depicting the goat as a path toward liberated sexuality, such as when Black Phillip accompanies Thomasin to the witches' sabbath, it here becomes a stand-in for Albrun's inability to escape a cross-generational cycle of child abuse.[47]

As in *The Witch*, untamed female reproduction figures as a potential threat to social order, since another young mother, Swinda (Tanja Petrovsky), warns Albrun about the "Jews" and "heathens" who come at night to impregnate Christian women. (Because Albrun admits that baby Martha has no father,

Swinda likely suspects Albrun's progeny to be such supernatural spawn.) Taken in by these gestures of friendship, Albrun is lured to a nearby hillside where Swinda and her husband accuse her of being a heathen and rape her, in a scene whose tight, lingering close-up on Albrun's terrified face recalls *The Virgin Spring* (1960). Upon returning to the cabin, Albrun finds baby Martha alive but her beloved goat mutilated.

Much as Jews and heathens in the early-modern period were also blamed for spreading the plague, her subsequent means of gaining retribution suggests that, even if she is a mentally ill woman who only believes herself to be a witch, she mistakes these naturally occurring pathogens for supernatural powers. Albrun plants a dead rat in the spring where Swinda and her husband collect their water; she then urinates on the rat, as if part of casting a curse, and returns home to ceremonially bathe and pray to her mother's skull. Since the germ theory of disease was not yet widespread during the fifteenth century (with the plague's spread more commonly attributed to miasma, or polluted air from decaying organic matter), Albrun's vengeance on her rapists derives less from holding anachronistic scientific knowledge about bacteria than from esoteric beliefs, presumably learned from her mother, in how to seemingly weaponize natural materials via witchcraft.

In the film's final two chapters, "Blood" and "Fire," Albrun and her baby enter a mossy forest where, her vengeance now achieved, she placidly consumes hallucinogenic mushrooms. (From the pagan rituals in *Midsommar* to all three witch-themed films discussed here, the ingestion of hallucinogenic flora is a recurring post-horror trope, associating unruly femininity with altered states of consciousness achieved via naturally occurring entheogens.) Unlike the film's other depictions of the forest as a largely inhospitable place, it now appears idyllic, full of gentle animal sounds as the tree branches high above her blur together. Upon waking, however, the darkened forest begins to take on more ominous overtones as she wanders into a nearby bog and drowns baby Martha; filmed from behind in a painfully long, slow-motion shot with Albrun centered in the frame, we simply see Albrun slip the nursing sling from her shoulder and hear the child's cries abruptly stop (Figure 5.3).

Dropping beneath the murky water and opening her eyes, Albrun sees hazy images of her adolescent self and her mother, both of which vanish into the green void as the screen becomes overlaid by increasingly abstract images of plant material and blood psychedelically commingling in the water. As Richard Armstrong notes, the mourning woman's connection with nature can be aestheticized via pastoral imagery that depicts the natural world as transcending the human (such as the upward shots of tall

Figure 5.3 Albrun drowns baby Martha in the bog before submerging into the murky water herself, in *Hagazussa: A Heathen's Curse*. (Source: Blu-ray.)

trees seen during her mushroom trip), even as her closeness with nature might also violate the conventional bounds of taste, by linking her with dirt and decay.[48] From the worms crawling on her bare feet in the forest to her subsequent immersion in the swampy muck, Albrun's misdirected mourning of her mother and child alike hence become visually linked to her too-closeness with the natural world.

Much as the recurring image of the snake recalls another biblical symbol of temptation, then, these final two chapters of *Hagazussa* do not so much embrace nature's beauty as dwell upon its abject and threatening qualities. Upon returning home to the cabin, a snake crawls across Albrun's resting body (as it had her mother's corpse) and she hears her mother's voice calling to her. Since baby Martha is not depicted as a "difficult" child (like *The Babadook*'s Samuel), Feigelfeld leaves Albrun's reasons for killing baby Martha more ambiguous – perhaps to prevent the next generation of women in her family from growing up similarly persecuted – but we are nevertheless left with another monstrous mother/daughter transgression as baby Martha joins her namesake in death. Were the murder of baby Martha not already reminiscent of *Eraserhead* (1977), the film takes a more grotesque turn when Albrun cooks and eats her child (a different version of the monstrous mother's consumption of her own child than the one suffered by Albrun upon her menarche). With her mental instability exacerbated by numerous traumas, Albrun may have finally acquiesced to the early-modern belief that witches kill and eat infants, even if there is nothing truly supernatural in her own acts of infanticide and cannibalism. Martha's cackling face becomes superimposed over Albrun's own vomiting visage as she realizes the gravity of her crimes, and the dead mother appears in the cabin as if the skull, as a symbol of mourning, has given birth to its former

Figure 5.4 Albrun spontaneously bursts into flames as the sun rises against the distant peaks, in the final shot of *Hagazussa: A Heathen's Curse*. (Source: Blu-ray.)

owner. Finally, Albrun runs to the top of a ridge where her eyes cloud over and, in an extreme long shot, she spontaneously bursts into flame as the sun rises over the distant, beautiful mountains (Figure 5.4).

Whereas *The Witch* ends on a cautiously optimistic note signaling Thomasin's unity with nature, Albrun's demise is closer to the ending of *Under the Skin*: a violated woman engulfed in flames as she disintegrates into the landscape. In *Hagazussa*, however, they are flames of her own making, as if hellish punishment for doing inhuman things to her child, rather than *Under the Skin*'s pathos over the misogynistic murder of an extraterrestrial who is actually in the process of becoming more "human." In interviews, Feigelfeld may have retrospectively attempted to link his film to popular feminist readings of *The Witch*, yet Kwasu Tembo argues that Albrun's story is ultimately one of trauma and tragedy recurring across several generations – especially if we follow Feigelfeld's own lead in elsewhere describing *Hagazussa* as less about witchcraft than the persecution of mentally ill women.[49] From an early-modern perspective, witchcraft and mental illness might have seemed similarly "unnatural," but the sublime Alpine landscape in *Hagazussa* offers its protagonist no real refuge. Unlike *The Witch*'s abrupt cut-to-black as Thomasin becomes one with the forest, *Hagazussa*'s most overtly supernatural moment – Albrun's immolation – does more to erase her from the pristine landscape altogether, as the long take of her fiery end continues over the closing credits. Following Laurel Zwissler's tempered reading of *The Witch*, I would argue that *Hagazussa*'s depiction of persecution, arguably rooted in both misogyny and ableism, merely points toward sources of historical oppression, but ultimately depicts Albrun's choice to kill her daughter as an even more solitary dead end than Thomasin's entry into the witches' coven. Hence, *Hagazussa*'s unrelentingly grim ending makes its visual connections between emotional and Alpine bleakness feel all the more oppressive for the viewer.

To close this section, we can briefly consider director Oz Perkins's first major studio film, *Gretel & Hansel*: a horror movie that feels superficially indebted to *The Witch* and *Hagazussa*, but whose attempt to retell the Grimm fairy tale as a "feminist" take (à la Angela Carter) on witchcraft represents a lackluster attempt to reconcile post-horror style with Hollywood narrative conventions – thereby throwing *Hagazussa*'s aesthetic minimalism and extreme negativity into sharp relief. Although featuring mystical imagery inspired by the films of Alejandro Jodorowsky and a compelling analog-synth score recalling *It Follows*'s (2014) score, Perkins's relatively slow and atmospheric approach to his source material is marred by Rob Hayes's derivative screenplay – especially an obtrusive, painfully expositional voiceover (a completely unnecessary addition that removes any shred of arthouse ambiguity from its protagonist's psychological development) – whose conventionally happy ending reinscribes classical narrative closure and ideological reassurance. In this regard, it significantly contrasts with the narrative ambiguity of Perkins's earlier post-horror films *The Blackcoat's Daughter* (2015) and *I Am the Pretty Thing That Lives in the House* (2016) (see Chapter 7).

Cast out by her mother, Gretel (Sophia Lillis) is now the story's lead character – hence her top billing in the title. After rejecting an early offer to work in a brothel, Gretel instead takes her younger brother Hansel (Sam Leakey) into the woods – though a Huntsman (Charles Babalola) warns her along the way of dangers in the forest. Much like William in *The Witch*, a male authority figure cautions a teenage woman against dark forces lurking in the woods – but the orphans neglect his advice and soon find the witch's house, its dinner table piled high with delectable treats. Presented as the archetypal hag, the witch Holda (Alice Krige) invites the orphans to stay with her as servants, but this is a ruse to fatten up Hansel while Gretel receives tutelage in becoming a witch herself.

As with *The Witch*'s Thomasin and Caleb, Gretel has a younger brother who wanders off into the woods and becomes ensnared by witchery, and as in *Hagazussa*, the film features a fraught mother–daughter relationship between two women accused of witchcraft. Not only does Gretel's menarche occur during her stay with Holda, but the witch empathizes with Gretel for having been similarly born with "second sight." Indeed, Gretel's own favorite folktale (shown in one of the film's few sequences not shot in a storybook-like 1.55:1 aspect ratio) turns out to have been the story of how Holda and her evil daughter were ostracized from their village for practicing the dark arts. Having now found a sort of replacement child in Gretel, Holda tells her that she must embrace and foster her supernatural skills in order to gain power over men, since they will already fear her, one way or another; that is, much as Gretel has already turned away from sexually submitting to men in the brothel, she is now encouraged to develop her witchcraft as a twisted sort of "feminist" empowerment. Gretel's training, for example, includes her use of a magical salve to bend tree branches toward her hand, in a scene that both removes epistemic hesitation (by confirming the presence of the supernatural), and also grants her a degree of active agency over the natural world that is more consistent with the characterization of classical Hollywood protagonists than most post-horror depictions of nature's cold indifference toward humans.

Harking back to *Hagazussa*'s depiction of intrafamilial cannibalism, Holda says Gretel must take the decisive step onto the "evil" path by consuming her brother – but, unlike Albrun, she ultimately refuses, instead using her newly developed powers to save her brother and kill Holda. With the evil witch now destroyed, the ghosts of the children that Holda ate are finally allowed to go into the afterlife, and in her closing voiceover, Gretel pledges only to use her magical powers for good. The film thus attempts to reconcile a superficially "feminist" message of female empowerment-via-witchcraft with a cloyingly broad embrace of family values that feels about as far from *Hagazussa*'s self-apocalyptic denouement as possible. Despite *Gretel & Hansel*'s veneer of audiovisual stylization evoking an "elevated" genre film, then, its thoroughly unambiguous script closes with pat moralism instead of *Hagazussa*'s disturbing nihilism. By resolving Gretel's inborn supernatural abilities as nothing to fear, while also upholding the Child as a sanctified figure of "reproductive futurism," nature is tamed and order is restored.[50]

Man the Bunkers

As I argued in Chapter 3, child protectionism is a more common theme in Hollywood-style horror films, compared to the cynicism toward the nuclear family seen in most post-horror films. Post-horror that foregrounds the natural landscape implicitly invokes these themes by asking whether the land's cultivation – especially by a father figure – can effectively serve the continuance of his family line. As noted above, William's family farm in *The Witch* represents a hubristic failure to "conquer" the wilderness, but that film is not alone in exploring this issue. While *Hagazussa* and *Gretel & Hansel* effectively pick up where *The Witch* leaves off, presenting two very different visions of a young woman's supernatural training, *A Quiet Place* and *It Comes at Night* refocus our attention on the patriarch's role in survivalist scenarios – but, again, to very different ideological purposes as this "bunker mentality" plays out.

Like *Gretel & Hansel*, *A Quiet Place* is a secondary post-horror film (if that) in its far closer adherence to Hollywood filmmaking traditions than *It Comes at Night*'s austere minimalism and nihilistic tone. Indeed, given a wide release by Paramount, *A Quiet Place* was a major box-office and critical success alike, while A24's *It Comes at Night* proved extremely divisive, acclaimed by many film critics but largely rejected by populist viewers. I would go so far as to argue that *A Quiet Place* earned discursive nomination as an "elevated" or "post-horror" film due more to its temporal proximity to more representative post-horror films than to its overall style. The film's central conceit – that remaining virtually silent is necessary to survive, following an extraterrestrial invasion by blind monsters that hunt humans via extremely sensitive hearing – may seem to subvert generic conventions by largely keeping its monsters offscreen and denying characters' ability to scream (as many appreciative critics observed). Yet the film's visual grammar still predominantly follows Hollywood conventions, including predictable narrative beats, average shot durations, and jump scares enhanced by the diegetic need for pensive silence. Indeed, many of the suspense-driven scenes of humans quietly hiding from snooping monsters closely recall previous Hollywood hits like *Jurassic Park* (1993) and *I Am Legend* (2007), while the *deus ex machina* revelation that the aliens can be killed with high-frequency noise owes as much to *War of the Worlds* (2005) and *Signs* (2002).

Per an onscreen title, the film opens on Day 83 after the invasion (a catastrophe depicted though flashbacks in the 2020 sequel), in which the Abbott family loses their youngest son, Beau (Cade Woodward), to the monsters while returning to their isolated farm from a scavenging expedition to a deserted supermarket. Notably, Beau dies because he disobeys his father Lee's (John Krasinski) instructions to leave behind the batteries for a toy rocket – an early dramatic moment that both reinforces how Father knows best and, in a meta-filmic sense, disciplines the audience's generic expectations that this horror film will be just another "noisy toy." Despite the film's visual resemblance to more populist horror films, its sound-centered premise registered most strongly during the theatrical viewing experience, encouraging the audience also to remain in hushed suspense – much as its critical discussion as a "smart" horror film was likely due in part to viewers' need to extensively read subtitles (a practice more often associated with art cinema than populist films) because of the characters' extensive use of American Sign Language.[51]

Like a post-horror film, *A Quiet Place* thus opens with the tragic loss of an immediate family member, but most of the narrative unfolds over a year later, with pregnant mother Evelyn (Emily Blunt) expecting a replacement child as life goes on with relatively little disruption. Although the coffin-like box that she builds to quietly house the crying infant briefly suggests that the new baby will represent a sort of post-apocalyptic death-in-life, the film's overall celebration of the nuclear family still posits children as keys to the future; as Evelyn earnestly tells her husband, "Who are we if we can't protect them?" Moreover, it quickly becomes apparent how daily life is structured by traditional gender roles: Lee has successfully cultivated a subsistence farm and engineered a security system for the homestead, while Evelyn prepares food and maintains their basement bunker. Ironically or not, Lee's patriarchal authority here echoes Krasinski's dual role as *A Quiet Place*'s director-star alongside his real-life wife Blunt – an onscreen pairing that was arguably a major draw in the film's box-office success.

As in *The Witch*, the family has an increasingly rebellious teenage daughter, Regan (Millicent Simmonds), who blames herself for her youngest brother's death and fears that her father no longer loves her. Yet, despite sharing a name with the possessed-hellion daughter in *The Exorcist* (1973), Regan is mostly obedient and does not significantly challenge parental authority. In addition, unlike *Hagazussa*'s depiction of disability (in that film, mental illness) as a "curse," Regan's deafness actually saves her family from destruction when she realizes that electronic interference from her cochlear implants can be amplified to kill the aliens – though these implants were built by her father, thus indirectly upholding the patriarch's role as ingeniously successful protector.

Unlike the failed farm in *The Witch*, *A Quiet Place* presents markers of (male) cultivation as an efficiently operating system, even when they occasionally create temporary sources of danger. When, for example, Regan and her brother Marcus (Noah Jupe) almost drown inside a grain silo while being chased by monsters, this threat of literally drowning in corn could hardly contrast more with the existential threat of starvation created by William's failed crops. And while *The Witch* depicts the woods as a site of potential danger and corruption, *A Quiet Place* instead posits a nearby waterfall as one of the few sites of refuge from the monsters, its natural roar providing cover for Lee and Marcus to speak aloud. Yet, even as this waterfall presages how a broken water line later floods the basement bunker shortly after Evelyn has given birth, the water's uncontrolled flow into their home proves more of a nuisance compared to the monsters' intrusion into the basement.

Lee is the only other member of the family who does not survive the film, sacrificing himself by yelling to divert the monsters away from Regan and Marcus during the film's climax. Nevertheless, *A Quiet Place*'s patriarch goes out as a heroic martyr, in marked contrast to William's death in *The Witch* as a pathetic victim of hubris. Although Evelyn and Regan both emerge as stronger characters in *A Quiet Place Part II*, the sequel's story about the remaining Abbott family fending off human intruders from their homestead also bears a closer narrative resemblance to Trey Edward Shults's *It Comes at Night*, a core post-horror text whose thoroughly downbeat story of thwarted survival casts severe doubt over who is allowed to man the bunkers during a post-apocalyptic scenario.

It Comes at Night opens with a pre-credit sequence, set to ominous strings and the sound of labored breathing, in which Sarah (Carmen Ejogo) mournfully tells her dying father Bud (David Pendleton) that he can let go. Wearing gas masks, Sarah's husband Paul (Joel Edgerton) and teenage son Travis (Kelvin Harrison Jr) take Bud into the woods surrounding their fortified home, euthanizing the old man with a gunshot before burning his body in a shallow grave to prevent the spread of a highly virulent pathogen. If *A Quiet Place* was intended as Krasinski's "love letter to his kids,"[52] Shults's film was, by his own admission, a cathartic response to his estranged father's rapid death from pancreatic cancer – thus tying it to the familial mourning themes explored in Chapter 3. During the writing process, he took inspiration from not only the apocalyptic arthouse dramas *Take Shelter* (2011) and *Melancholia* (2011), but also *The Shining*'s story of a family unraveling within a claustrophobically enclosed living space. While *A Quiet Place* depicts its post-apocalyptic survival bunker as a product of robinsonade ingenuity, the house in *It Comes* is a forest-shrouded stronghold whose deliberately confusing inner geography recalls the Overlook Hotel's labyrinthine structure, with far more of the film taking place within the house than outside of it.[53] Indeed, much as the Overlook's exterior hedge maze mirrors the hotel's haunted interiors, the unpainted but lacquered wooden walls and floors of the house and outbuildings in *It Comes* suggest that the densely surrounding woods – from which the film never offers us visual respite – have turned inward on the compound's inhabitants.[54]

Amid the many interchangeable rooms in the house, only one spot truly stands out: an ominous red door, located at the end of a long hallway near a reproduction of Pieter Bruegel the Elder's painting *The Triumph of Death* (*c*.1562); Bruegel's vivid panorama of the medieval plague's ravages not so subtly alludes to the reasons why this door to the outside world must remained locked at all times. The red door thus comes to symbolize the threshold between the "empty space" of "[l]imitless night" and the tentative security of the "ramified interior," especially as a recurring image in Travis's nightmares. For Gaston Bachelard, the door is such a primal dream image because it evokes "an entire cosmos of the Half-open," capable of representing so many different emotions (including fear, temptation, safety, isolation, freedom, and so on) that the story of one's whole life could be retold as an account of all the doors one has opened and closed.[55]

Meanwhile, the film's invisible threat – much to the frustration of a populist audience expecting that the titular "*It*" would be some sort of embodied monster (even a shapeshifting figure as in *It Follows*) – is closer to how Saige Walton describes *The Witch*'s symptoms of bewitchment as a sort of airborne contagion, a link that *Hagazussa*'s setting amid a pre-Enlightenment plague outbreak makes even more explicit.[56] Unlike the clear, sound-based logic of the monsters in the more populist *A Quiet Place*, "[t]he almost complete lack of a backstory, and only the bare minimum regarding the mechanics of the disease itself, serves to heighten the sense of anxiety that permeates" *It Comes*.[57] In addition to many extended scenes of Travis creeping around at night with a lantern, dialogue scenes often unfold in long takes, the camera slowly panning from one character to another, with minimal light sources emphasizing the characters' enclosure within the darkened house.

Of course, as with most post-apocalyptic narratives, much of the film focuses less on monstrous threats than on how human survivors adapt to their newfound precarity – which is another reason why *It Comes* may seem, for some viewers, like an ill fit with the "horror" genre proper. In the wake of her father's death, Sarah has doubts about Paul's pledge to keep their son safe, while Travis is more concerned with protecting the family dog, Stanley (a likely Kubrick allusion). Tensions mount when a younger man, Will (Christopher Abbott), breaks into the boarded-up house in search of food and water, presuming it to be uninhabited. After forcing Will to give him assurances that he is not infected, Paul argues with Sarah about whether Will and his own family should be allowed to join them in the compound for the sake of strength in numbers. Despite his preference for isolationism, Paul allows Will, his wife Kim (Riley Keough), and young son Andrew (Griffin Robert Faulkner) to move in, provided they adhere to Paul's rigid, almost cult-like system of order (including collective meals, no nocturnal excursions, locked-up guns, and so on). As Brandon Grafius observes, though, *It Comes* ultimately shares *The Witch*'s horrible consequences of an overbearing patriarch trying to tighten the boundaries around his already isolated home in a failed attempt to stave off invisible threats.[58]

Although the two families settle into a new normal together, it does not take long for these tenuous trust relationships to erode. Paul feels threatened watching a younger man teach his son how to do practical things like chopping wood (again, a potential symbol of fatherly impotence). Meanwhile, the younger couple Will and Kim bring an active sex life into the picture, and Travis also fantasizes about having sex with her. We learn that Paul was a history teacher in his former life, while Will was a construction worker – hinting at unspoken, class-based resentments about whose survival strategies will work best, much as the shut-in survivors in *Night of the Living Dead* (1968) are torn apart by unspoken racial tensions.[59] Finally, one night, Travis finds Andrew sleeping on the floor near the ajar red door, and potentially infects himself by helping Andrew to bed, shortly before he finds Stanley mortally wounded from an unknown cause. Before returning wounded, Stanley was last seen barking at something off in the forest before bolting after it (much like the fate of the family dog in *The Witch*); this image of Stanley sensing a threat in the natural world that the humans cannot see also appeared on the film's poster, further suggesting the forest's importance as a source of paranoia.

After the two families quarantine themselves in their bedrooms for several days, waiting to see if either child develops symptoms, Will confronts Paul at gunpoint on the staircase, commanding him to give his family a fair share of food and water for striking off on their own. Following a tense standoff that turns increasingly violent as a struggle between the family members spills outside, Sarah shoots Will in the back to save Paul from Will's blows. Paul shoots at Kim as she tries to flee, accidentally killing Andrew, and then coldly executes her as well. The outsider family may now be eradicated, restoring Paul's unchallenged authority, but Travis has already become sick and is quickly succumbing, so nothing has truly been accomplished. Much as Travis has failed to be Stanley's self-appointed protector, Paul has failed to protect his son and also decimated another family in the process. Harking back to the opening scene with her father, Sarah tells Travis that he is allowed to pass on, and he imagines himself walking out through the open red door as he dies.

The film ends with Paul and Sarah in the last of many symmetrically framed dinner-table scenes, with Travis's chair conspicuously empty (a common filmic means of signaling grief) as Shults cuts to black.[60] Unlike *The Witch*, the patriarch is left to live with the tragic consequences of his hubris, including the potential end of the family line he so desperately tried to preserve – but the cumulative effect more closely resembles *Hagazussa*'s oppressive nihilism than *A Quiet Place*'s emotional reassurance. As Grafius summarizes, "one thing that does arrive at night, repeatedly, is human intimacy. In the horrific world constructed by the film, this intimacy is always dangerous, and sometimes fatal."[61]

Throughout the film, nightmares also come at night, and these shifts into Travis's subjectivity are subtly marked by not only the rise of ominous music in a film that is otherwise largely unscored, but also a vertical narrowing of the aspect ratio from 2.40:1 to 2.75:1. However, Shults's most effective use of a selective aspect ratio occurs during a four-and-a-half-minute span between the armed standoff on the stairs and Paul's killing of Andrew. During this sequence, the aspect ratio slowly but steadily constricts from 2.40:1 to an exceptionally tight 3.0:1 ratio, its almost imperceptible pace obscured by the use of shakier, handheld cinematography within the increasingly chaotic scene. As Shults observes, this use of aspect ratio was not intended to call attention to itself, but rather to affectively ramp up the scene's tension while also implying that the film's nightmare sequences have finally blurred into reality.[62] For my purposes, it is notable that this aspect-ratio shift begins on the staircase between floors of the house, and continues out into the adjacent woods, visually collapsing the psychologically fraught inner space of the house into the danger of the surrounding landscape. Much like the long, wordless opening sequences that call our attention to depopulated landscapes in some post-horror films, shifts in the overall shape of the frame (as also used in *Gretel & Hansel*) help focus our attention on the immense settings that fall within it. This chapter's final example, *The Lighthouse*, uses both techniques to evoke a horrifically slow-building claustrophobia amid an oceanic landscape that could scarcely seem vaster.

Masculine Anxiety and Oceanic Dread

Much as he did with *The Witch*, Robert Eggers took great pains to capture the period authenticity of *The Lighthouse*'s 1890s New England setting, including the construction of a 70-foot working lighthouse on a rocky tip of Nova Scotia, and dialogue inspired by archival lighthouse keepers' journals and the novels of Herman Melville and Maine author Sarah Orne Jewett. Filmed in orthochromatic black-and-white with a horizontally constricted 1.19:1 aspect ratio (first used in 1926 by Fox's early sync-sound Movietone format), *The Lighthouse* also bears strong connections back to *The Shining*'s alcohol-fueled cabin-fever narrative and *There Will Be Blood*'s Gothicized spaces of masculine labor. Indeed, the protagonists' isolation on a barren coastal island, cut off from the mainland by stormy weather and surrounded by the imposing vastness of the Atlantic Ocean, marks an even more inhospitable setting than the mountains and forests explored earlier in this chapter; this is not a sublime landscape that men can productively cultivate, only warn others against its natural hazards. Indeed, as a male-only space where the closest thing to women are hallucinated mermaids, I would argue that this story of "two men . . . trapped in a giant phallus"[63] links the rocky outcrop's barrenness to non-reproductive desires, in the form of violent eruptions of (repressed) homoeroticism.

The film itself begins with the sounds of a foghorn and gulls as a steamship appears from the gray, foggy void of the sea, approaching the island where chief lighthouse keeper Thomas Wake (Willem Dafoe) and his much younger protégé Thomas Howard (Robert Pattinson) will take up their posts. Much as this long, wordless introduction (with Wake's ubiquitous farts heard long before any lines of dialogue) gives the viewer seven minutes to soak in the remote setting, we become additionally aware of the cramped aspect ratio when Howard bumps his head on the door frame (visually aligned with the edge of the camera frame) when first entering their upstairs sleeping quarters. Many subsequent scenes frame these two increasingly quarrelsome characters with little visual clearance above their heads, while isolated lanterns create extreme chiaroscuro lighting effects (not unlike many of the interior shots in *It Comes at Night*). Yet, even indoors, the ocean is an ever-dominating presence, linked to the old salt's attempted dominance over his second in command. Wake's first dialogue is a dinner toast (which Howard refuses to join) asking for the ocean's blessing; later in the film, Wake will invoke the sea gods in cursing Howard, calling for the younger man to be wholly consumed, body and soul, by the sea.

Tensions between the two men slowly build as Wake begins selectively enforcing the US Lighthouse Establishment's manual, by encouraging the taciturn Howard to drink with him in the evening, but refusing to allow Howard to take the overnight watch. Howard wonders about Wake's possessiveness over the top of the lighthouse, and resents being commanded to fill his time with menial but grueling tasks like a "housewife." Meanwhile, Howard takes out his pent-up anger on a one-eyed gull that repeatedly taunts him; filmed centered at ground level like the hare in *The Witch*, the gull is another one of Eggers's eerily personified animals as symbols of foreboding. Having not heeded Wake's superstitious prohibition about killing a seabird, the weather turns stormy immediately after the gull's death – a shift that strongly suggests, but does not entirely confirm, the presence of the supernatural.

Indeed, the film's central premise was inspired by an 1801 incident at Smalls Lighthouse off the coast of Wales, in which one of the two keepers (both named Thomas) died, forcing the other keeper to live with the decaying corpse (kept to avoid a murder accusation) while a storm kept the rescue vessel at bay. However, Eggers also drew fictional inspiration from Jean Grémillon's 1929 film *The Lighthouse Keepers*, itself an adaptation of a 1905 Grand Guignol play that ends badly when the son in a father–son lighthouse team goes mad from rabies, contracted just before their month-long post began.[64] Of course, *The Shining* also features a murderous father–son relationship – but, perhaps even more than *The Witch*, *The Lighthouse* bears a closer resemblance to an arthouse drama about folklore, paranoia, and repressed sexuality compared to *The Shining*'s generic closeness to films like *The Amityville Horror* (1979).

Unbeknownst to Wake, Howard has stolen the identity of his former timber foreman, Ephraim Winslow (Logan Hawkes), who was killed in a logging "accident" – much like the desperate and prospectless man (Kevin J. O'Connor) who steals the deceased Henry Plainview's identity in *There Will Be Blood*. (At times, Pattinson's accent also recalls Daniel Day-Lewis's accent as Daniel Plainview.) Promised that the more remote the lighthouse, the higher the pay, "Winslow" (née Howard) concedes to Wake that he "had enough of trees," but has simply swapped the seemingly infinite space of the deep Canadian forest for the immensity of the sea. Although told that his predecessor went mad and died after raving about merfolk and claiming to see St Elmo (patron saint of sailors) in the lantern beam, Howard becomes increasingly convinced that Wake killed his former second mate and used the body as lobster bait, especially since Wake keeps changing the stories about his past. Moreover, Wake keeps assuring him that he is receiving high marks in the chief's logbook for the lighthouse authorities, but Howard eventually finds the logbook unguarded and full of so many demerits that Wake has recommended his second mate's dismissal without pay. As with *It Comes*, more of the film occurs within the tightly enclosed spaces of the lighthouse station than outside, yet the sound of foghorns, wind, and waves is omnipresent. Indeed, as the storm grows fiercer, rain and crashing waves increasingly invade their living quarters, these raging waters also serving as a metaphor for the men's slippage into constant drunkenness that brings out buried secrets (including "Winslow's" true identity).

Whereas *The Shining* uses daily title cards to demarcate Jack's dissolution over about a week, *The Lighthouse*'s narrative is riven with temporal ellipses that make it impossible to truly tell how much time has passed. By the film's halfway point, the characters and audience alike are confused about how long they have been on the island; for instance, when the relief boat fails to arrive following a particularly drunken night, Howard thinks they simply slept in, while Wake corrects him that it has been weeks since the tender failed to land in the storm. Additionally, several times during the film, Howard slips into nightmares about the real Winslow's death, interspersed with erotic fantasies about a beached mermaid – all edited so that it becomes difficult to separate objective reality from his subjective states.

Later, shortly after Howard's confession about not trying to save his foreman, we see Wake destroy the emergency skiff with a pickaxe to prevent Howard from leaving without him, and then a tracking shot as the axe-wielding Wake limps through the mud after Howard – a sequence that visually recalls *The Shining*'s scenes of Jack sabotaging the snowcat, killing Dick Halloran (Scatman Crothers), and chasing Danny (Danny Lloyd) through the hedge maze. Yet, when they confront each other back inside, Wake accuses *Howard* of having smashed the skiff and chased him with an axe – thus undercutting what the viewer has just seen. Wake then goes on to gaslight Howard, goading the younger man with the thought that the whole lighthouse job has been Howard's hallucination while knee-deep in snow back in the Canadian forests. Both characters gradually emerge as unreliable narrators, but because Howard is framed throughout as the viewer's main locus of identification, the revelation that he may be the truly crazy one is especially disorienting.[65]

Although Howard angrily says that Wake's "Captain Ahab horseshit... sound[s] like a goddamn parody," *The Lighthouse* bears far closer connections to Melville's *Billy Budd, Sailor* (1891), especially in the homoerotic and almost sadomasochistic relationship that develops between men in the absence of women. Of course, Howard is a much less idealized character than Billy Budd and Wake is no John Claggart, but they are still "drawn together in a bond that renders desire indistinguishable from predation" as a "typifying gesture of paranoid knowledge."[66] At times the two men recall a bickering married couple (passive-aggressively straining each other's nerves, insulting the other's cooking, and so on), while other times witness a tender intimacy between the men (holding the other in his arms, dancing together, confessing secrets) – but these moments, such as a thwarted kiss, often lead to punches as the men attempt to phobically dispel the homoeroticism from their homosociality. Even the physical location of their duties within the lighthouse itself – Wake/top and Howard/bottom – suggest their relative positions of (sexual) power.

In a thematic reversal of *The Witch*'s wood-chopping as redirected erotic energy, each man's masturbation additionally represents a form of misspent labor – as Wake denotes in his logbook by jotting "habitual self-abuse" as a mark against Howard. The latter uses a scrimshaw carving of a mermaid, found tucked in a hole in his mattress (not unlike the love rune in *Midsommar*), as a masturbatory aid, while Wake reserves his utmost desire for the light itself. Howard spies up through the locked grate into the lantern room as he imagines his superior suddenly transformed into a tentacled creature (Figure 5.5). On the DVD/Blu-ray commentary track, Eggers describes Wake's dripping semen, oozing down before Howard's face, as "tentacle juice," indicating how this scene represents repressed homoeroticism taking monstrous form – but Eggers has elsewhere cited Mircea Eliade's comparative analysis of semen and/ as the "mystical light" of (pro)creation across many religious traditions (albeit depicted here as an unattempted or failed procreation, given the spilled seed).[67] Meanwhile, Wake's teasing descriptions of Howard as "pretty as a picture" with "eyes as bright as a lady," and as "a painted actress screaming in the footlights," hint at an underlying attraction – but whereas Melville's novella has Captain Vere as a mediating authority figure in the conflict between angelic sailor Billy Budd and repressed homosexual Claggart, only the quickly discarded lighthouse keepers' manual exists in this film.

Figure 5.5 Howard peers up into the lantern room as Wake's semen becomes "tentacle juice," in a moment mixing homoeroticism and horror in *The Lighthouse*. (Source: Blu-ray.)

Much as Billy lashes out at the cruel master-at-arms in the end – an act that proves fatal for both of them – *The Lighthouse*'s final scenes depict Howard violently reversing their earlier dominant/submissive power dynamic. Imagining himself attacking his martinet of a former logging foreman, Howard reduces Wake to the role of a subservient dog, telling him to "roll over" (a possible rape threat), and even leads him around on a leash. The displaced sexuality in this violence is visually conveyed by Eggers's montage editing, with hallucinatory overlaps between Howard's violent blows, shots of him fucking the mermaid, and shots where the strikingly handsome Winslow stands in for Wake. After attempting to bury Wake alive, Howard finally kills him with the pickaxe and, for the first time, fully recites Wake's opening toast, as though embracing the ocean's destructive power shortly before it does him in as well. Finally armed with the key to the lantern room, Howard enters as the Fresnel lens seems to magically open on its own – but, upon reaching into the light, it grows blindingly bright and he begins screaming. The fuzzed-out audiovisual distortion in this moment suggests that both the lamp and the film itself are (technological) limit points that Howard has transgressed, like a Lovecraft protagonist driven mad by looking upon a cosmic horror (recall his vision of the tentacled horror) that defies human comprehension. After falling backward down the lighthouse stairs, the final image is a long, slow backward tracking shot of Howard's broken, nude body on the rocks outside, his guts being pecked at by seagulls – until a cut-to-black, with an ironically jaunty sea jig playing over the closing credits (Figure 5.6).

Like Prometheus to Wake's Proteus, Howard meets his fate for trying to steal the mystical light, and Wake's earlier curse upon Howard is seemingly confirmed. In Eggers's post-horror films, both Thomasin and Howard trespass upon forbidden knowledge – but whereas she rises into the air, he falls from it, back toward the ocean far below. Unlike Lucile Hadžihalilović's *Evolution* (2015), a post-horror film whose extensive use of beautifully colorful underwater cinematography (filmed in the Canary Islands) complements its deeply Freudian narrative about a young boy's escape from his pre-Oedipal, "oceanic" mother (revealed to be, along with the other women in their seaside village, some sort of asexually reproducing sea creature), there are almost no underwater shots in *The Lighthouse*, save a brief shot of the mermaid in her element. Men may enter the cold Atlantic waters at their own peril, but they are ultimately kept at bay from its undersea realm, much as we are visually denied access to the ocean's depths – a mysterious expanse more often gendered "feminine" than "masculine" – as a hard division between the human and the non-human.[68] Perhaps it is no surprise, then, that when attacking Wake,

Figure 5.6 Howard meets his Promethean fate for attempting to steal the "mystical light," in the final shot of *The Lighthouse*. (Source: Blu-ray.)

Howard briefly imagines the old salt attired in seashells like Poseidon – as though the masculine sea god has finally been dethroned to make room for something else. Yet, regardless, the men repress their same-sex desires through a masculine violence that self-destructively turns inward on itself, instead of embracing the "feminizing" associations of male homosexuality (via its period-appropriate connotations of gender inversion) as a mysterious realm of experience beyond.

Although homosexuality in the 1890s was itself a horizon of previously forbidden knowledge only then coming into focus as a modern identity category, Eve Sedgwick posits that its violent repression at *Billy Budd*'s conclusion (and, I would add, in *The Lighthouse*) "imagin[es] a time *after the homosexual* [which] is finally inseparable from . . . imagining a time *after the human*."[69] That is, despite homosexuality being a naturally occurring phenomenon, its non-procreative desires have often been culturally linked with death as a supposed "crime against nature," so the history of homosexuality's attempted extermination also implies "a broader, apocalyptic trajectory toward something approaching omnicide."[70] As we will see in the next chapter, however, post-horror's depopulated landscapes might embrace the radical negativity of queerness as strategies for survival, even at an existentially trying moment when human life is increasingly defined by neoliberal capitalism and ecological destruction. While not all post-horror films depict the natural sublime, their powerful evocation of dread nevertheless suggests how "[t]he loss of identifiably human subjectivity shades into the looming extinction of humanity as a whole."[71]

Notes

1. Karl Schoonover, "What Do We Do with Vacant Space in Horror Films?" *Discourse*, 40, no. 3 (2018), pp. 345–6. Also see Adam Charles Hart, *Monstrous Forms: Moving Image Horror Across Media* (New York: Oxford University Press, 2020), ch. 2.
2. Julian Hanich, *Cinematic Emotion in Horror Films and Thrillers: The Aesthetic Paradox of Pleasurable Fear* (New York: Routledge, 2010), pp. 171, 175, 177, 194.
3. J. A. Bridges, "Post-Horror Kinships: From *Goodnight Mommy* to *Get Out*," *Bright Lights Film Journal*, December 20, 2018 <https://brightlightsfilm.com/post-horror-kinships-from-goodnight-mommy-to-get-out/>.
4. Tom Cochrane, "The Emotional Experience of the Sublime," *Canadian Journal of Philosophy*, 42, no. 2 (2012), pp. 125–6, 130–1, 146–7. Cf. Noël Carroll, *The Philosophy of Horror, or Paradoxes of the Heart* (New York: Routledge, 1990), pp. 240 n20, 241 n23.
5. Tarja Laine, *Feeling Cinema: Emotional Dynamics in Film Studies* (New York: Continuum, 2011), pp. 13–15; Rick Warner, "Kubrickian Dread: Echoes of *2001: A Space Odyssey* and *The Shining* in Works by Jonathan Glazer, Paul Thomas Anderson, and David Lynch," in *After Kubrick: A Filmmaker's Legacy*, ed. Jeremi Szaniawski (New York: Bloomsbury Academic, 2020), pp. 128–9, 139–40.
6. Warner, "Kubrickian Dread," 125–6, 128–9, 132–5.
7. On *The Shining*'s darkly comic violence, also see Laura Mee, *The Shining* (Leighton Buzzard: Auteur, 2017), p. 24.
8. Jason Sperb, *Blossoms and Blood: Postmodern Media Culture and the Films of Paul Thomas Anderson* (Austin, TX: University of Texas Press, 2013), pp. 205–6, 212, 234.
9. George Toles, *Paul Thomas Anderson* (Urbana, IL: University of Illinois Press, 2016), pp. 68–9. On *The Shining*'s music, also see Roger Luckhurst, *The Shining* (London: British Film Institute, 2013), pp. 75–80.
10. Saige Walton, "Air, Atmosphere, Environment: Film Mood, Folk Horror, and *The Witch*," *Screening the Past*, no. 43 (2018) <http://www.screeningthepast.com/2018/02/air-atmosphere-environment-film-mood-folk-horror-and-the-vvitch/>.
11. Warner, "Kubrickian Dread," 128–30.
12. Ara Osterweil, "*Under the Skin*: The Perils of Becoming Female," *Film Quarterly*, 67, no. 4 (2014), p. 44.

13. Ibid., p. 46.
14. Laine, *Feeling Cinema*, 15, 27 (quoted at p. 27).
15. Elena Gorfinkel, "Sex, Sensation, and Nonhuman Interiority in *Under the Skin*," *Jump Cut: A Review of Contemporary Media*, no. 57 (2016) <https://www.ejumpcut.org/archive/jc57.2016/-GorfinkelSkin/2.html>.
16. Michel Faber, *Under the Skin* (New York: Harcourt, 2000), pp. 273, 292–3, 310–11.
17. The post-horror film *The Untamed* (2016) similarly depicts a fog-shrouded countryside as the adoptive home for a sexualized extraterrestrial (albeit depicted as a tentacled monster, à la *Possession* (1981), rather than a seductive humanoid), housed in a small cabin that a small coterie of sexually repressed city dwellers repeatedly visit in order to experience superhuman sexual pleasures, despite the potential dangers of the id-like creature's lusts.
18. Osterweil, "*Under the Skin*," 46, 50. This ending differs from the novel's conclusion, in which the alien explodes herself with a bomb to avoid detection after becoming severely wounded in a car crash.
19. Gorfinkel, "Sex, Sensation, and Nonhuman Interiority."
20. See Carol J. Clover, *Men, Women, and Chainsaws: Gender in the Modern Horror Film* (Princeton, NJ: Princeton University Press, 1992), pp. 76–81; Barbara Creed, *The Monstrous-Feminine: Film, Feminism, Psychoanalysis* (London: Routledge, 1993), pp. 74–5; Erin Harrington, *Women, Monstrosity, and Horror Film: Gynaehorror* (New York: Routledge, 2018).
21. Gaston Bachelard, *The Poetics of Space*, trans. Maria Jolas (Boston: Beacon Press, 1994), pp. 185–6, 188 (quote at p. 188).
22. Tony Williams, *Hearths of Darkness: The Family in the American Horror Film* (Jackson, MS: University Press of Mississippi, 2014), p. 25–6.
23. Brandon Grafius, "Securing the Borders: Isolation and Anxiety in *The Witch*, *It Comes at Night*, and Trump's America," in *Make America Hate Again: Trump-Era Horror and the Politics of Fear*, ed. Victoria McCollum (London: Routledge, 2019), p. 120. Ironically, antinomianism (or individual "spiritual courage" to "go against the grain" of conventionally held beliefs) is a key characteristic of the so-called "Left-Hand Path" in modern magical traditions – hence how William's views, borne of pride, might share "heretical" territory with witchcraft, despite his obviously Puritanical worldview. See Nevill Drury, *Stealing Fire from Heaven: The Rise of Modern Western Magic* (New York: Oxford University Press, 2011), pp. 116, 125.
24. Kwasu D. Tembo, "The Left-Hand Path: On the Dialectics of Witchery in *The Witch* and *Hagazussa: A Heathen's Curse*," *Frames Cinema Journal*, no. 16 (Winter 2019) <https://framescinemajournal.com/article/the-left-hand-path-on-the-dialectics-of-witchery-in-the-witch-and-hagazussa-a-heathens-curse/>.
25. Hart, *Monstrous Forms*, 85–6.
26. Aviva Briefel, "Devil in the Details: The Uncanny History of *The Witch* (2015)," *Film & History: An Interdisciplinary Journal*, 49, no. 1 (2019), p. 14.

27. Ibid., pp. 7, 11–13.
28. Walton, "Air, Atmosphere, Environment."
29. The sin of "Onanism" was well-known to the Puritans, although before the eighteenth century, Onan's biblical sin was associated less with masturbation per se than selfishly spilling his seed without impregnating his dead brother's wife – that is, refusing to fulfill a familial obligation, at his father's request, to perpetuate his brother's genealogical line (and hence the future coming of the Messiah). See Thomas W. Laqueur, *Solitary Sex: A Cultural History of Masturbation* (New York: Zone Books, 2003), pp. 128–9.
30. Adam Scovell, *Folk Horror: Hours Dreadful and Things Strange* (Leighton Buzzard: Auteur, 2017), p. 102.
31. Briefel, "Devil in the Details," 8; Tembo, "The Left-Hand Path."
32. Hart, *Monstrous Forms*, 87–8.
33. Walton, "Air, Atmosphere, Environment." On the ergotism theory, see Emerson W. Baker, *A Storm of Witchcraft: The Salem Trials and the American Experience* (New York: Oxford University Press, 2015), pp. 109–10.
34. Adam Lowenstein, "The *Giallo*/Slasher Landscape: *Ecologia del Delitto*, *Friday the 13th*, and Subtractive Spectatorship," in *Italian Horror Cinema*, eds Stefano Baschiera and Russ Hunter (Edinburgh: Edinburgh University Press, 2016), pp. 133–5, 138.
35. Walton, "Air, Atmosphere, Environment"; Briefel, "Devil in the Details," 9.
36. It is also possible to read this ambiguous ending as being Thomasin's *own* imagined projection of fears about her future survival – such as interpreting Satan's appearance to her as simply part of a nightmare suffered while she is still asleep in the shed.
37. Walton, "Air, Atmosphere, Environment."
38. Briefel, "Devil in the Details," 8; Chloe Carroll, "'Wouldst Thou Like to Live Deliciously?' Female Persecution and Redemption in *The Witch*," *Frames Cinema Journal*, no. 16 (Winter 2019), <https://framescinemajournal.com/article/wouldst-thou-like-to-live-deliciously-female-persecution-and-redemption-in-the-witch/> (quoted).
39. Laurel Zwissler, "'I Am That Very Witch': On *The Witch*, Feminism, and Not Surviving Patriarchy," *Journal of Religion & Film*, 22, no. 3 (2018) <https://digitalcommons.unomaha.edu/jrf/vol22/iss3/6/>.
40. Ibid.
41. Ibid.
42. Sandra Huber, "Blood and Tears and Potions and Flame: Excesses of Transformation in Ari Aster's *Midsommar*," *Frames Cinema Journal*, no. 16 (Winter 2019), <https://framescinemajournal.com/article/blood-and-tears-and-potions-and-flame-excesses-of-transformation-in-ari-asters-midsommar/>.
43. Also see Valerie Rohy, "Ahistorical," *GLQ*, 12, no. 1 (2006), pp. 61–83; Heather Love, *Feeling Backward: Loss and the Politics of Queer History* (Cambridge, MA: Harvard University Press, 2007), ch. 1.

44. Tembo, "The Left-Hand Path."
45. Again, this is not unlike *The Eyes of My Mother*'s lonely female protagonist, who grows up to perpetuate a cycle of murderous violence after having lost her mother to a thrill killer as a child. In that film, though, she kills and/or captures people, sometimes keeping them as surrogate family members, in order to prevent them from abandoning her to her private grief on her deceased parents' isolated farm.
46. James George Frazer, *The Golden Bough: A Study in Magic and Religion*, 3rd edn, vol. IX (New York: Macmillan, 1913), pp. 275–80.
47. Tembo, "The Left-Hand Path."
48. Richard Armstrong, *Mourning Films: A Critical Study of Loss and Grieving in Cinema* (Jefferson, NC: McFarland, 2012), pp. 174, 187.
49. Tembo, "The Left-Hand Path."
50. See Lee Edelman, *No Future: Queer Theory and the Death Drive* (Durham, NC: Duke University Press, 2004). The ideology of reproductive futurism explains why the Female's refusal to save the infant from the rising tide in *Under the Skin* registers as so disturbing (Osterweil, "*Under the Skin*," 48).
51. Although one of many Hollywood films delayed by the 2019–21 coronavirus pandemic, it is notable that Krasinski, in an Instagram post, framed *A Quiet Place Part II*'s (2020) delayed release as an authorial choice tied to the collective viewing experience: "One of the things I'm most proud of is that people have said our movie is one you have to see all together. [. . .] As insanely excited as we are for all of you to see this movie . . . I'm gonna wait to release the film til we CAN all see it together!" (quoted in Tom Grater, "'A Quiet Place II' Global Release Delayed to Avoid Coronavirus Crisis – Update," *Deadline*, March 12, 2020 <https://deadline.com/2020/03/a-quiet-place-ii-delayed-coronavirus-crisis-1202880784/>).
52. Matt Miller, "John Krasinski's Second Act Didn't Pick Up Where Jim Left Off. You Mad?" *Esquire*, February 20, 2020 <https://www.esquire.com/entertainment/movies/a30898110/john-krasinski-a-quiet-place-2-politics-interview/>.
53. Jacob Hall, "'It Comes at Night' Director Trey Edward Shults on How 'The Shining' Inspired His New Cinematic Nightmare [Interview]," *SlashFilm*, June 7, 2017 <https://www.slashfilm.com/it-comes-at-night-trey-edward-shults-interview/>.
54. Produced under the revived Hammer brand, Veronika Franz and Severin Fiala's *The Lodge* (2019) bears a similar mix of influences: its titular snow-bound location harks back to *The Shining*, while its backstory about a suicide cult recalls *The Invitation* (2015). *It Comes at Night*'s Riley Keough also plays the cult's sole survivor, who soon emerges as a strangely threatening maternal figure – hence her similarity to the titular character in Franz and Fiala's *Goodnight Mommy* (2014). Much as the lodge's lacquered wood interior resembles the *It Comes* interiors, even Stanley, the dog in *It Comes*, finds a counterpart in *The Lodge*'s dog, Grady (a reference to the Overlook's ghostly caretaker).

55. Bachelard, *The Poetics of Space*, 222, 224, 230 (quoted at pp. 222, 230).
56. Walton, "Air, Atmosphere, Environment."
57. Grafius, "Securing the Borders," 122.
58. Ibid., pp. 119, 122.
59. Here we might recall the American history professors who build a repressive, Mennonite-inspired society in M. Night Shyamalan's *The Village* (2004) as an imagined refuge against the modern world, although Paul alludes to an expertise in ancient Roman history, perhaps suggesting his self-identification with imperial power.
60. Eugenie Brinkema, *The Forms of the Affects* (Durham, NC: Duke University Press, 2014), pp. 95–6.
61. Grafius, "Securing the Borders," 124.
62. Tasha Robinson, "Why the Director of *It Comes at Night* Hopes Audiences 'Don't Catch On' to His Technological Tricks," *The Verge*, June 8, 2017 <https://www.theverge.com/2017/6/8/15762548/it-comes-at-night-director-trey-edward-shults-krisha-interview-horror>.
63. Quoted in Katie Rife, "*The Lighthouse*'s Robert Eggers: 'Nothing Good Happens When Two Men Are Trapped in a Giant Phallus,'" *A. V. Club*, October 17, 2019 <https://film.avclub.com/the-lighthouse-s-robert-eggers-nothing-good-happens-w-1839071674>.
64. Alexandra Heller-Nicholas, "Grand Guignol, Early Cinema, and Robert Eggers' *The Lighthouse*," *Diabolique Magazine*, October 4, 2019 <https://diaboliquemagazine.com/grand-guignol-early-cinema-and-robert-eggers-the-lighthouse/>. Also see Paul Autier and Paul Cloquemin, "The Lighthouse Keepers (*Gardiens de phare*)," in Richard J. Hand and Michael Wilson, *Grand-Guignol: The French Theatre of Horror* (Exeter: University of Exeter Press, 2002), pp. 109–20.
65. Minus the emotional payoff of retributive glory, this moment is also similar to *Midsommar*'s ending, when the viewer's perception of Dani's mental state – very subtly called into question throughout the film – is markedly undercut (see Chapter 4).
66. Eve Kosofsky Sedgwick, *Epistemology of the Closet* (Berkeley, CA: University of California Press, 1990), p. 100.
67. See Mircea Eliade, "Spirit, Light, and Seed," *History of Religions*, 11, no. 1 (1971), p. 1–30; Robert Eggers, director's commentary track, *The Lighthouse* DVD/Blu-ray (Santa Monica, CA: Lionsgate, 2020).
68. Stefan Helmreich, "The Genders of Waves," *WSQ: Women's Studies Quarterly*, 45, no. 1/2 (2017), pp. 29–51. We might compare *The Lighthouse* with the fantasy/romance *The Shape of Water* (2017), whose closer generic resemblance to *Beauty and the Beast* (1740) than *Creature from the Black Lagoon* (1954) depicts an interspecies relationship between a human woman and amphibian man that has also been read as a "queer" romance (see Eddie Falvey, "Sexual Participation Within Fan Cultures: Considering a Sex Toy as a Mode of Reception for *The Shape of Water*," *Journal of Fandom Studies*, 7,

no. 3 (2019), pp. 245–59). Resembling a far more classical Hollywood film than *The Lighthouse*, *The Shape of Water* sports a conventional filmmaking style, melodramatically broad characterization, and well-worn plot beats, though the sympathetic monster becomes a locus of identification for many different Cold War-era outsiders. Its fairy-tale conclusion has the lovers reuniting in the safety of the ocean, where the mute woman's mysterious neck scars open into gills – thus confirming the film's earlier hints that she has been an amphibian herself all along. But by removing the taboo of interspecies contact and narratively banishing the creatures back beneath the waves, the film's happy ending reinforces a heterocentric logic befitting its stylistic classicism. However, whether or not we read the ending of either *The Lighthouse* or *The Shape of Water* as a final "containment" of queerness, the water line still separates human from non-human life.
69. Sedgwick, *Epistemology of the Closet*, 128 (original emphasis).
70. Ibid. In *The Witch*, the possessed Caleb's dying monologue also uses conspicuously homoerotic language to describe his fantasy of embracing Jesus as he passes into the afterlife – ironically suggesting that, according to a Puritan mindset, queerness can only be implicitly spoken on the way out of human existence.
71. Warner, "Kubrickian Dread," 140.

CHAPTER 6

Queer Ethics and the Urban Ruin-Porn Landscape: The Horrors of Monogamy in *It Follows*

> When there is torture, there is pain and wounds, physical agony, and all this distracts the mind from mental suffering, so that one is tormented only by the wounds until the moment of death. But the most terrible agony of all may not be in the wounds themselves but in knowing for certain that within an hour, then within ten minutes, then within a half a minute, now at this very instant – your soul will leave your body and you will no longer be a person, and that this is certain; the worst thing is that it is certain.
>
> – Fyodor Dostoyevsky, *The Idiot* (1869)

This epigraph by Dostoyevsky is the final dialogue uttered in *It Follows* (2014), read aloud by one of the main characters as she recuperates in a hospital bed following a violent ordeal at the end of writer-director David Robert Mitchell's critically acclaimed post-horror film, one of the cycle's most prominent early successes in crossing over to a wider audience. To be marked for imminent doom is, of course, a common enough occurrence in the horror genre, but Mitchell's film centers on more than the existential dread of one's own inescapable mortality. Despite J. A. Bridges's claim that post-horror films "are almost entirely sexless," *It Follows* – along with several other post-horror titles such as *Under the Skin* (2013) and *The Untamed* (2016) – is centrally concerned with the ethics of sexual contact within a dread-inducing landscape.[1] Although I argued in Chapter 2 that post-horror films' generalized eschewal of jump scares and explicit gore can make them seem closer to a "mind genre" than a "body genre," their alternate means of generating powerful viewing affects via narrative ambiguity, visual space, and stylistic minimalism also blurs any too-easy distinctions. *It Follows* aptly demonstrates this by focusing on sexuality as a source of horror centered around the body – albeit horror tied less to the sexual act itself than the moral implications of one's choices in sexual partners.

It Follows tells the story of Jay Height (Maika Monroe), a nineteen-year-old Detroit suburbanite who acquires a sexually transmitted curse from her boyfriend, Hugh (Jake Weary). After they first have sex, Hugh sedates her with chloroform and ties her up, forcing her to heed his bizarre instructions about the curse: she must "sleep with someone as soon as [she] can" in order to pass it along to another person (and on and on, like a chain letter), lest she be tracked down and killed by a ghostly entity – the titular "It" – that takes various human forms, slowly but perpetually walking toward her location. If It kills her, It will resume following Hugh or whoever else preceded each of them in the sexual chain. It follows only one person at a time, so maintaining a continual flow of transmission is necessary for survival. Aided by her younger sister Kelly (Lili Sepe) and friends Yara (Olivia Luccardi) and Paul (Keir Gilchrist), Jay attempts to locate Hugh while emotionally wrestling with whether and to whom to give the curse for her own protection. After eventually passing the curse to her unbelieving neighbor Greg (Daniel Zovatto) proves to be Greg's undoing once It catches up with him, Paul then volunteers his own body to Jay, perhaps more eager to have sex with his unrequited crush than to help the childhood friend with whom he experienced his first kiss. After a climactic confrontation in which It takes the form of the sisters' absent father, the film ends with Jay and Paul beginning a romantic relationship, unaware that It still follows them.

The monster in *It Follows* may be a supernatural being, but the film's true source of horror is living under a regime of sexual shame (one of the film's primary negative affects) wherein our heteronormative culture compels sexual subjects toward monogamy – even at the risk of their overall well-being. Although nearly all critics observed that the film's conceit was a clever reworking of the "have-sex-and-die" cliché commonly associated with the fate of disposable teenage characters in 1970s and 1980s horror films, far fewer critics grasped the film's most subversive implications: the curse would become moot in a society embracing the value of a multiplicity of sexual partners in conjunction with an ethos of open communication and mutual support. In other words, the characters' failings illustrate how the film's logic finds monogamy (serial or otherwise) as promising perpetual danger, whereas one's survival would be far better ensured through what Michael Warner has called an "ethics of queer life."[2] If *The Lighthouse* (2019), for example, hinted at the destructive potential of repressed homoeroticism, then *It Follows* illustrates, by way of negative example, the queerer lessons for survival that its monogamous protagonists ultimately fail to learn.

According to Eleanor Wilkinson, it is important to distinguish the rejection of monogamy from the rejection of "mononormativity" (that is, biases against non-monogamous relationships and people), because those who reject monogamy do not necessarily embrace politically radical or sex-positive values. (Think of serial infidelity, for example, as an unethical practice for people in a strictly monogamous relationship.) By the same token, the practice of polyamory is not necessarily transgressive if it remains wedded to a non-threatening neoliberal agenda that privileges personal choice and romantic love over political change and sexual "promiscuity." Hence, the queer political potential of non-monogamy resides in its challenge to mononormativity as a major bias dividing socially accepted sex from stigmatized sex.[3] This chapter's discussion of queer ethics in *It Follows* is thus less of a critique of monogamy in itself than mononormativity and its attendant institutions – but it is not the only structural inequality at work in the film.

Earlier in the film, the Dostoyevsky-reading Yara offers an even more suggestive quote from *The Idiot*: "I think that if one is faced with inevitable destruction – if a house is falling upon you, for instance – one must feel a great longing to sit down, close one's eyes, and wait – come what may." With its allusions to inexorable architectural devastation, this quote resonates with the film's setting in contemporary Detroit and its surrounding environs, evoking an aesthetic of ruination that links the once-prosperous city's spectacular decay to the decrepitude of dangerously outdated sexual norms. Consequently, the film's ethical questions about sex are ultimately inseparable from the film's setting, since *It Follows* "cultivates dread not through gory spectacle but rather a haunting *mise-en-scène* that indexes the social geography of everyday vulnerability."[4] In the previous chapter, I explored the natural sublime in post-horror films set in desolate, wild spaces, but this chapter uses a fine-grained analysis of a specific city to highlight the horrors of (sub)urban spaces as contact zones between sexual citizens.

Through the film's retro nods to the horror genre of the 1970s and 1980s and its proximity to the photographic aesthetic of "ruin porn," *It Follows* evinces an uncertain nostalgia for Detroit's pre-bankruptcy past, a period before the rampant privatization of the very sort of social services that would help promote a life-sustaining queer ethics of sexual health. Although the film's overall post-ironic aesthetic – especially elements of *mise-en-scène* drawn from different decades in a "promiscuous" manner, echoing the strategy for survival to which its protagonist only partly accedes – may appear to suggest a temporally ambiguous milieu, the film's contemporary political relevance came into sharper focus against the backdrop of its expanded nationwide release in 2015: a year that saw monogamy (and its tool of enforcement, sexual shame) reified across sexual lines in the United States.

Contagion, Queer Intimacies, and the Normative Couple

For some viewers, a horror film that depicts sexual partners callously spreading a deadly curse via intercourse might seem deeply sex-phobic – indeed, most of the film's reviewers understood its central conceit as tapping into "the fears of anyone who came of age during the AIDS plague years."[5] The threat of AIDS has, of course, long been allegorically linked to popular horror imagery, from crisis-era films like *The Thing* (1982), *The Hunger* (1983), and *The Fly* (1986) to perceptions of the AIDS-era gay man as Gothic vampire.[6] Allusions to that most infamously incurable and stigmatizing of sexually transmitted diseases abound in the critical reception of *It Follows*, but the film's queer lesson is less about the avoidance of sex than the management of risk. After all, according to the film's logic, those infected by the curse can survive only by successfully finding new sexual partners, versus remaining abstinent and living out the fatal consequences of one's prior sexual history.[7] The film scarcely acknowledges that Jay has any other option but to find new partners, yet her hesitance to move beyond a series of monogamous bonds ultimately proves her downfall as well. *It Follows* thus implies that having a sexual life is inevitable and always involves a certain negotiation of risk (emotional or otherwise) – but the film also suggests that the danger truly lies in the social attitudes that make one increasingly objectified and stigmatized as a consequence of one's sexual history.

The scene following Jay's infection in the back of Hugh's car – a moment prominently reproduced in the film's publicity materials and home-video covers – most blatantly emphasizes the unethical dimensions of this dynamic. After Jay wakes from the chloroform to find herself bound in a wheelchair perched on the upper levels of an abandoned factory, Hugh informs her that the supernatural entity will now follow her until she has sex with someone else; to forcefully prove his point, he waits until It – first seen here in the guise of an unidentified nude woman – follows them up into the factory. Mitchell's directorial decision to frame much of this scene through a camera mounted directly on the wheelchair, pointing back at Jay, emphasizes not only her vulnerability (the frame shaking as Hugh wheels her along the uneven floor) but also the narrative's suddenly sharpened focus on her sexual history (Figure 6.1).[8] As viewers, we cannot help but watch her alternately confused and terrified reactions as Hugh explains what little he knows about It – an explanation that he claims is for her own protection but that also amounts to a tremendous betrayal of her trust. Indeed, Leslie Hahner and Scott Varda note that Hugh's allegedly benevolent reasons for so brutally forcing Jay to hear him out are belied by a later scene where she and her friends locate Hugh to peaceably discuss the monster's threat as a collective group.[9]

Figure 6.1 In Detroit's abandoned Packard auto plant, Hugh/Jeff forcibly explains the curse to wheelchair-bound Jay as the monster approaches them in *It Follows*. (Source: Blu-ray.)

We learn that Jay was not a virgin at the start of the film — she says she already slept with Greg back in high school and it "wasn't a big deal" — so acquisition of the curse should not be seen as her character's "punishment" for premarital or non-procreative sex. Indeed, just before Jay arrives home with her newly acquired curse, we see Kelly, Yara, and Paul playing old maid on the front porch, the camera slowly zooming in on the Old Maid card; the game's goal of avoiding the mismatched card (personified by a decrepit, asexual spinster) ironically foreshadows the "game" that Jay will soon be forced to play in finding new sexual "matches" to inherit the curse.

Importantly, however, neither Hugh nor the film in general ever specify *which* sexual acts will successfully pass along the curse — thus opening plenty of space for queer speculation. Is heterosexual intromission the only option? Will same-sex partners do the trick? Do oral or anal sex count? What about non-genital forms of sexuality? Just how conventional and vanilla are the expectations of this paranormal entity, anyway? Although these speculations might strike some readers as silly or overly literal (it is never implied that Jay is anything but heterosexual), the film's fantastic conceit involving a causal relationship between sexual choices and supernatural consequences still raises provocative questions about what "counts" as sex and how, within the film's logic, sexual norms might be denaturalized by supernatural exigencies. Take, for instance, the fact that It can change genders at will — as we see later when the entity, hunting down Greg in the (queerly charged) form of an anonymous young man in long underwear, first breaks into Greg's house and then takes the form of his mother to trick him into opening his bedroom door.[10] When Jay finds It, still disguised as Greg's mother, writhing atop him in a fatal sexual embrace, the film may blatantly play on the horror of incest taboos, but it also illustrates a supernatural fluidity of identity that shows no apparent concern for upholding those cultural prohibitions.

Although we might think of the HIV seroconversion confession as a sort of analogue to the scene of Jay's captivity by Hugh (think of the urban legend about someone awakening from a one-night stand to find the scrawled message "Welcome to the world of AIDS"), this disturbing depiction of knowledge acquisition as a traumatic and sexualized event also finds analogues in common cinematic depictions of rape. When, for example, Hugh drops the barely conscious Jay in front of her house and speeds away, leaving her to collapse on her front lawn, it is difficult not to narratively read the preceding scene as a sort of "symbolic rape," even if the sexual intercourse occurring before her captivity was seemingly consensual, as she subsequently affirms to the police.[11] When Greg soon after expresses doubt about Jay's version of the events ("What did he really do to you?"), his callous question about sexual consent merely emphasizes that, for the viewer, the scene of Jay's captivity is likely to register in the overall narrative trajectory much like rape scenes commonly operate in other films. Moreover, much like the white supremacist tendency to disbelieve reports of racist violence against people of color (as noted in Chapter 4), rape culture's minimization of women's testimonies about sexual violence – as exemplified here by Greg's skepticism – represents another form of gaslighting writ large. As potentially stigmatizing events (especially when commonly, if erroneously, associated with entering into "unsafe" situations), both rape and seroconversion seemingly compel protagonists to relate their past sexual histories to other characters, even at the risk of extending their stigma when not believed.[12]

A useful point of comparison is Eric England's relentlessly grim body-horror film *Contracted* (2013), in which Samantha (Najarra Townsend), a young lesbian woman, is drugged and date-raped by a man at a party, leaving her infected with a mysterious disease that gradually transforms her into a zombie over the course of several days. In that film, the backseat of a car is again the scene of infection, and the protagonist's past sexual history with both men and women becomes a central plot point – although Samantha's eventual transformation into a rotting, deranged monster who brutally kills two other lesbian acquaintances in a fit of sexual frustration marks a particularly homophobic turn. Moreover, *Contracted*'s marketing tagline "Not Your Average One Night Stand" equates her (unambiguous) date rape with casual and consensual sex – a confusion made all the more possible by Samantha's repeated refusal throughout the film to identify her violation as rape (out of fears that her current girlfriend will leave her if she confesses she was with a man – apparently regardless of the issue of consent). Whereas *It Follows* and *Contracted* depict the act of sexual transmission in markedly different ways (consensual and non-consensual, respectively), both films similarly depict their narratives' inciting acts of transmission as a grave violation. Indeed, not unlike *Contracted*'s rape-apologist tagline, most film critics failed to connect Jay's ordeal to sexual violence – a critical blind spot that, as Hahner and Varda argue, bespeaks rape culture's prevalence.[13]

It is difficult to imagine films like *It Follows* or *Contracted* achieving a similarly horrific tenor with men as their central protagonists, given our cultural double standards against active female sexuality. But whereas *Contracted* eventually turns its teenage protagonist into an irredeemable monster destructively spreading contagion at will, *It Follows* far more sympathetically depicts the societal pressures placed upon sexually active women as threatening in their own right – much as *The Witch* (2015) portrays the historical roots of this sex-negativity in early-American Puritan values. In this sense, the film belongs to a recent strand of horror cinema that, as Pamela Craig and Martin Fradley argue, "foreground[s] troubled (and frequently female) teen protagonists and, implicitly, the films' empathetic focus on their physical, emotional, and psychological suffering." Not merely an updating of the 1970s and 1980s female victim-hero personified by the slasher cycle's oft-cited "Final Girl," these more recent films deploy melodramatic tropes to heighten the (implicitly teenage) viewer's investment in horror protagonists struggling with interpersonal relationships among the teenage set. Date rape, domestic abuse, and other "potential horrors of heteronormativity" resonate in these films, which also include renderings of female sexuality as a "curse" that young women must negotiate within a patriarchal culture – as in *Ginger Snaps* (2000), *Cursed* (2005), and *Teeth* (2007).[14] Furthermore, *It Follows* shares dramatic territory with independent films like *Welcome to the Dollhouse* (1996), *The Virgin Suicides* (1999), *Donnie Darko* (2001), *Elephant* (2003), and *Mysterious Skin* (2004) – all films that Craig and Fradley identify as "contemporary cinematic depictions of young American adults . . . specifically filtered through the horrors of the late-capitalist gothic imaginary."[15]

In *It Follows*, for instance, we first meet Jay while she relaxes in her suburban backyard pool (a setting foreshadowing the location of the film's climax), casually drowning an ant crawling on her arm and calling out several pre-teen neighborhood boys for spying on her from behind the bushes. This temporary idyll figures Jay as the sexualized object of an attention that first seems innocent but later becomes figured as a pervasively threatening force. Although she easily spots these boys lurking nearby, Jay is soon visually scanning her surroundings for It, whose obsessive pursuit follows from her sexual choices. Here and elsewhere in the film, the camera slowly zooms in toward Jay as she is watched, not only implicating the viewer in the monster's slow but continuous approach to its prospective victims but also reflecting Jay's accompanying need to look closely at her surroundings for the approaching threat. Mitchell's prevalent use of wide-angle lenses creates many deeply focused compositions, helping prevent the zooms from unduly flattening out the image. Several of his most striking shots also feature slow, 360-degree pans, emphasizing the characters' paranoid scanning of their surroundings for safety. The film's opening shot contains one such pan, already turning before it finds a human character to follow, and thus foreshadowing how the viewer will be subsequently expected to visually scan the whole frame.[16] Whereas some of the films discussed in the previous chapter focus the viewer's attention on landscape via unconventional or shifting aspect ratios, *It Follows* does likewise using camera movement and shot depth within its consistent 2.35:1 ratio. Hugh's description of the monster as being "very slow, but it's not dumb" could easily apply to *It Follows* itself, with the film's stately editing and narrative pace matching the entity's slow march across the depopulated (sub)urban milieu.

In a later scene, Jay is startled as one of the same neighborhood boys, spying from outside on her roof, bounces a rubber ball off the bathroom window where she stands scantily clad, fearfully staring at her nether regions – the apparent site of the curse's sexual transmission. Although the actual cause of the shockingly loud noise, which Jay (and we) might immediately ascribe to a surprise attack by the monster, turns out to be a comparatively banal instance of pre-adolescent voyeurism, the film repeatedly implies that what once may have seemed innocently sexual can quickly take sinister overtones when one lives under the stigma of contagion and sexual shame. Indeed, the use of static, long point-of-view shots during those few moments when the cursed stop long enough to scan their surroundings serve as a sort of refracted optics for their own shame: much as their sexual histories mark them as subject to social and self-surveillance, they must now survive by surveilling their once-safe environment for risks in return.

Likewise, in another scene, not coincidentally occurring just before the monster's intrusion, Paul and Jay reminisce about finding and laughing over some discarded porn magazines back when they were children – another instance of juvenile curiosity about sex initially serving as less of a disturbing primal scene than an innocent pursuit. But this memory later becomes echoed in the present when Paul and Jay find, in an abandoned

Detroit house where Hugh has been squatting, a stash of old porn magazines bookmarked by a photo featuring Hugh and an unnamed teenage girl posing in their high-school hallway. Here, the "shameful" domain of pornography literally envelops this once-wholesome image of Hugh and a past girlfriend, visually suggesting the tainted nature of his own sexual choices. Moreover, the discovered photo proves the vital clue that Jay and company will use to finally locate "Hugh" under his real name, Jeff, who is living with his mother in a well-to-do suburban home, where he explains how he contracted the curse during a one-night stand with an unknown woman from a bar. Like Jay, it seems that Hugh/Jeff was just as instrumentally used and discarded by the curse's previous owner out of calculated self-interest. He may have tried to warn Jay (again, out of self-interest, hoping that It would not kill her and revert to following him), but as long as the chain of deception continues on a one-to-one basis, the curse's transmission cannot help but seem deeply abusive instead of ethically sound.

Jay herself guiltily understands this when she seeks out new sexual partners once Greg's death causes the curse to revert to her. Instead of endangering another friend, she takes her mother's car to a nearby lake and gives herself to three random young men on an offshore boat. Although the film elides what actually transpires on the boat (and, again, it is unclear what kinds of sexual behavior will successfully transmit the curse), Jay is clearly upset by the experience – whether by the shame of her sexual submission or the knowledge of having just doomed them. We never learn whether she attempted to inform these men about the curse – and it does not seem likely that she attempted to submit them to the traumatizing experience of forced instruction that she herself underwent at Hugh/Jeff's hands. In an early version of the script, Jay turns back toward shore instead of knowingly dooming the men, but Joshua Grimm argues that Mitchell's elliptical editing in the finished film opens the scene to greater moral ambivalence by "counter[ing] Hugh's ignorant claim regarding how much easier it would be for her than him."[17] In my reading of this scene, therefore, it is no longer clear that "Jay assumes a moral culpability with whom she will pass the curse onto, demanding *fully informed consent* before she will even consider transference of the supernatural stalker."[18] In other words, if the non-consensual nature of her former boyfriend's actions cannot be reconciled with sexually ethical practices, then neither can Jay's attempt to move beyond the fatal chain of serial monogamy through this potential gangbang scenario if she is unable or unwilling to impart the seriousness of her sexual transmission to them. In any case, this unsettling effort merely proves a means of buying time, and It is soon back on Jay's trail. If there is a sure death sentence in *It Follows*, it resides at the intersection of monogamy and ignorance.

If abstinence is an unrealistic answer (as the film suggests), then the crucial problem here would require a twofold solution: more openness in sexual relations, in order to disperse the curse as efficiently as possible, and the need for properly educating and caring for those afflicted. This is not, then, so much a model of purely casual sexual relations as one of mutual investment in sexual well-being. According to the film's logic, those previously infected with the curse can still see It following the new recipients, so it logically follows that the more people previously infected, the more who will be able to monitor the approaching threat. Taken more literally, Grimm even hypothesizes that a social network or mobile app could be developed for infected users to constantly update each other on the monster's current whereabouts.[19] Although the curse might technically continue to follow a linear chain of transmission, open and rapidly shifting sexual interconnections would produce a more rhizomatic dispersal of risk – more akin to herd immunity to a communicable disease than solipsistic punishment for one's own sexual choices. Unlike the punishment of sexually active characters in so many horror films, the secret to ensuring one's safety in the world of *It Follows* would not reside in *no* sex but in *more* sex. The curse may seemingly follow the logic of a straight line,[20] but when so many straight lines overlap to form a complex web of sexual interconnection, any one line will appear far more bent (or, shall we say, *queered*).

Here I can finally return to the matter of queer ethics and the horrors that monogamy can produce. In his 1999 book *The Trouble with Normal*, Michael Warner argues that a queer ethics insists on forms of intimacy and care that are not limited to normative constructs like the nuclear family or the monogamous couple, instead embracing a far more multiplicitous range of erotic connections among partners, friends, and even strangers – all united in a community in which "one doesn't pretend to be *above* the indignity of sex."[21] And yet even though these fluid sexual relations were promoted as a consequence of queer people's historical exclusion from heteronormative institutions such as marriage, Warner finds contemporary gay and lesbian identity politics championing same-sex marriage as an assimilationist strategy that embraces dominant standards of monogamy. As he explains, one of queer culture's

> greatest contributions to modern life is the discovery that you can have both: intimacy and casualness; long-term commitment and sex with strangers; romantic love and perverse pleasure. [. . .] Straight culture has already learned much from queers, and it shouldn't stop now. In particular, it needs to learn a new standard of dignity, and it won't do this as long as gay people think that their "acceptance" needs to be won on the terms of straight culture's politics of shame.[22]

Although Warner incorrectly predicted that same-sex marriage would not likely come to pass in the United States, he nevertheless foresaw that, regardless of its eventual legality, the campaign for same-sex marriage would itself do "more harm" to the crucial insights of queer culture "than marriage could ever be worth."[23] Indeed, much as the origins and motivation of It in *It Follows* are never explained to viewers, monogamy circulates as Western society's unmarked norm, even to the point that "safe" forms of queerness can be appropriated beneath its auspices in support of mainstream gay and lesbian culture's "new homonormativity," which Lisa Duggan describes as a conservative assimilationist politics built on neoliberal standards of individual responsibility, privatization, and domestic normalization.[24] Eleanor Wilkinson notes, for instance, that even assimilationist discourses about polyamory have drawn inspiration from homonormativity by privileging deep romantic bonds, rather than sexual profligacy, as a "respectable and admirable" basis for sexual relationships with multiple partners.[25]

Ironically enough, the year of *It Follows*'s wide release saw two high-profile testaments to monogamy's entrenched status: the US Supreme Court's legalization of same-sex marriage in June 2015 and the August 2015 dump of hacked data from an estimated 37 million user accounts on the pro-infidelity social-networking website Ashley Madison (slogan: "Life is short. Have an affair") – a website whose existence demonstrates how non-monogamous practices need not be ethically responsible. Whereas the former event was widely celebrated by social liberals as a long-awaited milestone in sexual equality, widespread *Schadenfreude* at the latter event merely proved mononormativity's centrality in promoting an endemic culture of sexual shame.

Hence, it is not difficult to see how a sex-positive, non-monogamous queer ethics would help dispel the monstrous threat in *It Follows*. Lee Edelman argues that queerness should be defined not by an essentialist notion of same-sex-desiring identity but as an indeterminate, identity-defying quality marking a perpetual challenge to the dominant ideology of reproductive futurism. The titular threats in *The Birds* (1963), for example, do not symbolize homosexuality per se, but because the culturally denigrated figure of the queer is supposedly antithetical to the socially valorized figure of the Child and the normative family, "homosexuality inflects how [the birds] figure the radical refusal of meaning" that their unexplained but horrific presence connotes. If the Child is a symbolic figure representing the continuance of the (heterosexual) human species – hence the child-protectionist themes in most Hollywood films – and mobilized to repress various forms of non-procreative desire, then "whatever voids the promissory note, the guarantee, of futurity, precluding the hope of redeeming it, or of its redeeming us, must be tarred, and in this case feathered, by the brush that will always color it queer in a culture that places on queerness the negativizing burden of sexuality."[26]

Like Hitchcock's birds, then, *It Follows* presents a monstrous, free-floating threat whose lack of clear identity, eschewal of rational explanation, and perpetual death drive mark its own sense of queerness. But much like Edelman's reversal of homophobic edicts, the most ethical response would be for Jay to effectively beat the It monster at its own game, using her sexuality in far more multiplicitous ways than are permissible by the linearity of socio-sexual relations required of both monogamy and reproductive futurism. Her repeated attempts to save herself by passing on the curse may ironically recall reproductive futurism's use of procreation as fantasized defense against mortality, but so do the eventual deaths of her former partners testify to its inefficacy as a viable solution. Following Warner, if straight culture continues to have much to learn from queer culture, then these lessons would include eschewing the monogamous couple as a culturally ideal form, along with the various forms of sexual shame that police its boundaries – which, in the film, encourage the curse to be deceptively passed to unsuspecting victims while also inhibiting the afflicted from disseminating the curse in an informed way that would ultimately prove more efficacious to everyone involved.

Heteronormative understandings of sexual shame as an isolating, stigmatizing quality bear heavily on Jay and her friends, but queer theorists have also described shame as a contagious affect that queers the boundaries between self and other, because one can easily feel another person's shame and thereby become part of "collectivities of the shamed."[27] As David Caron explains, shame is normatively expected to motivate "internalized self-policing," since "it feels hyperindividuating. Yet this extreme singularity also enables the collective," creating ethical bonds when memories of one's own past or present shame are shared with others.[28] In Sally Munt's discussion of shame as a queer "structure of feeling" that is "intrinsically relational, correlative, and associative," forming a contagious web of attachments and disattachments between people, she suggests:

> Perhaps we can imagine an aesthetics or technology of the self that reinscripts [*sic*] the bio-power of bodies, that builds ethical futures out of shame, that perceives shame as a sort of muscle, an energy that can make things happen. Foucault claimed that there are no relations of power without a multiplication of resistances, and thus, to stay with the muscle analogy, sometimes a muscle must be "ripped" in order to extend; perhaps shame must be intensely endured in order that individuation, and hence new thoughts and feelings, can occur.[29]

Although the stigmatizing effect of Jay's sexual history gradually implicates her friends in potential danger from It once they begin interceding (sexually or otherwise) on her behalf, if the curse were more openly shared through "promiscuous" contact, including temporary intimacies with strangers, then it would cease to circulate as a marker of individual stigma and instead become subject to the more collective responsibilities necessitated by shared risk.

Here, especially, the film's resonance with AIDS anxieties gains greater relevance. At the time *It Follows* appeared on screens, media attention began addressing the slow-growing popularity of pre-exposure prophylaxis (PrEP) drugs, such as Truvada, that prevent HIV viral transmission altogether, thus reopening possibilities for queer sexual life that once seemed foreclosed by the threat of AIDS and the push toward same-sex marriage.[30] In Tim Dean's 2009 book *Unlimited Intimacy*, he argues that condom-less "bareback" sex has arisen as both a subcultural practice and a wellspring of erotic fantasy among male-desiring men seeking radically queer alternatives to homonormative drives toward assimilationism and conformity. Whereas a mainstream gay identity politics promotes the right to marriage and adoption by same-sex couples, the bareback subculture uses real or imagined HIV transmission to "breed" emergent forms of kinship that, by eroticizing a once-fatal disease, fall afoul of gay culture's newfound political correctness. As Dean notes, one of the unforeseen ironies of the AIDS crisis was how the threat of transmission inadvertently paved the way for widespread acceptance of same-sex marriage, precisely by encouraging male-desiring men to stay "safe" by restricting sexual fluid exchange within the bounds of monogamy.[31]

Made feasible by the post-1990s spread of protease inhibitors (which minimize HIV replication in the infected body), the rise of barebacking represents a queer ethics based around not only the shared risk of infection but also the openness to alterity once more commonly associated with "risky" behaviors like cruising.[32] Even if Dean tends to paint San Francisco's distinct barebacking subculture as full of tattooed, muscular, ultramasculine "power bottoms" embracing an ethos of self-sacrifice, recent advances like PrEP drugs help mitigate the sheer extent of the risk assumed by barebackers.[33] Nevertheless, these preventative medications also help open an ethics of queer life to far more than a subset of urban queer men – thus proving another important instance where queer culture could educate straight culture. Still, the fact that early PrEP users have often been stigmatized as "Truvada whores" serves as a reminder that, much as birth-control pills were initially denigrated as an unlimited "license to fuck" for straight women, it will not be easy to overcome the various forms of sexual shame that promote monogamy as a socially acceptable norm.[34]

Overall, then, *It Follows* appeared at a historical moment when a hetero-cum-homonormative model of monogamy was upheld as law of the land in its extension to gay and lesbian couples, while a countervailing trend saw the (partial) overcoming of longtime anxieties about the most infamously fatal of sex-borne diseases, opening fresh possibilities for sexual autonomy through multiplicitous intimacies. The film may not have been deliberately intended as a sociopolitical commentary on such shifts – indeed, David Robert Mitchell left the monster's motives and weaknesses nightmarishly unexplained and open to interpretation – but the place of queerness as a sort of structuring absence within the text, an unnamed but perpetually haunting presence, still speaks to the film's centrality within an emergent "structure of feeling" informed by queerness's lingering status as an indeterminate quality that, despite recent political shifts, cannot be fully incorporated into normative socialization.

Moreover, despite the horrific deaths resulting from Jay's efforts to pass on the curse, the film itself closes on a darkly (post)ironic note that undercuts the apparent restoration of monogamy – heterosexual or otherwise. Although Jay initially rebuffs Paul's offer to receive the curse, suspecting a mere excuse to consummate his longtime crush on her, her trust is established when Paul foments a plan to lure It to a deserted Detroit pool and electrocute It with disused household appliances. Despite the plan proving a disastrous failure when It (having taken the form of Jay and Kelly's absent father) refuses to enter the pool and Yara is wounded in the climactic tumult, the monster is temporarily dispelled with a well-placed bullet.[35] Thereafter falling back on another previously failed solution, Jay finally consents to have sex with Paul and transfer the curse to him – having apparently failed to learn that even serial monogamy will not dismantle the linear chain of transmission. In the post-coital moment, Paul asks if she feels any different, and she shakes her head no. "Do you?" she responds, as Paul sits in silent disappointment. While neither of them "feels any different" from transferring the curse to Paul, this pregnant line also suggests that the simmering sexual tension between them has had little emotional payoff through its anticlimactic consummation. We next see Paul driving past several prostitutes on a lonely street corner, mentally debating whether to pass along the curse to them – two women who, because of their stigmatized status as sex workers, are presumably disposable, or would at least succeed in passing the curse along to an unsuspecting client.

Figure 6.2 The "happy" monogamous couple as image of ruination: Jay and Paul walk down their suburban streets, unaware that It still follows them in the distance, in the final shot of *It Follows*. (Source: Blu-ray.)

The film closes, however, with a shot of Jay and Paul walking silently hand in hand down their quiet suburban streets, unaware that It is still approaching in the distance behind them (Figure 6.2). This open ending implies that Paul, portrayed throughout as a somewhat nerdy and hopeless romantic, could not go through with infidelity to Jay – even for purely instrumental reasons that would potentially save them both from impending danger. Casey Ryan Kelly optimistically reads this concluding image as Jay and Paul having agreed to shoulder their burden by keeping It following them in perpetuity, to prevent it from preying on Detroit's more precarious citizens.[36] Yet, rather than reading Jay and Paul as acquiescing to social responsibility by altruistically upholding their link in the chain of transmission, I more cynically interpret the ending shot as a warning to the viewer of what *not* to do in order to survive. Jay and Paul's future relationship is likely as flimsy as Paul's failed plan to trap It in the pool, so not only does the pathos of their earlier post-coital exchange cast doubt on this naively "romantic" final image, but the cruel optimism of monogamy has also implicitly sentenced the seemingly happy couple to death. It is, then, an image of monogamous, romantic love in ruination: a human-made edifice that still stands, but whose external visage betrays its fundamentally crumbling character, evincing a sort of melancholy beauty in its decay.

Furthermore, the sense of pathos we might experience at the film's conclusion is a cumulative effect of the film's larger use of setting: an evocative synthesis of its actual filming location and its use of retro signifiers to evoke both an urban and film-historical past that have each been subject to ambivalent forms of nostalgia. If these uses of setting merely served as proverbial window-dressing, they would not merit extended discussion, but they instead prove instrumental in lending the film an emotional and political weight that it might not otherwise possess, thereby enhancing its potential as a text that can be read as critiquing neoliberal economics and the traditional sexual mores subtending neoliberal privatization.

Ruin Porn and the Haunted Spaces of Detroit

Aside from the film's obvious twist upon the common convention that horny teenagers are the first to die in a 1970s or 1980s horror film, *It Follows* is rife with post-ironic allusions to that period of genre history, creating less of a hip, ironic retro-pastiche than a more subtle level of nostalgic ambience. In the film's first moments, for instance, a shapely teenage girl wearing a diaphanous camisole and high heels runs away from the as-yet-unseen entity, her attire and unlikely footwear slyly recalling the horror genre's history of scantily-clad female victims. Other scenes are more obvious citations of specific films: when Jay flees her community-college class after seeing It (in the form of an elderly woman in a hospital gown) walking toward her outside the window, the film recalls similar monster sightings during classroom scenes in both *Halloween* (1978) and especially *A Nightmare on Elm Street* (1984). Other *Nightmare*-inspired scenes come when Jay, disturbed by the encounter with the old woman, invites her friends to sleep over and stay up all night to keep watch; and when, once she has transferred the curse to Greg, she stays awake watching his house from her bedroom window, warning him too late of the approaching threat. Jay and Kelly's mother is an alcoholic, much like Nancy's mother in *Nightmare*, helping account for the conspicuous absence of concerned parents throughout much of the film. Composer Rich Vreeland's (aka Disasterpeace) analog synthesizer score adds to the overall retro vibe, at times recalling Air's electronic score for the 1970s-set *The Virgin Suicides* – another film about teenage girls and seemingly peaceful Michigan suburbs haunted by loss. And one of the film's alternate theatrical posters even features a hand-illustrated design (a terrified young woman looking in a rearview mirror) reminiscent of so many early VHS box covers and 1980s horror paperback novels.

Indeed, with its more somber focus on the emotional tribulations of teenage sexuality (including not only Jay's predicament but also Paul's jealousy over Jay initially passing him over for Greg), *It Follows* occupies a liminal territory between the horror genre and the sort of indie coming-of-age drama exemplified by Mitchell's previous Detroit-set feature, *The Myth of the American Sleepover* (2011). *It Follows* thus achieves much of its affective weight by grounding the recognizably realistic emotions of its contemporary teen characters within a generic framework that subtly colludes with many critics' "gloomy nostalgia" for 1970s horror as a more artistically and politically engaged period in genre history than the present moment might seem to be.[37] Paradoxically, then, the film's nostalgic nods toward a bygone past help affectively charge the emotional realism of its present-day characters by situating these recognizably realistic teenage protagonists within a diegesis suffused with other forms of (temporal) longing and angst borne of nostalgia, combined with the pathos of recognizing that, much like the film's falsely "happy" ending, the past was never as ideal as our various nostalgias might want to imagine.

It is, in this sense, particularly notable that the film's temporal signifiers gain more political relevance in regard to economic class and, by extension, the dramatic class disparities that have bedeviled Detroit and so many other postindustrial cities in the American Rust Belt. One of the most common critical observations about *It Follows* is the film's apparently promiscuous use of temporal signifiers, including (among others): a 1980s-style synth score, 1970s-era cars and kitchen appliances, clothes bearing 1980s touches, 1950s "creature features" like *Killers from Space* (1954) broadcast on rabbit-eared television sets, and a palm-size e-reader that does not actually exist (but is, as one critic evocatively puts it, "shaped like a pack of birth-control pills").[38] As Mitchell explains:

> There's a lot of things from the '70s and '80s, I think a lot of people feel like it's a period piece to that point, and it probably leans in that direction, but there are enough things from many different time periods to where you can't quite put your finger on when it's taking place. And that's the intention, it's like a dream or a nightmare.[39]

And yet, regardless of how critics and viewers may think the film gently blurs together multiple time periods, the appearance of these seemingly outdated temporal signifiers is actually far more reflective of class disparities – albeit class disparities that also resonate with sexual disparities.

Following Elizabeth Freeman, we can connect the film's temporal indeterminacy to its overall queer structure of feeling, as "in its dominant forms, class enables its bearers what looks like 'natural' control over their body and its effects, or the diachronic means of sexual and social reproduction. In turn, failures or refusals to inhabit middle- and upper-class habitus appear as, precisely, asynchrony, or time out of joint. And as denizens of times out of joint, queers *are* a subjugated class."[40] As though embarrassingly fixated on the past, the film's queering of temporalities thus echoes its overall tenor of sexual shame, because shame's mnemonic affect ("to remember shame is to experience it anew") creates "queer community [as] a community of spatial discrepancy and asynchronicity, where past and present are concurrent and in which we enjoy the pleasures of the collective and relive our original isolation at the same time."[41] Despite *It Follows*'s human characters being figured as heterosexual, then, their difficulties asserting "natural" control over their bodies and their bodies' effects affectively open onto the broader histories of sexual and economic loss that have found particular purchase in Detroit.

Although Jay and Kelly Height live in the suburbs (in the Oakland County municipality of Sterling Heights, to be precise) just outside Detroit's city limits, their home illustrates the fact that many suburb dwellers are not necessarily middle class – or at least as uniformly middle class as dominant cinematic depictions of the American suburbs tend to imply. If American movies generally tend to paint such a homogeneously classed image of the suburbs, it is little surprise that so many viewers (mis)read *It Follows*'s temporal signifiers as more of a stylistic idiosyncrasy than a barely exaggerated version of what many real-world homes of working-class suburban families actually look like. Step into many such homes and one is likely to find furniture or appliances that have not been updated since the 1970s, secondhand clothes and electronics purchased from garage sales and thrift stores, and all manner of outdated commodities commingling with a more limited number of newer models. The past persists out of economic necessity, not out of hipster affectation.

This contrast is made clear when we compare the resolutely working-class interior of the Height home with the typically bourgeois home of Greg's family just across the street: the latter's furniture, fixtures, and appliances all look modern and up-to-date, and when It breaks into both homes during the film, only Greg's house has a burglar alarm. While observing the flashing lights and commotion as the police interview Jay about her captivity by Hugh, one of Greg's family members even looks across the street and remarks, "Those people are such a mess." The class divide between the two homes, separated by a mere strip of pavement, could scarcely be more apparent in this disgusted judgment. Moreover, when Jay tells the police that she hasn't actually been inside Hugh/Jeff's supposed house (his squatter pad, rented under a false name) because he was allegedly ashamed of where he lived, it is not hard to see her respect for his hesitation as tacit acknowledgment of what she thinks is their shared economic underclass status.

In one of *It Follows*'s several moments of post-coital poignancy, Jay – lazing in the back of Hugh/Jeff's car, unaware that she has just received the curse – absentmindedly tells him about one of her younger teenage fantasies. She explains that she had wanted to simply drive away with her lover – not to any specific destination but simply in search of a sense of freedom – but "now that we're old enough, where the hell do we go?" This line, uttered just before Jay is sedated with chloroform and tied up by her deceptive boyfriend, could just as easily apply to her later relationship with Paul – a monogamous bond that, given the continued threat from It, is also not likely to go anywhere. The ability to get away is, of course, crucial to the film's plot – as is the centrality of cars as both a mode of transport and a symbol of Detroit's former glory. Greg owns his own car to take Jay and her friends to his family's hunting cabin on the lake, but Jay must either escape her supernatural pursuer on a bicycle or by borrowing her mother's car. Aside from car ownership as a class privilege, consider that the cursed might hypothetically hop on a cross-country or international flight to buy herself plenty of respite from It – but the fact that this option is never mentioned implicitly acknowledges its economic impossibility. Perpetual travel and multiple residences would render the threat of It largely moot, but this class luxury clearly does not exist for working-class denizens like Jay.

It is also notable that Jay acquires the curse during sex in the back of Hugh/Jeff's 1975 Plymouth Gran Fury – a formerly Detroit-made car – and that the trauma of her forced captivity and first sighting of It was filmed in the ruins of Detroit's Packard Automotive Plant, thus visually cementing the link between the horrific and Detroit's urban decay. Cinematographer Mike Gioulakis notes that Mitchell had initially planned to shoot this scene at a completely different building, but the filmmakers were quickly forced to change locations because of an active murder investigation occurring at the originally slated filming site.[42] Detroit's high violent crime rate may have impinged on the film's production, but by turning to what is one of the city's most commonly photographed locations for the creation of so-called ruin porn, the film actually ends up indexing the economic causes underlying so much of the city's rampant crime.

The recent neologism "ruin porn" refers to the primarily photographic discourse produced by tourists, urban explorers, and artists whose images find beauty in the decay of de-industrialized cities like Detroit.[43] Unlike the far longer and less controversial practice of aestheticizing ancient or pre-industrial ruins, ruin porn gains its allegedly "pornographic" tenor by encouraging sublime pleasure in viewing these decrepit, depopulated spaces and thereby glossing over the temporally proximate human lives ruined by the decline of urban industry. Aside from the moralistically overdetermined connotations of the term "porn" in this context,[44] ruin porn also tends to present an oversimplified visual rhetoric that focuses less on the root causes of industrial decay (the removal of manufacturing bases by corporate and state interests) than the after-effects of a seemingly inevitable decline. To its detractors, ruin porn thus evacuates urban sites of historical context, freezing them in a post-apocalyptic mortification that serves for little more than aesthetic contemplation by viewers who don't actually have to live there.[45]

In her study of Detroit as the quintessential site of ruin porn, Dora Apel summarizes this aesthetic's cumulative function as a politically conservative one:

> The images participate, wittingly or not, in constructing the dominant narrative of Detroit as a story about an eternal romantic struggle between culture and nature, or a natural downward spiral of historical progress. The romantic narrative is precisely, perversely, what yields the pleasure of the deindustrial sublime, containing and controlling the anxiety of decline provoked by the images through the safety and distance of representation. This mental mastery of the terrifying is the nature of the ruin imaginary. [. . .] Detroit ruin imagery thus performs a doubly reassuring function, suggesting either that the city is to blame for its own conditions or that this state of affairs is historically inevitable and no one is to blame. Either way, the dominant forces of capital as the real agents of decline become naturalized and the threat of fiscal austerities for many other towns and cities hidden from view.[46]

Although most of the film transpires in Detroit's northern suburbs, *It Follows* does trade in some of these images: from the aforementioned scene at the Packard plant, to the wide-angle shots of the deserted city streets that Greg's car glides down, to the abandoned house where Hugh/Jeff has hung old bottles and cans over the windows, a makeshift It alarm that could just as easily warn of the city's many homeless individuals and serial arsonists.

Sometimes critically lumped into the post-horror corpus, *Don't Breathe* (2016) similarly depicts Detroit's depopulated urban neighborhoods as a potential war zone where impoverished residents prey upon each other in an attempt to escape to friendlier climes. In that film, however, three teens (one of whom is played by *It Follows*'s Daniel Zovatto) attempt to rob a blind Gulf War veteran, only to find themselves trapped in his private stronghold against the surrounding urban decay, where he has been artificially inseminating captive women to bear a replacement daughter for his biological daughter (tragically killed in a traffic accident). Like *It Follows*, then, Detroit's lack of economic productivity is figured as a setting for monstrous forms of non-consensual reproduction. *Don't Breathe* also looks ahead to *A Quiet Place*'s (2018) narrative conceit, since the characters must remain silent to avoid detection by the blind man's heightened hearing, especially after the viewer's potential sympathies for the shut-in veteran have shifted following the revelation that he has been raping his own captives. Yet, much like its closest generic kin, *The People Under the Stairs* (1991), *Don't Breathe* ramps up to fast-paced action within the enclosed domestic space once the film's "true" monster(s) is revealed, whereas *It Follows* maintains a much slower pace befitting its characters' overall sense of drifting through their wider (sub)urban milieu.

As the friends drive past abandoned houses while trekking across the city limits to the public pool to do battle with the monster, Yara off-handedly remarks, "when I was a little girl, my parents wouldn't allow me to go south of 8 Mile [Road, the city's northern border]. And I didn't even know what that meant until I got a little older and I started realizing that's where the city started and the suburbs ended. And I used to think about how shitty and weird that was." "My mom said the same thing," Jay replies – but a whole history is implied in this simple exchange. Indeed, Adam Lowenstein suggests that one of the monster's most unnerving aspects is its utter indifference to the ideologically charged borders between urban and suburban spaces that the human characters still respect, as though It is a force representing Detroit's slow spatial reclamation from its former human inhabitants.[47]

Thomas Sugrue and Kevin Boyle both observe that Detroit's deindustrialization began following World War II, with major industries slashing jobs – especially the types of unskilled labor once held by African Americans, now performed through automation – or moving those jobs northward to the more affluent white suburbs. (Here we might recall *Get Out*'s (2017) opening depiction of white suburbs as racially exclusionary spaces, potentially unsafe for people of color.) As white flight continued, the effects of racism in employment and housing kept most African Americans from following those jobs to the suburbs, eventually creating what remains one of the most racially segregated cities in America.[48] According to a recent estimate, "While Detroit is almost 83 percent black, the neighboring white working-class suburbs are less than 2 percent black" with rates of unemployment and violent crime disproportionately higher in the increasingly depopulated city than surrounding areas.[49] With little cooperation existing between Detroit's black political leadership and the white suburbs, the city's decline has been more commonly blamed on its majority black population than the relocation of white-run industries over the late twentieth century.

Although the film is not dominated by images of ruin porn, those that do appear are tempered by a certain awareness of how "shitty and weird" (to put it mildly) dominant attitudes continue to be toward Detroit's disenfranchised racial underclass. When Jay, for example, peers out the window of Hugh/Jeff's abandoned house and sees a young black man walking around outside, she recoils with fear that It has once again found her – but this brief shot also contains a tinge of racial anxiety, given the historically black city's notoriety among its white neighbors. Black faces are only fleetingly seen throughout the film, a result not only of so much time being spent in Sterling Heights but also perhaps a reluctance on Mitchell's part to visually associate urban decay with blackness and thereby echo the racism that has long attributed Detroit's downfall to its black residents. After all, the film may visually associate Detroit's decay with the horrific, by repeatedly depicting the "Heights" (Jay and Kelly's surname) facing threats when they journey into the city and back, but the suburbs prove no safer from It.

Much of the debate over ruin porn concerns who has the right to produce it: exploitative outsiders with little or no understanding of Detroit's history versus local insiders capturing images of their city out of respect for its plight. Moreover, Detroit locals often take umbrage that ruin porn widely publicizes and exaggerates the city's problems, broadcasting a sense of helplessness and obscuring more optimistic signs of urban renewal. Small wonder, then, that a neighbor suspiciously eyes Jay and her friends as they enter the abandoned house; as much as the neighbor might be on the lookout for criminality, she could also mistake the teenagers for young ruin tourists in search of eerie locations (not unlike the filmmakers themselves). George Steinmetz suggests that "the largest group of non-locals participating in the representation of Detroit's ruins consists of white suburbanites who left the city or whose parents and grandparents fled a generation or two ago" – an adequate description of *It Follows* creator David Robert Mitchell. While ruin porn might, on some level, conjure nostalgia for a bygone Fordist era of economic prosperity and urban stability, Steinmetz sees this nostalgia as especially mutable because "most suburbanites have transferred their deeper investments, both psychic and economic, to the suburbs and beyond."[50] As one critic (and former Detroiter) astutely observed, "It doesn't strike me as coincidence that Mitchell, who grew up in suburban Oakland County, has his white heroine catch the curse in Detroit (while having sex in the parking lot of an abandoned factory), and that when the decay follows her to the suburbs, she flees further north with her friends, repeating a pattern started by her parents and grandparents."[51]

In this respect, the nostalgic aesthetic of *It Follows* – its mixture of temporal signifiers that locate the film in both the past and the present – may have more to do with idealizing a suburban past than an urban one. Yet the fact that those temporal signifiers also index present-day economic disparities within even the northern suburbs raises the specter of neoliberalism's broader divestment of capital from workers to corporate owners, of which Detroit's de-industrialization is only the most visible part. Furthermore, Apel argues that the insider-versus-outsider discourse about ruin porn is fundamentally flawed, because it is not possible to accurately discern a photographer's artistic intent when any image can foster multiple interpretations, from touristic exploitation to local appreciation.[52]

We might compare, for example, the Detroit of *It Follows* with Jim Jarmusch's genre hybrid *Only Lovers Left Alive* (2013), in which a depopulated Motown serves as temporary haven for a trio of globe-trotting, hipster vampires. Visiting prominent ruin-porn sites like the Packard plant and the Michigan Theater, they describe the abandoned city spaces as having become a "wilderness," but they are also conspicuously able to hop on a flight to Tangiers or Los Angeles at a moment's notice. On one hand, they have more in common with the "creative class" of predominantly young, white artists and entrepreneurs who, drawn by promises of cheap rent and images of romantic ruination, have settled in downtown Detroit over the past decade, creating "two different cities within Detroit, one a tiny thriving gentrified area of millennials and the other the devastated neighborhoods in most of the rest of Detroit, in a microcosm of the chasm of inequality nationwide."[53] On the other hand, though, the centuries-old vampires' privileged ability to survive indefinitely (even to the point of contemplating suicide), while offering wry commentary on the human species' broader environmental self-destruction, speaks more to Jarmusch's smugly ironic, Gen-X sensibility than the melancholy sense of precarity faced by *It Follows*'s young people, prematurely nostalgic for their own youth in the face of a foreshortened future, because saddled with larger post-Great Recession burdens than their generational predecessors.[54]

Detroit's rise and fall paralleled that of Fordism, the capitalist industrial system of standardized mass production and consumption that characterized much of twentieth-century America – before the post-1960s rise of neoliberalism's deregulated, globalized capitalism (buttressed by state support), widespread austerity measures, and privatization of public services drastically undercut the potential prosperity of working- and middle-class citizens. As such, it makes sense that many people drawn to latter-day Detroit's industrial ruins "experience the neoliberal, hyper-competitive present as intensely challenging and long for the days of Fordist working-class solidarity and cross-class coalitions of economic interest."[55] As Apel observes, neoliberalism's effects on everyday life have hit Detroit especially hard in the wake of the city's Chapter 9 bankruptcy proceedings in

June 2013, from the privatization of basic services (such as water, electricity, garbage disposal, mass transit) to the divesture of municipal assets and workers' pensions, to the further erosion of collective bargaining rights for labor unions. But in this regard, Detroit exemplifies, and serves as a warning of, the broader socio-economic inequalities that have become endemic under neoliberalism – hence the iconic role acquired by its much documented postindustrial ruins.[56]

And here we can finally conjoin the political relevance of *It Follows*'s haunted urban spaces to its possibilities for a queer ethics. As I suggested earlier, the film's monstrous threat would be assuaged by a turn away from monogamy and toward far more multiplicitous sexual contacts, engendering a community that does not disavow sexual shame and instead embraces shared risk through an ethical dynamic of open communication and collective responsibility (such as contact tracing). In his discussion of queer life in Times Square's once-numerous adult movie theaters, Samuel Delany describes such open sexual contact (as actualized in cruising spaces for public sex) as welcoming alterity and risk, which paradoxically makes urban life safer by fostering productive (if unpredictable) cross-racial and cross-class connections with strangers.[57] Likewise, Tim Dean updates and extends this argument to bareback sex's embrace of seroconversion risk as exemplifying a more ethical means of fostering community than the fear-based avoidance of social others.[58]

The connotations of ruin porn in *It Follows*'s Detroit setting become more notable (and even literalized) in this regard, as it was precisely the ruination of old urban centers that opened their economically impoverished spaces to reclamation by queer patrons forming covert communities organized around public sex. As Tim Edensor theorizes, postindustrial ruins become liberating spaces for all manner of licit or illicit play, "serv[ing] as erotic realms where sex can take place beyond prying eyes, but by virtue of their proximity to settled urbanity, these endeavors may also be charged with the frisson of forbidden practice."[59] In this sense, it is not difficult to see how postindustrial ruins' "spooky absent presence of the past, the ghosts that swarm through spaces of dereliction, producing the not quite comprehensible," could take on queer potentialities.[60] While *It Follows* depicts Detroit's abandoned Packard Plant as a horrific site through the scene of Jay's disturbingly non-consensual bondage, we might also imagine the city's many ruins as potential contact zones for the very sorts of open, consensual sexual contact that would help disperse the curse's threat (Figure 6.3). Rich Cante and Angelo Restivo note, for example, that the cruising grounds featured in urban-set gay porn films depict how "pornography seems to have invaded all of the 'useless' and

Figure 6.3 The monster's first appearance in *It Follows*, in the form of a nude woman inside the Packard plant, indexes both a ruin-porn aesthetic and the potential for such postindustrial spaces to be reclaimed for open, polyvalent sexual practices. (Source: Blu-ray.)

abandoned spaces of postmodern urban capitalism not yet ready to be made residential or legitimately commercial. In retrospect, we can see this uneven development as having been governed by a large-scale reorganization of capitalism toward dispersed, transnational modes of production and consumption."[61]

Yet it is also this ethical sense of community that has been endangered by neoliberalism's widespread privatization of social services – including sexual health services – in places like post-bankruptcy Detroit, where HIV infection rates have reached "crisis" levels.[62] Take, for instance, my earlier allusion to PrEP drugs like Truvada – a course of which cost about $1,500 per month in 2015 and, because more often associated with license for promiscuous sexual opportunities than with basic sexual rights, are not covered by many insurance plans. Aaron Braun notes that, whereas an earlier generation of queer activists like ACT UP demanded more democratic access to early anti-AIDS drugs like AZT, many of those older activists oppose PrEP drugs for encouraging non-monogamous sex, thus allowing access to PrEP drugs to remain a distinct class privilege while also stigmatizing users as non-homonormative. Consequently, "working-class and low-income people, predominantly people of color, are excluded from a crucial sector of the pharmaceutical industry that directly serves LGBTQ folk. Meanwhile, public figures resort to sexual moralizing that seeks to dismiss new drugs and thus the needs of those most affected."[63] Sarah Schulman notes that such symptoms of the "gentrification of gay politics" have accompanied the more familiar gentrification of urban spaces: much as the campaign for same-sex marriage accelerated with the homonormative displacement of risk via monogamy, the post-1970s gentrification of urban neighborhoods was facilitated by the dramatic rise in housing vacancies created by the AIDS epidemic's high death rate.[64] Even as a resident of Detroit's predominantly white, northern suburbs, Jay's working-class status in *It Follows* thus resonates with larger questions about the exclusionary transformation of urban environments and the related restriction of access to certain sexual health services. PrEP drugs may still be marketed primarily to gay men, but with more democratic means of access, their wider implications for sexual freedoms clearly extend beyond subcultural and class boundaries.

As austerity measures shift the purview of basic services from the public good to corporate control (and often higher prices in the process), it has become more common for sexual shame and civic shame to go hand in hand. Mark Padilla, for example, finds young Detroiters hoping to distance themselves from the "spatial stigma" associated with living in the city, even as many have also been forced by economic necessity into the stigmatizing realm of sex work (recall the prostitutes at the end of *It Follows*, which is also mentioned as the only other means of self-sufficiency available to *Don't Breathe*'s female protagonist). Because neoliberalism emphasizes individual responsibility instead of public interest, Detroit's most vulnerable citizens (not its outsourced corporations) shoulder the blame for the city's postindustrial decline, which compounds the sexual stigma assigned to citizens' sexual- and gender-nonconforming bodies.[65]

Perhaps it is no surprise, then, that *It Follows* nostalgically looks to the past for inspiration, even as its promiscuous pastiche of different periods contaminates any simple notion that the past was a wholly idyllic time. Although, for example, we might see the film's 1970s-era temporal signifiers as invoking a pre-AIDS period when cruising, swinging, and other forms of non-monogamous sex carried different, less fatal understandings of risk, that decade also saw the dramatic acceleration of Detroit's de-industrialization: "Detroit lost 5 percent of its jobs every year between 1972 and 1992, a rate of deindustrialization dramatically higher than that of the 1950s."[66] Viewed through a queer lens, its overall aesthetic of ruination mourns the lost collectivities of pre-AIDS queer subcultures and working-class solidarities alike – social bonds that once served as a bulwark against different varieties of shared vulnerability. After all, as Adam Lowenstein observes, "aloneness itself becomes a sign of potential monstrosity" in *It Follows*, since It most often takes the form of lone walking figures amid Detroit's depopulated landscape, instead of as active members of communal groups.[67]

Through its use of anachronism, *It Follows* therefore looks back to a period on the cusp of neoliberalism's post-1960s triumph, even as the immediately recognizable ruins of present-day Detroit belie any simplistic idealization of the past. By depicting its characters traversing the raced and classed borders between the northern suburbs and the decayed metropolis, *It Follows* traces an urban history whose widely circulated images of latter-day ruination cast ironic light on the film's characterization of monogamy itself as a monstrous edifice, threatening to fatally collapse at any moment upon the film's doomed lovers. But if these characters' unfortunate fates inadvertently offer us lessons in survival, as horror films so often do, those lessons are to be found in the polymorphous expressions of queer sexual community that, in a homonormative climate, have been seemingly consigned to a more naive, pre-assimilationist past.

Yet, if we follow Lee Edelman's suggestion that the "ethical burden" of queerness must be to embrace an existential refusal of future-oriented meaning, maximizing the live-for-today jouissance of ego-destroying sexual pleasure over the empty promises of future progress, then we are left at a political impasse.[68] Indeed, why pursue social or political change if, as *Only Lovers Left Alive*'s decadent vampires note, Earth itself is quickly becoming inhospitable to human life altogether? Whereas *It Follows* raises issues around the sexual uses of one's body, the films addressed in my final chapter move into the realm of existential dread on an even larger scale. In turning from this chapter's explicitly political analysis of sexual ethics toward some of post-horror's more metaphysical questions about the limits of human existence, we come full circle to post-horror's purported challenge to the genre's own limits.

Notes

1. J. A. Bridges, "Post-Horror Kinships: From *Goodnight Mommy* to *Get Out*," *Bright Lights Film Journal*, December 20, 2018 <https://brightlightsfilm.com/post-horror-kinships-from-goodnight-mommy-to-get-out/>.
2. Michael Warner, *The Trouble with Normal: Sex, Politics, and the Ethics of Queer Life* (New York: Free Press, 1999).
3. Eleanor Wilkinson, "What's Queer about Non-Monogamy Now?" in *Understanding Non-Monogamies*, eds Meg Barker and Darren Langdridge (London: Routledge, 2009), pp. 243–54.
4. Casey Ryan Kelly, "*It Follows*: Precarity, Thanatopolitics, and the Ambient Horror Film," *Critical Studies in Media Communication*, 34, no. 3 (2017), p. 5.

5. Chris Kaye, "The Unrelenting Pursuer in Horror Film *It Follows*," *Newsweek*, January 24, 2015 <http://www.newsweek.com/2015/02/06/unrelenting-pursuer-horror-film-it-follows-301761.html>.
6. See, among others, Ellis Hanson, "Undead," in *Inside/Out: Lesbian Theories, Gay Theories*, ed. Diana Fuss (New York: Routledge, 1991), pp. 324–40; Harry M. Benshoff, *Monsters in the Closet: Homosexuality and the Horror Film* (Manchester: Manchester University Press, 1997).
7. In this regard, *It Follows* breaks from American cinema's post-9/11 reinforcement of the George W. Bush-era pro-abstinence movement, as described in Casey Ryan Kelly, *Abstinence Cinema: Virginity and the Rhetoric of Sexual Purity in Contemporary Cinema* (New Brunswick, NJ: Rutgers University Press, 2016).
8. This visual linkage of sexually transmitted "curse" and the wheelchair may also subtly suggest HIV/AIDS's potential status as a chronic impairment.
9. Leslie A. Hahner and Scott J. Varda, "*It Follows* and Rape Culture: Critical Response as Disavowal," *Women's Studies in Communication*, 40, no. 3 (2017), p. 254.
10. The apparition's later sighting as an unidentified nude man standing atop the roof of Jay's house also plays into a queer reading of the monster's fluid appearance, as does Jay's gender-neutral name (short for "Jamie"). See Carol Clover's discussion of the androgynous names among the horror genre's "Final Girls" in *Men, Women, and Chainsaws: Gender in the Modern Horror Film* (Princeton, NJ: Princeton University Press, 1992), p. 40. Nude middle-aged to elderly people as visual sources of horror have also become a recurring trope in the films of Ari Aster and Robert Eggers, among other post-horror works.
11. Hahner and Varda, however, argue that Hugh's sex with Jay under false pretenses could be legally recognized as "rape by deception" ("*It Follows* and Rape Culture," 253).
12. Yet this parallel also has notable shortcomings: HIV is, after all, a known quantity, and thus perhaps more likely to stigmatize the recipient than Jay's mysterious curse would be, despite seroconversion not being the death sentence it once was (at least in developed nations with readier access to antiviral therapies). Likewise, It is a singular entity affecting only one person at a time, unlike HIV/AIDS as a disease affecting many people simultaneously.
13. Hahner and Varda, "*It Follows* and Rape Culture," 257–64.
14. Pamela Craig and Martin Fradley, "Teenage Traumata: Youth, Affective Politics, and the Contemporary American Horror Film," in *American Horror Film: The Genre at the Turn of the Millennium*, ed. Steffen Hantke (Jackson, MS: University Press of Mississippi, 2010), pp. 87, 88.
15. Ibid., p. 78.
16. Adam Charles Hart, *Monstrous Forms: Moving Image Horror Across Media* (New York: Oxford University Press, 2020), p. 149.
17. Joshua Grimm, *It Follows* (Leighton Buzzard: Auteur, 2018), p. 75.
18. Hahner and Varda, "*It Follows* and Rape Culture," 262 (original emphasis).

19. Grimm, *It Follows*, 87.
20. Ben Dalton, "*It Follows*: Horror in a Straight Line," *Intensities: The Journal of Cult Media*, no. 8 (2016), p. 90.
21. Warner, *Trouble with Normal*, 35.
22. Ibid., pp. 73, 74.
23. Ibid., p. 91.
24. Lisa Duggan, "The New Homonormativity: The Sexual Politics of Neoliberalism," in *Materializing Democracy: Toward a Revitalized Cultural Politics*, eds Russ Castronovo and Dana D. Nelson (Durham, NC: Duke University Press, 2002), pp. 175–94.
25. Wilkinson, "What's Queer," 247.
26. Lee Edelman, *No Future: Queer Theory and the Death Drive* (Durham, NC: Duke University Press, 2004), p. 149.
27. Douglas Crimp, "Mario Montez, for Shame," in *Gay Shame*, eds David M. Halperin and Valerie Traub (Chicago: University of Chicago Press, 2009), p. 72.
28. David Caron, "Shame on Me, or the Naked Truth about Me and Marlene Dietrich," in *Gay Shame*, 126, 127.
29. Sally R. Munt, *Queer Attachments: The Cultural Politics of Shame* (Burlington, VT: Ashgate, 2007), pp. 220–1.
30. For instance, see Christopher Glazek, "Why Is No One on the First Treatment to Prevent HIV?," *New Yorker*, September 30, 2013 <http://www.newyorker.com/tech/elements/why-is-no-one-on-the-first-treatment-to-prevent-hi-v>; Tim Murphy, "Sex without Fear," *New York*, July 13, 2014 <http://nymag.com/news/features/truvada-hiv-2014-7/>; Evan J. Peterson, "The Case for PrEP, or How I Learned to Stop Worrying and Love HIV-Positive Guys," *The Stranger*, November 12, 2014 <http://www.thestranger.com/seattle/the-case-for-prep-or-how-i-learned-to-stop-worrying-and-love-hiv-positive-guys/Content?oid=20991643>; and Ariana Eunjung Cha, "In New Study, 100 Percent of Participants Taking HIV Prevention Pill Truvada Remained Infection-Free," *Washington Post*, September 4, 2015 <http://www.washingtonpost.com/news/to-your-health/wp/2015/09/04/in-new-study-hiv-prevention-pill-truvada-is-startlingly-100-percent-effective/>.
31. Tim Dean, *Unlimited Intimacy: Reflections on the Subculture of Barebacking* (Chicago: University of Chicago Press, 2009), pp. 84–92.
32. Ibid., pp. 204–7, 210–11.
33. Ibid., pp. 52–6. More recently revisiting *Unlimited Intimacy* in light of Truvada's popularization, Dean questions whether barebacking on PrEP still counts as "barebacking" if the fantasy of viral transmission is rendered moot. More importantly, though, he criticizes how this purported sexual "freedom . . . depends on biomedical technologies and their unprecedented potential for monitoring the interior of our bodies" while extracting high profits from gay men. See Dean, "Mediated Intimacies: Raw Sex, Truvada, and the Biopolitics of Chemoprophylaxis," *Sexualities*, 18, no. 1/2 (2015), p. 241.

34. See David Duran, "Truvada Whores?," *Huffington Post*, November 12, 2012 <http://www.huffingtonpost.com/david-duran/truvada-whores_b_2113588.html>; Jim Burress, "'Truvada Whore' Stigma Endures Among Doctors and LGBTs," *The Advocate*, August 11, 2014 <https://www.advocate.com/health/2014/8/11/truvada-whore-stigma-endures-among-doctors-and-lgbts>; and Aaron Braun, "'Truvada Whores' and the Class Divide," *Pacific Standard*, August 17, 2015 <http://www.psmag.com/health-and-behavior/truvada-whores-and-the-aids-class-divide>.
35. Although Hugh/Jeff had earlier warned her that It might take the form of loved ones just to hurt her, it is never made clear why It specifically takes the form of Jay's father at this moment. One might speculate that Jay and Kelly's father is absent because he had an extramarital affair, possibly with someone else infected with the curse. (It is never made clear whether he is living or deceased.) Another common theory among film critics and fans has their father banished for past sexual abuse of his daughters – hence Jay's refusal to tell Kelly about what form she sees It take here – but the truth is ultimately left ambiguous.
36. Kelly, "It Follows," 13–14.
37. Craig and Fradley, "Teenage Traumata," 80.
38. Leslie Jamison, "It's Not Done," *Slate*, April 21, 2015 <http://www.slate.com/articles/arts/culturebox/2015/04/it_follows_and_the_transgressive_pleasure_of_the_horror_movie.single.html>.
39. Quoted in Meredith Woerner, "How *It Follows* Uses Dread and Beauty to Create the Perfect Monster Movie," *io9.com*, March 10, 2015 <http://io9.com/how-it-follows-uses-dread-and-beauty-to-create-the-perf-1690601352>.
40. Elizabeth Freeman, *Time Binds: Queer Temporalities, Queer Histories* (Durham, NC: Duke University Press, 2010), p. 19 (original emphasis). Freeman, for example, cites "T. S. Eliot's sexually frustrated J. Alfred Prufrock declaring himself to be 'Lazarus, come from the dead!'" as a queer literary character bound by multiple temporalities (7). This same line features prominently in *It Follows*, recited in the college classroom while Jay watches It approach in the guise of the elderly woman – not unlike *Hereditary*'s (2018) classroom discussion of tragic predestination as Paimon's influence on Peter grows.
41. Caron, "Shame on Me," 128, 129.
42. Gioulakis, interviewed in Matt Mulcahey, "'We Didn't Have to Add Too Much Creepiness': *It Follows* DP Mike Gioulakis," *Filmmaker Magazine*, March 31, 2015 <http://filmmakermagazine.com/93629-we-didnt-have-to-add-too-much-creepiness-it-follows-dp-mike-gioulakis/#.VfXB1nt8gQ0>.
43. For books of ruin porn specific to Detroit, see Yves Marchand and Romain Meffre, *The Ruins of Detroit* (Göttingen: Steidl, 2010); Andrew Moore, *Detroit Disassembled* (Bologna: Damiani/Akron Museum, 2010); Dan Austin, *Lost Detroit: Stories Behind the Motor City's Majestic Ruins* (Mount Pleasant, SC: Arcadia, 2010); and Julia Reyes Taubman, *Detroit: 138 Square Miles* (Detroit, MI: Museum of Contemporary Art, 2011).

44. Also see Helen Hester, *Beyond Explicit: Pornography and the Displacement of Sex* (Albany, NY: State University of New York Press, 2014).
45. Sarah Arnold, "Urban Decay Photography and Film: Fetishism and the Apocalyptic Imagination," *Journal of Urban History*, 41, no. 2 (2015), pp. 326–39. Arnold, for example, compares ruin porn to Victorian death photography, as both involve capturing mournful images of subjects too late to be saved but incapable of telling their own stories – much like the ghosts in *The Others* (2001).
46. Dora Apel, *Beautiful Terrible Ruins: Detroit and the Anxiety of Decline* (New Brunswick, NJ: Rutgers University Press, 2015), pp. 93, 100.
47. Adam Lowenstein, "A Detroit Landscape with Figures: The Subtractive Horror of *It Follows*," *Discourse*, 40, no. 3 (2018), pp. 361, 364–6.
48. Thomas J. Sugrue, *The Origins of the Urban Crisis: Race and Inequality in Postwar Detroit* (Princeton, NJ: Princeton University Press, 1996); and Kevin Boyle, "The Ruins of Detroit: Exploring the Urban Crisis in the Motor City," *Michigan Historical Review*, 27, no. 1 (2001), pp. 109–27.
49. Apel, *Beautiful Terrible Ruins*, 45.
50. George Steinmetz, "Harrowed Landscapes: White Ruingazers in Namibia and Detroit and the Cultivation of Memory," *Visual Studies*, 23, no. 3 (2008), pp. 217–18 (quote at p. 218).
51. Mark Binelli, "How *It Follows* Uses Detroit to Explore the Horror of Urban Decay," *Slate*, April 1, 2015 <http://www.slate.com/blogs/browbeat/2015/04/01/it_follows_how_the_new_movie_uses_detroit_to_explore_the_horror_of_urban.html>.
52. Apel, *Beautiful Terrible Ruins*, 23–4, 91–2.
53. Ibid., p. 34.
54. See Joni Hayward, "No Safe Space: Economic Anxiety and Post-Recession Spaces in Horror Films," *Frames Cinema Journal*, no. 11 (2017) <https://framescinemajournal.com/article/no-safe-space-economic-anxiety-and-post-recession-spaces-in-horror-films/>.
55. Steinmetz, "Harrowed Landscapes," 232.
56. Apel, *Beautiful Terrible Ruins*, 28–9, 33–4, 100.
57. Samuel Delany, *Times Square Red, Times Square Blue* (New York: New York University Press, 1999).
58. Dean, *Unlimited Intimacy*, 187–94.
59. Tim Edensor, *Industrial Ruins: Space, Aesthetics, and Materiality* (Oxford: Berg, 2005), p. 25. Edensor's refusal to identify the specific ruins he discusses has, however, been sharply criticized by other scholars; for example, High and Lewis: "In universalizing his gaze, Edensor strips these former industrial sites of their history and their geography just as surely as the departing companies, entrepreneurs, and trophy hunters stripped the sites of their assets." Steven C. High and David W. Lewis, *Corporate Wasteland: The Landscape and Memory of Deindustrialization* (Ithaca, NY: Cornell University Press, 2007), p. 60. Any optimistic consideration of postindustrial ruins as sites of anarchistic possibility should thus be counterbalanced by a more circumspect understanding of

the specific urban history (including the catastrophic impact upon local workers) behind each site.
60. Edensor, *Industrial Ruins*, 145.
61. Rich Cante and Angelo Restivo, "The Cultural-Aesthetic Specificities of All-Male Moving-Image Pornography," in *Porn Studies*, ed. Linda Williams (Durham, NC: Duke University Press, 2004), p. 162.
62. See Todd Heywood, "HIV in Detroit: Officials, Activists Agree It's a Crisis," American Independent Institute, March 19, 2012 <http://www.americanindependent.com/214111/hiv-in-detroit-officials-activists-agree-its-a-crisis>; Michigan Department of Community Health, "Annual HIV Surveillance Report: City of Detroit," Michigan Department of Health and Human Services, July 2014 <http://www.michigan.gov/documents/mdch/Detroit_July_2014_full_report_465194_7.pdf>.
63. Braun, "'Truvada Whores' and the Class Divide."
64. Sarah Schulman, *The Gentrification of the Mind: Witness to a Lost Imagination* (Berkeley, CA: University of California Press, 2012), pp. 27–8, 37, 115–16.
65. Mark Padilla, "Spatial Stigma, Sexuality, and Neoliberal Decline in Detroit, Michigan," *S&F Online*, 11, no. 1/2 (2012–13) <http://sfonline.barnard.edu/gender-justice-and-neoliberal-transformations/spatial-stigma-sexuality-and-neoliberal-decline-in-detroit-michigan/>.
66. Boyle, "Ruins of Detroit," 120–1.
67. Lowenstein, "A Detroit Landscape with Figures," 365.
68. Edelman, *No Future*, 47–8.

CHAPTER 7

Existential Dread and the Trouble with Transcendence

In this final chapter, I turn to four different post-horror films that, in addition to revisiting themes from earlier chapters, centrally explore issues of a more spiritual or metaphysical nature than *It Follows*'s (2014) bodily concerns about sexual contact as a strategy for survival when marked for approaching death. All of these films feature protagonists reduced to relative passivity by states of grief – but they also look toward possible ways out of grief through appeals to what might exist above and beyond the human. *A Dark Song* (2016) and *mother!* (2017) offer differing takes on religious belief, with *mother!* evincing a deep cynicism about the Judeo-Christian tradition, while *A Dark Song* offers a (very) qualified vindication of the types of occult practices quite literally demonized in most other horror films. Whereas *A Dark Song* ends with a sort of redemption – albeit after its protagonist abandons selfish ends for altruistic ones – *mother!* depicts an eternally recurring cycle of failed creation and subsequent destruction. Meanwhile, *A Ghost Story* (2017) and *I Am the Pretty Thing that Lives in the House* (2016) largely tell their minimalistic narratives from the ontological side of ghosts themselves, as spirits left behind to grieve the loss of their formerly human existence.

Notably, all of these films make extensive use of temporal ellipses to downplay the protagonists' experience of lived, human time in favor of cosmic or supernatural experiences of time. By evoking ambiguously fluid conceptions of time and history, these films implicitly turn our attention back toward the history of the horror genre itself, as an entity that post-horror only partially transcends. *A Ghost Story*'s titular protagonist is not only a melancholy wanderer across time, but also subverts the generic trope of the ghost as supernatural menace by visually marking him as a pathetic figure. *I Am the Pretty Thing*, by contrast, maintains more explicit links to the Gothic horror tradition – although its allusions to Alfred Hitchcock's *Psycho* (1960), by way of director Oz Perkins's father Anthony Perkins, also create a more ambivalent meditation on mortality and (generic) inheritance. Collectively exploring what might exist in another metaphysical plane of existence, the films in this closing chapter return us to the crux of post-horror's status as seemingly "elevated" above the rest of the horror corpus, even as the prospect of achieving such transcendence remains dubious at best.

A Dark Song: Grief as Angelic Conversation

Liam Gavin's *A Dark Song*, the story of a grieving mother who turns to high-ceremonial magic for vengeance against those who murdered her child, opens with an epigraph from Psalms 91: 11 – "For he shall give his angels charge over thee, to keep thee in all thy ways" – before an extreme long shot of Sophia (Catherine Walker) driving across a desolate Welsh landscape, not unlike the Scottish landscapes of *Under the Skin* (2013). After renting an isolated, Gothic manor house, Sophia enlists occultist Joseph Solomon (Steve Oram) to lead her through the "Abramelin operation," a months-long magical ritual for contacting one's Holy Guardian Angel (HGA) and, using the HGA's authority, binding "unredeemed" or demonic spirits to do one's bidding. Incidentally, Paimon is among the many kings and dukes of Hell called into service in this operation, but unlike *Hereditary*'s (2018) depiction of invoking Paimon through a combination of ritual magic and spiritualist parlor tricks, the medieval *Book of Abramelin*'s instructions require a far more ascetic endeavor, especially to keep these conjured spirits under control.[1] Hence Sophia's own process of striving toward "higher" supernatural contact overlaps with *A Dark Song*'s status as an elevated chamber drama for most of its duration, transcending even some of the familiar genre conventions still present in other post-horror films like *Hereditary*.

Almost unique among horror films for depicting occultism as a long and arduous process of personal transformation, *A Dark Song*'s narrative is structured by the course of the (here, semi-fictionalized) Abramelin operation itself, which Solomon, though conceding the "poor metaphor," describes as "a journey." Dispelling Sophia's assumption that the work will be a Kabbalistic exploration of "mental states," possibly involving "astral projection or runes" (such as the occult magic developed by the Hermetic Order of the Golden Dawn), he gradually leads her through a mix of prayer, meditation, fasting, sleep deprivation, and other endeavors, after they seal themselves inside the manor with a circle of salt. The film's overall pace is very slow and methodical, with only occasional signs of spooky emanations (such as creaking doors and unexplained thuds), to the point that, by halfway through its duration, Sophia herself is fed up with the lack of discernable progress as Solomon instructs her to begin the ritual cycle anew. In his glowing review, esoteric author Daniel Moler describes *A Dark Song* as "not a popcorn [horror] movie," but rather "high art, because the writer-director expects a little bit of effort out of the audience," including some background knowledge of esoteric texts. "Explanation will come, but you have to (like Sophia) be patient and endure the rituals and trials of initiation in order to attain it."[2]

Although Sophia is initially cagey about explaining her reasons for doing the working, first telling Solomon that it is "for love" (which he misinterprets as romantic love), she later reveals that she wants her HGA to deliver vengeance upon the "idiots" who, three years earlier, abducted and killed her young son Jack for an amateur occult ritual. Much like the mourning protagonists in Chapter 3, she displays post-traumatic symptoms around this loss (such as nightmares about child abduction), not only blaming herself for having been late to pick him up from day care, but also rejecting her Catholic faith because God's "goodness" has seemingly abandoned her to an unresolved grief that others cannot fathom.

While the actual Abramelin operation is supposed to be performed alone, by a man, and only after having comprehensively studied the instructions for six months before beginning, Solomon's role is closer to the master–disciple system described in another classic medieval grimoire, the *Key of Solomon*.[3] Indeed, Sophia's name is an obvious allusion to gaining knowledge, which Solomon describes as the underlying objective of doing occult work ("the point is to know . . . to see the architecture"), whereas his own name evokes the ancient Jewish king to whom the *Key of Solomon* and several other grimoires have been apocryphally attributed – but whom the *Book of Abramelin* actually chastises for misusing his arcane powers. As the film proceeds, we see multiple ways that Solomon breaks from the spiritual purity that the *Book of Abramelin* prescribes – whether through alcohol abuse, selling his magical craft, or using it for curiosity or entertainment value ("There's no point in going to the fairground if you're not going on any of the rides") – and he is eventually punished for his unholy transgressions.[4] Although the Abramelin operation's objective is more about enlisting unredeemed spirits into human service than asking one's HGA for "favors" (as *A Dark Song* suggests), both Sophia and Solomon seek ends for which the *Book of Abramelin* offers specific spells – vengeance for her and the power of invisibility for him – though neither one truly gets these things in the end.[5]

Much like *The Lighthouse* (2019), *A Dark Song* explores the almost (non-consensual) sadomasochistic power dynamic between two people locked inside together for months on end, with the more experienced person abusing his charge's trust; here, however, Solomon hints at class resentment by reasserting the value of his occult knowledge whenever "stupid, little posh girl" Sophia reminds him that she is paying for his services. Although genuinely fearful of the dark forces at work, Solomon's various attempts to psychologically and physically break her down to induce a visionary state of consciousness (such as instructing her to purge herself by ingesting a poisonous mushroom, not unlike the fungi in Chapter 5's witch-themed films) often takes a sadistic bent not found in actual occult grimoires. For instance, he exploits Sophia's relative ignorance about the ritual by convincing her to perform an act of "sex magic," but this is simply an excuse to get her to disrobe so that he can masturbate over her nudity. Such abuses reach their breaking point when he drowns and resuscitates her in the bathtub in an attempt to reach across the limits of mortality. Enraged, she confronts him in the kitchen, accidentally shoving him against a nearby knife, but he refuses to abort the ritual for his own safety. Believing that almost everyone is already "damned," and now confronted with a different means of existentially vanishing, Solomon finally sacrifices his own will to Sophia's goals, even as her own objectives become more altruistic over the course of the working.

As Solomon slowly dies from sepsis, the film creeps more decisively into horror territory, with Sophia increasingly alone within the manor as the electricity fails, shadowy figures begin appearing, and demons tempt her by speaking in her son's voice. Even when she breaks the salt circle and ventures on foot across the empty countryside in search of aid, she somehow finds herself circled back to the manor, unable to escape the ritual space as geography seems to fold in on itself. By the film's end, the unredeemed spirits appear as nude, clay-caked figures chasing Sophia through the house, but she escapes into a prayer room filled with heavenly light, where her HGA awaits (Figure 7.1). As flakes of gold rain down from the ceiling, the gigantic

Figure 7.1 Sophia asks her Holy Guardian Angel for the power to forgive, making an altruistic request at the end of *A Dark Song*. (Source: DVD.)

angel speaks to her in a thunderous voice (unintelligible to the viewer) – but, rather than finally asking for vengeance, she instead supplicates herself before the angel and asks for "the power to forgive."

Having perhaps rediscovered her faith (albeit via an unconventional path), the film concludes with a vindication of spirituality – although, ironically, Sophia's achievement in contacting the realm of spiritual transcendence occurs after the film itself has turned from more of a chamber drama into a horror film. Gavin wisely excised an original ending (included as a DVD/Blu-ray bonus feature), in which Sophia reconciles with her sister and sister's children at the seaside; he instead concludes with a bleaker final shot of Sophia flinching as a car passes her while she drives back to civilization. But even without the mawkish ending of Sophia embracing a proxy form of reproductive futurism via her sister's children, *A Dark Song* still ends with Sophia overcoming her grief in one of the post-horror cycle's few (semi-)successful turns toward spirituality – or at least mysticism – as a source of beneficial forces.[6]

Describing his film as "different territory" than the typical horror film, Gavin went so far as to deliberately avoid showing (in his words) actual "black magic" rituals in the film.[7] Superstition aside, Gavin's choice to impurely blend together bits from the *Book of Abramelin* and other medieval grimoires – with his production designers also drawing symbols from their knowledge of Reiki, Tarot, energy fields, and other esoteric practices[8] – is rather ironic, given Solomon's repeated disparagement of Sophia for reading "stuff on the Internet." Yet, even if we put aside how the film uniquely narrativizes the process of high-ceremonial magic (despite inaccurately depicting the specifically named Abramelin operation), we can still discern important differences between our two protagonists emerging as they form an unlikely détente. Whereas Solomon more closely personifies occultism's "Left-Hand Path," in which the magician egotistically quests toward self-deification, Sophia eventually lands closer to the "Right-Hand Path's" goal of subsuming one's ego into larger divine forces instead of becoming a god-like individual oneself.[9]

Rather than assuming the responsibility for assigning divine retribution over her son's death, she ends her mystical journey through the Abramelin operation by arriving at a more redemptive place, even as the film itself has arrived much more squarely in the horror genre by its conclusion. Hence, despite Gavin's stated focus on the "darkness" of occultism, horror's generic associations between occult practices and willful malevolence effectively serve as the final test which Sophia passes through, in order to transcend her all-too-human desires for vengeance. Ironically, though, *A Dark Song* itself fails to escape the genre's gravity during its final act, when monsters breech the same spiritual/generic threshold through which Sophia's newfound power of forgiveness has seemingly derived.

mother!: A Metaphysical Theater of Gendered Violence

Unlike *A Dark Song*'s ultimately redemptive vision of religious belief, Darren Aronofsky's *mother!* is blatantly skeptical about religion's power to be much more than a destructive force, not least toward women. Generically an amalgam of his two previous films, the psychological-horror film *Black Swan* (2010) and the biblical epic *Noah* (2014), *mother!* presents a Judeo-Christian allegory that, despite its artistic pretentions (or perhaps because of them), grows increasingly ham-fisted as the film proceeds – although this movement also coincides with the film's shift into generic territory beyond the horror film. While stylistically inspired by early Polanski, from *Repulsion*'s (1965) claustrophobically tight cinematography to a poster design clearly modeled upon the poster for *Rosemary's Baby* (1968), the underlying themes in *mother!* are closer to the same patriarchal-religious fears about female generativity and untamed landscapes discussed in Chapter 5 – albeit reframed around depicting "Mother Nature" (Jennifer Lawrence) as a figure of "God's" (Javier Bardem) combined love and neglect. (Since none of the characters are given specific names via dialogue, I will name them, for the sake of clarity, according to their most obvious biblical analogues.) Yet, even as the film's stylistic differences from the other films in this book – generating strong affects through assaultive means instead of contemplative ones – make it a secondary addition to the post-horror corpus, its formal strategies nonetheless speak to many of the same metaphysical concerns.

Boasting a $30 million budget, with major stars and considerable use of computer-generated imagery, *mother!* is also an outlier in the post-horror corpus due to its conspicuous lack of distanced cinematography throughout the story of a pastoral home devolving into a war zone. Matthew Libatique's handheld cinematography (as previously used in *Black Swan*) remains very close to Mother Nature's body throughout, as though she is followed by a suffocating force; by remaining so close to her, the camera often lingers on Jennifer Lawrence's natural beauty, which constantly shines through in spite of the pajamas she wears for much of the film. (At one point, her sheer shirt is criticized as "indecent," as if nature's sensuousness is a source of suspicion and disdain.)

Yet, with Lawrence coming off a string of successes in the crowd-pleasing *Hunger Games* franchise (2012–15) and David O. Russell's middlebrow dramedies – a major reason *mother!* received a wide multiplex release – audiences perhaps felt betrayed by her starring role as a predominantly passive and victimized protagonist. Indeed, *mother!* is the sole post-horror film to date to earn an "F" CinemaScore, though Aronofsky's obscurantist attack on Judeo-Christian religions arguably did as much to earn this widespread ire, including walkouts and angry outbursts from audience members. Populist viewers were not the only taste culture to offer very critical opinions, however, since some high-minded viewers also found Aronofsky's allegory alternately pretentious and hackneyed, to the point of tipping into unintentional camp – a criticism that *Black Swan*, his previous horror film about a histrionically tortured female protagonist, also earned.[10]

Effectively retelling the Bible from Creation to Apocalypse as a twenty-four-hour period in its protagonists' lives, *mother!* opens with a close-up of a woman's face staring into the camera as she is consumed by flames, followed by several shots of God walking through a burnt-out house as it miraculously restores itself to an inhabitable state. Finally, Mother Nature wakes in bed as a new morning dawns, calling out "Baby?" These images only retrospectively make sense when they recur at the film's end, as part of a seemingly eternal cycle of creation and destruction, each time with a different Mother Nature as a goddess torn asunder by the followers of God. He is depicted as an alternately naive and narcissistic poet, flattered that anyone cares enough to praise him for his creations, but not personally bothered enough to cast out the destructive invaders to whom he has given "dominion . . . over all the earth" (Genesis 1: 26).

Although all of the films discussed in this chapter depict a house as a character in its own right, *mother!* depicts the dilapidated old house, with a fetus growing within the walls, at the center of an Edenic landscape with no surrounding traces of human life. Attempting to prove her value to him, Mother Nature works to renovate God's existing home ("I want to make a paradise") instead of simply building a new one. Despite her premonitions of the inferno to come, she keeps working as best as possible as interlopers begin to arrive – first "Adam" (Ed Harris) and then "Eve" (Michelle Pfeiffer) – who are soon revealed to be God's devotees, dismissive of the maternal goddess's efforts. In an allusion to human existential crisis, Adam explains that he is dying and desperately wanted to meet God before the end – but he and Eve are cast out of the poet's study (Garden of Eden) for accidentally breaking a mysterious jewel that they were forbidden to touch. Yet, this transgression is soon joined by a further sin as newly arrived "Cain" (Domhnall Gleeson) kills "Abel" (Brian Gleeson), and Abel's blood soaks into the deep structure of the house, leaving a yonic hole in the floorboards which suggests that Mother Nature will be falsely blamed for this originary act of masculine violence. As a flock of mourners arrive, they trespass throughout the house, even attempting to make it over themselves, until driven out by the Great Flood after disregarding Mother Nature's warnings about sitting on an unstable kitchen sink.

As the rest of the film plays out, jumping from Genesis to the Gospels at its halfway point, God keeps gaslighting Mother Nature by professing love, but always making excuses for the increasingly chaotic and entitled zealots to remain there. Much as the less confident romantic partner in Chapter 4's films is induced to keep making concessions that trap them in an emotionally abusive relationship, Mother Nature submits to rough sex with God and immediately becomes pregnant with the Messiah – an act that inspires God to finally overcome his writer's block and produce a New Testament. But this new work leads to a long line of pilgrims who invade the house, making themselves all-too-comfortable and tearing it apart in search of souvenirs of their devotion.

If the first half of the film occupies generic territory somewhere between early Polanski, the "Bluebeard" folktale, and the discomforting home-invasion horror of *Funny Games* (1997), *mother!*'s second half suddenly veers into the war movie by looking askance at a major religious tradition in order to play up its most violent implications. Riots and warring factions soon break out, with armed police and military forces taking over the house as refugees and political prisoners brutally suffer (Figure 7.2).[11] Despite being repeatedly praised as the creator's "inspiration," the cultists violently attack the expectant mother for now occupying the latter side of the virgin/whore dichotomy. Extending the biblical allegory, *mother!*

Figure 7.2 Mother Nature stumbles through her former house, now turned into a devastated warzone, during the last act of *mother!* (Source: Blu-ray.)

thus explores – and partly critiques – the traditionally gendered relationship between male artist and female muse, with God's Herald (Kristen Wiig) and worshipful followers depicted as the poet's agent and rabid fans.

Although most of *mother!*'s second half depicts the man-made horrors of war instead of the horror genre's typical subject matter, the cultists' accidental killing and sacramental eating of the newly born baby, literalizing Communion's "body of Christ" in gory detail, is perhaps the film's most disturbing moment. While the lead Zealot (Stephen McHattie) proclaims Mother Nature's screams to be "the sound of humanity" in the face of death, the fatal attack on Christ-as-child repudiates Christianity's own uses of reproductive futurism (that is, promises of a heavenly rebirth for true believers). Yet, rather than following God's lead in forgiving the zealots for murdering her child, Mother Nature violently destroys the house and all of its invaders by exploding a tank of heating oil which she had first found hidden in the basement while investigating the rot left by Abel's blood. With Adam's discarded lighter now used for the catastrophic ignition, humanity's original sins have sown the seeds for the destruction they finally face when their corrosive quest to overcome existential crisis – by neglecting the natural world in hopes of supernatural deliverance – has gone too far.[12]

Unlike *A Dark Song*'s Sophia, then, Mother Nature refuses to forgive those responsible for her grief, but *mother!* ends on a far more Pyrrhic note, with its protagonist destroying herself in the process. Aronofsky's fiery denouement is not unlike *Midsommar*'s (2019) story of a gaslighting relationship finally severed by its largely passive, female protagonist's final, defiant act of (semi-)agency – but Mother Nature ultimately fares worse than the potentially maddened Dani. Her self-immolation does not take God down with her; rather, the male deity emerges from the inferno unscathed and, in a final gesture of supplication, she lets him reach into her scorched chest cavity to extract a new jewel from her heart – the former version of which he had described as a source of creative inspiration, a treasure left behind in the ashes of an earlier fire. She may resent not having been enough to satisfy him, and he admits that he can do nothing else save create – but even if Mother Nature destroys humanity in order to let the natural world regenerate itself without them, God is still presented with a blank slate for new acts of creation. The film ends with virtually the same images from the beginning: the burnt shell of the house regenerating itself to its previously dilapidated form, and a new Mother Nature waking (her question "Baby?" again confusing romantic and parental love) as the cycle repeats anew.

In *Marine Lover of Friedrich Nietzsche*, Luce Irigaray rejects the concept of "eternal return" (the philosophical idea that, across the infinitude of space-time, a finite number of events will endlessly recur) as a masculinist fantasy that "pleasure is the return of the same, and if everything returns 'one more time,' that is to say 'for ever and ever,'" then "for your eternity, everything should always turn in a circle, and that within that ring I should remain – your booty." Instead, Irigaray posits that women should abandon the male-controlled terrestrial world in favor of philosophically championing the ocean's depths as a feminine realm not subject to patriarchal control.[13] As I suggested in Chapter 5, for instance, *The Lighthouse*'s sexually repressed men remain excluded from those immemorial waters through their resistance to male homosexuality's associations with feminization. A feminist critique of the eternal return thus goes hand in hand with a critique of men's perpetual desire to dominate the natural world, whose "feminine/untamed" fertility has been subjected to "masculine/civilizing" attempts at control since the ancient rise of patriarchal cultures.

By upholding the ancient associations between nature and femininity, then, Aronofsky seemingly echoes Mary Daly's ecofeminist argument that gynocentric, nature-worshipping religions were largely stamped out (or pushed into the realm of occultism) by the rise of Abrahamic religions.[14] Yet, Maggie Nelson observes that, even though there is nothing new about pointing out how "a repressed, symbolic matricide" is "a hallmark of patriarchal religion, culture, and psychology," male artists who insist on violently exposing that history often do so by reproducing the trope of the suffering woman – even to the point of implicitly attacking the maternal as a source of socialization that supposedly must be uprooted en route to engaging with cosmically transcendent issues.[15] In other words, like Linda Williams's argument (discussed in Chapter 4) about the suffering black body as a trope reproduced in both racist and anti-racist melodramas,[16] the figure of the suffering woman can be used for both feminist and anti-feminist purposes, even to the point of ambiguity over a given work's political intent.

Christianity, in particular, has a tradition of depicting self-sacrifice and bodily mortification as a means toward spiritual transcendence – but what looks to a true believer like divine suffering might look like meaningless cruelty to a more skeptical observer. Nelson, for instance, cites Lars von Trier's *Breaking the Waves* (1996) as a film whose "cruelty does not lie in any ability to strip away cant or delusion, but rather in an ability to construct malignant, ultimately conventional fictions that masquerade as parables of profundity, or as protests against the cruelties of the man's world in which we [women] must inevitably live and suffer." Presented so histrionically as to verge on campiness, Von Trier's Christ-like female protagonist Bess (Emily Watson), who sacrifices herself for her husband's good, is already too close to the everyday reality of living in a misogynistic society that the film's criticism of the local Christian patriarchs registers as deeply disingenuous.[17] Following Nelson, then, I would argue that Aronofsky's Mother Nature is only a shade away from Bess, since her voluntary (self-)destruction of the world does not ultimately dethrone the patriarchal God who eternally continues on unshaken.

As easy as it would be to primarily locate *mother!*'s attempt to transcend the horror genre in its decisive mid-film move into the war movie, I also include it in this chapter because of its distinct inspiration from Antonin Artaud's concept of the "Theater of Cruelty," which he described as an "alchemical" and "metaphysical" theater that should assault the audience's senses by revealing, among various dark and cosmic forces, "the first carnage of essences that appeared in creation."[18] In other words, rather than positioning itself outside or adjacent to the horror genre on the level of content, *mother!*'s formal strategies, especially its assaultive generation of negative affect, derive more from avant-garde intent. Although Artaud's ideas about aesthetic "cruelty," inspired as much by Balinese theater as by French surrealism, are notoriously difficult to put into practice, Aronofsky's film displays an Artaudian emphasis on loading the *mise-en-scène* with brutally symbolic meaning that pummels the viewer's senses in order to circumvent intellectual distanciation, treating characters as archetypes or mythic figures instead of psychologically interiorized individuals, with an overall objective of driving audiences into a purgative frenzy. For instance, dialogue like Mother Nature's "I'll just get started on the apocalypse" is far closer to Artaud's desire to distill spoken language to mythic incantations instead of plausibly naturalistic speech – hence these awkwardly blunt lines also risk being read as unintentionally campy among viewers who refuse to surrender themselves to the film's sensory assault.

Indeed, Artaud's suggested subject matter for the inaugural Theater of Cruelty included "The Story of Bluebeard" and a "Tale by the Marquis de Sade" alongside the "Fall of Jerusalem" and an "Extract from the *Zohar*" – which together evoke the mix of misogynistic violence and religious/mystical themes present in *mother!*[19] Meanwhile, Aronofsky's use of the artist/muse relationship as an allegory for God/Nature suggests Artaud's belief that restoring a metaphysical dimension to theater could rip the veil from an uncanny system of cosmic forces that ancient and non-Western cultures had recognized through theater, but which has been forgotten or repressed in modern Western society:

> Where alchemy, through its symbols, is the spiritual Double of an operation which functions only on the level of real matter, the theater must also be considered as the Double, not of this direct, everyday reality of which it is gradually being reduced to

a mere inert replica – as empty as it is sugar-coated – but of another archetypal and dangerous reality [. . .] For this reality is not human but inhuman, and man with his customs and his character counts for very little in it.[20]

With the theater director now doubling as master of sacred ceremonies, the Great Work of theater also becomes a magical operation. Much as alchemy has historically relied on a theatrical language of metaphysical symbols and gestures, Artaud directly compares his avant-garde strategies to the tradition of Hermetic magic also seen in *A Dark Song* (recall the rain of gold flakes) – a means of reducing and transmuting base material by personally achieving a higher spiritual state.[21]

Yet, as Nelson argues, when cruel artists ambush and terrorize a potentially unsuspecting audience (as Aronofsky arguably did with *mother!*'s multiplex viewers) in order to strip away the falsities of religion or whatever else is their target, these artists ironically assume a Messianic approach to art-making that "underestimates the capacities and intelligence of most viewers, and overestimates that of most artists."[22] Of course, for male artists to anoint themselves among the enlightened few might seem particularly disingenuous, especially when such "higher" efforts contrast with their own failures to transcend the messiness of all-too-human entanglements. For instance, despite Aronofsky's public assertions that the 2010 breakup of his nine-year relationship with Rachel Weisz (the star of his metaphysical science-fiction film *The Fountain* (2006)) did not inform *mother!*, the film's opening shot of the previous version of Mother Nature closely resembles Weisz. Moreover, Aronofsky began dating Jennifer Lawrence, who stars as the "replacement" Mother Nature, during the film's production – but they split during the film's post-release press junket because (according to Lawrence) she was "doing double duty of trying to be a supportive partner" while he became obsessed with the scathing critical response.[23] This extratextual information, of course, casts the film's abusive artist/muse relationship in a darkly ironic light, not least due to Aronofsky's apparent pretentions to be a God-like creator himself. Even though Artaud advocated, in his typically oblique way, "a theater difficult and cruel for myself first of all,"[24] it is difficult to know whether Aronofsky intended *mother!* to serve as a self-critique – especially since, for some viewers, his environmental/spiritual message seemed far more masturbatory than (pro)creative.

In a larger sense, Thomas Ligotti (a writer whose non-academic philosophy is far more pessimistic than Nietzsche's nihilism, lacking even the eternal return's glint of hope) argues that rampant vandalism of the natural environment serves, like religious belief in a redemptive afterlife, as merely an adjunct to humanity's existential disavowal of death. According to Ligotti, we humans are the only species to have evolved a consciousness of our own mortality, but therefore we need to delude ourselves that we are far more than another animal destined to die. Consequently, aligning oneself with a political cause like environmentalism is ultimately no more valid than a religious belief in an awaiting afterlife, since both are exercises in future-oriented thought that gloss over the inevitability of one's own demise.[25] Furthermore, where *mother!* looks askance at God's compulsion to create anew, no matter the destructive toll on lower beings along the way, Ligotti's anti-humanist stance invalidates the whole idea that art or other human (pro)creations can be anything but vain attempts at elevating oneself over the natural fact of mortality. Rather, "If we vanished tomorrow, no organism on this planet would miss us. Nothing in nature needs us," and hence "absent us there is nothing of the supernatural in the universe."[26] But if neither artistic posterity nor the concept of supernatural deities would survive our wholesale extinction, then what purpose – if any – can each of us have in the grand span of cosmic time?

A Ghost Story: Wandering Across Time and Genre

Ligotti's extreme pessimism might not seem directly relevant, were he not best known as an acclaimed author of horror fiction in the Lovecraftian tradition. For Ligotti, without the uniquely human sense of consciousness-qua-mortality, we would have developed neither the concept of the "supernatural" nor the dread-inducing sense of "atmosphere" (a particularly privileged part of post-horror cinema) that marks supernatural horror fiction in general. This is why death, as a transition to the inherently unknowable state of non-existence from which each of us emerged and will return, often seems "more like a visitation from a foreign and enigmatic sphere, one to which we are connected by our [repressed] consciousness" of mortality.[27] Humans created supernatural fiction in order to express the sense that something deeply "wrong" lurks behind the scenes of life – a conclusion that philosophical pessimists like Ligotti might already arrive at without any superstitious belief in actual supernatural forces. Rather, our ability to entertain a *sense* of the supernatural as "what should not be" exists independently of personal beliefs in an actual supernatural realm, which is why "the supernatural may be regarded as the metaphysical counterpart of insanity, a transcendental correlative of a mind that has been driven mad" by our paradoxical place in an indifferent universe.[28]

According to Ligotti, H. P. Lovecraft's great contribution to supernatural fiction was his elaboration of ancient and extraterrestrial "cosmic horrors" emerging from beyond human space-time, and utterly indifferent to the value of human life or moral concepts like "good" and "evil." We may all exist like characters in a Lovecraft story, vaguely suspecting that we have no permanence in a chaotic universe, but we still remain enrapt by the details of our own life-narratives, despite ultimately knowing how our stories must end at the grave.[29] Yet, Adam Charles Hart notes how, for as much as his narrators run up against encounters with the indescribable, Lovecraft's cosmic horror fiction still relies on the narrative trope of the monster to give at least partial shape to the unfathomable entities whose mere existence so often drives Lovecraft's protagonists nearly mad. This means that, even though his monsters do not evoke the reader's empathy, there is still something inherently reassuring about the figure of the monster as a formal locus for fears, anxieties, and forces that we may be unable to fully comprehend or articulate.[30]

Even though it bears little generic resemblance to the supernatural horror fiction of Lovecraft or Ligotti, David Lowery's *A Ghost Story* speaks to many of the same existential/cosmic concerns through its transformation of the monster into an existential wanderer across time. More than simply depicting the ghost as a pathos-inspiring figure by virtue of a human's untimely death – there is, after all, no shortage of such melancholy spirits haunting the history of horror literature and cinema – Lowery radically deflates the ghost's generic role as archetypal spook by depicting it as a mere actor beneath a white sheet, like a young child's Halloween costume or a *Scooby Doo* villain. If *mother!* amps up the action to a ludicrous degree via the war genre, *A Ghost Story*'s titular character is generically underwhelming to the point of humor. Yet, after a few potential chuckles upon the ghost's first appearance, the film soon drains this response across a glacially slow portrait of ennui among both the living and the dead. Whereas the leisurely narratives of *A Dark Song* and *mother!* are still noticeably dynamic at times, the final two films discussed in this chapter are, by comparison, extremely minimalistic and perhaps best evince the influence of "slow cinema" on the post-horror corpus (as discussed in Chapter 2). Indeed, these two films seem to play out in "ghost time" instead of "human time"; months, decades, and even centuries of human history pass fluidly via temporal ellipses, whereas the duration of specific (lived) moments feels interminably stretched.

Signaling its modernist influences with an epigraph from the opening lines of Virginia Woolf's 1921 short story "A Haunted House," *A Ghost Story* also immediately marks its high-art aspirations via an antiquated 1.33:1 aspect ratio, with vignetted corners like a Victorian-era photograph. Like several of the post-horror films discussed in Chapter 5, this constricted visual frame paradoxically calls our attention to the preponderance of spatially distant imagery throughout, similarly capturing cosmic imagery like overhead galaxies alongside mundane scenes of domestic life in a lower-middle-class home. A young married couple, identified in the end credits only as "C" (Casey Affleck) and "M" (Rooney Mara), go about their normal life, but are awoken one night by the loud, discordant sound of something striking the piano that a previous tenant had left in the living room – the first indication that they may not be alone in the suburban house. Notably, the film reunites Affleck and Mara from Lowery's previous film, *Ain't Them Bodies Saints* (2013); much as *mother!* becomes more interesting in light of extratextual information about the romance between its director and star, *A Ghost Story*'s barely sketched couple seems to gain additional characterization via this intertextual link.

The film's inciting event comes when C dies in a car crash, just outside their driveway; the accident itself is not shown, only a long shot of the house as the camera slowly pans over to see the destruction, as the morning mist drifting across the scene is now revealed to be smoke. M visits the morgue to identify his body and, after she leaves the room, the camera lingers on the empty space for what feels like an eternity before the Ghost of C sits up beneath the white sheet. This three-minute-long take, filmed from the hallway outside the room, exemplifies Lowery's use of extended-duration shots that may seem completely static, but where there is often an almost imperceptible degree of camera movement, thus requiring the viewer to perform an active search for meaning within these shots' minimalistic form (not unlike the disembodied pans and wide-angle shots in *It Follows*). Indeed, the Ghost's blankness also turns him into a figure onto which the viewer must project emotion, since he displays only scant gestures for much of the film – including in this first scene of wandering the institutionally blank hospital halls, and hesitating to enter a glowing portal (presumably to the afterlife) that opens in one of the walls, before returning home.

Meanwhile, M resembles the mourning female protagonists described by Richard Armstrong, especially in the "anti-action" of haunted widows whose grief is so powerful that it shades into nausea.[31] In M's central scene, she spends five unbroken minutes sitting on the kitchen floor as she eats (and then vomits) an entire chocolate pie left by a sympathetic realtor – this masochistic act of gorging and purging a would-be comforting treat presented as a long take while the Ghost looks on from the background, as if mourning the loss of both his wife and his own ability to intercede in the living world. In subsequent scenes, as M packs up and prepares to move out, the Ghost's passive spectatorship largely mirrors our own, fixed within the diegetic house as the typical experience of (cinematic) time seems to become increasingly irrelevant. This almost absurd fixity within the haunted house is exemplified when the Ghost of C has a silent, subtitled conversation with another ghost, visible through the window of a nearby house. Much as the voices of the living are largely muffled or indistinct during most of *A Ghost Story*, this silent conversation reveals the ghosts to be waiting for someone to return – even if they do not necessarily remember who – and are only able to move on when they realize that the longed-for person is not coming back.

Indeed, several new tenants pass through the house before a wrecking crew eventually demolishes it to make room for urban expansion. First is a Latino family whose happy gatherings the Ghost disrupts, in a rare moment of supernatural rage, with thrown dishes and falling books – one of the only "scary" things the Ghost ever does throughout the film.[32] Next are some white hipsters, one of whose parties the Ghost attends in a long scene that notably begins with a guy jokingly invoking the ghosts of this "haunted house" to help him perform a card trick (some simple sleight of hand, rather than the proper magic discussed earlier this chapter) to impress a young woman.

The Ghost then listens in on a six-minute, drunken monologue delivered around the kitchen table by a man who expresses extreme skepticism about the value of existence, especially if the acquisition of money or love will not give anyone a substantially longer lifespan than anyone else. Using the readily hummable melody of Beethoven's "Ode to Joy" as his example, he expounds about how the best art was once created to exalt God, but how concerns about personal posterity have increasingly motivated human creations, from art to children, in a secular world. (This musical example is especially poignant because indie musician Will Oldham plays this character, credited only as "Prognosticator.") He continues with speculations about the future, noting how this famous melody may perhaps survive a cataclysmic collapse of the human population if it momentarily gives the survivors "something other than fear and hunger and hate" to think about – or it may even be taken into outer space by future humans escaping Earth's environmental destruction – but this will only be a temporary respite because the Sun will eventually die and the universe will expand, destroying all existing matter.

Hypothetically asking which of the partygoers has children, he flippantly announces, "Your kids are going to die – yours too," thus connecting the end of human creation to Ligotti's anti-natalist belief that it is more ethical *not* to procreate. The Prognosticator dejectedly concludes:

> You can write a book but the pages will burn. You can sing a song and pass it down. [. . .] You can build your dream house, but ultimately none of that matters any more than digging your fingers into the ground to bury a fence post. Or fucking – which I guess is just about the same thing.

Much as *mother!* expresses skepticism about the value of art (God's creation as "poetry") if it is all destined to end in utter destruction, the Prognosticator hints at the apocalyptic "end times" to come when there are no more humans left to remember our former presence on Earth as an existentially conscious species (much less remember Lowery's film, Oldham's music, Ligotti's philosophy, the book you are currently reading, ad infinitum).

The Prognosticator's speech is thus remarkably close to Ligotti's philosophical pessimism, given his rejection of humanist values like art or love ("Let's leave love out of this [. . .] This is just science") as any more lasting in human memory than the earlier branches of one's family tree in the face of an indifferent universe. Dylan Trigg argues that this "seductive image of a ruined Earth," as a living organism that flourishes again once humans are extinct, is a "posthuman phantasy" that may well encourage "humility in the present." Yet, its romanticization of human-made ruins paradoxically reinscribes a very humanist way of anthropomorphizing the natural world's own "overcoming of adversity."[33] In other words, this common fantasy of Mother Nature triumphant in a not-too-distant, post-human future effectively serves as a larger geological version of "ruin porn" – albeit operating as the flip side of ruin porn's tendency to ignore or obscure the adversity suffered by such ruins' earlier human occupants (as discussed in the previous chapter).[34]

Indeed, shortly after the Prognosticator's monologue, at some indistinct point in the future, bulldozers tear down the Ghost's now-abandoned house, just as he is about to extract from a door frame a folded-up scrap of paper on which M had written a message before moving out (a ritual she had begun practicing when moving houses as a child). Over the remaining half-hour of *A Ghost Story*, the homeless Ghost wanders across various landscapes (evincing Lowery's oft-noted influence from early Terrence Malick films) while temporal ellipses in the narrative become more marked. He drifts through an industrial building site for a skyscraper under construction, and by the time he reaches the roof of the now-finished edifice, he peers out over a futuristic urban skyline.

But, after leaping from the roof in an apparent suicide plunge, the Ghost awakens on the same site centuries earlier, as a family of white settler-colonists arrives in the Old West via covered wagon. While the Ghost lingers around this scene, he watches the father hammering stakes for building their modest homestead – a callback to the Prognosticator's earlier/future comparison between burying a fence post, building a dream house, and propagating a family – much as the Ghost watches the settler family's youngest daughter burying a hidden message under a rock, as if a precursor of M's own childhood somewhere down the generations. Yet these potentially hopeful images are undercut when the Ghost suddenly sees the aftermath of the settler family's abrupt massacre by Native Americans, with the Texas grassland soon growing over the family's corpses as nature reclaims the clearing.

Although this Old West interlude suggests *A Ghost Story*'s brief generic shift into the western, the film concludes back in the same modern-day house where it began, with a generic return to domestic romance/drama as the Ghost watches C and M first moving in. Like another vision of eternal return, C now effectively watches himself in his former life, while the viewer finally receives some belated backstory about the married couple. A struggling musician, C seems strangely fixated on remaining in the house instead of moving to a new home; only able to vaguely explain that they have "history" there, he appears to be holding M back from some form of future career advancement, since she frustratedly responds, "Not as much as you think." Overheard by the Ghost, C finally concedes to her that they can leave – which is just before the Ghost angrily strikes the piano, as a sort of future-perfect-tense gesture or warning to his living self not to leave and thereby fulfill his fated demise.

Seemingly trapped in an endless cycle of death and ghostly resurrection, the film finally ends with the Ghost successfully pulling the hidden note from the wall, reading the message (its contents kept from the viewer), and then the sheet collapsing to the floor as though C has finally been able to move on. Indeed, the Ghost's form as a blank white sheet evokes the folded white note itself, both depicted as messages left behind in wait for the proper recipient – which also alludes back to the film's Woolf epigraph. Like the walled-in note, Woolf's narrator in "A Haunted House" imagines a ghostly couple searching her house for "buried treasure," and wakes with a start, realizing that the ghosts are looking for "[t]he light in the heart."[35] Ironically, then, even though the Prognosticator's monologue serves as more of *A Ghost Story*'s centerpiece than C and M's faintly sketched relationship, Lowery's implicit message second-guesses the Prognosticator's Ligottian pessimism by positing that heterosexual love will somehow transcend time and space. Or, Lowery at least implies some tiny measure of comfort if, despite its unexpected brevity, C and M's abruptly curtailed romance will eternally recur at some further point(s) in cosmic time.

Hence *A Ghost Story* may ventriloquize Ligottian pessimism via the Prognosticator's monologue but, as Ligotti himself argues, horror fiction can also sublimate existential anxieties into "tamed" artistic forms, allowing horror audiences to entertain but ultimately disavow how a sense of the supernatural effectively makes us all puppets of our own delusions

EXISTENTIAL DREAD AND TROUBLE WITH TRANSCENDENCE   231

of "mattering." For Ligotti, this containment function is especially true when so many works of horror fiction "promoted as vehicles of a 'dark vision' finish up by lounging in a warm bath of affirmation, often doing a traitorous turnabout in their closing pages or paragraphs."[36] With C's upbeat music playing over *A Ghost Story*'s closing credits, it is thus difficult not to see Lowery pulling his metaphysical punches (even if this film was marketed as less of a "dark vision" than a melancholy one). Additionally, the Ghost's visual form as a child's costume version of a ghost rather than an unfathomable Lovecraftian entity hints at an underlying belief in reproductive futurism by figuring the supernatural as the unthreatening creation of perpetually emerging generations of humans yet to come, rather than a reminder of the human species' impending extinction (a period that Donna Haraway has dubbed, in an unintended nod to Lovecraft's most famous monster, the "Chthulucene").[37]

Overall, both *A Dark Song* and *A Ghost Story* offer glimpses of hope, with (respectively) the force of parental and romantic love able to transcend death, but whether these glimpses are merely examples of "cruel optimism" is open to philosophical debate. According to Lauren Berlant, cruel optimism names those affective attachments to future hopes that impede our full recognition of living in a constant state of crisis under neoliberal precarity. Whereas "traumatic" personal/social upheavals marked the shocks of twentieth-century life (as discussed in Chapter 3), narrative tropes about trauma are less sufficient to account for the temporal impasses created by the endemic feeling of drifting from one precarious state to another in the twenty-first century.[38] Apropos of post-horror cinema, Berlant cites the waning of traditional genres, and especially the waning of generic narratives about creating/restoring the "good life," as cultural sites where cruel optimism might be more readily recognized for what it is.[39] Indeed, according to Lowery, "I wanted to engage with the archetypes and iconography of ghost films and haunted house movies, without ever crossing over into actually being a horror film," although many critics still labeled it one.[40]

Even as its pathos-laden Ghost traverses a narrative that seems so detached from the horror genre as to be scarcely considered part of it, his wandering through pre-industrial building sites (Figure 7.3) recalls *It Follows*'s post-industrial ruin-porn imagery (also a symptom of neoliberal precarity, as I argued in the previous chapter), while the Old West scene evokes the earlier settler-colonial period depicted in *The Witch* (2015). In effect, the Ghost seems to roam through the distinctive landscapes of two earlier post-horror films, only to end up back in the domestic romance/drama as a site that nominally becomes more "horrific" when intertextually

Figure 7.3 Somewhere in the future, the Ghost stands in an industrial building site on the grounds of his former home, evoking a ruin-porn aesthetic extended to a cosmic scale, in *A Ghost Story*. (Source: Blu-ray.)

read in relation to the rest of the core post-horror corpus. Still, even as the Ghost's posthumous (non-)existence was created by the singular event of a traumatic death, his invisible, drifting longueurs amid an unstable world filled with insecurity and impermanence might *feel* remarkably resonant with many viewers' experience of precarious life today.

Nevertheless, if Lowery's underlying message here is that love – and, by extension, art – might somehow survive the test of time, then we might ponder whether the horror genre's cross-pollination with other genres, such as post-horror's aforementioned affinities with (melo)dramas and mourning films, is its own best hope to carry on into whatever is left of human history/memory's increasingly tenuous existence on Earth. Yet, unlike the populist recognition and acclaim still enjoyed by Beethoven's "Ode to Joy," it is difficult to imagine divisively minimalistic post-horror films like *A Ghost Story* being similarly carried forward by more than a taste-based subset of film viewers. In my final analysis of a post-horror text, however, I will examine a film whose intertextual allusions to one of the horror genre's best-known films attempts a less "cosmic" and far more personal act of memorialization.

I Am the Pretty Thing That Lives in the House: Trapped in the Old House of Genre

In Oz Perkins's film *I Am the Pretty Thing That Lives in the House*, we again have the figure of the ghost as existential wanderer, but contained within the more familiar generic home of Gothic horror. Although a relatively simple story, its elaboration via three women's overlapping voice(over)s, spread across the past, present, and future of an old Massachusetts house, invites the viewer to ponder the temporal layers that can commingle within a single generic setting. Indeed, through indirect allusions to arguably the most influential "old dark house" in modern horror cinema – the Bates house in *Psycho* – *I Am the Pretty Thing* meditates on whether finding oneself preserved in and through the horror genre itself is a more valuable way to seek posthumous remembrance than the durability of familial memory alone.

Perkins's debut post-horror feature, *The Blackcoat's Daughter* (2015), had earned positive reviews upon its premiere at the Toronto International Film Festival, but did not secure distribution beyond the festival circuit until released as a video-on-demand title in February 2017 – shortly after *I Am the Pretty Thing* premiered on Netflix on October 26, 2016.[41] The latter film received positive reviews from most critics, though some found its narrative too threadbare to carry a feature-length film – a not-unwarranted criticism for a film whose scant plot might seem more appropriate to a short film, but is here hypnotically stretched via very slow camera movements, extensive slow motion and de-focused cinematography, and long fade-outs. Given these stylistic traits, it has unsurprisingly received disproportionately low audience scores, not least because its very wide accessibility as a Netflix Original Movie brought an unconventionally minimalistic film before casually browsing subscribers during Halloween season, when even the most occasional horror viewers might be in the mood to stream some spooky fare. But, like the other films discussed in this chapter, *I Am the Pretty Thing* gains added poignancy from intertextual connections that might not be readily apparent to many viewers, especially those with less cultural capital.

The film opens with an enigmatic voiceover by Lily Saylor (Emma Wilson), the live-in nurse for a famed horror author, Iris Blum (Paula Prentiss), who suffers from dementia. Although we see Lily first arriving to take the job, her voiceover posthumously narrates much of the film, telling us that she did not survive until her next birthday, and then poetically ruminating on her current state as a ghost.[42] Even from the first night, Lily begins hearing low, rhythmic thumping coming from somewhere in the house and notices a patch of black mold starting to grow on one of the downstairs walls. Several more mildly spooky things happen over the following year, but none that is surely supernatural in origin. Nevertheless, Lily's ghostly voiceover, her voice sounding choked-off and distant, comes and goes throughout the film, periodically reminding the viewer that she is fated to die before the film is over – even if we do not yet know how it will happen.

After a temporal ellipsis of eleven months, the executor of Ms Blum's estate, Mr Waxcap (Bob Balaban), visits and gently refuses to pay for renovations while Blum is still alive, reserving the estate's money for eventually turning the house into a retreat for women writers. Despite Lily's assertion that she is deathly sensitive to horror fiction, he also seems slightly resentful that Lily has not read any of Blum's books – not even her best-known novel, *The Lady in the Walls*. Nevertheless, he explains that Ms Blum's strange habit of referring to Lily as "Polly" might be the demented author confusing Lily with the similar-sounding name of *The Lady in the Walls'* protagonist, Polly Parsons. Refusing to spoil the novel's conclusion, Waxcap describes Blum's "deliberate choice to leave off the presumably horrific ending" as, in Blum's words, not a mere artistic choice but an "obligation" to the book's titular subject. Lily's suspended comprehension of the novel's ending therefore echoes our own uncertainty over how Lily herself will become a ghost by the end of *I Am the Pretty Thing*.

Trying to solve this mystery, Lily attempts to read *The Lady in the Walls*, whose author explains to the book's reader that the following story was dictated by the ghost of Polly Parsons; the ghost, however, was unable or unwilling to reveal the circumstances of her own death, so Blum has omitted the ending "out of respect for the dead." Nevertheless, *I Am the Pretty Thing*'s viewer is shown more about Polly's (Lucy Boynton) demise than Blum herself learned: shortly after moving into the newly constructed house in 1812, Polly's husband had killed the blindfolded woman with an axe, sealing the body inside a downstairs wall before fleeing town. Like the folded-up note in *A Ghost Story*, Polly's white-dressed corpse is less "buried" than merely given a "hiding place," as *The Lady in the Walls* phrases it.

Finding a sealed box marked "Polly," Lily then reads young Iris Blum's (Erin Boyes) journal about the ghostly dictation that inspired her famous 1960 novel. As Lily learns, Polly's memory of her own murder seemed less like recalling an event than trying to remember a song that she once heard – as though, like *A Ghost Story*'s diatribe about "Ode to Joy," the affective pull of the semi-remembered thing might mnemonically outweigh conventional understandings of importance. Rather, the ghost remains tied to the house not simply because a violent event befell her, but because she sees yet is unable to recognize herself anymore. Indeed, dementia's symptomatic loss of the ability to identify loved ones or even loss of one's own identity means that the elderly Ms Blum now inhabits a deep epistemic void akin to the ghosts' inability to recognize themselves. As the young Blum's journal notes, "Surely this is how we make our own ghosts. We make them out of ourselves," not unlike Ligotti's argument that we are all like characters in a supernatural horror story, fascinated by the marvelous and uncanny details while remaining willfully ignorant of the fact that they will conclude with mortality's fulfillment, sooner or later.

"The pretty thing you are looking at . . . is me," Polly remarks in the first lines of *The Lady in the Walls*, just as Lily repeats this same line in her own voiceover as the film both opens and closes. These lines hark back to one of elderly Ms Blum's few moments of dialogue, as she refers to Lily as one of "[y]ou poor, pretty things whose prettiness holds only one guarantee. Learn to see yourself as the rest of the world does and you'll keep. But left alone, with only your own eyes looking back at you, then even the prettiest things will rot." Shortly afterward, Lily's ghostly voiceover, noting that her premature death will soon come, offers another recurring refrain: "It is a terrible thing to look at oneself and, all the while, see nothing." Much as the eponymous protagonist of *mother!* is defined solely in relation to her husband's patriarchal power, Polly and Lily are somehow defined by their "prettiness" in society's eyes, but they are left with fewer ways to autonomously define their own identities. This makes it all the more difficult for their ghosts to move on, once confronted with the realization that their now-ended lives were so superficially valued – whereas the average-looking Ms Blum took a different route, becoming an author whose works would hopefully last for posterity.

Lily's death finally arrives when she clearly sees Polly's ghost for the first time – the specter pacing through the house with its head turned backward on its body, as if simultaneously caught between forward and backward temporalities – and suddenly dies of fright. The ghost's revelation to Lily thus literalizes what Eve Sedgwick describes as one of Gothic fiction's unifying conventions: the most violent, horrific, and supernatural moments occur upon the breach of an imprisoning wall.[43] Like the time loop at the end of *A Ghost Story*, Lily's ghost slowly descends the stairs and sees her own corpse collapsed near the front door, not yet grasping the significance of this sight. Now neglected, Ms Blum expires sometime thereafter, and as Lily's ghost explores the rest of the house wondering what has happened, she peers into Ms Blum's writing room and is suddenly back in the past, watching the young author pause at the typewriter, having felt a ghostly presence. Small wonder, then, that the elderly woman so easily conflated the two ghosts that have been left (as Lily's ghost says) "pressed deeply in place, like type on paper." In her closing voiceover, Lily explains that she will remain in the haunted house until she can catch another glimpse of Polly – but, like the black mold on the entombing wall, until then she will "let [her]self rot."

Although Lily had not yet known that Ms Blum's confusion over the name "Polly" foreshadowed her own future as a ghost, another recurring motif in their overlapping voices echoes the same conclusion across different time periods: a house where a death has occurred cannot be bought or sold by the living, only borrowed from its ghostly inhabitants. This sentiment is visually reflected in a pair of images that bookend the film: a slow pan across the sleeping members of a newly arrived family, the ghost's blinkered gaze resembling a dim flashlight beam; and a slow-motion image of one of the two ghosts (Polly or Lily) moving against a black void, their actions streaked like the supposed "ectoplasm" captured in Victorian-era spirit photography. The film's closing image of Lily's ghost, pulling from her mouth what appears to be a rope of cheesecloth or muslin, directly evokes such spiritualist hoaxes – as though Perkins, in a deliberate stroke of ambiguity, wants to both confirm and disprove the ghosts' ontological status.

Yet, this overarching idea of ghosts becoming trapped within the old Gothic house, as if becoming historical works of horror fiction themselves, lends itself to a more intimate reading of a film that contains multiple allusions to Oz Perkins's actor father, Anthony, forever associated with his role as *Psycho*'s Norman Bates. Unlike the biblical and literary epigraphs noted elsewhere in this chapter, Perkins's film opens with the director's onscreen dedication to his father – "For A. P., who gave me an old house" – implying that his father's memory has also bequeathed *Psycho*'s legacy to his son. In addition, one of *I Am the Pretty Thing*'s voiceovers contains the line "shook their heads and clucked their [thick] tongues," a paraphrase of Norman's parlor-room monologue to Marion Crane (Janet Leigh); while Iris Blum is played by Paula Prentiss, who costarred with Anthony Perkins during the original Broadway run of *The Star-Spangled Girl* (1966); and Blum's most famous work, *The Lady in the Walls*, even shares a 1960 copyright date with Hitchcock's *Psycho*. Given these references, we can read *I Am the Pretty Thing* as a deeply personal work by a director paying loving homage to his famous father, while nevertheless trying to escape from the long film-historical shadow cast by his father's most iconic role.

Anthony Perkins even briefly appears in his son's film, when Lily watches the pre-*Psycho* actor in *Friendly Persuasion* (1956) on television – a role that earned him a Golden Globe award for Best New Star of the Year, vindication of the career potential that his post-*Psycho* typecasting unfortunately curtailed. Indeed, Ms Blum's lone speech about "learn[ing] to see yourself as the rest of the world does" immediately precedes the scene of Lily watching that film on television. The sheer proximity between Blum's thematically important dialogue and the *Friendly Persuasion* clip suggests how Lily's fate to become a ghost who looks at, but does not see, herself is much like how Perkins became trapped within *Psycho*'s reputation. Because primarily defined as an actor, he is closer to the "pretty things" who cannot see what awaits them, celebrated for their visual appeal and yet unaware of how their ghostly preservation in texts that persist beyond their death might continue to haunt the living.

As *I Am the Pretty Thing*'s writer-director, however, Oz is closer to Ms Blum's authorial role: trying to be his own person despite feeling "obligated" to honor such an important source of inspiration.[44] Although less literally than with *The Lady in the Walls*, his film was dictated to him by a sort of "ghost," in the form of his father's memory – especially in light of Anthony's premature death from AIDS complications in 1992, only two years after portraying Bates for the final time in *Psycho IV: The Beginning* (1990). Furthermore, Lily's opening monologue describes Blum as the author of "the kinds of thick and frightening books that people buy at airports and supermarkets" – with even *The Lady in the Walls* having become adapted as (in Mr Waxcap's words) a "not very good movie" – which suggests that her work is closer to populist tastes than high art. (Her surname may be an allusion to Jason Blum, founder of Blumhouse Productions, the company responsible for many of the horror genre's most audience-pleasing hits during the same years that the more divisive post-horror cycle arose.) Perkins's "elevated" film acknowledges, then, that more popular works of horror – ranging from *Psycho* to Blumhouse's stable of paranormal-themed movies – might be as capable of containing hidden depths about mortality and remembrance as an artistically self-conscious work like *I Am the Pretty Thing*, depending on how viewers take them up.

Like the nexus of genre and aesthetics that has haunted the post-horror corpus throughout this whole book, this tension between populism and art also harks back to *Psycho*'s very mixed reception upon its initial release in 1960. Made by a very popular director, *Psycho* was a "prestige" horror hit at the box office, but some horror-skeptic critics and older viewers denounced the film as too violent and sexually lurid, a blot on Hitchcock's reputation. Its critical reappraisal as an artistic masterpiece, and one of the horror genre's most influential films, occurred gradually over the following decades – partly driven by critics' much greater distaste toward the 1970s and 1980s slasher films whose sensationalistic mixtures of sex and violence may have been influenced by *Psycho* but made Hitchcock's film seem a comparative model of aesthetic restraint.[45] Indeed, these questions about lasting reputation literalize some of the same anxieties around familial-cum-generic inheritance addressed in Chapter 3. For example, Janet Leigh's daughter, Jamie Lee Curtis, became a scream queen with her breakthrough role as *Halloween*'s (1978) "Final Girl" Laurie Strode, while Oz Perkins played the young Norman Bates in *Psycho II* (1983) as a child. Critically rejected but financially successful, Universal's *Psycho* sequels represent a fascinating moment when influence within the modern horror genre effectively folded in on itself: whereas many of the early slasher films directly looked to Hitchcock's film for inspiration, this belated turn to sequelizing *Psycho* over two decades after its initial release was largely driven by a major Hollywood studio trying to cash in on the box-office successes of independently produced slasher movies like *Halloween*.

Again, this would be little more than intertextual trivia if it did not imply, per *I Am the Pretty's Thing*'s dedication, that Anthony Perkins's son might also end up, like Norman himself, feeling similarly trapped in the generic world of *Psycho*. As William Rothman observes, "Part of *Psycho*'s myth is that there is no world outside its own, that we are fated to be born, live our alienated lives, and die in the very world in which Norman Bates dwells."[46] Moreover, as Mr Waxcap explains to Lily, Ms Blum intended to leave behind a "house of stories" as her posthumous gift to the world – much as, I would argue, the horror genre is itself a sort of "house" filled with the ghosts of old stories (such as *Psycho* and its kin) that continue to haunt post-horror films like this one.

Yet, where *A Ghost Story* undercuts the Prognosticator's skepticism about the longevity of human memory with a final turn toward romantic sentimentality and the Ghost's passage into the afterlife, *I Am the Pretty Thing* partially conceals Perkins's heartfelt homage to his father beneath layers of ambiguity, from its poetic voiceovers to its ostensibly bleak ending with Lily remaining in ghostly purgatory. In other words, both films register a certain degree of not just affect but *affection* – though Lowery's film ultimately wears its heart on its sleeve, while Perkins's downbeat mood piece strikes a far more ambivalent tone. Hence, Perkins seems to be asking whether finding oneself "walled inside" the horror genre's own realm of perpetual recurrence, remaining there as a ghostly presence, would be such a bad thing – especially if it might offer a greater means of achieving posterity than the more private, individualized process of remembering predecessors on one's own family tree.

EXISTENTIAL DREAD AND TROUBLE WITH TRANSCENDENCE   239

Following Thomas Ligotti, I would argue that the horror genre will remain relevant for as long as human beings find something strangely comforting about the difference-in-repetition that its long history of generic texts offers.[47] Hence, there is still something vaguely hopeful about *I Am the Pretty Thing*'s attempt to balance existential anxiety with familial love. Rather than transcending the horror genre by refusing to properly inhabit it, as *A Ghost Story*'s cosmic romance aspires to do, Perkins settles into more comfortably dwelling within the genre, despite the potential "rot" lurking in the old and oft-denigrated storytelling structure. True enough, memory itself will not exist after environmental or cosmic destruction wipes out the last of the human species. But until then – much as young Ms Blum gives voice to Polly through her novel and journal, and Lily later gives voice to the elderly author by reading her works – both generations of Perkins, father and son, exist as ghostly echoes speaking to each other across different historical moments and different aesthetic/taste strata. And perhaps that small, temporary measure of posterity is all that anyone can hope for.

In the End . . .

The preceding section may seem like both an abrupt and gloomy way to end a book about a film cycle that was inaugurated less than a decade ago, and which is still unfolding as of this writing. Yet, it is precisely the in-progress state of this new wave of horror cinema that offers more questions than answers about continuing influence and long-term posterity – the very issues that *I Am the Pretty Thing* raises. Beyond arguing that "elevated" or "post-horror" films constitute one of the most important developments in the genre during the 2010s, it would be disingenuous for this first full-length study of the cycle to come to any grandiose prognostications about the industrial longevity and longitudinal appeal of these films, especially while the cycle's first wave is mid-crest. By both evoking a longer tradition of art-horror cinema and also crossing over to wider audiences (albeit with mixed success), some earlier post-horror works – such as *It Follows*, *The Witch*, and *Get Out* (2017) – have already seemed to garner canonical status within the larger genre, while time will tell about the longer reception tail of other texts. Nonetheless, much as I have argued in earlier chapters that post-horror themes often speak to a preoccupation with familial resemblances and natural generativity, the cycle's stylistic hybridization of both art and horror cinema may well sow the seeds for future generic developments.

Of course, whether horror-skeptic critics and populist audiences follow those future developments remains to be seen. After all, as elaborated in

Chapter 2, post-horror cinema has become a historically significant trend *because* of its divisiveness among taste cultures, from major film critics' inadequate attempts to name its minimalistic form to the grassroots efforts by Rotten Tomatoes users at cautioning prospective viewers away from the films' less entertaining affects, like feelings of grief. Meanwhile, some of the most recent post-horror films to date, such as *The Lodge* (2019) and *Gretel & Hansel* (2020), evince – for better or worse – as much influence from previous films in the cycle as from the wider web of "slow," "smart," and "indie" cinema that provided significant early inspiration for post-horror's emergence.

On one hand, this is a common enough trajectory for film cycles that emerge within an existing genre: as soon as a "core" style or formula crystallizes and can be emulated, the cycle's initial energy begins to wane across subsequent, increasingly methodical iterations. On the other hand, the box-office underperformance of *The Lodge* and *Gretel & Hansel* – the follow-up efforts from the directors of *Goodnight Mommy* (2014) and *I Am the Pretty Thing*, respectively – also demonstrates post-horror's continuing difficulties in bridging the gap between art-cinema severity and populist tastes. The former is an exceedingly bleak film, very much in the vein of *It Comes at Night* (2017), and its wide release was repeatedly delayed before being scaled back to a limited theatrical run, while the latter is a mediocre attempt to merge "elevated" style with "hollywooden" themes (as noted in Chapter 5). Hence, whether post-horror films eventually retract back to their pre-2014 home in the specialty market for art and independent cinema, especially if wide multiplex releases no longer prove profitable, will likely also be a factor in the cycle's longevity – or at least its overall visibility.

Even if the post-horror boom proves to be an approximately decade-long cycle – with its austere style as another iteration of the genre's major currents periodically recalibrating toward less gratuitous thrills, as well as an outgrowth of art-horror's long history – the sense of lingering dread that these films so powerfully generate may well extend to the genre itself by casting a stylistic and affective shadow over horror cinema for years to come. During that time, there will surely be plenty more critical and scholarly ink spilled about the post-horror phenomenon – since it is, after all, a cycle whose prominence has been driven by critical conversation – but hopefully this book has provided a fruitful way into the "elevated" style, political themes, and fraught reception of films located at the productive (albeit divisive) overlap between art and genre.

EXISTENTIAL DREAD AND TROUBLE WITH TRANSCENDENCE   241

Notes

1. Because Gavin used Samuel Liddell MacGregor Mathers's 1897 English translation of the *Book of Abramelin* as his source material, Sophia attempts a six-month Abramelin working, whereas a more complete 2006 translation clarifies that it is actually an eighteen-month procedure. See Abraham von Worms, *The Book of Abramelin: A New Translation*, eds and trans. Georg Dehn and Steven Guth (Lake Worth, FL: Ibis Press, 2006).
2. Daniel Moler, "Not Your Hollywood Kind of Magic (A Film Review of A DARK SONG)," *Daniel Moler: Words, Images, Esoterics* (blog), June 20, 2017 <https://www.danielmolerweb.com/post/2017/06/20/not-your-hollywood-kind-of-magic-a-film-review-of-a-dark-song>.
3. *The Book of Abramelin*, 39–40, 82–83. Cf. *The Key of Solomon (Clavicula Salomonis)*, eds and trans. Samuel Liddell MacGregor Mathers and Joseph H. Peterson, Esoteric Archives, accessed April 19, 2020 <http://www.esotericarchives.com/solomon/ksol.htm>.
4. *The Book of Abramelin*, 81, 84, 128–9.
5. Ibid., pp. 159–60, 173–5. As the *Book* notes, nefarious people could attempt to use word squares to cast spells for quick results, but these unenlightened efforts will come to naught without the HGA's guidance (p. 199).
6. See Lee Edelman, *No Future: Queer Theory and the Death Drive* (Durham, NC: Duke University Press, 2004), a book that complements the anti-natalist philosophy of Thomas Ligotti, discussed below.
7. "Interview with Director Liam Gavin," *A Dark Song* DVD bonus features (Los Angeles: IFC Films, 2017); Richard Whittaker, "DVDanger: *A Dark Song*," *Austin Chronicle*, April 30, 2017 <https://www.austinchronicle.com/daily/screens/2017-04-30/dvdanger-a-dark-song/>; Gavin, interviewed in Michael Muncer, "Occult Pt. 21: *A Dark Song* (2016)," *The Evolution of Horror* (podcast), accessed April 21, 2020 <https://www.evolutionofhorror.com/occult-pt-21>. Among *A Dark Song*'s many derivations from the actual Abramelin operation are a ritual progression through five elemental circles, the performance of rituals in different rooms, the use of pentacles (rather than just magic squares), and their attempts to cast spells before making contact with the HGA.
8. Conor Dennison (production designer), personal communication, April 30, 2020.
9. See Nevill Drury, *Stealing Fire from Heaven: The Rise of Modern Western Magic* (New York: Oxford University Press, 2011), pp. 78–81, 116. Indeed, Solomon's assertion that the Abramelin operation is about much darker forces than exploring God via the Tree of Sephiroth suggests his closer allegiances with the Tree of Qliphoth, or the "negative" energy counterparts in the Kabbalistic tradition – these latter energies also corresponding with the Left-Hand Path (122–5).
10. See Adrienne L. McLean, "If Only They Had Meant to Make a Comedy: Laughing at *Black Swan*," in *The Last Laugh: Strange Humors of Cinema*,

ed. Murray Pomerance (Detroit, MI: Wayne State University Press, 2013), pp. 143–61; Julia Mendenhall, "Cult Cinema and Camp," in *The Routledge Companion to Cult Cinema*, eds Ernest Mathijs and Jamie Sexton (New York: Routledge, 2020), pp. 194–6.
11. Although Aronofsky has not been shy about connecting the underlying biblical allegory to his own environmentalism, whether these war scenes were intended as the Jewish-American auteur's commentary on Israeli–Palestinian relations is unclear – albeit strongly implied. For example, see Anne Thompson, "'Mother!': Darren Aronofsky Answers All Your Burning Questions About the Film's Shocking Twists and Meanings," *IndieWire*, September 18, 2017 <https://www.indiewire.com/2017/09/mother-darren-aronofsky-explains-mythology-allegory-bible-jennifer-lawrence-1201877848/>.
12. The *Wendehorn* rune on Adam's lighter, derived from the same Elder *Futhark* runic language depicted in *Midsommar* (another film about cycles of death and rebirth), alludes to a union of female and male forces that also symbolizes the conjunction of life/creation and death/destruction.
13. Luce Irigaray, *Marine Lover of Friedrich Nietzsche*, trans. Gillian C. Gill (New York: Columbia University Press, 1991), pp. 8–12 (quoted at pp. 10, 11). Cf. Friedrich Nietzsche, *Thus Spoke Zarathustra: A Book for All and None*, trans. Walter Kaufmann (New York: Penguin Books, 1978).
14. See Mary Daly, *Gyn/Ecology: The Metaethics of Radical Feminism* (Boston: Beacon Press, 1978).
15. Maggie Nelson, *The Art of Cruelty: A Reckoning* (New York: W. W. Norton, 2011), pp. 17, 72, 168 (quoted at p. 168).
16. Linda Williams, *Playing the Race Card: Melodramas of Black and White from Uncle Tom to O. J. Simpson* (Princeton, NJ: Princeton University Press, 2001), pp. 20, 44, 308.
17. Nelson, *The Art of Cruelty*, 176–7, 195–7 (quoted at p. 196).
18. Antonin Artaud, *The Theater and Its Double*, trans. Mary Caroline Richards (New York: Grove Press, 1958), p. 31.
19. Ibid., p. 99.
20. Ibid., p. 48.
21. Ibid., pp. 48–9, 51–2, 60, 70, 73.
22. Nelson, *The Art of Cruelty*, 116.
23. Jennifer Lawrence, interviewed in *Variety*, "Actors on Actors: Jennifer Lawrence and Adam Sandler (Full Video)," YouTube, November 28, 2017 <https://www.youtube.com/watch?v=hzCeq0-Vd1U>.
24. Artaud, *The Theater and Its Double*, 79.
25. Thomas Ligotti, *The Conspiracy Against the Human Race: A Contrivance of Horror* (New York: Penguin Books, 2018), pp. 4, 27–8, 64–5, 120–1, 145, 148–9, 158, 168, 213.
26. Ibid., p. 214.
27. Ibid., pp. 173, 185, 204, 209 (quoted at p. 209).

28. Ibid., pp. 39, 41, 203 (quoted at p. 203). Having spent much of his life confined to asylums, Artaud would likely concur with Ligotti's assessment that a sense of the supernatural can be correlative to insanity.
29. Ibid., pp. 194–7, 210. Also see Eugene Thacker, *Tentacles Longer Than Night: Horror of Philosophy*, Vol. 3 (Alresford: Zero Books, 2015).
30. Adam Charles Hart, *Monstrous Forms: Moving Image Horror Across Media* (New York: Oxford University Press, 2020), pp. 136–9.
31. Richard Armstrong, *Mourning Films: A Critical Study of Loss and Grieving in Cinema* (Jefferson, NC: McFarland, 2012), pp. 22–3, 31–2, 98, 127.
32. Because the Ghost's sheeted appearance also recalls a Ku Klux Klan robe, his misplaced anger toward these supposed interlopers might suggest racist implications – especially since the subsequent white tenants experience little more ghostly influence than flickering lights – although the Ghost's later pose of indifference toward an Indigenous tribe's (arguably justifiable) massacre of white settlers also complicates such a reading.
33. Dylan Trigg, *The Thing: A Phenomenology of Horror* (Alresford: Zero Books, 2014), pp. 145–6. On the horror genre as a means of attempting to imagine the "world-without-us," also see Eugene Thacker, *In the Dust of This Planet: Horror of Philosophy*, Vol. 1 (Alresford: Zero Books, 2011).
34. For example, consider the title of Nikolaus Geyrhalter's ruin-porn documentary *Homo Sapiens* (2016), a series of static shots of abandoned places around the world, which provides no context for what is being filmed or why these human-built places were left behind.
35. Virginia Woolf, "A Haunted House," in *A Haunted House and Other Short Stories* (New York: Harcourt, 1944), p. 5.
36. Ligotti, *The Conspiracy Against the Human Race*, 14, 76, 80, 140, 156–7, 175, 211 (quoted at p. 140).
37. See David H. Fleming and William Brown, "Through a (First) Contact Lens Darkly: *Arrival*, Unreal Time, and Chthulucinema," *Film-Philosophy*, 22, no. 3 (2018), pp. 359–61.
38. Lauren Berlant, *Cruel Optimism* (Durham, NC: Duke University Press, 2011), pp. 1–11. Neoliberal precarity is therefore closer to Laura S. Brown's concept of "insidious trauma" (see Chapter 3), albeit felt by an increasingly wide swath of people compared to insidious trauma's association with socio-economic minorities.
39. Ibid., pp. 6–7.
40. Lowery, quoted in Steve Rose, "How Post-Horror Movies are Taking Over Cinema," *The Guardian*, July 6, 2017 <https://www.theguardian.com/film/2017/jul/06/post-horror-films-scary-movies-ghost-story-it-comes-at-night>.
41. Indeed, his sophomore film's visibility on Netflix convinced A24 to belatedly pick up *The Blackcoat's Daughter* for a limited theatrical release during spring 2017, appearing on A24's release slate between *The Witch* and *It Comes at Night* (2017).

42. Unlike the distractingly obtrusive and overly expositional voiceover in Perkins's *Gretel & Hansel* (2020), as discussed in Chapter 5, *I Am the Pretty Thing*'s frequent use of voiceover feels appropriately ambient within Ms Blum's "house of stories," with certain repeated refrains evoking mystery instead of blatantly explaining characters' thoughts.
43. Eve Kosofsky Sedgwick, *The Coherence of Gothic Conventions* (New York: Methuen, 1986), p. 13.
44. Oz's brother Elvis Perkins also composed the film's moody music, largely consisting of detuned and reverberating piano chords that rise up from the soundtrack's ambient buzz of crickets, cicadas, and rain.
45. Among others, see Stephen Rebello, *Alfred Hitchcock and the Making of Psycho* (New York: St. Martin's Griffin, 1990), pp. 160–72; Robert E. Kapsis, *Hitchcock: The Making of a Reputation* (Chicago: University of Chicago Press, 1992), pp. 58–64, 159–76; Janet Staiger, *Perverse Spectators: The Practices of Film Reception* (New York: New York University Press, 2000), pp. 179–87.
46. William Rothman, *Hitchcock: The Murderous Gaze*, 2nd edn (Albany, NY: State University of New York Press, 2012), p. 263.
47. Also see David Church, "Afterword: Memory, Genre, and Self-Narrativization; or, Why I Should Be a More Content Horror Fan," in *American Horror Film: The Genre at the Turn of the Millennium*, ed. Steffen Hantke (Jackson, MS: University Press of Mississippi, 2010), pp. 235–42.

Selected Bibliography

Abbott, Stacey. "High Concept Thrills and Chills: The Horror Blockbuster." In *Horror Zone: The Cultural Experience of Contemporary Horror Cinema*, ed. Ian Conrich. London: I. B. Tauris, 2010, pp. 27–44.

Abraham, Nicolas, and Maria Torok. *The Shell and the Kernel: Renewals of Psychoanalysis*, Vol. 1, ed. Nicholas T. Rand. Chicago: University of Chicago Press, 1994.

Abramson, Kate. "Turning Up the Lights on Gaslighting." *Philosophical Perspectives*, 28 (2014), pp. 1–30.

Ahmed, Sara. *The Cultural Politics of Emotion*, 2nd edn. Edinburgh: Edinburgh University Press, 2014.

Andrews, David. *Theorizing Art Cinemas: Foreign, Cult, Avant-Garde, and Beyond*. Austin, TX: University of Texas Press, 2013.

Apel, Dora. *Beautiful Terrible Ruins: Detroit and the Anxiety of Decline*. New Brunswick, NJ: Rutgers University Press, 2015.

Armstrong, Richard. *Mourning Films: A Critical Study of Loss and Grieving in Cinema*. Jefferson, NC: McFarland, 2012.

Arnold, Sarah. *Maternal Horror Film: Melodrama and Motherhood*. New York: Palgrave Macmillan, 2013.

Arnold, Sarah. "Urban Decay Photography and Film: Fetishism and the Apocalyptic Imagination." *Journal of Urban History*, 41, no. 2 (2015), pp. 326–39.

Artaud, Antonin. *The Theater and Its Double*, trans. Mary Caroline Richards. New York: Grove Press, 1958.

Austin, Dan. *Lost Detroit: Stories Behind the Motor City's Majestic Ruins*. Mount Pleasant, SC: Arcadia, 2010.

Autier, Paul, and Paul Cloquemin. "The Lighthouse Keepers (*Gardiens de phare*)." In *Grand-Guignol: The French Theatre of Horror*, eds Richard J. Hand and Michael Wilson. Exeter: University of Exeter Press, 2002, pp. 109–20.

Avery, Dwayne. *Unhomely Cinema: Home and Place in Global Cinema*. London: Anthem Press, 2014.

Bachelard, Gaston. *The Poetics of Space*, trans. Maria Jolas. Boston: Beacon Press, 1994.

Baker, Emerson W. *A Storm of Witchcraft: The Salem Trials and the American Experience*. New York: Oxford University Press, 2015.

Balanzategui, Jessica. "*The Babadook* and the Haunted Space Between High and Low Genres in the Australian Horror Tradition." *Studies in Australasian Studies*, 11, no. 1 (2017), pp. 18–32.

Barefoot, Guy. *Gaslight Melodrama: From Victorian London to 1940s Hollywood*. London: Continuum, 2001.

Benshoff, Harry M. *Monsters in the Closet: Homosexuality and the Horror Film*. Manchester: Manchester University Press, 1997.

Berenstein, Rhona J. *Attack of the Leading Ladies: Gender, Sexuality, and Spectatorship in Classic Horror Cinema*. New York: Columbia University Press, 1996.

Berlant, Lauren. *Cruel Optimism*. Durham, NC: Duke University Press, 2011.

Blake, Linnie. *The Wounds of Nations: Horror Cinema, Historical Trauma, and National Identity*. Manchester: Manchester University Press, 2008.

Bordwell, David. "Intensified Continuity: Visual Style in Contemporary American Film." *Film Quarterly*, 55, no. 3 (2002), pp. 16–28.

Bordwell, David. "The Art Cinema as a Mode of Film Practice." In *Critical Visions in Film Theory: Classic and Contemporary Readings*, eds Timothy Corrigan, Patricia White, and Meta Mazaj. Boston: Bedford/St. Martin's, 2011, pp. 558–71.

Bourdieu, Pierre. *Distinction: A Social Critique of the Judgment of Taste*, trans. Richard Nice. Cambridge, MA: Harvard University Press, 1984.

Boyle, Kevin. "The Ruins of Detroit: Exploring the Urban Crisis in the Motor City." *Michigan Historical Review*, 27, no. 1 (2001), pp. 109–27.

Braun, Aaron. "'Truvada Whores' and the Class Divide." *Pacific Standard*, August 17, 2015, <http://www.psmag.com/health-and-behavior/truvada-whores-and-the-aids-class-divide>.

Brennan, Teresa. *The Transmission of Affect*. Ithaca, NY: Cornell University Press, 2004.

Bridges, J. A. "Post-Horror Kinships: From *Goodnight Mommy* to *Get Out*." *Bright Lights Film Journal*, December 20, 2018 <https://brightlightsfilm.com/post-horror-kinships-from-goodnight-mommy-to-get-out/>.

Briefel, Aviva. "Devil in the Details: The Uncanny History of *The Witch* (2015)." *Film & History: An Interdisciplinary Journal*, 49, no. 1 (2019), pp. 4–20.

Briefel, Aviva. "Parenting Through Horror: Reassurance in Jennifer Kent's *The Babadook*." *Camera Obscura*, 32, no. 2 (2017), pp. 1–27.

Brinkema, Eugenie. *The Forms of the Affects*. Durham, NC: Duke University Press, 2014.

Brown, Kimberly Nichele. "'Stay Woke': Post-Black Filmmaking and the Afterlife of Slavery in Jordan Peele's *Get Out*." In *Slavery and the Post-Black Imagination*, eds Bertram D. Ashe and Ilka Saal. Seattle, WA: University of Washington Press, 2020, pp. 109–23.

Brown, Laura S. "Not Outside the Range: One Feminist Perspective on Psychic Trauma." *American Imago*, 48, no. 1 (1991), pp. 119–33.

Brown, Michael. "The Problem with 'Post-Horror.'" *Overland*, May 15, 2019 <https://overland.org.au/2019/05/the-problem-with-post-horror/>.

Buerger, Shelley. "The Beak That Grips: Maternal Indifference, Ambivalence, and the Abject in *The Babadook*." *Studies in Australasian Cinema*, 11, no. 1 (2017), pp. 33–44.
Calef, Victor, and Edward M. Weinshel. "Some Clinical Consequences of Projection: Gaslighting." *Psychoanalytic Quarterly*, 50, no. 1 (1981), pp. 44–66.
Cante, Rich, and Angelo Restivo. "The Cultural-Aesthetic Specificities of All-Male Moving-Image Pornography." In *Porn Studies*, ed. Linda Williams. Durham, NC: Duke University Press, 2004, pp. 142–66.
Caron, David. "Shame on Me, or the Naked Truth about Me and Marlene Dietrich." In *Gay Shame*, eds David M. Halperin and Valerie Traub. Chicago: University of Chicago Press, 2009, pp. 117–31.
Carpenter, Amanda. *Gaslighting America: Why We Love It When Trump Lies to Us*. New York: Broadside Books, 2018.
Carroll, Andrew. "Horror Means Horror: The Fallacy of 'Elevated Horror.'" *Headstuff*, March 28, 2019 <https://www.headstuff.org/entertainment/film/elevated-horror-get-out-us/>.
Carroll, Chloe. "'Wouldst Thou Like to Live Deliciously?' Female Persecution and Redemption in *The Witch*." *Frames Cinema Journal*, no. 16 (Winter 2019) <https://framescinemajournal.com/article/wouldst-thou-like-to-live-deliciously-female-persecution-and-redemption-in-the-witch/>.
Carroll, Noël. *The Philosophy of Horror, or Paradoxes of the Heart*. New York: Routledge, 1990.
Caruth, Cathy. *Unclaimed Experience: Trauma, Narrative, and History*. Baltimore, MD: Johns Hopkins University Press, 1996.
Cherry, Brigid. "Gothics and Grand Guignols: Violence and the Gendered Aesthetics of Cinematic Horror." *Participations: Journal of Audience & Reception Studies*, 5, no. 1 (2008) <http://www.participations.org/Volume%205/Issue%201%20-%20special/5_01_cherry.htm>.
Christian, Laura. "Of Housewives and Saints: Abjection, Transgression, and Impossible Mourning in *Poison* and *Safe*." *Camera Obscura*, 19, no. 3 (2004), pp. 93–123.
Church, David. "Afterword: Memory, Genre, and Self-Narrativization; or, Why I Should Be a More Content Horror Fan." In *American Horror Film: The Genre at the Turn of the Millennium*, ed. Steffen Hantke. Jackson, MS: University Press of Mississippi, 2010, pp. 235–42.
Clover, Carol J. *Men, Women, and Chainsaws: Gender in the Modern Horror Film*. Princeton, NJ: Princeton University Press, 1992.
Cochrane, Tom. "The Emotional Experience of the Sublime." *Canadian Journal of Philosophy*, 42, no. 2 (2012), pp. 125–48.
Coleman, Robin R. Means. *Horror Noire: Blacks in American Horror Films from the 1890s to Present*. New York: Routledge, 2011.
Collins, Jim. *Architectures of Excess: Cultural Life in the Information Age*. New York: Routledge, 1995.

Collins, K. Austin. "Jordan Peele's *Us* is Just a Horror Movie, and That's a Good Thing." *Vanity Fair*, March 22, 2019 <https://www.vanityfair.com/hollywood/2019/03/jordan-peeles-us-dont-overthink-it>.

Craig, Pamela, and Martin Fradley. "Teenage Traumata: Youth, Affective Politics, and the Contemporary American Horror Film." In *American Horror Film: The Genre at the Turn of the Millennium*, ed. Steffen Hantke. Jackson, MS: University Press of Mississippi, 2010, pp. 77–102.

Creed, Barbara. *The Monstrous-Feminine: Film, Feminism, Psychoanalysis*. London: Routledge, 1993.

Crimp, Douglas. "Mario Montez, for Shame." In *Gay Shame*, eds David M. Halperin and Valerie Traub. Chicago: University of Chicago Press, 2009, pp. 63–75.

Crowley, Aleister. *The Book of the Goetia of Solomon the King* [1904]. Leeds: Celephaïs Press, 2003.

Dalton, Ben. "*It Follows*: Horror in a Straight Line." *Intensities: The Journal of Cult Media*, no. 8 (2016), pp. 88–93.

Daly, Mary. *Gyn/Ecology: The Metaethics of Radical Feminism*. Boston: Beacon Press, 1978.

Danielsen, Shane. "The Elevated Horror of Ari Aster's 'Hereditary.'" *The Monthly*, June 2018 <https://www.themonthly.com.au/issue/2018/june/1527775200/shane-danielsen/elevated-horror-ari-aster-s-hereditary#mtr>.

Davis, Blair, and Kial Natale. "'The Pound of Flesh Which I Demand': American Horror Cinema, Gore, and the Box Office, 1998–2007." In *American Horror Film: The Genre at the Turn of the Millennium*, ed. Steffen Hantke. Jackson, MS: University Press of Mississippi, 2010, pp. 35–57.

Davis, Glyn. "The Speed of the VCR: Ti West's Slow Horror." *Screen*, 59, no. 1 (2018), pp. 41–58.

Davis, Wade. *The Serpent and the Rainbow*. New York: Simon & Schuster, 1985.

Dean, Tim. "Mediated Intimacies: Raw Sex, Truvada, and the Biopolitics of Chemoprophylaxis." *Sexualities*, 18, no. 1/2 (2015), pp. 224–46.

Dean, Tim. *Unlimited Intimacy: Reflections on the Subculture of Barebacking*. Chicago: University of Chicago Press, 2009.

Delany, Samuel. *Times Square Red, Times Square Blue*. New York: New York University Press, 1999.

De Luca, Tiego, and Nuno Barradas Jorge. "Introduction: From Slow Cinema to Slow Cinemas." In *Slow Cinema*, eds Tiago de Luca and Nuno Barradas Jorge. Edinburgh: Edinburgh University Press, 2016, pp. 1–21.

De Villiers, Nicholas. "Leaving the Cinema: Metacinematic Cruising in Tsai Ming-liang's *Goodbye, Dragon Inn*." *Jump Cut*, no. 50 (2008) <https://www.ejumpcut.org/archive/jc50.2008/DragonInn/>.

Doane, Mary Ann. *The Desire to Desire: The Woman's Film of the 1940s*. Bloomington, IN: Indiana University Press, 1987.

Downing, Lisa. "On the Fantasy of Childlessness as Death in Psychoanalysis and in Roeg's *Don't Look Now* and Von Trier's *Antichrist*." *Lambda Nordica*, 16, no. 2/3 (2011), pp. 49–68.

Drury, Nevill. *Stealing Fire from Heaven: The Rise of Modern Western Magic*. New York: Oxford University Press, 2011.
Due, Tananarive. "*Get Out* and the Black Horror Aesthetic." In Jordan Peele, *Get Out: The Complete Annotated Screenplay*. Los Angeles: Inventory Press, 2019, pp. 8–15.
Duggan, Lisa. "The New Homonormativity: The Sexual Politics of Neoliberalism." In *Materializing Democracy: Toward a Revitalized Cultural Politics*, eds Russ Castronovo and Dana D. Nelson. Durham, NC: Duke University Press, 2002, pp. 175–94.
Edelman, Lee. *No Future: Queer Theory and the Death Drive*. Durham, NC: Duke University Press, 2004.
Edelstein, David. "Now Playing at Your Local Multiplex: Torture Porn." *New York*, January 26, 2006 <http://nymag.com/movies/features/15622/>.
Edensor, Tim. *Industrial Ruins: Space, Aesthetics, and Materiality*. Oxford: Berg, 2005.
Edwards, Kyle. "'House of Horrors': Corporate Strategy at Universal Pictures in the 1930s." In *Merchants of Menace: The Business of Horror Cinema*, ed. Richard Nowell. New York: Bloomsbury Academic, 2014, pp. 13–30.
Edwards-Behi, Nia. "A Response to Post-Horror." *Wales Arts Review*, July 9, 2017 <https://www.walesartsreview.org/cinema-a-response-to-post-horror/>.
Egan, Kate. *Trash or Treasure? Censorship and the Changing Meanings of the Video Nasties*. Manchester: Manchester University Press, 2007.
Ehrlich, David. "The Evils of 'Elevated Horror': *IndieWire* Critics Survey." *IndieWire*, March 25, 2019 <https://www.indiewire.com/2019/03/elevated-horror-movies-us-1202053471/>.
Eliade, Mircea. "Spirit, Light, and Seed." *History of Religions*, 11, no. 1 (1971), pp. 1–30.
Faber, Michel. *Under the Skin*. New York: Harcourt, 2000.
Falvey, Eddie. "Sexual Participation Within Fan Cultures: Considering a Sex Toy as a Mode of Reception for *The Shape of Water*." *Journal of Fandom Studies*, 7, no. 3 (2019), pp. 245–59.
Fischer, Lucy. *Cinematernity: Film, Motherhood, Genre*. Princeton, NJ: Princeton University Press, 1996.
Fitzgerald, Jonathan D. "Sincerity, Not Irony, is Our Age's Ethos." *The Atlantic*, November 20, 2012, <https://www.theatlantic.com/entertainment/archive/2012/11/sincerity-not-irony-is-our-ages-ethos/265466/>.
Flanagan, Matthew. "Towards an Aesthetics of Slow in Contemporary Cinema." *16:9*, 6, no. 29 (2008) <http://www.16-9.dk/2008-11/side11_inenglish.htm>.
Fleming, David H., and William Brown. "Through a (First) Contact Lens Darkly: *Arrival*, Unreal Time, and Chthulucinema." *Film-Philosophy*, 22, no. 3 (2018), pp. 340–63.
Fletcher, John. "Primal Scenes and the Female Gothic: *Rebecca* and *Gaslight*." *Screen*, 36, no. 4 (1995), pp. 341–70.
Foucault, Michel. "Nietzsche, Genealogy, History." In *The Foucault Reader*, ed. Paul Rabinow. New York: Pantheon Books, 1984, pp. 76–100.

Frazer, James George. *The Golden Bough: A Study in Magic and Religion*, 3rd edn. New York: Macmillan, 1913.

Freeman, Elizabeth. *Time Binds: Queer Temporalities, Queer Histories*. Durham, NC: Duke University Press, 2010.

Freud, Sigmund. "Mourning and Melancholia." In *The Standard Edition of the Complete Psychological Works of Sigmund Freud*, Vol. XIV, ed. James Strachey. London: Hogarth Press, 1964, pp. 243–58.

Freud, Sigmund. *The Interpretation of Dreams*, 3rd edn. New York: Macmillan, 1913.

Freud, Sigmund. "The Uncanny." In *The Standard Edition of the Complete Psychological Works of Sigmund Freud*, Vol. XVII, ed. James Strachey. London: Hogarth Press, 1955, pp. 219–52.

Frey, Mattias. *Extreme Cinema: The Transgressive Rhetoric of Today's Art Film Culture*. New Brunswick, NJ: Rutgers University Press, 2016.

Frey, Mattias. "Introduction: Critical Questions." In *Film Criticism in the Digital Age*, eds Mattias Frey and Cecilia Sayad. New Brunswick, NJ: Rutgers University Press, 2015, pp. 1–20.

Frey, Mattias. "The New Democracy? Rotten Tomatoes, Metacritic, Twitter, and IMDb." In *Film Criticism in the Digital Age*, eds Mattias Frey and Cecilia Sayad. New Brunswick, NJ: Rutgers University Press, 2015, pp. 81–98.

Frey, Mattias. *The Permanent Crisis of Film Criticism: The Anxiety of Authority*. Amsterdam: Amsterdam University Press, 2014.

Fusco, Katherine. "*Hereditary* and the Monstrousness of Creative Moms." *The Atlantic*, July 11, 2018 <https://www.theatlantic.com/entertainment/archive/2018/07/hereditary-and-the-monstrousness-of-creative-moms/564815/>.

Gibbs, Alan. *Contemporary American Trauma Narratives*. Edinburgh: Edinburgh University Press, 2014.

Gildersleeve, Jessica. *Don't Look Now*. Leighton Buzzard: Auteur, 2017.

Gordon, Avery F. *Ghostly Matters: Haunting and the Sociological Imagination*. Minneapolis, MN: University of Minnesota Press, 2008.

Gorfinkel, Elena. "Sex, Sensation, and Nonhuman Interiority in *Under the Skin*." *Jump Cut: A Review of Contemporary Media*, no. 57 (2016) <https://www.ejumpcut.org/archive/jc57.2016/-GorfinkelSkin/2.html>.

Grafius, Brandon. "Securing the Borders: Isolation and Anxiety in *The Witch*, *It Comes at Night*, and Trump's America." In *Make America Hate Again: Trump-Era Horror and the Politics of Fear*, ed. Victoria McCollum. London: Routledge, 2019, pp. 119–28.

Graves, Stephanie A. "Jordan Peele's *Get Out* (2017) – Smart Horror." In *Horror: A Companion*, ed. Simon Bacon. Oxford: Peter Lang, 2019, pp. 127–34.

Greven, David. *Representations of Femininity in American Genre Cinema: The Woman's Film, Film Noir, and Modern Horror*. New York: Palgrave Macmillan, 2011.

Grimm, Joshua. *It Follows*. Leighton Buzzard: Auteur, 2018.

Gripsrud, Jostein. "'High Culture' Revisited." *Cultural Studies*, 3, no. 2 (1989), pp. 194–207.
Hahner, Leslie A. and Scott J. Varda. "*It Follows* and Rape Culture: Critical Response as Disavowal." *Women's Studies in Communication*, 40, no. 3 (2017), pp. 251–69.
Hanich, Julian. *Cinematic Emotion in Horror Films and Thrillers: The Aesthetic Paradox of Pleasurable Fear*. New York: Routledge, 2010.
Hanich, Julian. *The Audience Effect: On the Collective Cinema Experience*. Edinburgh: Edinburgh University Press, 2018.
Hanson, Ellis. "Undead." In *Inside/Out: Lesbian Theories, Gay Theories*, ed. Diana Fuss. New York: Routledge, 1991, pp. 324–40.
Harrington, Erin. *Women, Monstrosity, and Horror Film: Gynaehorror*. New York: Routledge, 2018.
Hart, Adam Charles. *Monstrous Forms: Moving Image Horror Across Media*. New York: Oxford University Press, 2020.
Hartman, Saidiya. *Lose Your Mother: A Journey Along the Atlantic Slave Route*. New York: Farrar, Straus, & Giroux, 2008.
Hawkins, Joan. "Culture Wars: Some New Trends in Art Horror." *Jump Cut*, no. 51 (2009) <https://www.ejumpcut.org/archive/jc51.2009/artHorror/>.
Hawkins, Joan. *Cutting Edge: Art-Horror and the Horrific Avant-Garde*. Minneapolis, MN: University of Minnesota Press, 2000.
Hawkins, Joan. "'It Fixates': Indie Quiets and the New Gothics." *Palgrave Communications*, 3:17088 (2017), doi: 10.1057/palcomms.2017.88.
Hayward, Joni. "No Safe Space: Economic Anxiety and Post-Recession Spaces in Horror Films." *Frames Cinema Journal*, no. 11 (2017) <https://framescinemajournal.com/article/no-safe-space-economic-anxiety-and-post-recession-spaces-in-horror-films/>.
Heffernan, Kevin. *Ghouls, Gimmicks, and Gold: Horror Films and the American Movie Business, 1953–1968*. Durham, NC: Duke University Press, 2004.
Heller-Nicholas, Alexandra. "Grand Guignol, Early Cinema, and Robert Eggers' *The Lighthouse*." *Diabolique Magazine*, October 4, 2019 <https://diaboliquemagazine.com/grand-guignol-early-cinema-and-robert-eggers-the-lighthouse/>.
Helmreich, Stefan. "The Genders of Waves." *WSQ: Women's Studies Quarterly*, 45, no. 1/2 (2017), pp. 29–51.
Hester, Helen. *Beyond Explicit: Pornography and the Displacement of Sex*. Albany, NY: State University of New York Press, 2014.
High, Steven C., and David W. Lewis. *Corporate Wasteland: The Landscape and Memory of Deindustrialization*. Ithaca, NY: Cornell University Press, 2007.
Hills, Matt. "An Event-Based Definition of Art-Horror." In *Dark Thoughts: Philosophic Reflections on Cinematic Horror*, eds Steven Jay Schneider and Daniel Shaw. Lanham, MD: Scarecrow Press, 2003, pp. 138–57.
Hills, Matt. "Attending Horror Film Festivals and Conventions: Liveness, Subcultural Capital, and 'Flesh-and-Blood Genre Communities.'" In *Horror Zone: The Cultural Experience of Contemporary Horror Cinema*, ed. Ian Conrich. New York: I. B. Tauris, 2010, pp. 87–101.

Hills, Matt. "Para-Paracinema: The *Friday the 13th* Film Series as Other to Trash and Legitimate Film Cultures." In *Sleaze Artists: Cinema at the Margins of Taste, Style, and Politics*, ed. Jeffrey Sconce. Durham, NC: Duke University Press, 2007, pp. 219–39.

Hills, Matt. *The Pleasures of Horror*. London: Continuum, 2005.

Hirsch, Joshua. *Afterimage: Film, Trauma, and the Holocaust*. Philadelphia, PA: Temple University Press, 2004.

hooks, bell. *Black Looks: Race and Representation*. Boston: South End Press, 1992.

Horek, Tanya, and Tina Kendall (eds). *The New Extremism in Cinema: From France to Europe*. Edinburgh: Edinburgh University Press, 2011.

Hu, Jane. "Can Horror Movies Be Prestigious?" *The Ringer*, June 15, 2018 <https://www.theringer.com/movies/2018/6/15/17467020/hereditary-elevated-horror-get-out-a-quiet-place-the-witch>.

Huber, Sandra. "Blood and Tears and Potions and Flame: Excesses of Transformation in Ari Aster's *Midsommar*." *Frames Cinema Journal*, no. 16 (Winter 2019) <https://framescinemajournal.com/article/blood-and-tears-and-potions-and-flame-excesses-of-transformation-in-ari-asters-midsommar/>.

Hunter, I. Q. *British Trash Cinema*. London: British Film Institute, 2013.

Irigaray, Luce. *Marine Lover of Friedrich Nietzsche*, trans. Gillian C. Gill. New York: Columbia University Press, 1991.

Jaffe, Ira. *Slow Movies: Countering the Cinema of Action*. London: Wallflower Press, 2014.

Jancovich, Mark. "'Antique Chiller': Quality, Pretention, and History in the Critical Reception of *The Innocents* and *The Haunting*." In *Cinematic Ghosts: Haunting and Spectrality from Silent Cinema to the Digital Era*, ed. Murray Leeder. New York: Bloomsbury Academic, 2015, pp. 115–28.

Jancovich, Mark. "'A Real Shocker': Authenticity, Genre, and the Struggle for Distinction." *Continuum: Journal of Media & Cultural Studies*, 14, no. 1 (2000), pp. 23–35.

Jancovich, Mark. "Beyond Hammer: The First Run Market and the Prestige Horror Film in the Early 1960s." *Palgrave Communications*, 3:17028 (2017), doi: 10.1057/palcomms.2017.28.

Jancovich, Mark. "Bluebeard's Wives: Horror, Quality, and the Gothic (or Paranoid) Woman's Film in the 1940s," *Irish Journal of Gothic and Horror Studies*, no. 12 (2013), pp. 20–43.

Jancovich, Mark. "Genre and the Audience: Genre Classifications and Cultural Distinctions in the Mediation of *The Silence of the Lambs*." In *Horror: The Film Reader*, ed. Mark Jancovich. London: Routledge, 2002, pp. 151–62.

Jancovich, Mark. "Relocating Lewton: Cultural Distinctions, Critical Reception, and the Val Lewton Horror Films." *Journal of Film and Video*, 64, no. 3 (2012), pp. 21–37.

Jarvis, Michael. "Anger Translator: Jordan Peele's *Get Out*." *Science Fiction Film and Television*, 11, no. 1 (2018), pp. 97–109.

Kaplan, E. Ann. *Trauma Culture: The Politics of Terror and Loss in Media and Literature*. New Brunswick, NJ: Rutgers University Press, 2005.

Kaplan, E. Ann, and Ban Wang. "Introduction: From Traumatic Paralysis to the Force Field of Modernity." In *Trauma and Cinema: Cross-Cultural Explorations*, eds E. Ann Kaplan and Ban Wang. Hong Kong: Hong Kong University Press, 2004, pp. 1–22.

Kapsis, Robert E. *Hitchcock: The Making of a Reputation*. Chicago: University of Chicago Press, 1992.

Kelly, Casey Ryan. *Abstinence Cinema: Virginity and the Rhetoric of Sexual Purity in Contemporary Cinema*. New Brunswick, NJ: Rutgers University Press, 2016.

Kelly, Casey Ryan. "*It Follows*: Precarity, Thanatopolitics, and the Ambient Horror Film." *Critical Studies in Media Communication*, 34, no. 3 (2017), pp. 234–49.

Kendrick, James. "A Return to the Graveyard: Notes on the Spiritual Horror Film." In *American Horror Film: The Genre at the Turn of the Millennium*, ed. Steffen Hantke. Jackson, MS: University Press of Mississippi, 2010, pp. 142–58.

Kerner, Aaron Michael. *Torture Porn in the Wake of 9/11: Horror, Exploitation, and the Cinema of Sensation*. New Brunswick, NJ: Rutgers University Press, 2015.

Kerner, Aaron Michael, and Jonathan L. Knapp. *Extreme Cinema: Affective Strategies in Transnational Media*. Edinburgh: Edinburgh University Press, 2017.

Key of Solomon, The (Clavicula Salomonis). Ed. and trans. Samuel Liddell MacGregor Mathers and Joseph H. Peterson. Esoteric Archives. Accessed April 19, 2020 <http://www.esotericarchives.com/solomon/ksol.htm>.

Knight, Jacob. "There's No Such Thing as an 'Elevated Horror Movie' (And Yes, 'Hereditary' is a Horror Movie)." *SlashFilm*, June 8, 2018 <https://www.slashfilm.com/elevated-horror/>.

Konstantinou, Lee. *Cool Characters: Irony and American Fiction*. Cambridge, MA: Harvard University Press, 2016.

Kruger, Marie. "Trauma and the Visual Arts." In *Trauma and Literature*, ed. J. Roger Kurtz. Cambridge: Cambridge University Press, 2018, pp. 255–69.

Laine, Tarja. *Feeling Cinema: Emotional Dynamics in Film Studies*. New York: Continuum, 2011.

Laine, Tarja. "Traumatic Horror Beyond the Edge: *It Follows* and *Get Out*." *Film-Philosophy*, 23, no. 3 (2019), pp. 282–302.

Lanckman, Lies. "'I See, I See . . .': *Goodnight Mommy* (2014) as Austrian Gothic." In *Gothic Heroines on Screen: Representation, Interpretation, and Feminist Enquiry*, eds Tamar Jeffers McDonald and Frances A. Kamm. New York: Routledge, 2019, pp. 171–83.

Laqueur, Thomas W. *Solitary Sex: A Cultural History of Masturbation*. New York: Zone Books, 2003.

Lewis, Sophie. "The Satanic Death-Cult is Real." *Commune*, no. 4 (Fall 2019) <https://communemag.com/the-satanic-death-cult-is-real/>.

Leys, Ruth. *Trauma: A Genealogy*. Chicago: University of Chicago Press, 2000.

Ligotti, Thomas. *The Conspiracy Against the Human Race: A Contrivance of Horror*. New York: Penguin Books, 2018.

Lloyd, Christopher. "'I Told You Not to Go into That House': *Get Out* and Horror's Racial Politics." In *Make America Hate Again: Trump-Era Horror and the Politics of Fear*, ed. Victoria McCollum. London: Routledge, 2019, pp. 108–18.

Love, Heather. *Feeling Backward: Loss and the Politics of Queer History*. Cambridge, MA: Harvard University Press, 2007.

Lowenstein, Adam. "A Detroit Landscape with Figures: The Subtractive Horror of *It Follows*." *Discourse*, 40, no. 3 (2018), pp. 358–69.

Lowenstein, Adam. *Shocking Representation: Historical Trauma, National Cinema, and the Modern Horror Film*. New York: Columbia University Press, 2005.

Lowenstein, Adam. "Spectacle Horror and *Hostel*: Why 'Torture Porn' Does Not Exist." *Critical Quarterly*, 53, no. 1 (2011), pp. 42–60.

Lowenstein, Adam. "The *Giallo*/Slasher Landscape: *Ecologia del Delitto*, *Friday the 13th*, and Subtractive Spectatorship." In *Italian Horror Cinema*, eds Stefano Baschiera and Russ Hunter. Edinburgh: Edinburgh University Press, 2016, pp. 127–44.

Luckhurst, Roger. *The Shining*. London: British Film Institute, 2013.

Luckhurst, Roger. *The Trauma Question*. New York: Routledge, 2008.

Marchand, Yves, and Romain Meffre. *The Ruins of Detroit*. Göttingen: Steidl, 2010.

Martin, Daniel. "Japan's *Blair Witch*: Restraint, Maturity, and Generic Canons in the British Critical Reception of *Ring*." *Cinema Journal*, 48, no. 3 (2009), pp. 35–51.

Massumi, Brian. *Parables for the Virtual: Movement, Affect, Sensation*. Durham, NC: Duke University Press, 2002.

McKinnon, Rachel. "Allies Behaving Badly: Gaslighting as Epistemic Injustice." In *The Routledge Book of Epistemic Injustice*, eds Ian James Kidd, José Medina, and Gaile Pohlhaus, Jr. New York: Routledge, 2017, pp. 167–74.

McLean, Adrienne L. "If Only They Had Meant to Make a Comedy: Laughing at *Black Swan*." In *The Last Laugh: Strange Humors of Cinema*, ed. Murray Pomerance. Detroit, MI: Wayne State University Press, 2013, pp. 143–61.

McMurdo, Shellie. "The Problem with Post-Horror." *In Media Res*, March 4, 2019 <http://mediacommons.org/imr/content/problem-post-horror>.

McNally, Richard J. *Remembering Trauma*. Cambridge, MA: Harvard University Press, 2003.

Mee, Laura. *The Shining*. Leighton Buzzard: Auteur, 2017.

Mee, Laura. "*The Shining* and the Spectre of 'Elevated Horror.'" *In Media Res*, March 8, 2019 <http://mediacommons.org/imr/content/shining-and-spectre-elevated-horror>.

Mendenhall, Julia. "Cult Cinema and Camp." In *The Routledge Companion to Cult Cinema*, eds Ernest Mathijs and Jamie Sexton. New York: Routledge, 2020, pp. 190–7.

Middlemost, Renee. "Babashook: *The Babadook*, Gay Iconography, and Internet Cultures." *Australasian Journal of Popular Culture*, 8, no. 1 (2019), pp. 7–26.

Moore, Andrew. *Detroit Disassembled*. Bologna: Damiani/Akron Museum, 2010.
Munt, Sally R. *Queer Attachments: The Cultural Politics of Shame*. Burlington, VT: Ashgate, 2007.
Nayar, Sheila J. "Epistemic Capital: The Etiology of an 'Elitist' Film Canon's Aesthetic Criteria." *Post Script*, 29, no. 1 (2009), pp. 27–44.
Nelson, Maggie. *The Art of Cruelty: A Reckoning*. New York: W. W. Norton, 2011.
Newman, Michael Z. "Indie Culture: In Pursuit of the Authentic Autonomous Alternative." *Cinema Journal*, 48, no. 3 (2009), pp. 16–34.
Nietzsche, Friedrich. *Thus Spoke Zarathustra: A Book for All and None*, trans. Walter Kaufmann. New York: Penguin Books, 1978.
Nowell, Richard. *Blood Money: A History of the First Teen Slasher Film Cycle*. London: Continuum, 2011.
Odén, Birgitta. "Ättestupan – Myt eller Verklighet?" *Scandia: Tidskrift för Historisk Forskning*, 62, no. 2 (1996), pp. 221–34.
Osterweil, Ara. "*Under the Skin*: The Perils of Becoming Female." *Film Quarterly*, 67, no. 4 (2014), pp. 44–51.
Paciorek, Andy. "The Last Laugh: The Comedic Nature of Folk Horror." In *Folk Horror Revival: Field Studies*, 2nd edn, eds Andy Paciorek, Grey Malkin, Richard Hing, and Katherine Peach. Durham, UK: Wyrd Harvest Press, 2018, pp. 536–42.
Padilla, Mark. "Spatial Stigma, Sexuality, and Neoliberal Decline in Detroit, Michigan." *S&F Online*, 11, no. 1/2 (2012–13) <http://sfonline.barnard.edu/gender-justice-and-neoliberal-transformations/spatial-stigma-sexuality-and-neoliberal-decline-in-detroit-michigan/>.
Patton, Elizabeth A. "*Get Out* and the Legacy of Sundown Suburbs in Post-Racial America." *New Review of Film and Television Studies*, 17, no. 3 (2019), pp. 349–63.
Pederson, Joshua. "Trauma and Narrative." In *Trauma and Literature*, ed. J. Roger Kurtz. Cambridge: Cambridge University Press, 2018, pp. 97–109.
Peele, Jordan. *Get Out: The Complete Annotated Screenplay*. Los Angeles: Inventory Press, 2019.
Peirce, Alison. "The Feminine Appeal of British Horror Cinema." *New Review of Film and Television Studies*, 13, no. 4 (2015), pp. 385–402.
Perkins, Claire. *American Smart Cinema*. Edinburgh: Edinburgh University Press, 2012.
Pheasant-Kelly, Fran. "Trauma, Repression, and *The Babadook*: Sexual Identity in the Trump Era." In *Make America Hate Again: Trump-Era Horror and the Politics of Fear*, ed. Victoria McCollum. London: Routledge, 2019, pp. 81–94.
Poll, Ryan. "Can One *Get Out*? The Aesthetics of Afro-Pessimism." *Journal of the Midwest Modern Language Association*, 51, no. 2 (2018), pp. 69–102.
Pye, Douglas. "Movies and Tone." In *Close-Up 02*, eds John Gibbs and Douglas Pye. London: Wallflower Press, 2007, pp. 1–80.
Quandt, James. "Flesh and Blood: Sex and Violence in Recent French Cinema." *Artforum*, 42, no. 6 (2004), pp. 126–32.

Quigley, Paula. "*The Babadook* (2014), Maternal Gothic, and the 'Woman's Horror Film.'" In *Gothic Heroines on Screen: Representation, Interpretation, and Feminist Enquiry*, eds Tamar Jeffers McDonald and Frances A. Kamm. New York: Routledge, 2019, pp. 184–98.

Radstone, Susannah. "Trauma Theory: Contexts, Politics, Ethics." *Paragraph*, 30, no. 1 (2007), pp. 9–29.

Rebello, Stephen. *Alfred Hitchcock and the Making of Psycho*. New York: St. Martin's Griffin, 1990.

Reiff, Michael C. "Mediating Trauma in Jennifer Kent's *The Babadook*." In *Terrifying Texts: Essays on Books of Good and Evil in Horror Cinema*, eds Cynthia J. Miller and A. Bowdoin Van Riper. Jefferson, NC: McFarland, 2018, pp. 120–31.

Renner, Karen J. *Evil Children in the Popular Imagination*. New York: Palgrave Macmillan, 2016.

Reyes Taubman, Julia. *Detroit: 138 Square Miles*. Detroit, MI: Museum of Contemporary Art, 2011.

Rich, Adrienne. *On Secrets, Lies, and Silence: Selected Prose 1966–1978*. New York: W. W. Norton, 1979.

Rich, Jennifer A. "Shock Corridors: The New Rhetoric of Horror in Gus Van Sant's *Elephant*." *Journal of Popular Culture*, 45, no. 6 (2012), pp. 1310–29.

Rohy, Valerie. "Ahistorical." *GLQ*, 12, no. 1 (2006), pp. 61–83.

Rose, Steve. "How Post-Horror Movies are Taking Over Cinema." *The Guardian*, July 6, 2017, <https://www.theguardian.com/film/2017/jul/06/post-horror-films-scary-movies-ghost-story-it-comes-at-night>.

Rothman, William. *Hitchcock: The Murderous Gaze*, 2nd edn. Albany, NY: State University of New York Press, 2012.

Royle, Nicholas. *The Uncanny*. Manchester: Manchester University Press, 2003.

Sarkis, Stephanie. *Gaslighting: Recognize Manipulative and Emotionally Abusive People – and Break Free*. Boston: Da Capo, 2018.

Scahill, Andrew. *The Revolting Child in Horror Cinema: Youth Rebellion and Queer Spectatorship*. New York: Palgrave Macmillan, 2015.

Schoonover, Karl. "What Do We Do with Vacant Space in Horror Films?" *Discourse*, 40, no. 3 (2018), pp. 342–57.

Schulman, Sarah. *The Gentrification of the Mind: Witness to a Lost Imagination*. Berkeley, CA: University of California Press, 2012.

Schwab, Gabriele. *Haunting Legacies: Violent Histories and Transgenerational Trauma*. New York: Columbia University Press, 2010.

Sconce, Jeffrey. *Haunted Media: Electronic Presence from Telegraphy to Television*. Durham, NC: Duke University Press, 2000.

Sconce, Jeffrey. "Irony, Nihilism, and the New American 'Smart' Film." *Screen*, 43, no. 4 (2002), pp. 349–69.

Sconce, Jeffrey. "'Trashing' the Academy: Taste, Excess, and an Emerging Politics of Cinematic Style." *Screen*, 36, no. 4 (1995), pp. 371–93.

Scovell, Adam. *Folk Horror: Hours Dreadful and Things Strange*. Leighton Buzzard: Auteur, 2017.

Sedgwick, Eve Kosofsky. *The Coherence of Gothic Conventions*. New York: Methuen, 1986.
Sedgwick, Eve Kosofsky. *Epistemology of the Closet*. Berkeley, CA: University of California Press, 1990.
Seigworth, Gregory J., and Melissa Gregg. "An Inventory of Shimmers." In *The Affect Theory Reader*, eds Gregory J. Seigworth and Melissa Gregg. Durham, NC: Duke University Press, 2010, pp. 1–25.
Sexton, Jamie. "US 'Indie-Horror': Critical Reception, Genre Construction, and Suspect Hybridity." *Cinema Journal*, 51, no. 2 (2012), pp. 67–86.
Shaviro, Steven. "Prophecies of the Present." *Socialism and Democracy*, 20, no. 3 (2006), pp. 5–24.
Shoos, Diane L. *Domestic Violence in Hollywood Film: Gaslighting*. New York: Palgrave Macmillan, 2017.
Shouse, Eric. "Feeling, Emotion, Affect." *M/C Journal*, 8, no. 6 (2005) <http://journal.media-culture.org.au/0512/03-shouse.php>.
Shrum, Wesley. "Critics and Publics: Cultural Mediation in Highbrow and Popular Performing Arts." *American Journal of Sociology*, 97, no. 2 (1991), pp. 347–75.
Skvarla, Robert. "Among Us: On Jordan Peele and Elevated Horror." *Diabolique Magazine*, March 27, 2019 <htps://diaboliquemagazine.com/among-us-on-jordan-peele-and-elevated-horror/>.
Snelson, Tim. "'From Grade B Thrillers to Deluxe Chillers': Prestige Horror, Female Audiences, and Allegories of Spectatorship in *The Spiral Staircase* (1946)." *New Review of Film and Television Studies*, 7, no. 2 (2009), pp. 173–88.
Snelson, Tim. *Phantom Ladies: Hollywood Horror and the Home Front*. New Brunswick, NJ: Rutgers University Press, 2015.
Sobchack, Vivian. "Bringing It All Back Home: Family Economy and Generic Exchange." In *The Dread of Difference: Gender and the Horror Film*, ed. Barry Keith Grant. Austin, TX: University of Texas Press, 1996, pp. 143–63.
Spadoni, Robert. "Carl Dreyer's Corpse: Horror Film Atmosphere and Narrative." In *A Companion to the Horror Film*, ed. Harry M. Benshoff. Malden, MA: Wiley Blackwell, 2014, pp. 151–67.
Spadoni, Robert. "Horror Film Atmosphere as Anti-Narrative (and Vice Versa)." In *Merchants of Menace: The Business of Horror Cinema*, ed. Richard Nowell. New York: Bloomsbury Academic, 2014, pp. 109–28.
Sperb, Jason. *Blossoms and Blood: Postmodern Media Culture and the Films of Paul Thomas Anderson*. Austin, TX: University of Texas Press, 2013.
Staiger, Janet. *Perverse Spectators: The Practices of Film Reception*. New York: New York University Press, 2000.
Steinmetz, George. "Harrowed Landscapes: White Ruingazers in Namibia and Detroit and the Cultivation of Memory." *Visual Studies*, 23, no. 3 (2008), pp. 211–37.
Stern, Robin. *The Gaslight Effect: How to Spot and Survive the Hidden Emotional Manipulation Others Use to Control Your Life*. New York: Harmony Books, 2018.

Sugrue, Thomas J. *The Origins of the Urban Crisis: Race and Inequality in Postwar Detroit*. Princeton, NJ: Princeton University Press, 1996.

Tafoya, Scout. "The Pain Needs to Mean Something: On Horror and Grief." *RogerEbert.com*, August 26, 2019 <https://www.rogerebert.com/balder-and-dash/the-pain-needs-to-mean-something-on-horror-and-grief>.

Taussig, Michael T. *Mimesis and Alterity: A Particular History of the Senses*. New York: Routledge, 1993.

Tembo, Kwasu D. "The Left-Hand Path: On the Dialectics of Witchery in *The Witch* and *Hagazussa: A Heathen's Curse*." *Frames Cinema Journal*, no. 16 (Winter 2019) <https://framescinemajournal.com/article/the-left-hand-path-on-the-dialectics-of-witchery-in-the-witch-and-hagazussa-a-heathens-curse/>.

Thacker, Eugene. *In the Dust of This Planet: Horror of Philosophy*, Vol. 1. Alresford: Zero Books, 2011.

Thacker, Eugene. *Tentacles Longer Than Night: Horror of Philosophy*, Vol. 3. Alresford: Zero Books, 2015.

Thomas, Richard. "The H Word: How *The Witch* and *Get Out* Helped Usher in the New Wave of Elevated Horror." *Nightmare Magazine*, February 2019 <http://www.nightmare-magazine.com/nonfiction/the-h-word-how-the-witch-and-get-out-helped-usher-in-the-new-wave-of-elevated-horror/>.

Thornton, Sarah. *Club Cultures: Music, Media, and Subcultural Capital*. Middletown, CT: Wesleyan University Press, 1996.

Todorov, Tzvetan. *The Fantastic: A Structural Approach to a Literary Genre*, trans. Richard Howard. Ithaca, NY: Cornell University Press, 1975.

Toles, George. *Paul Thomas Anderson*. Urbana, IL: University of Illinois Press, 2016.

Tomkins, Silvan S. *Affect, Imagery, Consciousness: The Complete Edition*. New York: Springer, 2008.

Trigg, Dylan. *The Thing: A Phenomenology of Horror*. Alresford: Zero Books, 2014.

Tryon, Chuck. *Reinventing Cinema: Movies in the Age of Convergence*. New Brunswick, NJ: Rutgers University Press, 2009.

Tzioumakis, Yannis. "'Independent,' 'Indie,' and 'Indiewood': Towards a Periodization of Contemporary (Post-1980) American Independent Cinema." In *American Independent Cinema: Indie, Indiewood, and Beyond*, eds Geoff King, Claire Molloy, and Yannis Tzioumakis. London: Routledge, 2013, pp. 28–40.

Vause, Erika. "Critically Acclaimed Horror Film of the 2010s or Your Ph.D. Program?" *McSweeney's Internet Tendency*, August 12, 2019 <https://www.mcsweeneys.net/articles/critically-acclaimed-horror-film-of-the-2010s-or-your-phd-program>.

Vickroy, Laurie. *Reading Trauma Narratives: The Contemporary Novel and the Psychology of Oppression*. Charlottesville, VA: University of Virginia Press, 2015.

Von Worms, Abraham. *The Book of Abramelin: A New Translation*, ed. and trans. Georg Dehn and Steven Guth. Lake Worth, FL: Ibis Press, 2006.

Wada-Marciano, Mitsuyo. "Showing the Unknowable: *Uncle Boonmee Who Can Recall His Past Lives*." In *Cinematic Ghosts: Haunting and Spectrality from*

Silent Cinema to the Digital Era, ed. Murray Leeder. New York: Bloomsbury Academic, 2015, pp. 271–89.

Waldman, Diane. "'At Last I Can Tell It to Someone!': Feminine Point of View and Subjectivity in the Gothic Romance Film of the 1940s." *Cinema Journal*, 23, no. 2 (1984), pp. 29–40.

Waller, Gregory A. "Made-for-Television Horror Films." In *American Horrors: Essays on the Modern American Horror Film*, ed. Gregory A. Waller. Urbana, IL: University of Illinois Press, 1987, pp. 145–61.

Walsh, Andrea S. *Women's Film and Female Experience, 1940–1950*. Westport, CT: Praeger, 1984.

Walton, Saige. "Air, Atmosphere, Environment: Film Mood, Folk Horror, and *The Witch*." *Screening the Past*, no. 43 (2018) <http://www.screeningthepast.com/2018/02/air-atmosphere-environment-film-mood-folk-horror-and-the-vvitch/.

Wampole, Christy. "How to Live Without Irony." *New York Times*, November 17, 2012 <https://opinionator.blogs.nytimes.com/2012/11/17/how-to-live-without-irony/.

Warner, Michael. *The Trouble with Normal: Sex, Politics, and the Ethics of Queer Life*. New York: Free Press, 1999.

Warner, Rick. "Kubrickian Dread: Echoes of *2001: A Space Odyssey* and *The Shining* in Works by Jonathan Glazer, Paul Thomas Anderson, and David Lynch." In *After Kubrick: A Filmmaker's Legacy*, ed. Jeremi Szaniawski. New York: Bloomsbury Academic, 2020, pp. 125–45.

Wilkinson, Eleanor. "What's Queer about Non-Monogamy Now?" In *Understanding Non-Monogamies*, eds Meg Barker and Darren Langdridge. London: Routledge, 2009, pp. 243–54.

Williams, Linda. *Playing the Race Card: Melodramas of Black and White from Uncle Tom to O. J. Simpson*. Princeton, NJ: Princeton University Press, 2001.

Williams, Raymond. *Marxism and Literature*. New York: Oxford University Press, 1977.

Williams, Tony. *Hearths of Darkness: The Family in the American Horror Film*. Jackson, MS: University Press of Mississippi, 2014.

Williams, Zoe. "The Final Irony." *The Guardian*, June 27, 2003 <https://www.theguardian.com/theguardian/2003/jun/28/weekend7.weekend2>.

Wilson, Emma. *Cinema's Missing Children*. London: Wallflower Press, 2003.

Wood, Robin. *Hollywood from Vietnam to Reagan . . . and Beyond*. New York: Columbia University Press, 2003.

Woolf, Virginia. *A Haunted House and Other Short Stories*. New York: Harcourt, 1944.

Zinoman, Jason. "Home Is Where the Horror Is." *New York Times*, June 7, 2018 <https://www.nytimes.com/2018/06/07/movies/hereditary-horror-movies.html>.

Zwissler, Laurel. "'I Am That Very Witch': On *The Witch*, Feminism, and Not Surviving Patriarchy." *Journal of Religion & Film*, 22, no. 3 (2018) <https://digitalcommons.unomaha.edu/jrf/vol22/iss3/6/>.

Index

Abraham, Nicolas, 89, 91
Abramelin operation, 214–18, 241n
Abramson, Kate, 102, 107, 116, 120
Absentia, 14, 32–3
academia, 4–5, 20, 108–9, 112, 137n, 140n, 240
Academy Awards, 41, 46, 100n, 104, 122
Act of Seeing with One's Own Eyes, The, 9
ACT UP, 205
aesthetics *see* style
affect, 1, 3, 7, 9–13, 15–21, 27–8, 30–1, 34, 37–9, 42, 50, 56–7, 68–72, 74, 80–1, 83, 92, 102, 114–15, 122, 133–4, 142–4, 146–7, 149, 161, 168, 181–2, 197–8, 218, 231–2, 234, 238, 240
Affleck, Casey, 227
Afro-pessimism, 126, 131
AIDS *see* HIV/AIDS
Ain't Them Bodies Saints, 41, 227
Air (band), 196
alchemy *see* magic; occultism
Alien, 80
ambiguity, 8, 11–12, 15–16, 19, 32, 36, 44, 46, 50, 71–2, 96n, 115, 134–5, 155, 159, 161, 177n, 181, 183, 189, 210n, 213, 236, 238; *see also* epistemic hesitation
American Film Market, 40
Amityville Horror, The (1979), 170
Amulet, 14
Anderson, Paul Thomas, 36, 145
Anderson, Victoria, 134
Anderson, Wes, 36
Andersson, Patrik, 112
Andrews, David, 40
Angel Street *see* Gas Light: A Victorian Thriller
Annabelle, 33
Annabelle: Creation, 52
Antichrist, 9

antinomianism, 150, 156, 176n
Anvari, Babak, 98n
Apel, Dora, 200, 203
Apprehension Engine, 1–2
Armstrong, Richard, 21, 69, 71–4, 79, 84, 86, 92–3, 158, 227
Arnold, Sarah, 73, 211n
Aronofsky, Darren, 218, 221–4, 242n
Artaud, Antonin, 223–4, 243n
art cinema, 1, 3, 6, 8–11, 13, 15–16, 18–21, 23n, 24n, 28–9, 34–5, 37, 40–4, 48–9, 52–3, 55–6, 69–71, 74, 76, 83, 86, 88, 94–5, 161, 164–5, 215, 239–40
art-horror, 3, 8–10, 12, 15, 24n, 27–9, 31, 40, 42, 50–1, 57, 72, 103, 239–40
arthouse theaters, 2, 7–8, 13, 19, 31, 33, 41, 52, 54, 57, 70, 80–1, 86
Ashley Madison (website), 191
Aster, Ari, 9, 47, 86, 88–90, 92–3, 95, 80n, 100n, 103, 108, 111–12, 117, 143, 208n
atmosphere, 7, 17–18, 29, 43, 142, 145–6, 161, 225
attention economy, 35
A24, 41–2, 57, 71, 111, 149, 163, 243n
A24 Podcast, The, 88
auteurism, 39, 42–3, 48–50, 55–7, 93, 236–7
Autumn Sonata, 88
avant-garde, 9, 145–6, 148, 223–4
A. V. Club, The, 34
AZT, 205

Babadook, The, 2, 8, 12, 14, 20–1, 47, 68, 70–1, 75–81, 83–5, 92, 96n, 98n, 121, 130, 151, 155, 159
Bachelard, Gaston, 150, 166
Bailey, Jason, 55
Balanzategui, Jessica, 81
Barefoot, Guy, 106
Beauty and the Beast, 179n

INDEX

Beethoven, Ludwig van, 228, 232, 234
Being John Malkovich, 125
Berberian Sound Studio, 14, 17
Bergfilm, 144
Bergman, Ingmar, 88
Berlant, Lauren, 231
Berlinka, Dan, 53–4
Berlioz, Hector, 144
Billson, Anne, 33
Billy Budd, Sailor, 171–4
Bird Box, 25n
Birds, The, 30, 191–2
Blackcoat's Daughter, The, 14, 30, 41–2, 96n, 161, 233, 243n
Black Lives Matter, 39, 122–3, 128, 131
Black Swan, 218–19
Blair Witch, 41
Blair Witch Project, The, 17
"Bluebeard" tale, 105–6, 220, 223
Blumhouse Productions, 40–1, 237
Blum, Jason, 237
Blunt, Emily, 164
body genres, 50, 181
Book of Abramelin see Abramelin operation
Bordwell, David, 8–9, 16
Bourdieu, Pierre, 51
Boyle, Kevin, 201
Brahms, Johannes, 82, 145
Bram Stoker's Dracula, 43
Branch Davidians, 117
Braun, Aaron, 205
Breaking the Waves, 222–3
Brecht, Bertolt, 9
Breillat, Catherine, 10
Bridges, J. A., 36, 68, 86, 181
Briefel, Aviva, 16, 151
Brinkema, Eugenie, 68, 71–2, 74, 79, 92
Brody, Richard, 46, 48, 56
Brown, Kimberly Nichele, 126
Brown, Laura S., 75, 123, 243n
Brown, Michael, 45
Bruegel the Elder, Pieter, 165
Buerger, Shelley, 80
Bush, George W., 208n
Buzzfeed, 35
Byrne, Gabriel, 88

Cabinet of Dr. Caligari, The, 8, 75, 83
Cabin in the Woods, The, 38, 125

Calef, Victor, 107
Cannibal Holocaust, 51
canon, 4, 43–4, 48, 50–1, 54, 239; *see also* taste
Cante, Rich, 204
capital, cultural, 4–5, 9, 19–20, 28–9, 34, 42, 44–5, 48–9, 51–2, 121, 127, 134, 233; *see also* taste
capital, economic *see* class
capitalism, 30, 36, 54, 95, 149, 175, 187, 200–6; *see also* class, neoliberalism
capital, social, 35–6, 45
capital, subcultural, 5–7, 19–20, 23n, 28–9, 35, 37, 45, 49–54, 57; *see also* fans
Carlos, Wendy, 144
Carnival of Souls (1962), 72
Caron, David, 192
Carpenter, John, 29
Carrie (1976), 19, 88, 154
Carroll, Andrew, 35
Carroll, Noël, 16–17, 24n, 144
Carter, Angela, 161
Caruth, Cathy, 74–6, 92
Castle, William, 47, 64n
catharsis, 90, 95, 115–17, 121, 155, 165
Cat People (1942), 43
Caught, 73
C'est La Vie, 100n
Changeling, The, 69
Childish Gambino, 123, 139n
Christensen, Benjamin, 153
Christianity, 13, 16, 114, 142, 150–1, 153–7, 159, 176n, 177n, 179n, 180n, 213, 215, 218–25, 228, 242n
Chthulucene, 231
CinemaScore, 10, 52, 219
cinematography, 11–12, 17, 29–30, 32, 36, 72–3, 76, 86–7, 90, 94, 100n, 108–9, 112, 114, 119, 121, 127, 142, 144–53, 156–8, 160–3, 166, 168–9, 173, 184, 188, 199–200, 218–19, 226–7, 233, 236
cinephilia, 29, 31, 51
class, 22, 31, 36, 49, 104, 118, 121–2, 127, 167, 197–207, 215, 227
Clockwork Orange, A, 9
Clover, Carol, 208n
Cochrane, Tom, 144
Collette, Toni, 88, 95, 100n
Collins, K. Austin, 56
Columbia Pictures, 47

colonialism, 12, 16, 30, 126, 142, 150, 155–6, 229–31, 243n
comedy, 8, 13, 18, 23n, 36, 38–9, 42, 46, 56, 113, 122, 131–5, 145, 219, 226
Conjuring, The, 33, 54
Contracted, 186–7
Costa, Pedro, 30
Craig, Pamela, 187
Crawl, 95
Creature from the Black Lagoon, 179n
Cries and Whispers, 72
Crimson Peak, 32–3
critics, 1–13, 15–17, 19–20, 23n, 27–9, 31, 33–6, 42–57, 68, 71, 80–1, 85, 100n, 122, 128, 131–2, 134–5, 137n, 143, 163, 181, 184, 197, 202, 210n, 219, 224, 233, 237–40
cruel optimism, 126, 195, 231
Cukor, George, 105
Cure for Wellness, A, 32
Cursed, 187
Curtis, Jamie Lee, 238
cycle, 1, 3, 8, 24n, 28–9, 32, 36, 70, 86, 142, 181, 217, 239–40

Daly, Mary, 222
Danielsen, Shane, 46
Dark Song, A, 14, 22, 101n, 213–18, 221, 224, 231, 241n
Davis, Glyn, 29, 31–2
Day-Lewis, Daniel, 170
Dean, Tim, 193, 204, 209n
Deathdream, 69
Delany, Samuel R., 204
Demme, Jonathan, 46
deserts, 145–6
Diabolique Magazine, 55
Diagnostic and Statistical Manual, 74–5
disability, 13, 75, 84–7, 105, 107, 127, 136n, 145, 147, 155–6, 158, 160, 164, 180n, 225, 235, 243n
discourse *see* critics
disgust, 1, 7, 9–11, 16, 53, 102, 144
dissociative identity disorder, 85, 87
distribution, 2, 6, 8, 13, 23n, 25n, 31–3, 40–1, 49, 52, 54, 70–1, 80–1, 111, 122, 149, 233, 240, 243n; *see also* arthouse theaters, multiplex theaters, Netflix
Doane, Mary Ann, 73

Doctor Sleep, 33, 55
documentary, 16, 132, 243n
Donnie Darko, 187
Don't Breathe, 14–15, 200–1, 206
Don't Look Now, 9, 43, 73–4, 83, 90–2
Dostoyevsky, Fyodor, 181, 183
Dracula (1931), 43
Dragonwyck, 73
drama, 13, 21, 30–1, 38, 40–1, 45–6, 74, 81, 86, 95, 145, 165, 197, 214, 216, 219, 230–1
dread, 1, 12–13, 17–18, 36–7, 102, 110, 134–5, 142, 144–5, 149, 175, 181, 183, 207, 225, 240
drive-in theaters, 41
Duggan, Lisa, 191
Duggan-Smith, Tony, 1–2

Edelman, Lee, 191–2, 207
Edelstein, David, 34
Edensor, Tim, 204, 211n
editing, 11–12, 29, 36, 72–4, 79, 92, 112, 119, 121, 151, 171, 173, 188–9, 233
Edwards-Behi, Nia, 48, 52, 56
Eggers, Robert, 37, 41–2, 48, 55, 57, 88, 142, 150, 153–4, 168–70, 172–3, 208n
Elephant, 31, 187
"elevated horror," 2–3, 8, 10, 12, 15, 20, 27–8, 31, 43–5, 48–56, 63n, 86, 122, 162–3, 214, 237, 239–40
Eliade, Mircea, 172
Eliot, T. S., 210n
elitism, 3, 19, 28, 31, 45, 49, 51–4, 134; *see also* taste
Enemy, 14, 99n
England, Eric, 186
entertainment, 6–7, 11, 19, 31, 43, 53–4, 57, 69, 72, 95, 102, 106, 122, 135, 144, 240
environmentalism, 175, 203, 207, 219, 221, 224–5, 228–9, 231, 239, 242n
epistemic hesitation, 12–13, 16, 19, 21, 32, 39, 42, 72, 83, 87, 103, 105, 107, 110, 113, 115–17, 120, 122–3, 125, 131, 133, 135, 138n, 155, 162, 171, 179n, 235; *see also* fantastic, the
epistemic violence *see* epistemic hesitation, gaslighting
Eraserhead, 9, 159
ergotism, 16, 153

EST, 120
eternal return, 213, 219, 221–2, 224, 230, 238
Evolution, 14, 173
excess, 34, 72, 74
existentialism, 13, 22, 31, 33, 164, 175, 181, 207, 213, 216, 219, 221, 224–6, 228–30, 233, 239
Exorcist, The, 43, 47, 79–80
exploitation cinema, 9, 23n, 29, 47, 49, 53–4, 81, 238
extinction *see* environmentalism
extreme cinema, 10, 54
Eyes of My Mother, The, 14, 68, 156, 178n
Eyes without a Face, 9

Faber, Michel, 146, 148
Facebook, 35
fairy tales, 111–12, 137n, 153, 161, 180n
family, 13, 21–2, 32, 47, 49, 55, 57, 68–71, 73–94, 96n, 98n, 101n, 102–3, 108, 115, 120, 136n, 138n, 143, 145, 147, 150–67, 177n, 190, 196, 210n, 213, 215, 217, 219–21, 228–9, 231, 233, 238–40
fans, 2–7, 10, 16, 20, 28–9, 34–6, 42, 44–5, 48–57, 210n
Fantasia Film Festival, 40
Fantastic Fest, 40, 145
fantastic, the, 16, 19, 42, 83, 95, 235
Farrow, Mia, 47
Feigelfeld, Lukas, 155, 157, 159–60
feminism *see* gender
Fessenden, Larry, 29
Fiala, Severin, 70, 100n, 178n
film festivals, 2, 31, 33–4, 39, 42, 52, 54, 57, 233
film noir, 73
Final Destination (2000), 95
Final Girls, The, 38
Fischer, Lucy, 70
Flanagan, Matthew, 29–30
Flanagan, Mike, 32–3
Fly, The (1986), 184
Fordism *see* capitalism
forests *see* wilderness
form *see* style
Foster, Jodie, 46
Foucault, Michel, 192
Fountain, The, 224

Fox Film Corporation, 168
Fradley, Martin, 187
Frankenstein (1931), 43, 125
Franz, Veronika, 70, 100n, 178n
Frazer, James George, 116
Freeman, Elizabeth, 197, 210n
Freud, Sigmund, 68, 74–5, 78, 84, 87, 89–90, 92–3, 100n, 147, 173
Frey, Mattias, 28, 34
Friday the 13th (1980), 69
Friedkin, William, 47
Friendly Persuasion, 236–7
Fukunaga, Cary Joji, 12
Funny Games (1997), 9, 85, 220
Fusco, Katherine, 93

gangster film, 8, 46
Gaslight (1944), 73, 104–6, 110, 114–15, 129, 136n
Gas Light: A Victorian Thriller, 104–5
gaslighting, 13, 21, 36, 39, 96, 102–12, 114–24, 128–35, 136n, 143, 155, 171, 186, 220–1
Gavin, Liam, 214, 217, 241n
Geddes, Colin, 40
gender, 13, 21, 49, 70, 75–7, 80, 88, 93–4, 98n, 104, 106–7, 113, 116, 119, 123, 135, 138n, 143–4, 149–51, 154–7, 159–64, 166–8, 171–4, 187, 193, 206, 218–24, 235, 242n
"Generation X," 37–8, 203
genre, 1–13, 15–22, 24n, 27–35, 37–40, 42–57, 68–74, 76, 80–2, 85–6, 94–5, 105, 107, 110–11, 114, 121–4, 127, 129, 132–3, 135, 142–5, 149, 151, 162–3, 166, 181, 183, 187, 196–7, 203, 207, 213–14, 216–18, 220–1, 223, 226, 230–3, 237–40, 243n
German Expressionism, 75
Get Out, 2, 6, 13–15, 20–1, 38, 40, 46, 55–6, 100n, 104, 110, 113, 122–35, 139n, 143, 147, 201, 239
Geyrhalter, Nikolaus, 243n
Ghost Story, A, 13–14, 22, 30, 41, 213, 226–32, 234–5, 238–9
giallo film, 17
Ginger Snaps, 187
Girls, 125
Girl Walks Home Alone at Night, A, 9
Gioulakis, Mike, 199

Glazer, Jonathan, 146, 149
Godfather, The, 46
Golden Globe Awards, 132, 237
Goodbye, Dragon Inn, 31
Goodnight Mommy, 8, 14–15, 21, 68, 70–1, 76, 79, 81–6, 91–2, 100n, 121, 143, 178n, 240
Google, 35
Gordon, Avery, 126
gore, 9, 17, 27, 30, 32–4, 49, 53–4, 94, 129, 181, 183; *see also* disgust
Gorfinkel, Elena, 149
Gothic, the, 32, 37, 43, 72–6, 78, 80–2, 86, 98n, 104–6, 132, 143–4, 150, 168, 184, 187, 213–14, 233, 235–6; *see also* "new Gothic"
GQ, 35
Grafius, Brandon, 150, 166, 168
Grand Guignol, 170
Grant, Charles L., 32
Graves, Stephanie, 37, 127
Great Recession, 203
Greenwood, Jonny, 145–6
Grémillon, Jean, 170
Gretel & Hansel, 14, 21, 143, 149, 161–3, 168, 240, 244n
Greven, David, 73
grief, 13, 21–2, 32, 43, 47, 55, 68–81, 83–7, 89–96, 98n, 102–3, 110, 118–22, 124, 151, 156, 158–9, 164–5, 167, 178n, 213, 215, 217, 220, 227, 240
Grimm Brothers, 161
Grimm, Joshua, 189–90
Gripsrud, Jostein, 51
Guardian, The, 3, 31, 34
Guess Who's Coming to Dinner?, 129

Hadžihalilović, Lucile, 173
Hagazussa: A Heathen's Curse, 14, 21, 68, 96n, 143, 149, 155–62, 164, 166, 168
Hahner, Leslie, 184, 187
Halloween (1978), 29, 123, 196, 238
Halloween (2018), 6, 50
hallucinogens, 110–11, 113, 158–9, 216
Hamilton, Patrick, 104–5
Hammer Films, 74, 178n
Haneke, Michael, 85
Hanich, Julian, 18, 37, 110, 134, 142
Haraway, Donna J., 231
Hart, Adam Charles, 19, 151, 153, 226
Haunting of Hill House, The, 33

Haunting, The (1963), 17, 43, 72
Hawkins, Joan, 9–10, 12, 31–3, 36, 42, 57
Häxen, 153
Hayes, Rob, 161
Haynes, Todd, 31, 36
Heaven's Gate (cult), 118
Heffernan, Kevin, 47
Hereditary, 2, 12, 14–15, 18, 21, 34, 41, 44, 46, 50, 55, 68, 70–1, 75, 86–95, 100n, 103, 110–11, 115, 125, 150, 155, 210n, 214
Hermetic Order of the Golden Dawn, 214
Herzog, Werner, 156
High, Steven C., 211n
Hills, Matt, 9, 17, 50, 83
Hiroshima Mon Amour, 72, 74
Hitchcock, Alfred, 73, 192, 213, 236–8
HIV/AIDS, 36, 184, 186, 193–4, 204–6, 208n
Hollywood, 6, 8, 10, 12, 15, 18–19, 23n, 25n, 29, 34, 37, 39–41, 43–4, 49, 55, 70–2, 79–81, 86, 106, 136n, 161–3, 178n, 180n, 191, 198, 237, 240
Hollywood Foreign Press Association, 132
Hollywood Reporter, The, 57
Homicidal, 47
homonormativity, 140n, 190–1, 193–4, 205–7
Homo Sapiens, 243
Hopkins, Anthony, 46
horror
 body, 149
 cosmic, 22, 149, 173, 223, 225–6
 found-footage, 40
 East Asian, 32–3
 folk, 110–14, 116, 133, 143, 153, 170
 Gothic *see* Gothic, the
 meta-horror, 38
 paranormal, 12, 32, 41, 54, 80–1, 85–6, 213, 216–17, 231, 237
 post-apocalyptic, 12, 15, 21, 25n, 36, 143, 163–6, 200
 psychological, 7, 218
 slasher, 17, 29, 32, 123, 187, 238
 "torture porn," 27, 32–4, 40, 54, 80–1, 85–6, 113
 vampire, 184, 203, 207
 zombie, 17, 126–7, 186
 see also art-horror, fans, genre, post-horror

horror-friendly viewers, 4–6, 16, 19–20, 27–8, 34, 44, 49, 51–2; *see also* fans, populism
horror-skeptic viewers, 4, 10, 16, 20–1, 23n, 27–8, 43–7, 49–52, 54, 122, 237, 239; *see also* critics
Hostel, 27, 51, 111–12
Hough, Q. V., 51
Hour of the Wolf, 8–9
House of the Devil, 14, 29
Huber, Sandra, 116
Hu, Jane, 52
Hunger, The, 184
Hunger Games, The, 218

I Am Legend, 163
I Am the Pretty Thing That Lives in the House, 2, 12–14, 22, 30–1, 161, 213, 233–40, 244n
Idiot, The, 181, 183
incest, 88–9, 111, 115, 151, 157, 186
"indie horror," 2, 20, 28, 39–40, 42, 54
In Fabric, 41
Innkeepers, The, 14, 29
Innocents, The, 43, 72
Insidious, 33, 80
Instagram, 178n
Internet Movie Database, 6, 10
Invisible Man, The (2020), 136n
Invitation, The, 14–15, 21, 104, 110, 118–22, 127, 129, 131, 138n, 139n, 178n
Irigaray, Luce, 221–2
irony, 22, 36–9, 80, 82, 145, 194, 196, 203, 224, 230; *see also* post-irony
It: Chapter One, 6, 12, 50, 55
It: Chapter Two, 6, 46, 55
It Comes at Night, 2, 11–12, 14–15, 17, 21, 41, 47, 143, 163, 165–70, 178n, 240, 243n
It Follows, 2, 8, 11–15, 18–20, 22, 29–30, 38, 50, 70, 166, 181–207, 208n, 210n, 213, 227, 231, 239

Jaffe, Ira, 30
Jancovich, Mark, 45–6, 73
Jarmusch, Jim, 38, 203
Jarvis, Michael, 123, 127, 129
Jessabelle, 33
Jewett, Sarah Orne, 168
Jodorowsky, Alejandro, 161

Judaism, 157–8, 213, 215, 218–19, 222–3, 242n
jump scares, 10–12, 15, 18–19, 27, 30, 33–4, 46, 50, 55, 79, 90, 94, 127, 151, 163, 181, 188
Jurassic Park, 163

Kabbalah, 214, 241n
Kaplan, E. Ann, 75, 94
Karlqvist, Martin, 112
Keener, Catherine, 125
Kelly, Casey Ryan, 195
Kendrick, James, 32–3
Kent, Jennifer, 47, 70
Keough, Riley, 178n
Key & Peele, 122, 133
Key of Solomon, 215
Killers from Space, 197
Killing of a Sacred Deer, The, 14, 41
King, Stephen, 55, 66n
Knight, Jacob, 51
Korven, Mark, 1–2, 18, 146
Krasinski, John, 164–5, 178n
Krisha, 41
Kubrick, Stanley, 55, 66n, 143–4, 166
Kurosawa, Kiyoshi, 33
Kusama, Karyn, 118

Lanckman, Lies, 82
landscape, 21–2, 108, 110, 135, 142–50, 152–4, 156–62, 164–5, 167–71, 173–5, 176n, 178n, 181, 188, 207, 214, 216, 218–19, 222, 229–30; *see also* deserts, mountains, oceans, postindustrial ruins, suburbs, wilderness
Last House on the Left, The (1972), 51
Laine, Tarja, 74, 144
Lawrence, Jennifer, 218, 224
Leigh, Janet, 238
Let the Right One In, 14
Levi, Mica, 146
Levin, Ira, 47, 124–5
Lewis, David W., 211n
Lewis, Sophie, 113
liberalism, 13, 122–4, 127–9, 131–2, 134, 140n, 191
Lighthouse, The, 14, 22, 37, 41, 48, 143, 168–74, 179–80n, 182, 215, 222
Lighthouse Keepers, The, 170

Ligotti, Thomas, 224–6, 228–31, 235, 239, 241n, 243n
Lionsgate, 40–1
Lodge, The, 14, 100n, 138n, 178n, 240
Lovecraft, H. P., 173, 225–6, 231
Lowenstein, Adam, 154, 201, 206
Lowery, David, 41, 226–7, 229–32
Luckhurst, Roger, 74

McKinnon, Rachel, 107, 125
McMurdo, Shellie, 45
magic, 87, 101n, 112, 116, 162, 176n, 125, 176n, 214–17, 223–4, 228, 241n; *see also* occultism, witchcraft
Magnolia, 36
mainstream *see* populism
Malick, Terrence, 229
Malleus Maleficarum, 154
Mama, 80
Manson, Charles, 121
Mara, Rooney, 227
marketing, 6, 11, 19, 41–3, 47, 49, 54–5, 104, 111, 134, 145, 167, 184, 186–7, 196, 218, 224
Martha Marcy May Marlene, 121
Martin, Daniel, 32
Martin, Trayvon, 123
Marvel Studios, 53
masturbation, 152–3, 171–2, 177n, 216, 224
Mathers, Samuel Liddell MacGregor, 241n
Mee, Laura, 44
melancholia, 68, 78–9, 91
Melancholia, 165
Méliès, Georges, 78
melodrama, 42, 69, 72–6, 93–4, 111, 132, 180n, 187, 222, 232
Melville, Herman, 168, 171–2
mental illness *see* disability
midnight movies, 42
Midsommar, 14, 21, 41, 95, 103–4, 108–21, 131, 133, 137n, 143, 151, 155, 158, 172, 179n, 221, 242n
"Millennials," 37–8, 203
mimesis, 116–17
Ming-liang, Tsai, 31
minimalism, 10–11, 13, 15, 21, 29, 50, 55, 57, 71, 81, 85–6, 102, 112, 122, 142, 146, 163, 181, 213, 226, 232–3, 240

Miramax, 39
mise-en-scène, 12, 17, 72–4, 93–4, 127, 153, 167, 183, 197, 217, 223
Mitchell, David Robert, 11, 41, 181, 188, 194, 197, 199, 202
MMMD, 156
mode, 8, 21, 68, 135
modernism, 3, 8–9, 35, 44, 51, 69–70, 72, 74, 79, 81–2, 85–6, 118, 226; *see also* art cinema, avant-garde
Moler, Daniel, 215
monogamy, 22, 182–3, 189–95, 199, 204–7
mononormativity, 182–3, 191
Moonlight, 41
mother!, 14–15, 22, 213, 218–26, 235
motherhood *see* family
mountains, 144, 155–8, 160–2, 169
mourning films, 13, 21, 69–70, 79, 84–6, 92–3, 95, 103–4, 119, 121, 227, 232
multiplex theaters, 1–2, 6, 10, 13, 18, 27, 33, 42, 52, 54, 71, 134, 178n, 219, 224, 240
mumblecore, 29
Munt, Sally R., 192
Murai, Hiro, 139n
music, 1, 6, 11, 18, 90, 94, 108, 114, 144–6, 150, 156, 161, 165, 168, 173, 196–7, 228–30, 244n
musical film, 132
Mysterious Skin, 187
Myth of the American Sleepover, The, 41, 197

narrative, 7–8, 11–13, 15–19, 21, 29–30, 36, 44, 50, 55, 68–74, 76, 79–80, 83, 86, 95, 96n, 100n, 106, 110, 115, 121–2, 129–33, 135, 143, 156–8, 161–3, 165, 170–1, 180n, 181, 184, 186–8, 195, 200, 214, 216, 219, 221, 226, 229, 231, 233–6, 238
Nelson, Maggie, 222–4
neoliberalism, 22, 175, 183, 203–7, 231, 243n
Neon Demon, The, 14–15, 17
Netflix, 2, 25n, 31, 33, 80, 233, 243n
"new Gothic," 32, 36; *see also* Gothic, the
New Hollywood era, 41
"New Sincerity," 37
New York, 34

New Yorker, 46
New York Times, 2, 30, 68
Nietzsche, Friedrich, 221–2, 224
Nightmare on Elm Street, A (1984), 196
Night of the Living Dead, 41, 53, 130, 167
Night Tide, 8
Noah, 218
nostalgia, 22, 183, 196–7, 202–3, 206

Obama, Barack, 124, 130
oceans, 22, 142–4, 147, 168–70, 173–4, 180n
occultism, 75, 87–9, 91, 93–4, 101n, 116, 125, 132, 149, 158, 213–17, 222–4, 241n
Oculus, 33
Oldham, Will, 228–9
Only Lovers Left Alive, 14, 38, 203, 207
Osterweil, Ara, 146, 149
Others, The, 32, 83, 211n
Owens, Jesse, 132

Packard Automotive Plant, 199, 202–5
Padilla, Mark, 206
paganism, 103, 112, 114, 118, 143, 150–2, 158, 169, 222
Pan's Labyrinth, 9
paracinema, 9
Paramount Pictures, 163
parody, 38
pastiche, 196, 206
Pattinson, Robert, 170
Payne, Alexander, 36
Peele, Jordan, 38, 46–7, 55–6, 122–35
Peeping Tom, 43, 47
Penderecki, Krzysztof, 145–6, 150
People Under the Stairs, The, 201
Perkins, Anthony, 44, 213, 236–9
Perkins, Claire, 39
Perkins, Elvis, 244n
Perkins, Oz, 44, 46, 161, 213, 233, 236–9, 243n, 244n
Personal Shopper, 14–15
pessimism (philosophy), 224–6, 228–31
Pet Sematary (1989), 69
Pet Sematary (2019), 55–6
Pheasant-Kelly, Fran, 79
Polanski, Roman, 47, 79, 218, 220
Poll, Ryan, 123, 129, 131
polyamory, 183, 191, 207

populism, 2, 6–7, 11, 13, 16–19, 23n, 27, 29, 31, 34, 37, 42, 44–6, 48, 50–7, 69, 80, 86, 95, 122, 130, 134, 144, 151, 163–4, 166, 215, 219, 232–3, 237, 239–40; *see also* Hollywood, taste
pornography, 4, 12, 23n, 188–9, 199, 204
Possession, 9, 176n
postcolonialism, 126
post-horror, 3, 6–9, 12–15, 17–22, 27–57, 68–71, 74–6, 81, 83, 85–6, 94–5, 102–4, 108, 111–12, 120, 122, 126, 131, 133–5, 142–6, 149, 156, 158, 161–3, 165, 168, 173–4, 181, 183, 207, 208n, 213–14, 217, 219, 225–6, 231–3, 237–40
  core/primary, 13–15, 20, 45, 68, 71, 81, 86, 165
  peripheral/secondary, 13–15, 20, 68, 71, 163, 218
postindustrial ruins, 22, 38, 183, 199–207, 211n, 229, 231
post-irony, 37–8, 142, 183, 194, 196, 203
postmodernism, 37, 205
post-traumatic stress disorder (PTSD), 74–5, 78–9, 91–2, 98n, 103, 110, 215
Powell, Michael, 43, 47
pre-exposure prophylaxis (PrEP) drugs, 193, 205–6, 209n
Prentiss, Paula, 236
"prestige horror," 2, 11, 20, 28, 31, 34, 43–9, 51, 54, 57, 72, 237
print media, 4, 28, 34–5
Psycho (1960), 43, 73, 80, 213, 233, 236–8
Psycho II, 238
Psycho IV: The Beginning, 237
Pugh, Florence, 117
Pulse (2001), 33
Punch-Drunk Love, 36
Purge, The, 122
Puritanism *see* Christianity
Pye, Douglas, 11, 42

queer ethics, 22, 181–4, 189–90, 192–3, 204–5, 207
queerness *see* sexuality
"quiet horror," 31–4
Quiet Place, A, 2, 6, 14–15, 17, 21, 25n, 40, 93, 143, 163–6, 168, 200
Quiet Place Part II, A, 163, 165, 178n
Quigley, Paula, 80

race, 13, 21, 49, 57, 75, 104, 107, 113, 122–35, 140n, 145, 167, 186, 201–7, 222, 228, 243n
Radcliffe, Ann, 144
rape, 79, 148, 157–8, 173, 186–7, 200–1, 208n, 210n
Radstone, Susannah, 75
Raw, 14
Ray Noble and his Orchestra, 145
realism, 8, 16, 30, 126, 151, 153–4, 168, 197
Rebecca (1940), 72–3, 104–6, 110, 129
reception *see* critics, horror-friendly viewers, horror-skeptic viewers, fans
Reddit, 50
Reiff, Michael, 78
Reiki, 217
Relic, 14
religion *see* Christianity, Judaism, paganism, occultism, spirituality
reproduction, 13, 21, 69–70, 91, 143, 150–2, 157–8, 162, 169, 172, 174, 185, 191–3, 200, 218, 224–5, 228, 231, 239
reproductive futurism, 69, 162, 164, 178n, 191–2, 217, 221, 231
Repulsion, 8, 78, 218
Restivo, Angelo, 204
Rich, Adrienne, 106
Ringu, 32
Roeg, Nicolas, 73
Rosemary's Baby, 29–30, 43–4, 47–8, 64n, 69, 76, 78–9, 89, 103, 124, 127, 139–40n, 144, 154, 218
Rose, Steve, 3, 31, 34, 49
Roth, Eli, 85
Rothman, William, 238
Rotten Tomatoes, 6, 10, 52, 240
Royle, Nicholas, 84
ruin porn, 199–201, 203–4, 206, 211n, 229, 231–2, 243n; *see also* postindustrial ruins
Russell, David O., 218

Sade, Marquis de, 223
Salò, or the 120 Days of Sodom, 9
Safe, 31, 36, 127
Sarkis, Stephanie, 109, 117
Saw, 27
Schulman, Sarah, 205

Schwab, Gabriele, 91
science fiction, 8, 46, 56, 146, 149, 224
Sconce, Jeffrey, 9, 36–7, 42
Scooby Doo, 226
Scovell, Adam, 110, 113
Scream, 32, 38
Sedgwick, Eve Kosofsky, 174, 235
Sexton, Jamie, 39, 42, 57
sexuality, 13, 22, 43, 57, 75, 80, 107, 108–9, 113, 116, 120, 137n, 140n, 147–8, 151–3, 157, 167, 169–74, 176n, 179–80n, 181–98, 200, 204–7, 209n, 213, 215–16, 220, 222, 228, 230, 237–8
shame, 13, 107, 125, 181, 183, 188–94, 198, 204, 206
Shape of Water, The, 137n, 179–80n
She Dies Tomorrow, 14
Shining, The (1980), 29–30, 33, 43–4, 55, 66n, 69, 79, 143–6, 149–50, 156, 165, 168, 170–1, 178n
shock, 1, 7, 9–10, 30, 37, 90, 102; *see also* jump scares
Shoos, Diane L., 106, 132
Shults, Trey Edward, 41, 47, 165, 168
Shyamalan, M. Night, 179n
Signs, 163
Silence, The, 25n
Silence of the Lambs, The, 43, 46
Sinister, 33, 80
Sixth Sense, The, 32, 43, 83, 100n
Skvarla, Robert, 55–6
slavery, 126–8, 130–1, 140n
slow cinema, 10, 18, 29–31, 36, 59n, 226, 240
"slow horror," 2, 20, 28–34
smart films, 36, 42, 127, 240
"smart horror," 2–3, 20, 28, 34, 37–9, 44, 163
Sobchack, Vivian, 69
social media, 1, 5–6, 20, 28, 34–6, 50–1, 108–9, 190–1
Solondz, Todd, 36
Sono, Sion, 10
Sophocles, 90, 100n
sound, 1, 15, 17–18, 32, 79, 90, 119, 121, 156–9, 161, 163, 165–6, 168–70, 188, 200, 216–17, 227–8, 233–4, 244n
Spadoni, Robert, 17
Sperb, Jason, 145

Spiral Staircase, The, 43, 72–3
spiritualism, 93–4, 214, 236
spirituality, 22, 101n, 110, 115–16, 150, 172, 213, 216, 218, 222, 224–5
Star-Spangled Girl, The, 236
Steinmetz, George, 202
Stepford Wives, The (1975), 124–5
Stern, Robin, 107, 109
Strange Thing About the Johnsons, The, 89
structure of feeling, 38, 192, 194, 197
style, 1–3, 5–13, 15–16, 18, 19–20, 22, 27–8, 30–1, 33–40, 44, 50–3, 55–7, 69, 71–2, 74–5, 79, 95, 119, 121–2, 127, 129–30, 142, 156, 162–3, 181, 188, 198, 218, 223, 233, 239–40; *see also* cinematography, editing, *mise-en-scène*, narrative
subgenre *see* cycle, horror
sublime, the, 135, 143–9, 156–7, 160, 169, 175, 183, 199–200
subtractive spectatorship, 154
suburbs, 38, 81, 122–4, 147–8, 182–3, 187–9, 195–6, 198, 200–3, 206–7, 227
Sugrue, Thomas, 201
Sundance Film Festival, 2, 39, 71
suspense film, 8, 30, 46, 105
Suspiria (1977), 53
Suspiria (2018), 14–15
Sverigedemokraterna (Swedish Democrats), 113
Swallow, 14
Sybil, 85
sympathetic magic, 116

Tafoya, Scout, 95
Take Shelter, 165
Tarkovsky, Andrei, 88
Tarot, 217
taste, 1–7, 9–10, 19–20, 23n, 28–9, 31, 33–4, 37, 44–5, 48–54, 56–7, 81, 86, 120–1, 125, 127–9, 134–5, 142, 146, 159, 198, 219, 232, 239; *see also* critics, elitism, fans, populism
Tarr, Béla, 30
Taussig, Michael, 116
Teeth, 187
Telegraph, The, 33
Tembo, Kwasu D., 155, 160
temporality *see* time

Tenant, The, 9
Texas Chain Saw Massacre, The (1974), 41, 51, 53
Theater of Cruelty, 223–4
themes, 3, 8, 11, 13, 15–16, 20–1, 31–2, 35, 37, 41, 49, 55–6, 69–71, 86, 102–3, 143, 148, 150, 162, 171, 191, 213, 218, 239–40; *see also* family, gaslighting, grief, shame
There Will Be Blood, 36, 145–6, 149, 168, 170
Thing, The (1982), 184
thriller film, 46–7, 55–6, 99n
time, 11–13, 18–19, 30, 44, 73–4, 91, 145, 149–50, 170–1, 183, 197–8, 202, 206, 213–15, 226–7, 229–33, 235–6, 239
Tingler, The, 47
Todorov, Tzvetan, 16, 83, 103
Toles, George, 145
Tomb of Ligeia, The, 69
Tomkins, Silvan, 13
tone, 11, 43, 56, 85, 111–12, 163
Torok, Maria, 89, 91
Toronto International Film Festival, 2, 40, 233
trailers *see* marketing
Transportation Security Administration, 128, 130
Trapp Family, The, 82, 86
trauma, 21, 46, 49, 55, 68, 70–1, 74–6, 78–9, 83–7, 90–2, 95, 103, 105, 111, 123–5, 128, 131, 143, 151, 156–7, 159–60, 186, 189, 199, 231–2, 243n; *see also* grief
Trigg, Dylan, 229
Triumph of Death, The, 165
Trouble Every Day, 9
Trump, Donald, 130, 140n
Truvada, 193, 205, 209n
Tucker and Dale vs. Evil, 38
Turistas, 111
Twitter, 55
2001: A Space Odyssey, 46, 145–6

Ugetsu, 8
uncanny, the, 16, 32, 68, 73, 76, 80, 82, 84, 87, 94, 99n, 100n, 103, 118–19
Un Chien Andalou, 9, 146
Uncle Boonmee Who Can Recall His Past Lives, 31

Uncle Tom's Cabin, 128, 132
Under the Shadow, 14, 98n
Under the Skin, 2, 14, 145–9, 160, 176n, 178n, 181, 214
Universal Pictures, 40, 238
Untamed, The, 14, 176n, 181
Us, 14, 39, 46, 55–6
US Lighthouse Establishment, 169
US Supreme Court, 191

Vampyr, 8
Van Sant, Gus, 31
Varda, Scott, 184, 187
Vertigo, 73
VICE, 35
Village, The, 179n
Villeneuve, Denis, 99n
Virgin Spring, The, 158
Virgin Suicides, The, 187, 196
Von Trapp, Maria, 82
Von Trier, Lars, 10, 222–3
Vodou, 127
Vreeland, Rich, 18, 196

Wake in Fright, 81
Waldman, Diane, 106
Walsh, Andrea, 106
Walt Disney Company, The, 53
Walton, Saige, 146, 153, 166
Wang, Ban, 75
Wan, James, 33
war film, 8, 220–1, 223, 226
Warner, Michael, 182, 190–2
Warner, Rick, 144, 146
War of the Worlds, 163
Weerasethakul, Apichatpong, 31
Weinshel, Edward M., 107
Weisz, Rachel, 224

Welcome to the Dollhouse, 187
We Need To Talk About Kevin, 80
Wes Craven's New Nightmare, 38
western film, 230
West, Ti, 29, 31–2
Whitford, Bradley, 125
Wicker Man, The (1973), 110–11, 114
wilderness, 21–2, 81, 135, 142–3, 146, 148–9, 156, 161–2, 164–5, 169–70, 183, 203
Wilkinson, Eleanor, 182, 191
Williams, Allison, 125
Williams, Linda, 132, 222
Williams, Raymond, 38
Williams, Tony, 69, 150
Wilson, Emma, 90
Wise, Joshua, 30
witchcraft, 16, 21, 93, 143, 149–62, 176n, 216; *see also* occultism
Witch, The, 1–2, 8, 11–16, 18–21, 41–2, 48, 50, 70, 112–13, 142–3, 149–57, 160–71, 180n, 187, 231, 239, 243n
Wolf Creek, 81
Wolf Creek 2, 81
Wolfe, April, 49
Woman in Black 2: Angel of Death, The, 33
woman's film, 72–5, 93, 103–6
Women of Trachis, 90, 100n
Woolf, Virginia, 226, 230

YouTube, 111

Zinoman, Jason, 47, 53, 68
Zoller Seitz, Matt, 27, 45
Zovatto, Daniel, 200
Zwissler, Laurel, 154–5, 160

EU representative:
Easy Access System Europe
Mustamäe tee 50, 10621 Tallinn, Estonia
Gpsr.requests@easproject.com

www.ingramcontent.com/pod-product-compliance
Lightning Source LLC
Chambersburg PA
CBHW052105230426
43671CB00011B/1935